AIRWORK

AIRWORK
A HISTORY

KEITH McCLOSKEY

For my daughters
Amelia, Camilla, Laura

Cover illustrations. Front, top: AS.4 Ferry G-ACFB (via Peter Amos);
front, below: A Vickers Viking at the Gatwick open day, 10 July 1948
(Royal Aero Club). *Back*: Spitfire F.22s and a de Havilland Hornet at
Gatwick, *c.* 1952 (Tom Pharo via Air Britain)

First published 2012

The History Press
The Mill, Brimscombe Port
Stroud, Gloucestershire, GL5 2QG
www.thehistorypress.co.uk

© Keith McCloskey, 2012

British Library Cataloguing in Publication Data.
A catalogue record for this book is available from the British Library.

ISBN 978 0 7524 7972 9

Typesetting and origination by The History Press
Printed in Great Britain

CONTENTS

FOREWORD

The story of Airwork and its numerous activities and undertakings is an extremely large one. So large, in fact, that many of the thirty-nine chapters in this book could be easily expanded into books in their own right. It is the story of the vision of two men, Alan Muntz and Nigel Norman, who saw that there was more to just flying planes for pleasure and taking passengers from one place to another. They were in the right place at the right time to capitalise on the huge public, commercial and military interest in flying, primarily by focusing on providing the facilities and opportunities for everything that was needed to get an aircraft into the air, from providing flying lessons to selling the aircraft to engineering support to even designing the airports they would use.

In interviews of former Airwork employees for this book (several in their eighties and nineties), time and again the same expression would be used: 'Airwork were a cut above the rest.' The pride of Airwork employees, from the apprentices of 1930s Heston to the 'Airworkies' of Saudi Arabia in the late 1960s and early 1970s, and the 'Thumrait Thuggies' of the late 1970s, 1980s and 1990s in Oman, is quite apparent.

Frederic Alan Irving Muntz 1899–1982. (Mrs Nicolette Baring)

Sir Henry Nigel St Valery Norman 1897–1943. (Sir Torquil Norman)

Some areas are well covered and there is little to add; I have drawn on the works done in these areas with the kind permission of their authors. I have also uncovered previously unpublished information gained from former Airwork employees and the private papers of Alan Muntz, very kindly provided by his youngest daughter Mrs Nicolette Baring, to whom I am deeply grateful. Overall what I have tried to do is to put together the first published account of Airwork from its beginnings to the present day and to include employees in that account. The company still exists and continues (mainly in Oman), although it has more or less passed into history.

Airwork became Britain's largest immediate post-war airline; in a different political climate to the one in which they operated in the post-war era (i.e. one which did not suffocate private enterprise), one can only guess at what they might have achieved and what form the company would be in today without the dead hand of the state hampering virtually their every move.

Airwork had always been an organisation that involved itself in the social side of aviation. This was prevalent at both Heston and Misr-Airwork. Perhaps not quite as grand as some of the Heston or Cairo evenings, the annual Airwork dinner dances held for employees at the various depots were very much enjoyed by staff. Sports were another area in which employees showed great enthusiasm, from the Airwork Renfrew football team of the 1940s to the Airwork Rhodesia football team in the 1960s. Airwork Rhodesia presented the air force with a trophy for six-a-side soccer to be played for each year.

The book is also a tribute to men who worked in arduous conditions overseas and whose feelings can be summed up by one Airwork employee, Tony Allen, in Saudi Arabia in the early 1970s, who said:

I have to say that I did get home sick and lonely at times despite having made many friends. On occasion, two or three of us would stroll down to the Airport terminal building on a sultry evening, with no alcohol we would take our Mirandas and Seven-Ups to the viewing veranda and wait for the weekly arrival of BOAC's VC10, a little reminder of England. We would watch the unlucky ones disembark and the lucky ones make their way across the apron to the luxury of the airliner in its smart blue and white livery and the speedbird logo on the tail fin. To see it lift off and climb away in the dusty evening sky was a melancholy feeling and did nothing to alleviate home sick blues.

Keith McCloskey
Berkshire

ACKNOWLEDGEMENTS

I must firstly mention Mrs Nicolette Baring. Nicolette is the youngest daughter of Alan Muntz and she has given me complete access to her late father's papers, diaries and photographs. Many mysteries were cleared up for me and this would have been a far lesser book without her kind and tireless help. I would also like to mention Louis Curl who has laid all the groundwork for an in-depth study of Airwork; John Hancock of Babcock International – the guardian of what little remains of Airwork's history; and Alan Holloway who has kindly given me full access to his late father's (Sydney Holloway) remarkable photographs and unpublished manuscript of his autobiography *The Prototype Man: A Profile of S.A. Holloway and his Aviation 1932–1992*.

I would like to thank Jennifer Scanlan for permission to reproduce some of the Ecuador chapter, John Havers for permission to reproduce the 1947 Taif Mission section, and R.A. Scholefield for the Barton and Sabre repair material. I would like to specially mention Major General Angus I. Ramsay CBE DSO and the Beit Trust for full access to their archives and their very kind financial assistance in the preparation of this book.

I have been given photos and help on a number of chapters from Peter Amos, Maurice Wickstead, Malcolm Fillmore; also Paul Becker for help with his late father's work for the Alan Muntz design team, Carole Brooks for her kind help with RUAC and Zimbabwe, Bryan Collins for the labyrinth of Airwork company history and Fison-Airwork, John Odlin, Peter Gray, Helen King and Ted Weinel. Also, Neil Aird, Geoff Ambrose, Norman Anyon, Martin Val Baker (Valentine Baker's grandson), Helen Balkwill-Clark, John Barnes, Rob Belcher, Sqn Ldr J. Blanche (RAuxAF Historian & Archivist), Peter Carter, Peter Casling, Tom Cooper, Madame Mimi Di Castro, Bob Crouden, Antoin Daltun, John Davis, Andrew Dawrant (Royal Aero Club), Ian Doig, Mike Draper, Karen Dunn (*Crawley Observer*), Allan Ellis, Peter Farrow, Anthony Fitzgerald, Barry Flahey, Peter Foster, Nick Gardner, Peter-Michael Gerhardt, Les Ginger, David Griffin, William Guinness (the son of Loel Guinness), Guy Halford-MacLeod, Mike Hamence, Peter Hamlin, Dave Hann, Reg Havers, Ian Hawkridge, Dave Homewood, Ray Hooper, Lester Hope, Rita Huggins (for her brilliant detective work), Tony Hyatt, Markham Jackson, G.A. Jones, Bjorn Larsson, Clive Laudham, Barry Leeming, Chrissy McMorris of The History Press, Dave Newnham, Sir Torquil Norman (son of Nigel Norman), Peter Norris, Robin Norton, Mike Phipp, Brian Powell, Bob Pugh, Eleanor Pulfer (Slough Museum), Douglas Revell, Air Vice Marshal Sir John Severne, Ray Shoebridge, John Skinner, Jonathan Smith (Archivist & Modern Manuscript Cataloguer, Trinity College, Cambridge), Peter Smith, Major Gary E. Sparks (Ret.), Brian Stead, Les Steel-Smith, Ron Tannock, Bill Taylor, Dennis 'Rusty' Theobald, Iain Todd, Phillip Treweek, William Turnbull, Steve Twigg (Marketing Director, Capita Symonds), Bill Van Heerden, Guy Warner, Dave Welch, Tom Wenham, Martin Wieuest and Allan G. Williams.

Also Carl Bastin and Leah Monahan for help with the technical side of PCs and photos, and Triona McCloskey for proof reading.

Last but not least, I want to mention two remarkable men who have provided valuable background: Joe Connolly and S.J. (John) Smith. Joe joined Airwork at Heston in 1938 and John joined the Alan Muntz Company in 1940. Joe is the last living person of the original batch of thirty-plus Airwork employees that went up to Renfrew from Heston on the day war broke out. John is also one of the very few left from that time and recalls being bought his first beer in the RAF mess in the Heston Jackaman Hangar by Squadron Leader A.E. Clouston.

EARLY DAYS

1

AIRWORK'S FOUNDERS

Both founders had followed similar paths: they went to Cambridge University; both served in the army in the Great War; both described themselves as engineers; and, importantly, both were fascinated by flying. In respect of flying, they were both involved in aviation tragedies, the first taking the life of Nigel Norman himself and the other taking the life of Alan Muntz's son.

Before either of them had reached the age of 30, they both left secure, well-paid jobs to follow their vision. Despite their many detractors, their idea was to create the best aerodrome near London.

FREDERIC ALAN IRVING MUNTZ[1]

Alan Muntz was born on 7 June 1899 at Leek in Staffordshire. His parents were Albert Irving Muntz (who was an army major) and Jessica Challinor.

The Muntz family were émigrés who were persecuted landowners and aristocracy originally from Poland, and left that country to move to eastern France. With the French Revolution, the family again moved and settled in the Birmingham area. Alan Muntz's great-grandfather and great-uncle were both Birmingham-based industrialists and Members of Parliament. George Frederic Muntz, his great-grandfather, was MP for Birmingham from 1840 until his death in 1857 and his great-uncle Philip Henry Muntz was also an MP for Birmingham from 1868 to 1885. Philip Muntz was the second mayor of Birmingham. George Muntz owned Muntz Rolling Mills which was very successful and Muntz steel plates were used in a wide variety of areas but particularly in sheathing ships' bottoms. One notable ship that was sheathed in Muntz metal was the *Cutty Sark*. A report issued by the Cutty Sark Society on 31 December 1963 mentions the pressing problem of replacing the 'wasted Muntz metal plates on the bottom of the ship'. These original plates had been on the vessel for eighty-five years. When replaced, sections of these original plates, along with engraved certificates, were sent to surviving members of the Muntz family including Alan Muntz, with each section carrying the original stamp of the Muntz name.

Alan Muntz attended Horris Hill prep school near Newbury followed by Winchester College where he performed well.

During the First World War Alan Muntz joined the Royal Engineers as a second lieutenant on 30 March 1918 and saw service in France. Although the war had interrupted the studies of many young men, he went on to study for a BA in Mechanical Sciences at Trinity College, Cambridge in 1919, gaining his degree in 1922. Previous to gaining his degree, an announcement in the *London Gazette* on 19 September 1921 stated he had relinquished his commission with the rank of second lieutenant. He had spent six weeks in the summer of 1920 undertaking practical work in the Horseley Bridge & Engineering Company in Tipton gaining engineering experience in the fitting shop, pattern shop and foundry.

During his time at Cambridge he was to meet two people who would become good friends and business partners, namely Nigel Norman and Roderick Denman. He was a classical scholar but unusually also possessed a keen mathematical mind which he put to good use in his engineering work. His profession in his passport was given as 'Engineer'.

After gaining his degree, he joined the Anglo-Persian Oil Company on 18 September 1922 at their Croydon branch on a salary of £250 p.a. (per annum) during his training period. This position was arranged through the Appointments Board of Cambridge University. Upon

1 Referred to in this book as Alan Muntz.

completion of his training period he was appointed circuit manager at the Croydon branch on 30 April 1923, at a salary of £350 p.a. He went on within the Anglo-Persian Oil Company to work with the company (which later became the Anglo-Iranian Oil Company and then British Petroleum) in Basra, Iraq, gaining knowledge and contacts that would serve him well in future years. He left the Anglo-Persian Oil Company in 1928 to join Nigel Norman in building the Airwork organisation.

Family Life

Although he lived in a number of locations in Britain including London and Amport near Andover, he spent a large part of his early life (over twenty years) at Ecchinswell House near Newbury, where his father was closely involved in local life as a district councillor and vice-chairman of Kingsclere and Whitchurch Rural District Council (amalgamated into Basingstoke District Council in 1974) for many years, resigning in 1944. Alan Muntz himself had political ambitions in 1944 and entertained the idea of putting himself forward as a prospective Conservative MP in a constituency within reach of London. However, although he completed a candidate's form, he never proceeded with the application.

He was married three times. His first marriage was to Mary Harnett in July 1923. They had three children: Scilla (b. 2 January 1925), Jasmine (b. 8 July 1927) and Colin Lee Irving (b. 23 March 1929). His son Colin was to follow Alan into aviation, gaining an RAeC (Royal Aero Club) Aviator's Certificate (No. 26754) on 12 September 1950 at the London Aeroplane Club. Colin then joined the RAF and was posted to 600 (City of London) Squadron at Biggin Hill with the rank of flying officer. He was tragically killed in a flying accident near Chelsfield in Kent on 25 April 1953 at the age of 24. He was flying Gloster Meteor F.8 WF747 when the aircraft lost its hood and the ejector seat operated. The aircraft flew on but then dived into the ground. Colin Muntz was found in the ejector seat 7 miles away from the aircraft crash point. He is buried at Biggin Hill Cemetery (Grave No. 189).

Alan Muntz (right) with HRH Duchess of York, the late Queen Mother, at Heston during the King's Cup Air Race in 1934. (Royal Aero Club)

Alan Muntz's second marriage was to the daughter of the 7th Marquess of Londonderry, Lady Margaret Frances Anne Vane-Tempest-Stewart on 21 November 1934. Lord Londonderry was the Secretary of State for Air at this time. It was not a happy union and they divorced in 1939. The divorce caused a certain degree of animosity between Alan Muntz and his former father-in-law, particularly as Lord Londonderry had refused to give his permission for the marriage.

His third marriage and, as it turned out, his happiest, was to Marjorie Strickland in October 1948. His third wife was eighteen years younger than himself and had grown up in Ceylon (modern-day Sri Lanka). They had a daughter, Nicolette Mary Irving (b. 23 December 1950), and he also gained two stepsons (Anthony and Jonathan Fitzgerald) whose father had tragically died. It is a measure of the kind of man Alan was that he took on his new wife's bereaved sons and brought them up as his own, paying for them to be educated at Ampleforth.

In his private life Alan Muntz was considered to be a quiet and gentle man by everybody who met him. He generally trusted everybody he met. It was often said that he was a gentleman in both senses of the word.

He enjoyed playing golf, becoming a member of Berkshire Golf Club, Ascot and Swinley Forest Golf Club, where he made a hole-in-one at the eighth hole on 15 April 1957, an achievement of which he was rightly proud.

Career

Alan had always been interested in aviation although his astigmatism had prevented him from joining the Royal Flying Corps. His attendance at the Light Aeroplane Show at Lympne in the summer of 1926 persuaded him to start flying. He became an associate (No. 19) of the Royal Aeronautical Society on 13 April 1926.

He learned to fly with the Henderson School of Flying at Brooklands in 1927, gaining A Licence No. 1534 on 5 August 1927, and bought his first aircraft the following year, DH.60X Moth G-EBWT, which he registered in March 1928. Alan Muntz flew as many visiting Heston aircraft as possible. He also had DH.60X Moth G-EBQH and DH.80A Puss Moth G-ABNC registered in his name.

He was a member of the Institution of Mechanical Engineers and an Associate Fellow of the Royal Aeronautical Society.

In 1954 he was awarded the silver medal of the Institute of Marine Engineering and in 1958 was admitted to the Freedom of the Guild of Airline Pilots and Air Navigation and to the Livery and Freedom of the City of London.

Final Years

Alan Muntz retired in 1974. He was an ardent Francophile and in his own words he 'emigrated' to France in early 1976 to live in Seillans in Fayence. In his final years he returned to live first at Amport near Andover and finally in Canon Street, Winchester, where he died of heart failure on 7 March 1985. He was cremated and buried at his beloved Winchester College at St Michael's church, Culver Road, Winchester.

SIR HENRY NIGEL ST VALERY NORMAN[2]

Nigel Norman was an exceptionally gifted and driven man. Born in London on 21 May 1897, he was the only child of Rt Hon. Sir Henry Norman, 1st Baronet of Honeyhanger, Surrey, and Menie Muriel Dowie. He had a half-sister, Rosalind, and two half-brothers, Willoughby and

2 Referred to in this book as Nigel Norman.

Anthony, children of his father and his second wife, Lady Fay Aberconway. As well as being a former MP for Blackburn and a JP, his father, Sir Henry, had a number of aviation interests and was a founder member of the Royal Aero Club. He had also dined with the Wright brothers and was a member of 601 Squadron (Auxiliary Air Force) City of London. Both Nigel Norman's mother and father were also writers and explorers.

He was educated at Horton School, Chipping Sodbury, before going on to Winchester in 1910.

Family Life

Nigel Norman himself became 2nd Baronet of Honeyhanger in 1939. He married Patricia Moira Annesley (the eldest daughter of Lieutenant Colonel William Annesley DSO CMG) in 1926 and they had three sons (Mark, Desmond and Torquil).

Each of his sons made their mark in aviation. His eldest son Mark (b. 8 February 1927 and who inherited the family title) flew with 601 Squadron as a pilot and later became sales director of Britten-Norman.

His second son Desmond (b. 13 August 1929) attended the de Havilland Technical School in 1947, where he met John Britten. He qualified as an aeronautical engineer in 1950 and completed his National Service in the RAF (including demonstrating the Gloster Meteor F.8 and serving in 601 Squadron, going on to SBAC as a test pilot). In 1953 he founded Britten-Norman with John Britten. With another partner, Jim McMahon, they started the successful company, Crop Culture, developing the revolutionary Micronair rotary atomiser. Another company they formed was Hovertravel and a significant amount of research was carried out on hovercraft by the company. Desmond Norman went on to design aircraft, the Britten-Norman Islander being his most well-known aircraft. There was also the Trislander, the BN.3 Nymph (redeveloped as the Freelance) and the later Firecracker (which was beaten by the Embraer Tucano in the competition to become the RAF trainer) and the Fieldmaster Cropsprayer in 1981. Like his father before him he became a CBE in 1970. He died on 23 November 2002.

Nigel Norman's third son, Torquil (b. 11 April 1933), also served in 601 Squadron and was involved with the music world in the 1960s, owning the Roundhouse theatre at Camden Lock. He established the company Bluebird Toys which has been very successful. He too has a great interest in aviation and flies DH.90 Dragonfly G-AEDU, which is based at Rendcomb.

Nigel Norman with his sons Desmond (seated) and Mark (turning propeller) playing with a model aircraft he had built for them in which they were often seen at Heston. The registration G-WAWP stood for 'God Willing And Weather Permitting'. (Royal Aero Club)

Nigel Norman was a sensitive and thoughtful man as shown in his passion for writing poetry (a passion he shared with Alan Muntz). He also had a great interest in the countryside and enjoyed fly-fishing and deer stalking.

Career

The advent of the First World War interrupted Nigel's education. After attending Sandhurst he served in the Royal Artillery as a second lieutenant (he was commissioned on 27 October 1915) in France. He was commissioned as a lieutenant on 6 March 1918 and was attached to the army Signals Service (then part of the Royal Engineers). In 1919 he left the army and went up to Trinity College, Cambridge, where he gained a BA in Mechanical Sciences in 1921. He was awarded the MA in 1939 (MAs were normally awarded as a matter of course after three years from the BA, but the long gap to 1939 is unexplained). From 1922 to 1928, he worked for the Metropolitan Railway, but aviation was to become an overriding passion.

Although Nigel Norman had been at Winchester at the same time as Alan Muntz, Nigel was three years older than Alan and was in a different house. They did not become firm friends until they met again at Cambridge University. They shared the running costs of a second-hand Avro 504K until they could both afford their own aircraft.

Nigel became a private aeroplane owner in 1926 and he held the Royal Aero Club Aviator's Certificate No. 8000. This was gained at the de Havilland School of Flying at Stag Lane, Edgware, on 4 June 1926. The type flown was a DH.60. The index card states his then current address as 3 Rex Place, South Street, London W1. His profession was given as 'Engineer'.

He joined the Auxiliary Air Force in 1926 as a pilot officer and served with 601 (City of London) Squadron. He became a squadron leader in November 1931. In March 1940 he became a temporary wing commander and was promoted to temporary group captain in June 1942. In the following year he was appointed acting air commodore.

On the civilian side, Nigel Norman was asked in early 1943 if he would consider becoming the first chairman of BOAC. His response was to say 'Come back after the War'. He also owned a number of aircraft including Avro 548 G-EBPJ, DH.60G Moth G-AAHI, DH.60 G-EBWY (fitted with Handley Page slots), DH.80A Puss Moths G-AAZM and G-AAZN, and DH.85 Leopard Moth G-ACNN.

He became a director of Aerofilms Ltd, Britain's first commercial aerial photography company which had been founded in 1919. Aerofilms were later involved with the PRU

Nigel Norman with DH.85 Leopard Moth G-ACNN which was registered to him from November 1933 until 12 May 1940 when it was impressed as AX861. (Royal Aero Club)

(Photographic Reconnaissance Unit) at Heston during the war. Additionally, he was a Fellow of the Royal Aeronautical Society, a member of the Aviation Committee of the London Chamber of Commerce and a member of the Council of the Air Registration Board, on which body he sat as chairman of the Design & Construction Panel.

In the same year in which he was tragically killed (1943), Nigel Norman was awarded a CBE.

His partnership with Alan Muntz was to give great impetus to their impact on the aviation world. The formation of Airwork and the establishment of Heston Air Park are covered separately in later chapters. However, despite the energy expended on these enterprises, Nigel Norman still found time and energy to become a co-partner with Alan Muntz and Graham Dawbarn in the firm of Norman, Muntz and Dawbarn Aeronautical Consulting Engineers (see Chapter 3).

Crash of Lockheed Hudson IIIA FH168, 19 May 1943

It is tragic that Nigel Norman met his death through aviation. In 1943, he was being flown to North Africa from Netheravon. He had just been appointed to Air Chief Marshal Sir A.W. Tedder's staff and was to attend an Airborne Forces Planning Conference in the Middle East to help prepare for the invasion of Sicily. Air Commodore Norman possessed particular expertise in parachute and glider assaults. On 19 May 1943, he boarded Lockheed Hudson 111A FH168 of 38 Wing RAF at RAF Netheravon. 38 Wing had been formed at Netheravon to provide a link with the 1st Parachute Brigade at Bulford Camp. The Hudson crew were mainly French-Canadians (Royal Canadian Air Force personnel). The pilot was Flight Lieutenant R.H. Jesse, navigator Pilot Officer Arthur Rotenburg and the wireless operator/air gunner was Flight Sergeant G. Russell. The four other occupants were passengers and included Wing Commander R.W. Hurst, Squadron Leader E.W. Armstrong and Corporal H.A. Palmer.

The journey was a long one and the Hudson landed at RAF St Eval in Cornwall to top up with fuel. After take-off the Hudson encountered difficulties with the port engine catching fire. About 7 miles south of RAF St Eval, two local farmers observed the aircraft dipping to the left and losing height. The Hudson attempted a landing in a field at Crugoes Farm, Blackcross, about 180m south-west of the St Columb Royal Observer Corps post. The aircraft just cleared a hedge, hit the ground, bounced and slewed across the field. A wing broke off, as did part of the tail, and the aircraft ended up partly on top of a hedge. Initially there was little fire, although the left-hand wing was broken and beginning to burn. The right-hand wing was almost over a gate, which caused part of the aircraft to be off the ground. The two farmers who had witnessed the crash were quickly on the scene, as was Royal Observer member George Gregory. Two occupants exited the aircraft through a hole in the underside. Fire was beginning to take hold while the farmers looked after two injured survivors. George Gregory rescued four additional crew members. George's promptness in obtaining medical aid no doubt helped save lives. All the survivors were suffering from broken limbs. After the rescue of six occupants, the aircraft burst into flames.

One of the farmers, Bill Richards, claimed that he remembered seeing the remaining occupant, Nigel Norman, fighting to get out of the burning cockpit. Thereafter, Bill Richards always maintained that Nigel did not die in the crash itself and with courage it may have been possible to save him. However, as the fire had taken hold, no further rescue attempts were made and Nigel Norman died in the blaze. It is believed that, having been seated in the cabin, he went forward to the cockpit to help when the engine problem started, thereby putting himself in jeopardy and most likely would have survived had he stayed in the cabin.

It was a tragic end and had Nigel Norman survived the war one can only guess at how he could have brought his talent and energy to focus on the fortunes of Airwork.

His ashes were scattered in Clifferdine Wood near Rendcomb, an area he had grown up in and loved. An oak memorial bench with an inscription to his memory can be found at the Main Ride, Clifferdine Wood. It can be reached by a short walk from the A435 Cirencester to Cheltenham road.

2

COMPANY DEVELOPMENT

1928–1960

Alan Muntz had been given £5,000 by his father to finance his time at Cambridge University and further education, but by 1928 he still had this sum intact and available. Nigel Norman and Alan Muntz considered they needed a total of £50,000 to establish the company and Heston. Promises had been obtained for a further £20,000 to add to the £5,000 sum held by Alan Muntz when Nigel Norman's stepfather, Major Edward Fitzgerald, offered to put up the balance of £45,000 on condition that he was the only other shareholder and that Nigel would be part-time chairman in the new company. Alan Muntz spoke to the other potential backers and then proceeded with Major Fitzgerald's offer. Airwork Limited came into being on 2 September 1928 and was officially registered on 11 October 1928 with a capital of £45,000 in £1 shares. Listed as first directors were H.N. St Valery Norman and F.A.I. Muntz with F.A.I. Muntz also shown as company secretary. The solicitors were Pettit, Walton & Co. of Leighton Buzzard. Airwork Limited were listed as 'Manufacturers of and dealers in aeroplanes, flying machines, airships and aerial conveyances of all kinds, and the component parts thereof, garage and hangar keepers, aerodrome proprietors, cinematograph proprietors and film makers, etc'.

While Heston Air Park was being prepared for operations, the office for the new company was Albion Lodge, Albion Road in Cranford, Middlesex.

Additionally, Roderick P.G. Denman joined Airwork in the autumn of 1929 and was appointed a director in June 1931.

However, within a relatively short period of time, the problem of financing was to appear again.

Since the establishment of the company, Airwork had expanded rapidly. Major Edward Fitzgerald had promised an addition of £30,000 to pay for the additional buildings at Heston as a result of the new business since the official opening in July 1929. These buildings were under construction with the injection of funds to pay for them due in October 1929. However, Major Fitzgerald became caught up in the stock market crash in the USA at the end of September 1929 and was unable to pay. Lord Cowdray and his finance company Whitehall Securities stepped in and provided the funds, along with further injections of finance when required. Later, Lord Cowdray's brother, the Hon. Clive Pearson, would form British Airways, with its headquarters at Heston. As a matter of interest, at the time of Lord Cowdray's assistance, his daughter Yoskyl was learning to fly with the Airwork School of Flying.

The other saviours of Airwork were the Guinness family. Despite the financial help from Lord Cowdray and Whitehall Securities, further problems had arisen in the autumn of 1929, with the formation of National Flying Services, created by the government to provide subsidised flying tuition, which was serious competition for Airwork. A lean time followed with both Nigel Norman and Alan Muntz paying themselves £700 p.a. for a number of years. In April 1933, Alan Muntz flew to France with Nigel Norman's half-sister Rosalind. She suggested they call in on Benjamin Guinness at Piencourt in Normandy (which had its own airstrip). As a result of this visit Alan Muntz met the presidents of two French industrial conglomerates (see Chapter 3) who would be of great help to the Alan Muntz Company and, importantly, Benjamin Guinness put a very substantial amount of capital into Airwork with his son T.L.E.B. Guinness (known hereafter as Loel Guinness) also providing further capital and joining the Board of Directors. Loel Guinness joined the Airwork Board of Directors in January 1935 along with the Pearsons/ Whitehall Securities representative John Lister Walsh.

Loel Guinness, of the banking and brewing family, was an important addition to the Board of Directors, being deeply passionate about flying as well as having the necessary business acumen to help take the company forward. He was a member of the Royal Aero Club and his aircraft were maintained by Airwork. Airwork design staff had also made a personalised modification for his DH.90 Dragonfly by extending the aircraft's control wheel downwards so that he could rest his forearms on his knees and keep one or both hands on the wheel whilst in flight. Loel Guinness was to stay with Airwork and help guide the company through to the merger with Hunting Clan, joining the Board of Directors of BUA (British United Airways) in due course.

John Walsh (who was already a director of Whitehall Securities Corporation Ltd) from the Pearson Group also had a great interest in aviation and the Pearson Group had numerous other aviation-related business interests including United Airways. Whitehall Securities played a significant role in aviation in the 1930s. The corporation was owned by the Pearson family and run by Lord Cowdray, who continued to run the very profitable business established by his father.

Engine work at Heston had proved to be a useful source of income and Airwork Engine Service Ltd was established on 31 May 1932 to concentrate on that activity.

The running of Heston itself was not financially sustainable and eventually Nigel Norman and Alan Muntz were able to convince the Air Ministry to buy Heston on 25 November 1937 for £220,000. Airwork were granted a seven-year lease on certain hangars and buildings so they could continue to operate the aircraft-servicing and repair organisation and provide ground services to other operators. The Air Ministry's plans were to use Heston as an alternative to Croydon and as a terminal for British Airways services to Scandinavia and Paris, and basically to allow Airwork to manage it.

After the purchase of Heston by the Air Ministry in 1937, Alan Muntz resigned as managing director and was replaced by Myles Wyatt. Alan Muntz took on the role of deputy chairman and was still very active in Airwork activities, but was starting to focus more on getting the Alan Muntz Company established.

Airwork General Trading Co. Ltd

On 23 December 1936, Airwork General Trading Co. Ltd was registered with a nominal capital of £100 in £1 shares to take over the company's engineering and servicing work. The registered address of the new company was Heston Airport but the principal base was to be at the new premises later taken on in 1938 at Gatwick, with further facilities at Whitchurch and Heston. The founding directors of Airwork General Trading Co. Ltd were Henry N. St V. Norman, F.A.I. Muntz, Roderick P.G. Denman, Loel Guinness and John L. Walsh (all Airwork Ltd directors).

The official objectives of the new company were 'To carry on the business of manufacturers, assemblers and repairers of aircraft, aero-engines etc., and to enter into an agreement with Airwork Limited'.

In effect, the forming of the new company was a reorganisation and expansion of the Airwork Service Department. All the equipment and personnel were transferred to Airwork General Trading and a new plant for general engineering, sheet-metal work and machining was purchased. F.H. Hinton, who was previously manager at Whitchurch and later works manager at Heston, was made general manager. In February 1937, W.G. Andrews who was managing director of Airwork Engine Service Ltd, was made managing director of Airwork General Trading Co. One of the main intentions in forming Airwork General Trading, however, was also to seek work outside the area of aviation, although many of Airwork's most lucrative contracts were to continue in aviation maintenance and contracting work. Nevertheless, some employees of the organisation did not view it as a step in the right direction, with particular criticism levelled at 'the production of baby carriages' (Dunkley Prams). However, the company was doing well at this stage. By 1938, the Airwork sales organisation was the largest of its kind in the British Isles and the looming war gave plenty of scope for work on behalf of the government.

The War Years & Beyond

With the pressure on facilities at Heston in 1939, Airwork had to move their offices to Fernleigh, Wood Lane, Iver Heath, Buckinghamshire, in October 1939 prior to moving in October 1940 to much larger facilities at Westbrook House, 134 Bath Road in Hounslow. Here they set up offices and workshops but were close enough to Heston to maintain their link with the airfield and their smaller representation there, including the Alan Muntz Company which had remained at Heston.

During the war, the Airwork organisation employed a total of 2,400 staff and the untimely death of Nigel Norman in 1943 saw Loel Guinness replace him as chairman.

Post-war, Airwork established a head office at 15 Chesterfield Street, London W1, with overspill offices at nearby Queen Street. In January 1947, part of the management team moved from the Chesterfield Street offices and from Westbrook House, 134 Bath Road, Hounslow, to Langley airfield, where the company had established itself with airline activities based at Blackbushe from 1947.

A new head office was opened at 35 Piccadilly, London W1 in 1957 with a small showroom on the ground floor promoting the West African services (which came under the control of Markham Jackson, the Brompton Road Town Terminal manager). The Piccadilly offices passed on to BUA with Myles Wyatt having his main office there.

The mid-1950s saw a flurry of activity of shipping lines investing in various independent airlines. In February 1954 the shipping line Furness Withy (who operated to the USA, Canada, Australia, New Zealand and the Mediterranean) bought a 60 per cent shareholding in Airwork. This was carried out in association with another shipping company, Blue Star Line Ltd, who in June 1954 announced that it had bought a substantial share in Airwork and appointed two directors to Airwork's board. Blue Star Line operated to Australia, New Zealand, South America, South Africa and the North American Pacific coast.

In early 1956 Sir Archibald Hope (who joined in 1945) stepped down as joint managing director, leaving Myles Wyatt as sole managing director and chairman. The reason he gave for stepping down was the 'continuing restrictions on the activities of private airlines'. He remained on the Board of Directors, however.

In September 1956 Airwork took over Transair, with Transair continuing to operate as a wholly owned subsidiary company. Two Airwork representatives (Airwork directors Myles Wyatt and R.L. Cumming) joined the Transair Board of Directors.

In 1957 Airwork Services Ltd was created to acquire and concentrate on non-airline activities which had previously been undertaken by Airwork General Trading Ltd.

In 1958 Freddie Laker decided to sell Channel Air Bridge, Air Charter and Aviation Traders to Airwork for £600,000 cash plus a further £200,000 subject to stock valuation. The sale was concluded in 1959 when the three companies joined the Airwork group.

In November 1958 Morton Air Services were bought out (along with their subsidiary Olley Air Services) by Airwork but continued with the same identity, and the routes and services remained unchanged. There was speculation at the time that Morton were looking for a financial injection due to the added costs in establishing themselves at Gatwick after having to leave their Croydon base. A statement by Morton's chairman, Captain T.W. Morton, in December 1958 repudiated this, although he was not prepared to give the reason for the takeover by Airwork.

Airwork moved to Hurn in 1959 from Langley and Blackbushe, from which time Hurn became the main base. Also in 1959 the company acquired the entire share capital of Bristow Helicopters.

By 1959, Airwork had become the largest privately owned UK airline and, combined with Transair, were operating a large European freight, mail and passenger network.

Formation of BUA

The year 1960 was one of major changes for Airwork's airline and air transport activities. In April 1960, the merger was agreed between Airwork, the British & Commonwealth Shipping

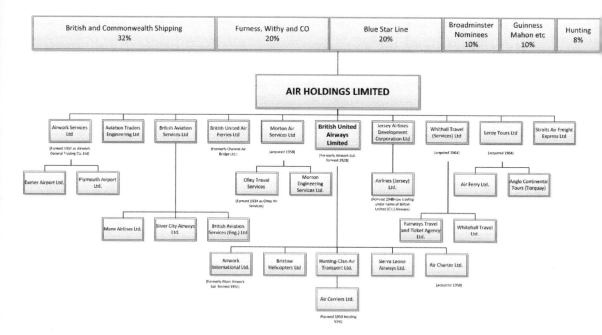

The original shareholding companies which made up the Air Holdings Group. Some of the companies forming the group joined after its formation. (Leah Monahan)

Group and Hunting Clan's air transport activities, which were to be formed into one new company named British United Airways Ltd, with over 3,000 employees and a fleet of fifty-two aircraft. Air Charter, Transair, Morton Air Services and Olley Air Services were absorbed into the new BUA. In addition, the Fison-Airwork and Bristow Helicopters operations were eventually merged with a total fleet of fifty-four helicopters (Fison had already relinquished its interest in Fison-Airwork, which became Airwork Helicopters). Alan Bristow was asked by Myles Wyatt to manage Airwork Helicopters. Both Airwork Services Ltd and Airwork Services Training retained their identities and continued to operate as individual entities.

The official date of the formation of BUA was 1 July 1960, although Airwork had changed its name to British United Airways on 19 May 1960, with the other airlines coming in on 1 July 1960. The name for the new airline had come from the original United Airways (later becoming the first British Airways with the amalgamation of United Airways, Hillman's and Spartan Airways), which Whitehall Securities allowed to be used with the addition of 'British'. Shipping lines held 72 per cent of the shares in the new group. The lines were Blue Star and Furness Withy from the Airwork side and British & Commonwealth from the Hunting Clan side. Meanwhile, Loel Guinness owned 10 per cent and Whitehall Securities owned 10 per cent, while the balance of 8 per cent was held by the Hunting Group. The dominant shareholders were the Cayzer family through their British & Commonwealth holding. The main board members (representing the largest shareholdings) were Sir Nicholas Cayzer, the Hon. Anthony Cayzer and Clive Hunting.

Myles Wyatt became the chairman and Freddie Laker became the managing director. Departures from the new organisation included Maurice Curtis, the managing director of Hunting, Gerald Freeman who had founded and run Transair, and the co-founder of Airwork, Alan Muntz. On 20 May 1960, Alan Muntz tendered his resignation from the Board of Directors and offered the company the opportunity to purchase his 3,000 Airwork shares, which was accepted.

Post-Merger

At Hurn the new headquarters building was occupied in October 1961. With the changes brought about by the formation of BUA and the Air Holdings Group, Airwork at Hurn were known as Airwork Services Ltd. In addition to the FRU (Fleet Requirements Unit) activities, Hurn became the company's new headquarters.

The Air Holdings Group was incorporated on 3 November 1961 as a holding company for the entire share capital of BUA and British Aviation Services, together with their former subsidiaries. The Group's headquarters was the former Airwork Ltd Head Office at 35 Piccadilly in London. The eight main companies which made up the Air Holdings Group were: Airwork International Ltd; Airwork Services Ltd; British Aviation Services Ltd; British United Airways Ltd; Channel Air Bridge Ltd; Morton Air Services Ltd; Silver City Airways Ltd; and Straits Air Freight Express Ltd of New Zealand.

On 23 January 1962 an announcement was made to the effect that the shareholders of British Aviation Services stock would exchange their shares for Air Holdings shares, with the result that Silver City Airways was absorbed into BUA. Jersey Airlines also became part of the Air Holdings Group on 20 May 1962.

In 1967 British Air Transport Ltd became British Air Transport Holdings, which became the holding company for Airwork International.

In March 1968 Airwork International, which was the parent company of Bristow Helicopters, merged with BUA and British & Commonwealth. Whilst remaining part of British & Commonwealth, Bristow Helicopters ceased to be part of the Air Holdings Group (of which Airwork formed the major part).

In May 1976 the aircraft design and modification facilities of Aviation Traders (Engineering) Ltd began to trade under the name of Britavia Ltd (separated from Avialift Products) based at Southend, still under the control of the Air Holdings Group.

In January 1980 Airwork Services Ltd changed its name and reverted to the original Airwork Ltd.

Bricom bought all the aviation companies including Airwork from British & Commonwealth in 1988 for over £380 million. British & Commonwealth then bankrupted themselves with the purchase of Atlantic Computers Ltd. Bristow Helicopters bought themselves out of the Bricom Group in 1991 and also bought AST (Air Service Training) Perth at the same time, as Bricom wished to dispose of it.

Short Brothers Ltd of Belfast, which was part of the Canadian Bombardier group of companies, became the new owners of Airwork Ltd in October 1993, with Airwork becoming part of Bombardier Defence Services Ltd.

A further takeover by the Vosper Thorneycroft group in June 2000 saw Airwork come under the VT Aerospace umbrella. VT Aerospace was itself taken over when it became part of the Babcock Wilcox Group, with Airwork coming under Babcock International. Since the mid-1990s, the Airwork name has all but disappeared, other than for the ongoing Oman contract.

3

ASSOCIATED COMPANIES

Both Nigel Norman and Alan Muntz had various business interests and held directorships outside Airwork, the following being the most significant.

NORMAN & DAWBARN

In July 1933 the partnership of Norman, Muntz and Dawbarn was formed by Nigel Norman and Alan Muntz with the architect Graham Dawbarn. They established their offices at 43 Grosvenor Place, London SW1. They had already designed the layout and buildings at Heston and a number of other airports. The intention of forming the architectural partnership was so that this side of the business would be kept separate from the business operations of Airwork Ltd. Alan Muntz left the partnership in 1937 to concentrate on his new company.

The partnership was involved in the planning of UK airports at Wolverhampton, Birmingham, Brooklands, Portsmouth, Perth, Manchester (Ringway), Jersey, Guernsey and the Gatwick Beehive, as well as in a report prepared in 1933 on a suitable civil airport for Edinburgh which recommended Gosford Park to the east of the city.

The partnership worked with Essex County Council in 1936 for airport planning for the county, which centred on a 'Class I' airport at Fairlop Plain, Ilford. The scheme included a relief airport at Berechurch near Colchester and extended Southend to a Class I airport with subsidiary airports at Chelmsford and Bishops Stortford. Reservation of Class II airport sites at Brentwood, Billericay, Clacton and Braintree were proposed along with a suitable site to serve Tilbury, Orsett and Grays Thurrock to be identified and provisionally reserved.

Nigel Norman travelled extensively to Africa, India, Europe and North America in the course of his work for Norman & Dawbarn, designing airport terminals at Lydda (Palestine) and Lusaka, among many others.

The partnership continued with Nigel Norman's name after his tragic death in 1943. In April 2005 Norman & Dawbarn was acquired by Capita Symonds and renamed Capita Norman & Dawbarn. The Capita Norman & Dawbarn name was dropped in 2007 when all the architecture practices were merged under the same brand name, Capita Architecture. The business continued to grow as a major UK consultancy and all the businesses and divisions were consolidated under the Capita Symonds name in January 2011, dropping the Capita Architecture name.

ALAN MUNTZ & COMPANY LTD

During a visit to Benjamin Guinness in France in April 1933, Alan Muntz was introduced by a guest, Count Horodyski, to the president of the large French industrial group Société Alsacienne de Contructions Mécaniques and the president of the Société Lyonnaise des Eaux et de l'Éclairage (this was later nationalised to become Électricité de France). Alan Muntz was to work closely with both of these groups with the formation of the Alan Muntz Company in 1937, initially in the free-piston engine invented by the Paris-based Argentine lawyer and inventor Raul Pescara (fully Raul Pateras Pescara de Castelluccio, Marquis of Pateras-Pescara). Alan Muntz was keen to continue development of the engine and establish his own patent for it. Work had already been carried out on the engine by both French groups and the Alan Muntz Company provided technical assistance (particularly in regard to internal combustion). Both French companies were cut off by the war but Alan Muntz was able to gain British Government support along with assistance from the Anglo-Persian Oil Company's engine research branch.

Leslie Baynes was the chief designer for the company. He was known at Heston as 'The Baron'. The nickname related to an anecdote involving Baynes in his car (a Lagonda) talking his way out of an awkward situation with the local constabulary by giving his name as 'Baron Baynes'. Once the police 'realised' he was a baron (he wasn't) he was allowed to proceed without further ado. Baynes was assisted by a talented team which included Viv Billings and Richard Becker; they produced many interesting designs and concepts.

Initially, the Alan Muntz Company design offices were located in the loft area/upper floor of the Jackaman Hangar and accessed via outside stairs on the east side. After the RAF moved in, the stairs on the west side gave access to the RAF mess. The RAF eventually took over the whole of the Jackaman Hangar and the Alan Muntz Company relocated to a small factory-type facility on the north side of Heston Aerodrome, with the design team working from a blister hangar on the south side.

A development contract from the Admiralty allowed the use of the Admiralty Engineering Laboratory at West Drayton for developing a free-piston gas generator (US75) capable of one-third of the output of the French unit (GS34) for use in motor torpedo boats. A later development contract from the MAP (Ministry of Aircraft Production) was given for a similar unit (CS75) to be developed for use in long-range aircraft. Leslie Baynes came up with a design for a flying boat which was larger than the Short Sunderland in which the CS75 would be installed. Whilst the flying-boat project was not proceeded with, it led to the development of Muntz Direct Flow Air Valves.

The Engine Design Office of the company moved to factory premises in Feltham to enable testing work to be carried out, although the aircraft design work continued at Heston under Leslie Baynes. The company moved to Langley Aerodrome in February 1952.

A number of interesting projects were worked on. Among them were: a contract from the Ministry of Supply to design and modify Rolls-Royce Merlin engines to run on gas; the Converter plane, also known as the Baynes Heliplane which never passed beyond the design stage; the prototype Carden-Baynes small twin-pusher light aircraft employing Carden modified Ford engines (work halted with the outbreak of war); the Baynes Carrier Wing (also known unofficially as the Bat) which started as a concept to add wings to a Vickers-Armstrong light tank. Leslie Baynes' approach to this concept was to take away the tail and have the vertical control surfaces incorporated in the wingtips, which was, in effect, a flying wing without any need for a fuselage or undercarriage as the vehicle's tracks or wheels would be enough undercarriage in itself. The controls of the wing were projected into the tank and the wings would be dispensed with upon landing. The aerodynamic properties of flying wings had not been fully studied at this stage. The Air Ministry did not like the concept because of the lack of a tail and rejected the idea. However, Lord Beaverbrook overruled the decision and a contract was given for a one-third-size scale model (eventually given the serial RA809). Although Baynes, Richard Becker and Viv Billings of the Alan Muntz Company had carried out this portion of the research, the actual construction of the wing was given to Slingsby Sailplanes Ltd of Kirkbymoorside with the testing carried out at Sherburn-in-Elmet. Despite useful trial flights undertaken by Robert Kronfeld and Eric Brown, nothing further came of the project. Richard Becker from the design team made a number of trips to Kirkbymoorside to supervise the building.

Only one prototype of the Youngman-Baynes Hi-Lift G-AMBL was built under the auspices of the Alan Muntz Company. Syd Holloway was responsible for the wind tunnel tests and the aircraft was handed over to Heston Aircraft Ltd for completion with its first flight on 5 February 1948.

Another project was a very large ground searchlight, developed in conjunction with GEC Wembley. This particular project, like the Turbinlite (see below), was overtaken by the development of more accurate and reliable centrimetric airborne interception.

The Turbinlite/Aerial Target Illumination

The idea for the airborne searchlight to equip night fighters came from Sidney Cotton who enlisted the help of William Helmore and they took out joint patents on the idea (Patent Nos GB 574970 & GB 574118). Patent No. GB 575093, also taken out jointly by both men, was for navigation lights to help accompanying aircraft keep station, which was adopted for the Turbinlites. Air Commodore Helmore took over the development work to improve the concept into the Turbinlite.

The design team at the Alan Muntz Company was tasked with producing a design for a searchlight to be placed in the nose of a Douglas Havoc carrying the primitive air interception

First flight of Boston Turbinlite Prototype W8254, July 1941. L to R: Richard W. 'Dick' Becker, Dennis Roberts, Leslie 'Baron' Baynes and Bruce Benson, all Alan Muntz Co. design team. Squadron Leader A.E. Clouston is in the cockpit. (Paul Becker)

unit and used in conjunction with Hawker Hurricanes to act as night fighters to hunt German bombers. The fighters would keep on station with the Havoc with the aid of station-keeping lights, shining directly on to white strips on both sides of the Turbinlite's mainplane.

Under Leslie Baynes, the design work was carried out by chief draughtsmen on the project, Viv Billings and Richard Becker. The project was originally known as Air Target Illumination (ATI) but then became known as the Helmore or Helmore Turbinlite or just Turbinlite, before finally ending up as the Hunter.

In conjunction with the research laboratories at GEC (General Electric Corporation), they came up with a workable plan to fit what was at the time the most powerful searchlight in the world into the nose of a Douglas Havoc. This required forty-eight 12v batteries (manufactured by Peto & Radford), weighing 1,920lb (870kg), to be fitted into the bomb bay of the aircraft. The batteries were designed to discharge in under twelve seconds. The power consumption of the light was 1,400 amps (compared to 150 amps of the later Leigh Light). A para-elliptical reflector projected a horizontal sausage-shaped beam of 30 degrees divergence, 950yds (868m) wide at a range of 1 mile (1,609m). At the suggestion of Leslie Baynes, the flat nose of the aircraft had a 'Townend' ring fitted to counteract turbulence and drag along with the resulting speed reduction. Wind tunnel tests at RAE Farnborough showed that with the 'Townend' ring fitted the loss of airspeed was only just over 5mph (8km/h).

A.E. Clouston's 1422 Flight at Heston carried out the flight development phase. At this point, Clouston had been promoted on 1 June 1941 to acting squadron leader. The first four aircraft (Douglas Boston IIIs) were fitted out by Airwork at Heston by the end of July 1941, with a further sixteen completed shortly afterwards by the Heston Aircraft Company. Components were provided to Airwork by the Heston Aircraft Company and Vickers-Armstrong. The remaining aircraft were modified and fitted out at the Burtonwood repair depot. Nine flights were established to undertake training at Heston and ten squadrons comprising almost 100 aircraft (Douglas Havocs and Bostons) were formed.

The Turbinlite was not a great success, however, and was superseded by centimetric airborne interception fighters which could get within firing range without the aid of a searchlight. Only five intercepts were made from the five squadrons equipped with the Turbinlites.

Turbinlite Mosquito

The drawback of the Havoc Turbinlite was the aircraft's lack of armament. As de Havilland Mosquitos entered squadron service, one (W4087) was made available for conversion to a Mosquito Turbinlite. Again, the nose of the aircraft was flat with a fairly small oval shape with a 'Townend' ring. The standard cannon installation was retained, however, with the alignment of the guns depressed forty minutes to miss the nose structure which was scalloped around the gun ports. The carbon arc was reflected from a para-elliptical mirror which projected a sausage-shaped beam. Small elevator movements allowed the pilot to sweep the beam above and below any potential target.

As with the Havoc Turbinlite, the batteries for the Mosquito version were a considerable weight (half a ton) and were located in a removable box suspended below the main spar by means of latches to a cross tube which projected from both sides of the box. Latches at the front and rear of the box kept it in place. The box itself could be replaced with the aid of a scissors torpedo trolley in between flights.

As a concept, the Mosquito Turbinlite was not proceeded with and did not enter service unlike the Havoc Turbinlite.

Helmore 39in Torpedo

The Channel dash (Operation Cerberus) on 11 February 1942 of the German pocket battleships *Scharnhorst* and *Gneisenau* prompted Helmore to go into the offices of the Alan Muntz Company the following morning and suggest methods of sinking them. What developed from this was a proposal by GEC to use a charge fitted to a torpedo which would lift the torpedo over torpedo nets. This, however, was not practical and the project aim was changed to have the torpedo dive below the nets using radio commands.

The torpedo was restricted in size to the capacity of a Lancaster bomb bay, which meant a diameter of 39in (1m) and a weight limit of 5 tons. The torpedo was to be capable of being dropped by air with a warhead of 1 ton of RDX explosive and having a 25-mile (40km) range. The torpedo was to be dropped by an Avro Lancaster with a de Havilland Mosquito acting as a command aircraft, controlling the torpedo by radio.

A scale model using a 21in (53cm) Torpedo was modified to develop the control system, with the test being conducted at the Queen Mary Reservoir at Staines. An RAF rescue launch being used for recovery was holed above the water line when the model went off course.

One of the problems that had to be overcome was that the torpedo used a 550bhp Meteor tank engine (developed from the Merlin engine) which required fuel and air. In order to maintain trim, a system using a bag and valve was designed to replace the fuel used with sea water.

In addition, the Alan Muntz design team produced a retractable tubular mast with inflatable tubular shutters which were activated by water pressure switches on the mast. The pressure switches on the mast controlled the air shutters on the masthead when water threatened to spill down into the engine. Once the ambient air was cut off by the shutters, air was released from 2,000psi air bottles. This compressed air feed was necessary to keep the engine running through waves and its final dive below nets.

After the torpedo had been launched, the mast was rotated to the erect position so it could be controlled by the Mosquito. The top of the mast carried a hemispherical radio antenna with the hydraulic actuator for the mast acting as a shock absorber in case of impact and rotated the mast 90 degrees so it lay flush with the body of the torpedo after the command to dive was given.

Apart from the Alan Muntz Company, there were numerous other parties and contractors involved: RAE Farnborough for stabilisation and control; GEC for provision of the mast and radio control; Stones of Deptford for provision of the hull and propellers; Dowty for hydraulics; Ricardo for the engine; plus others.

The complexity of the whole project meant that it was not ready before the end of the war and with the large costs involved it was another project which unfortunately never came to full fruition.

Baynes Aircraft Interiors Ltd

In 1954 Alan Muntz became chairman of Baynes Aircraft Interiors Ltd which was established as a subsidiary of the Alan Muntz Company. Baynes Aircraft Interiors specialised in aircraft furnishings. Leslie Baynes had notable artistic qualities which he put to good use in the contracts won by the company for aircraft interior work. In fact, on some sub-contracts, such as Aer Lingus and Vickers-Armstrong, it was a stipulation that the aircraft interior work be carried out only by Baynes Aircraft Interiors Ltd. Other work included the design and building of the Bristol Brabazon crew rest area. There was substantial work from Bristol Aircraft and the granting of a contract for work on the Bristol Britannia kept the company going for a number of years.

Rotachute

The leading designer and researcher for the Rotachute and in the field of rotary wing design was the Austrian Raoul Hafner. After he had been interned briefly, Hafner began work at the Central Landing Establishment, Ringway, on the Rotachute, which he designed to carry a man using a two-bladed rotor which was to be strapped to the soldier's back. The original design of a harness to be strapped to the soldier's back was dropped in favour of a machine consisting of a rotor atop a tubular metal frame on which the soldier would sit. A fin gave stability and a control column was fitted to enable the rotor to be tilted. Prototypes of the rotary wing glider were ordered from both Airwork General Trading at Hounslow and F. Hills & Sons Ltd in Manchester.

4

HESTON[1]

Nigel Norman and Alan Muntz regularly flew their de Havilland Moths from London to visit Nigel Norman's stepfather, Major Edward Fitzgerald, at his home near Cirencester. In his own words, Alan Muntz stated:

---

1   This chapter describes only civil activities.

Flying my Gipsy Moth soon brought home to me the crying need for an aerodrome within easy reach of London possessing aircraft housing and servicing facilities for light aircraft. Hence the search for a suitable site (mostly by air) and much careful budgeting to justify the essential financial backing.

The aerodrome at Heston will forever be linked with the Airwork name. The story of Heston can be divided into roughly four phases: the golden age of private flying from 1929 to 1934/35; the commercial development of the airport and approach to war from 1933/34 to 1939; the war years 1939 to 1945; and, finally, the decline and official closure from 1945 to 15 May 1947. Probably more than anything, Heston will be remembered as being described as the 'Ascot of Flying' or 'The Aerial Ascot'. At a Household Brigade Flying Club aviation meeting in 1931 which was closed to the public, *Flight* reported:

Messrs Norman and Muntz must, figuratively speaking, be rubbing their hands with glee when they saw so many of just the sort of people they set out to cater for gathered together on their aerodrome. Airwork Ltd have always made it their policy to encourage the people who consider themselves well up the social scale and who can afford more or less what they want in the way of aircraft.

An overview of Heston in the early 1930s. The central building with the control tower contained offices, a restaurant, flying clubs and the Airwork Flying School. (Royal Aero Club)

Heston was chosen as the site for the new aerodrome and was initially named Heston Air Park, being renamed Heston Airport in September 1931. The site was close to Cranford, 1½ miles (2.4km) to the west of Heston. The Airwork office was located at Albion Lodge in Cranford.

Nigel Norman had travelled to Poland and Germany gathering data on aerodromes prior to the purchase of the Heston field. He had been particularly impressed by what he saw in Poland and said that the countryside he saw was very flat and well suited to the building of aerodromes. The land Nigel Norman and Alan Muntz had surveyed for the future aerodrome was used as orchards and market gardens, and was surrounded by fields except to the north where there was housing, the Great Western Railway line and the Grand Union Canal. Otherwise, in all respects the location was ideal.

Once the land had been purchased, work started immediately on levelling, drainage and clearance. They were assisted by Alan Muntz's father who was experienced in this type of work at the family farm and estate at Stype Grange near Hungerford in west Berkshire. Immediately after the clearance and preparation of the land, Nigel Norman made a number of landings on the airfield in his DH.60 Moth G-EBWY. There were two small 'humps', which were levelled, but otherwise he was very happy with the site.

Once completed, the entrance to the aerodrome was from Cranford Lane and the short concrete road led to the central building which was flanked by hangars. The hangars and airport buildings were all located to the south of the landing areas.

BUILDINGS & FACILITIES

Alan Muntz and Nigel Norman set about buying as much of the land as they could with an eye to further land purchases later when expansion required it. In September 1928, 67 acres of land were bought for £10 per acre.

Heston Air Park was formally opened on 6 July 1929 by the Minister of Aviation, Lord Thomson, accompanied by Sir Sefton Brancker, the director general of Civil Aviation. Prior to the official July opening, the airfield had already been in use whilst the finishing touches were being put to the facilities. Heston was the first privately owned public airport in the UK and boasted excellent facilities for private flying.

The initial size of the field was 600 x 450yds (549 x 411m), with room to increase to 800 x 800yds (731 x 731m), and space to accommodate parking for 120 aircraft. Heston also had the first all-concrete hangar in England measuring 100 x 80ft (30.5 x 24.4m). The concrete hangar had a wide door opening and the upper level (with reinforced concrete floors) was turned over for use as offices, stores and workshops. This became known as the 'Jackaman' Hangar after Maurice Jackaman who had influenced the design. Alongside the large concrete hangar was a line of smaller hangars, in effect aircraft garages which the owners of light aircraft could rent to store their aircraft with the wings folded. There was room for twenty light aircraft in these 'lock-ups' with room for another fifteen if there was pressure on space. Demand was so great for this type of storage that plans were made for another similar hangar within six months of the aerodrome opening.

A prominent feature of the new air park was the refuelling installation on the apron outside the hangars which was able to deliver all grades of fuel at a rate of 25 gallons (114 litres) per minute.

In keeping with its image of the most up-to-date facility of its kind, shortly after its opening Heston was also equipped with the first of a new type of aerodrome transmitter and receiver with half a kilowatt of power to maintain telegraphic and wireless communication over a range of 300 miles (483km).

The main central building contained club rooms, viewing verandas, a restaurant, offices and a control tower. Nigel Norman had a keen interest in design and designed the furniture for the club as well as involving himself closely with the running of the restaurant.

1929/30

In the summer of 1929, a customs official was temporarily stationed at the air park mainly in connection with the aero show of 1929 to enable private owners and air taxis to clear customs for the Continent, the aim being to reduce congestion at Croydon. Twenty-eight aircraft were cleared in total, all of which would have otherwise had to go to Croydon (in the summer, an average of twenty aircraft cleared customs at Croydon every week). By the end of 1929, approval was given for permanent customs representation at Heston and a separate building was constructed for this function. Heston thereby became the first private commercial airport in the UK to have such a facility. By September 1930, 416 aircraft had cleared customs at Heston.

In addition to the hangar, concrete was also a feature of the apron which was constructed on a new principle: the preparation of diamond-shaped slabs of pre-prepared concrete slotted into place on prepared ground to form the new apron. This made it much easier to replace if any portion sank or was cracked.

By September 1930, demand for hangar space had increased to such an extent that two more lock-up hangars had been constructed next to the first lock-up hangar so the three were in a row together.

To assist night-flying, mobile floodlighting was used from 1930 and this was gradually improved over the next five years with fixed floodlights.

1932

At the end of March 1932 new hotel-style accommodation was opened. The facilities included a lounge and eight bedrooms, each with its own bathroom. The charge was half a guinea per night per room. There was also a large dormitory available as a pilot's barracks.

1933

In December 1933 En-Tout-Cas Co. (Syston) Ltd was engaged to carry out work on preparation of the 38 acres of land on the eastern side of the aerodrome being negotiated for purchase.

A service hangar was built on the other side of the main central building.

1934

In 1934 a further 38 acres of land were finally bought to give a total of 105 acres for the landing area. This was a considerable expansion. This extra land extended the airfield to the north-east which gave an east–west run of 700yds (640m) and a north-east–south-west run of 1,000yds (914m).

In December 1934, in order to assist aircraft whose blind-flying instruments did not come into operation until after take-off, a white dotted chalk line was painted across the aerodrome on a compass bearing of 85 degrees (more or less directly east–west). The line was bisected by a double cross-line 20ft (6.1m) long, with single white cross-line marks each quarter of the total distance of 805yds (736m). Ten cubic yards of chalk were used in making the line and the method adopted, after a preliminary theodolite survey, was for the two parties to start at opposite ends of the aerodrome. On meeting in the middle, the two lines were only 1½in (3.75cm) apart.

AS.4 Ferry G-ACFB; in the background is the Airwork Flying School's Avro Club Cadet G-ACHP. (Via Peter Amos)

1935

A significant amount of building work took place in 1935. Modifications were made to the passenger station to separate incoming and departing passengers due to the increasing numbers. A block of glass-fronted showrooms was built on to the west of the concrete hangar. Two squash courts were constructed to the south of the concrete hangar.

However, the major event of 1935 for Heston and a major boost to the Airwork operation was the official opening of the new Airwork Central Repair Station just to the west of the control tower building, which was opened on Friday 19 July 1935 by the Secretary of Air, Sir Philip Cunliffe-Lister. Described by *Flight* magazine as a 'Giant' hangar, it had been designed by Norman, Muntz and Dawbarn with steelwork framing by Boulton and Paul, and the contracting work was carried out by McLaughin and Hardy. The new facilities provided 32,450sq. ft (3,015sq. m) of unobstructed floor area with a door area of 200 x 30ft (61 x 13.6m). Around three sides of the new hangar were workshops including a cleaning room, engine shop, woodwork shop, fabric shop, battery and electrical equipment room, normalising room, first-aid room and a paint shop. The paint shop was separated from the rest of the facility by a fireproof door and was well ventilated.

To make way for the grand new hangar and offices, the small hangars accommodating Henly's and Brian Lewis were demolished and these two companies moved to a new hangar on the north-west side of the airport close to the Heston Aircraft Company facility.

During the year other improvements included the expansion of the landing area by 45 acres; the construction of a new block of offices for the airlines and to improve night-flying; and the installation of two Chance floodlights (each of 1.25 million candlepower) to supplement the Chance-Airwork Shadow Bar. There was also now floodlighting operated from the control tower on the eastern and southern boundaries and the north-west corner of the airport. The Shadow Bar was kept for use in emergencies. The floodlighting was worked according to wind direction, with the bar facing incoming pilots switched off. New boundary lighting, which was designed to give pilots an indication of perspective, was also installed at the end of February.

The additional acreage allowed landing runs of 2,100ft (640m) east–west and 3,000ft (915m) north-east–south-west.

Towards the end of 1935, a Lorenz blind-approach system was installed by Standard Telephones & Cables, who held the UK rights for the German equipment. The work, according to plans drawn up by Airwork's technical director Roderick Denman, was completed early in the new year of 1936. Heston was the first British airport to have this equipment and a full-scale test was made on 10 February 1936 by a Ju.52 of Lufthansa. The following month, a Lufthansa Ju.52 diverted from Croydon due to fog but was able to land at Heston using the Lorenz system.

In addition, Airwork had fitted the Lorenz receiving equipment to the Standard Telephones & Cables DH.80 Puss Moth G-AAZX for demonstration purposes, the first aircraft on the British register to be so equipped.

1936

In October 1936 Airwork instructed Alfred Savill & Son to put up 26 acres for sale on the eastern side of the airport. Whilst the approach from the Lorenz Beam was from this direction, the usage of this area of land was hampered by the fact there was a paling and public footpath through it. The footpath was a right of way that only an Act of Parliament could remove, so it was decided to relocate the Lorenz Beacons to offer a different line of approach and to sell the land. The significance of these 26 acres was that since September 1935 the Air Ministry had been considering a fast diesel rail service to Heston from Paddington, using the 26 acres of land as an air and rail terminus. There was pressure on the land for housing and, with the problem created by the footpath, Airwork decided just to sell the land with provisos regarding the height of any new buildings. Housing was eventually built on the land. At this stage expansion to the north and south of the airport was still possible.

1937

The Alan Muntz Company facility in North Hyde Lane by the side of Berkeley School playing field was built in 1936–37.

The Airwork Service Department offered complete overhauls on all types of engines and airframes with the additional service of damaged aircraft being collected from anywhere in the UK by a salvage team and brought back to Heston for repair. A woodmill was also run at Heston by Airwork, which offered aviators the opportunity to buy wood and have it properly prepared for use in the building of aircraft and for aircraft repairs.

The Airwork Supply Department also offered the facility of designing, supplying and erecting any size or type of hangar within the UK. As well, the directors of Airwork were given approval by the Air Council to act as consultants in aerodrome design and construction, in addition to the selection and layout of suitable sites. This was an area that was to take up a large proportion of Nigel Norman's time in the early to mid-1930s.

A fog line was laid down at Heston and was used by regular services in low visibility.

1938

Improvements were made to the bad-weather approach system which included a VHF radio beacon beyond the western edge of the airfield, and coloured approach lighting to runway 09/27 was installed to supplement the Lorenz system.

With the arrival of British Airways at the end of May 1938, the Airwork Service Department was moved to a hangar at the eastern end of the apron and the Airwork office staff were accommodated in a large single-storey building on the right of the entrance drive. A new traffic office was constructed on the site of the old one and was in use by early June 1938.

1939

When Airwork were in total control of Heston, they worked out detailed plans for considerable expansion of the airport that would have taken in land to the east, west and almost as far south as the Bath Road. The terminal buildings were to have been relocated to the northern boundary. Landing runs of 6,000ft (1,829m) to 6,480ft (1,975m) would have been possible with the extended boundaries and proposals were made to lay hard runways. After the Air Ministry bought Heston, they proposed similar plans in March 1939 to expand the airport. New land had already been bought to the south, east and west, and the intention was to improve and extend Heston, not just in line with those of a 'Standard Airport' but a 'Super Standard Airport'. In order to carry out the full expansion, it would have been necessary to close Cranford Lane along with roads adjacent to the western boundary.

HOUSEHOLD BRIGADE FLYING CLUB

The Household Brigade Flying Club, which was known as the Guards Flying Club, moved into Heston from Brooklands (taking over three rooms on the first floor of the central building at Heston). The move was prompted by lack of space at Brooklands. The club brought an air of exclusivity with them which added to the image that Heston projected of a place where the upper classes could meet, socialise and indulge in their shared interest of flying.

On 22 July 1931 the Guards Flying Club held an aviation 'meeting'. Heston was closed to the public for the day and a distinguished array of visitors attended including HRH the Prince of Wales. He presented the trophy to the winner of the Gwyn Madocks Cup, the annual landing competition held by the Guards Flying Club. Imperial Airways Handley Page HP.42 *Hadrian* G-AAUE made an over-flight of the aerodrome during the meeting.

The 1932 display on 18 May started with the final of the annual competition for the Gwyn Madocks Cup. However, the show had more of a military flavour to it with participants including the Armstrong Whitworth 16, Hawker Fury and Fairey Firefly. Also included was a flypast by Westland Wapitis of 601 Squadron. On the civil side, there was a demonstration of traffic control with four de Havilland Moths operating to instructions from the control tower to their wireless receiving sets (a light model manufactured by Standard Telephones & Cables Ltd), plus a demonstration of the flying capabilities of the Comper Swift.

The club took delivery of DH.60G Gipsy Moth G-AALK in July 1932. The aircraft was painted in new colours and fitted with a new Airwork Mk III windscreen. The Gipsy Moth remained registered in the original owner's name and was maintained by Airwork.

The annual general meeting of the club was held on 29 May 1935, which included a night-flying display and joy rides by Spartan Air Lines and Jersey Airways among others.

OLD ETONIAN FLYING CLUB

An Old Etonian Flying Club with its base at Heston was first proposed in July 1933. The originators of the idea were J.A.H. Burge and H.S. Burge with the backing and support of the Provost of Eton, Lord Londonderry (the Secretary of State for Air) and Sir Philip Sassoon. The club was also advised and supported by Air Vice Marshal A.E. Borton. A temporary committee was formed of the master of Semphill, Lord Apsley, Mr R.R. Ovey and Airwork director Roderick Denman. One aircraft, DH.60G Gipsy Moth G-AAFY, was purchased and made ready for use by 19 January 1934 and an arrangement was made with Airwork for the provision of maintenance and instruction at special rates. Approximately 300 members joined the club, with around 130 of them becoming flying members. Both the Old Etonian and the Household Brigade Flying Club were located in rooms beneath the control tower but were both moved to new club rooms in the western extension of the club house, which was opened in 1935. A second aircraft, Miles M.2H Hawk Major G-ACYX, arrived in November 1936. A number of Old Etonians offered the use of their landing grounds, including the Duke of Montrose at Buchanan Castle, Earl Fortescue at Minehead and Air Vice Marshal Borton near Maidstone.

AIRWORK SCHOOL OF FLYING

The late 1920s and 1930s was a period of great public interest in private flying and the Airwork School of Flying found that it had plenty of business from its opening day on 1 July 1929. Within the first year of operation, 1,000 hours of flying instruction had been undertaken with 142 pupils, twenty-three of whom qualified for their 'A' licences. By September 1930, the number of flying instructional hours had increased considerably, to 3,209 hours with seventy-four 'A' licences obtained.

Three Avro Cadets delivered to the flying school at the end of June 1933 had already accumulated seventy hours of flying time between them, a week after they had been delivered.

The noted aviator Valentine Henry Baker MC AFC became chief pilot and chief instructor for Airwork at Heston in April 1929. He brought to his new position at Airwork considerable aviation experience and in particular flying instruction experience. After leaving the RNAS (Royal Naval Air Service), he had been a flying instructor in the RFC (Royal Flying Corps) (and later the RAF) at Turnberry, Catterick and Cramlington, followed by civilian experience representing Vickers-Armstrong for three years in the Dutch East Indies as a flying instructor and also in Santiago, Chile. This was followed by spells as flying instructor for the Lancs Aero Club and he had held the post of chief flying instructor at the London Aeroplane Club, Stag Lane Aerodrome, Edgware.

The Airwork School opened under Baker's guidance and became the most famous in Britain. Up to the time of his death in 1942, of his 15,000 hours' accumulated flying time, 9,000 of these were gained at Heston. Among his more notable pupils were the Duke of Windsor (then the Prince of Wales), the Duke of Kent, former Air Minister Lord Londonderry, Lord Lloyd and Amy Johnson. 'Bake', as he was known, resigned his position with Airwork to go on to form the Martin-Baker Aircraft Company with his friend James Martin. Valentine Baker was assisted at Heston by John J. Parkes, who had come to Airwork from de Havilland and eventually became the service manager for Airwork.

One innovation for the flying school was the installation of radio-telephony equipment in the control tower in November 1929 which was used for flight instruction, with receivers fitted in the aircraft. Sir Sefton Brancker inaugurated the radio-telephony equipment in the control tower which had been manufactured at the nearby Graham Amplion Ltd, St Andrews works, in Slough. At this point, however, communication was only one-way, with the instructors on the ground talking to pupils in the air. Heston had the distinction of being the first in the UK to provide this facility. The first flying school aircraft to have a receiver fitted was DH.60G Tiger Moth G-AACY and was used for the Amplion Radio trials before being fitted to the other aircraft. G-AACY was entered for the MacRobertson Air Race in 1934 but withdrew. A sister aircraft, G-AACV, left the flying school after being purchased by Treasure Recovery Ltd to look for treasure in the Cocos Islands.

The flying school grew in popularity year on year. For instance, the May 1934 figures were 94 per cent up on the same month in the previous year despite high winds restricting some flying during the month. Overall, the flying hours for 1933 had been up by 50 per cent on the 1932 figures.

A number of well-known people learned to fly with the school and one of the first and perhaps more unusual guests was the Italian world heavyweight boxing champion Primo Carnera, who said the de Havilland Moth piloted by Valentine Baker was the only thing that had made light work of his weight when he visited in October 1929. A noteworthy pupil of the flying school was Dr J.E. Thomson who gained his 'A' licence at the age of 69½ years in 1934.

Another feature of flying lessons at the Airwork Flying School was the opportunity to learn how to fly an Autogiro. The school used an Autogiro in early 1930 and the first two pupils were both women, which was surprising given that the Autogiro was considered to be 'heavy' on the controls. One of the ladies was the Heston Aerodrome press secretary and the other was Miss Rosalind Norman, the half-sister of Airwork's co-founder Nigel Norman. She had learned to fly at Heston and was managing director of a company (Model Transport Company) based in Brooks Mews in London, which made scale models, particularly of aircraft.

Valentine Baker left Airwork in November 1935 and was replaced by Brian A. Davy.

In early 1935 the Air Ministry gave approval for the Airwork Flying School to carry out training for instrument flying; the chief flying instructor Brian Davy had already taken a number of pupils through the complete course by early March of that year on an Avro Cadet which had been fitted with Reid & Sigrist instruments. The final tests included spins and recovering the aircraft from difficult positions. The tests culminated in a hooded cockpit over a 50-mile triangular course which was terminated within gliding distance of Heston. Successful pupils gained an unofficial certificate. The area for cloud flying for the Airwork Flying School pupils extended north to Northolt, west to High Wycombe and Henley, and south almost to Brooklands. Only one pupil at a time was allowed to practise flying in cloud within this area, with aircraft from other schools keeping clear of the clouds within the boundaries.

The flying school was moved in 1935 to a new western extension of the club house.

One of the Airwork Flying School instructors, Paul B. Elwell, won the Thanet Air Race on 21 August 1937 flying Taylorcraft J.2 Cub G-AESK.

In August 1938, the Airwork Flying Club was moved to Denham airfield in Buckinghamshire due to ever-increasing pressure on space at Heston. Brian Davy left Airwork as chief flying instructor in March 1938.

AIRWORK WORKING CONDITIONS

Airwork expected the very highest of standards of workmanship from their employees in keeping with the image they projected of being Britain's leading centre for private flying and related activities, including maintenance. A good idea of what was expected from their employees was given by Syd Holloway, who joined Airwork in 1932 as a hangar boy at Heston. At the time, the service manager was Aubrey Burke who expected the very best from his staff at all times. There were many keen youngsters working for Airwork during this period including George Hawkins, Bill Kelly, Harold Jones, Dizz Allen, Norman Philips and Jimmy Gent, and they were all terrified of doing something wrong and getting the sack.

On one occasion Syd Holloway and Tom Pearce (an inspector) were compass swinging an Avro 504. Tom Pearce had to return to the hangar and left strict instructions that Syd was to hold on to the tail (on a trestle) as it was a windy day. This Avro 504 had been fitted with an exhaust hooter and Syd went forward to have a look at it. The wind caught the tail and knocked over the trestle which went through the fuselage of the aircraft. Petrified, Syd awaited the call for a dressing down and the sack from Aubrey Burke, but no call came. With no job card, the 504 was quickly repaired and he assumed the near disaster had been kept from the manager.

This view of working conditions was endorsed by another Airwork employee, Joe Connolly who joined Airwork as an apprentice at Heston in 1938. He recalled the very strict procedures and discipline. An accidental spillage of oil on the apron or hangar floor, for instance, would result in instant dismissal.

Against this, the company also took a paternalistic view towards their employees. Work tended to be slack during the winter months and Airwork were one of the few organisations in the industry which did not lay off workers during slack periods. Nonetheless, the image presented by Airwork was of an organisation that knew what they were doing and that anyone seeking advice or help would know that they were in the best hands.

PRIVATE & COMMERCIAL FLYING & OTHER ACTIVITIES

From the opening day, Heston was popular with private fliers and air taxi operators. At any one time during the first year of operation, up to fifty-seven aircraft were present on the aerodrome; also within the first year of operation, fifty-one different types of aircraft had visited. Membership of the air park could be provided for both flying and non-flying members for a fee of £2 2s and an annual subscription of £1 1s.

Airwork promoted Heston as providing first-class facilities for private flying, servicing and maintenance. Although commercial activities built up as time went on, the private flier was always catered for. For instance, in June 1936 Mr H. Addinell was appointed by Airwork to attend personally to all matters connected to the servicing of privately owned aircraft.

1929

The King's Cup and Siddeley Trophy Air Race from Heston to Glasgow (Renfrew) and Edinburgh (Dunbar as the turning point) and back was held over 5 and 6 July 1929. There were sixty entries but only forty-one final participants, and the race was won by Captain Neville Stack. Shortly after this a garden party organised by the Royal Aero Club was held on 20 July 1929. Over seventy aircraft attended with Nigel Norman, Alan Muntz and Valentine Baker acting as hosts for the event at which Civilian CAC Coupe Mk I G-AAIL made its debut. Another visitor of interest was the twin-engine Junkers General Purpose Monoplane SE-ABP.

Other aviation companies that moved into the new air park included: Brian Lewis & C.D. Barnard Ltd (who made Heston their headquarters); S.T. Lea Ltd; and International Aviation Ltd. Initially, there was representation at Heston for the following aircraft and manufacturers: de Havilland (Puss Moth and Gipsy Moth); Comper; Bluebird; Avro Avian; Klemm; and Breda. James Hunter Ltd of Chester opened their London depot at the air park to provide civil contracting services for work on aerodromes. The firm had originally been contracted to prepare the ground at Heston.

1930

The year 1930 started with a demonstration of an Autogiro, Cierva C.19 Mk II G-AALA. Flown by Flight Lieutenant A.H.C.A. Rawson and Sir Sefton Brancker, the C.19 demonstrated its capabilities to an assembled crowd of onlookers in a stiff wind. Flight Lieutenant Rawson was the Autogiro Company's test pilot.

Touring in groups was a significant part of the Heston social scene. An example was the European Easter tour organised by Airwork in 1930. With Alan Muntz, Nigel Norman and Captain Valentine Baker, a group of ten aircraft departed Heston on 17 April 1930 to visit Brussels, Cologne, Frankfurt, Munich, Salzburg, Vienna, Prague, Dresden, Berlin and Amsterdam. An engineer accompanied the group to attend to any problems.

On 9 October 1930, Wing Commander Charles Kingsford Smith departed Heston in an Avro 'Avian Sports' G-ABCF (named *Southern Cross Junior*) for an attempt on the London to Australia record, held by Bert Hinkler. He beat Hinkler's record by a third off the time, completing the 10,000 miles (16,093km) in nine days, twenty-one hours and forty minutes. Kingsford Smith's record lasted only eighteen months.

1931

On 28 October 1931 at 1.40 p.m. Prime Minister Ramsay MacDonald arrived at Heston by air in a Gipsy Moth, piloted by Mr Geoffrey Mahoney and taxied to the back of the lock-up hangars. The prime minister was greeted by Alan Muntz (Nigel Norman was in the USA), and he asked Muntz who had won the election contest in the Seaham Division which had just been contested.

Foreign guests clearing customs for the 'Weekend Aerien' held over the first weekend of September 1932. The Airwork logo sign on top of the concrete Jackaman Hangar is just visible. Customs facilities were first introduced at Heston in March 1930. (Royal Aero Club)

At this stage the election result was still not known and their discussion was interrupted by the arrival by air of Ishbel MacDonald, Ramsay MacDonald's daughter, and Delia Crossley.

It is worth noting that Nigel Norman's 1931 trip to the USA was most productive, having flown over 7,000 miles (11,265km) within the USA without mishap in a Puss Moth inspecting airports and landing grounds. He returned by sea from New York on the SS *Lapland* on 30 October 1931.

Other aviation activities in 1931 included two air races, one to Cramlington on 30 May 1931 and the other to Cardiff on 19 September 1931.

In keeping with its importance, the air park was renamed Heston Airport from 6 September 1931.

Two notable visitors to Heston in 1931 were Amy Johnson on 27 May, who flew on to a display at Brooklands, and the arrival on 24 June of the Italian Air Minister, General Italo Balbo.

By 1931–32, Heston was second only to Croydon in importance to civil flying in the UK. The Airwork Sales and Service operation was expanded with company concessionaires for de Havilland aeroplanes. Airline operations were also starting at this time.

1932

As stated earlier, from its very beginning Heston Airport attracted members of high society who were keen either to learn how to fly or to associate themselves with the social side of flying in those days. For example, to take one week in July 1932, on 20 July the Marquess of Donegal qualified for his 'A' licence at the Airwork Flying School, followed two days later by Lady Howard de Walden and Viscount Maldon, the son of the Earl of Essex. The previous day, 21 July, Lady Hay-Drummond-Hay departed Heston for Berlin and Amsterdam in her DH.80A Puss Moth G-ABEL and on the Sunday (24 July) Brigadier General A.C. Lewin, ADC to King George V, stayed at the airport hotel in order to start early at 8 a.m. to practise his flying skills in a Puss Moth. An interesting visitor during that July week was Lieutenant Robert Hirszbandt of the Polish air force, who arrived in RWD-2 SP-ADG. A group of seven aircraft (with the Hon. Drogo Montagu amongst the party) left Heston for an aviation meeting at Deauville on 23 July. That afternoon Heston played host to a visit from over 150 members of the Hounslow Central and Hounslow West Ward Ratepayers' Association. Two Puss Moths provided joy rides for the group and, whilst they had tea, they were welcomed by Nigel Norman with the aid of a loudspeaker. Co-director Roderick Denman then gave a talk on different types of aircraft and this was then followed by the Airwork Flying School's chief instructor, Captain Valentine Baker, giving an example of 'crazy flying'. That same afternoon the Countess of Haddington gave her husband a flight, he being her first passenger. On any one day in the central building's club sitting room it was said one 'could see the son of a Liberal Statesman getting ready to take his new Klemm to Cambridge or a man and his wife about to fly to the East coast with their golf clubs before returning to Heston in time for the theatre that evening'.

Despite the conscious attempt to promote the 'society' element of Heston, the general public was also catered for. From May 1932 the public could buy season tickets to watch the activities from the veranda with tea and other refreshments available.

Henly's, the car dealers, opened aircraft showrooms and a flying school with free tuition offered to their customers in the summer of 1932.

By this time Heston was designated as a diversionary airfield for Croydon, which meant that Imperial Airways airliners were seen from time to time. HP.42 G-AAXE *Hengist* was diverted to Heston from Croydon on 18 February 1932.

1933

During the first six months of 1933, the Airwork Service Department carried out 1,160 jobs from inspections to complete rebuilds. The activities of the Service Department were outlined in a booklet entitled *Weft Snarl* published by the company in mid-1933.

In 1933 the first private ATC (air traffic control) system was set up along with a self-briefing meteorological service and radio-telephony service.

The Sales Division of Airwork started to dispatch aircraft for the Egyptian air force which was a direct result of the visits to Egypt by Alan Muntz.

Airwork's engine service section also specialised in work on cars. In the summer of 1933 Prime Minister Ramsay MacDonald, Lord Trenchard and Home Secretary Sir John Gilmour had cylinder and crankshaft work carried out on the engines of their cars.

On 12 April 1933 scheduled summer air services from Heston to Ryde and Cowes on the Isle of Wight were started by Spartan Airlines with Spartan Cruiser G-ABTY operating the first service. The service became daily from 12 May 1934. The fare was 28s single and 55s return.

During the year 2,932 people had passed through customs, a 57 per cent increase on 1932.

Also in 1933 the Scottish cotton millionaire Major Jack Coates paid to have the RII 'Revoplane' sent to Heston for the Austrian Raoul Hafner to work on (Coates had been financing Hafner's work on helicopter and Autogiro design since 1930).

There were another two visits to Heston by HP.42s of Imperial Airways during 1933. HP.42 G-AAXD *Horatius* diverted in January and G-AAXE *Hengist* was diverted from Croydon on 31 December 1933, both due to fog.

By the end of 1933, 240 people were employed in all parts of the airport.

1934

By 1934, more commercial services were starting to operate from Heston, bringing in much-needed revenue. A new service began on 28 January 1934 when Jersey Airways began flying DH.84s on a once-daily scheduled service to the Channel Islands. This was an extension to the Jersey–Portsmouth service with the flight starting times having to be altered three times in every fortnight because of tides. The service started in Jersey on the beach opposite the Grand Hotel in St Helier.

A new twice-daily service to the Isle of Wight was opened by Portsmouth, Southsea & Isle of Wight Aviation on 1 May 1934, initially with their Westland Wessex G-ABVB and thereafter with DH.84 Dragons to maintain a four-times-a-day schedule at peak periods. The fare was the equivalent to the first-class rail fare over the route.

Heston became an intermediate stop (along with Nottingham and Le Touquet) on the Scottish & Provincial Airways new twice-daily Leeds (Sherburn Aerodrome) to Paris service from 6 August 1934. This service was operated in conjunction with Wallace Arnold Tours Ltd of Leeds.

BANCO opened a scheduled service to Berck for Le Touquet on 18 May 1934 with Ford 5AT-C G-ABHF. This was followed by services to Pourville on 23 June and Deauville on 12 July using Ford 5AT-C G-ABHO (named *Voyager*) and Ford 4AT-E G-ABEF (named *Vagabond*). These BANCO services were popular with passengers wishing to spend an extended weekend over the Channel, and the services operated at full or near-full capacity during the summer months.

The effect of these new services, bolstered by strong growth in private flying, saw total movements at Heston rise to 3,284 in August 1934. The summer months (May to August) of 1934 saw a colossal 500 per cent increase in passenger numbers clearing customs compared to summer 1933 (7,626 passengers compared to 1,557 the previous summer).

October 1934 was a notable month for Airwork at Heston. The company had some involvement in the 1934 England–Australia MacRobertson Air Race. The Airwork staff showed their professionalism when, on 12 October 1934, the Granville R-6H NX14307 entered for the race arrived at Heston for a number of important and very urgent modifications to be carried out on the aircraft before the race started from Mildenhall. Six Airwork engineers along with three mechanics, who had come over from the USA with the aircraft, worked day and night on the modifications which included rearrangement of the dashboard instruments to allow dual control and extending the exhaust pipe down underneath the fuselage. The exhaust spouted flames which dazzled the pilot when flying at night. Navigation and landing lights were also fitted. To allow enough time for the work to be carried out, the Royal Aero Club had granted an extension to Tuesday 16 October 1934 for the Granville R-6H to present itself at Mildenhall. The work was completed in time. Wesley Smith, the pilot to the owner of the aircraft, Miss Jacqueline Cochran, complimented the Airwork engineers by stating that the name on the nose of the aircraft QED meant *Quite Easily Done*. The compliment was gracefully accepted by the Airwork engineers. Another entrant for the race was a Lockheed DL-1A Vega G-ABGK named *Puck* flown by Jimmy Woods, which called into Heston on its way to Mildenhall. However, the aircraft's undercarriage was damaged on landing, though happily this was repaired by Airwork engineers in time for the race. Airwork sent a lorry and two engineers over to Mildenhall from Heston in order for them to supervise any work required on both aircraft. Jacqueline Cochran herself arrived at Heston on Tuesday 16 October 1934 and flew to Mildenhall with her pilot Wesley Smith. Unfortunately in the race itself they were forced to retire at Bucharest.

That same month, two second-hand Percival P.1 Gulls (VT-AFU and VT-AFV) were fitted out by Airwork in order to bring them up to an acceptable standard for use by Indian National Airways, who were going to use them for high-speed passenger and mail services.

An important visit was made on 14 October 1934 by Alderman S. Goodby, the Lord Mayor of Birmingham. He was accompanied by the Birmingham City engineer and members of the council which was at the time considering the establishment of a municipal aerodrome at Elmdon. They inspected the control tower, which had just installed a new system of two-way radios, hangars and Aerodrome Hotel. The municipal aerodrome, which was established at Elmdon on 1 May 1939, became Birmingham International Airport. That Heston was being looked at by other municipalities is due to the fact that the ATC, radio telephone and meteorological services were of such a high standard that by April 1935, the Air Ministry was considering the standardisation of these services for other aerodromes using Heston as the model.

Further to his experimental work with the ARII 'Revoplane' in 1933, Raoul Hafner continued his experimental work at Heston and in 1934, in association with Airwork (and his own newly formed company), produced the ARIII version (a gyroplane) which first flew in 1935 and was registered G-ADMV. Airwork had gained considerable experience of service work on Autogiros and, in addition to their work on construction of the first C.30 P wingless model, they had two of the older type of Autogiros under reconstruction at Heston in the autumn of 1934.

1935

In April 1935 Airwork took over Henly's aviation department and set up a new sales department under John J. Parkes with Dudley Page as assistant sales manager and staffed by Richard L'Estrange Malone, Mark Lacayo and James B. Turnbull.

On 9 March 1935 a DC-2 of Swissair came from Croydon to check Heston's suitability for operations. On board were a number of guests including the Swiss ambassador.

Among new services offered were North Eastern Airways, which operated a route from Heston to Leeds and Newcastle (Cramlington) using two Airspeed Envoys from Monday 8 April 1935 to the end of July 1935. The intention was to extend the route to Edinburgh (Turnhouse), although permission was gained for only one flight followed by a short period of service later.

Another route started on 1 May 1935 when United Airways launched a twice-daily service to Blackpool (Stanley Park) with connections to the Isle of Man (Hall Caine) and Carlisle (Kingstown).

Airwork also provided maintenance, repairs and turnarounds on a contractual basis for some of the airlines using Heston.

Before the Lorenz came into service, ATC at Heston was taken over from Airwork by the Air Ministry on 11 November 1935.

Total aircraft movements in 1935 were 33,962, 49 per cent of which were by commercial aircraft, a significant move away from the purely private flying carried out in the early days of the aerodrome.

1936

At Heston, 1936 was a very active year for Airwork. A review of the year showed that 4,132 job cards had been issued by the Service Department. These included 107 CoA (Certificate of Airworthiness) overhauls and fifty complete engine overhauls. Outstanding jobs completed during the year included equipping the Smith's Instruments DH.84 Dragon G-ADOS 'Flying Showroom' with a pneumatic automatic pilot and many instruments (inside transparent boxes) plus the rebuilding of wings for the HP.42 and Atalantas of Imperial Airways. Another complex job, which involved a significant amount of drawing-office work, was the equipping of DH.84 Dragon II G-ACNI which had been purchased from the Airwork Sales Department by the Irish Free State. The work on G-ACNI included fitting a radio, camera, bomb racks, trapdoors, troop accommodation, provision for parachutes, navigation, landing and signalling lighting plus a drogue target and winch. The aircraft was the first twin-engine aircraft to be delivered to the Irish Air Corps and the first aircraft of 1 Reconnaissance & Bomber Squadron. Given serial number 18, the Dragon was used as a target tug and for photographic assignments.

Export sales had done particularly well during the year with aircraft sold to Europe, Egypt, India, North and South America, and Australia.

The start of the year saw a portion of the British Airways fleet arrive on Saturday 11 January 1936 to make Heston their temporary headquarters after Stapleford Abbotts was heavily waterlogged by inclement weather. The aircraft and crews were still using Heston a month later in mid-February.

In April 1936 Air Commerce secured a two-year contract to fly Gaumont-British films to airfields throughout the UK for onward dispatch to local cinemas. Both Air Commerce and Gaumont-British jointly occupied the former radio building in the centre of the approach drive at Heston Airport.

A 'Weekend Aerien' held at the end of July and beginning of August 1936 brought eighty-five aircraft carrying 145 people from thirteen countries to Heston. Bad weather delayed some arrivals, which had to divert, but the crews that reached Heston enjoyed a number of aviation and sightseeing activities. Twenty-five aircraft flew to Cambridge for a tour of the city and a reception was held in London at Londonderry House by Lord and Lady Londonderry for the visitors.

A demonstration was given at Heston on 2 September 1936 by a Miles Whitney Straight to Kamal Elawi Bey and Raymond Grant-Govan. Both men represented associate Airwork companies. Kamal Elawi Bey was Misr-Airwork's managing director and Raymond Grant-Govan was the managing director of Indian National Airways. The aircraft was viewed as a possible trainer in Egypt, and in India as a pilot training aircraft and also for carrying mails for Indian National Airlines. The Airwork Sales Department later obtained Whitney Straight G-AEVA as a demonstrator.

For the whole of the summer of 1936, Alan Muntz used Puss Moth G-ABEM to commute from Heston to and from his cottage at Ecchinswell near Newbury, providing, as he put it: 'at the end of a tiring day, a most refreshing 25 minutes of carefree flying. No traffic tensions, no police traps and no cloud problems, the route being down the Bath Road valley. Of course this route was ideal for such commuting, my office being on the airport itself.' He also used G-ABEM to fly over to Ostend for dinner in his dinner jacket.

1937

One area in which Airwork were briefly involved was the supply of aircraft to both warring sides in the Spanish Civil War. For the Republicans, Airwork provided DH.84 G-ACEV and DH.89A G-ADDF. For the Nationalists, Airwork provided DH.89A G-ACPN and G-ADCL. The deliveries of these aircraft to both sides took place in 1936 and 1937.

During the first week of April 1937, Zlin XII OK-TBK was demonstrated to Airwork, who agreed to handle sales and maintenance of the trainer in the UK for the Czech manufacturer, Zlin. Prospective purchasers of the aircraft were asked to get in touch with the Airwork Sales Department at Heston. Priced at £350 in the United Kingdom, there appeared to be little interest in the aircraft.

1938

British Airways had moved from Heston to Gatwick in June 1936. However, they returned to Heston in the last week of May 1938 after flooding forced them out of Gatwick in February 1937 (Gatwick was closed for several weeks from 7 February 1937 due to the severe water-logging) and they were temporarily based at Croydon before returning to Heston.

The main routes operated by British Airways, with six Electras and three Ju.52s, were the daily except Sunday Heston–Hamburg–Copenhagen–Stockholm (Viking Royal Mail Express) and the six times daily Paris services.

Short S.16 Scion 2 G-AEZF, built under licence by Pobjoy Airmotors & Aircraft Ltd. G-AEZF started life as a floatplane for Elder Colonial Airways in West Africa before being converted to a landplane in 1941. (Alan Holloway)

The first Lockheed 14 G-AFGN for British Airways arrived from Southampton on Saturday 3 September 1938 to be used to South America via West Africa. However, it was first used to fly non-stop from Heston to Stockholm (Bromma) and return on 18 September 1938.

Prime Minister Neville Chamberlain flew from Heston to Munich to see Adolf Hitler during the Munich Crisis on three occasions. The first trip was in British Airways Lockheed 10A Electra G-AEPR on 15 September 1938 with the following two flights made in British Airways Lockheed 14 G-AFGN on 22 and 29 September 1938. It was on this last trip that he made his famous 'Peace for our time' speech outside 10 Downing Street. It is interesting to note that in an era of great interest in aviation the prime minister had never flown before his first flight to see Hitler. The place where the prime minister appeared before TV cameras at Heston is now close to the car-parking area of the westbound service area at the Heston M4 services station.

Channel Air Ferries opened a Heston–Shoreham–Isle of Wight (Bembridge)–Bournemouth–Bristol–Cardiff route which operated from 21 February 1938.

The intermittent 'Inner Circle' service flown between Heston, Gatwick and Croydon by Air Dispatch was extended to Hatfield. This service, which had started as a four times a day service between Heston and Croydon in April 1935 by Commercial Air Hire, had not lived up to its expectations, with the proposal of an 'Outer Circle' service to London aerodromes being added but not coming to fruition. The operation had deteriorated to more or less 'on demand' as opposed to a regular scheduled service and the route application for 1939 was withdrawn by Air Dispatch.

Airwork were appointed the main selling agents in Great Britain for Miles Aircraft and obtained Miles M.17 Monarch G-AFGL as a demonstrator, fitting it with a R Sensand de Lavaud variable pitch propeller. A letter from Airwork to *Aeroplane* corrected a report regarding the sale of Miles Monarchs by Messrs W.S. Shackleton; the sale had been taken over from W.S. Shackleton by Airwork.

1939

Jersey & Guernsey Airways took delivery of DH.95 Flamingo G-AFUE in May 1939 for proving flights to the Channel Islands from both Heston and Eastleigh.

In April 1939 British Airways restarted Heston–Brussels, Heston–Frankfurt–Budapest and Heston–Berlin–Warsaw services. Even with the threat of impending war, British Airways opened a new Heston–Stavanger–Stockholm–Helsinki route on 28 August 1939 using Lockheed 14s.

On 1 September 1939 British Airways started moving their aircraft over to Bristol (Whitchurch) for safety to be further away from potential attack, Whitchurch having been requisitioned by the Air Ministry just two days earlier. At virtually the same time Airwork moved thirty of its staff up to Renfrew in Scotland on 3 September 1939, the day war was declared. The five aircraft that were being worked on followed up to Renfrew a couple of days later leaving a staff of forty-four in place at Heston.

On the declaration of war, Heston was taken over by the National Air Communications organisation prior to its use by the RAF.

The ex-M&SAF (Midland & Scottish Air Ferries) airspeed ferry G-ACFB which had lain at Heston was left there as it had no CoA. It was eventually dismantled and moved for use by air cadets at Halton.

Sidney Cotton

Frederick Sidney Cotton, known as Sidney Cotton, was an Australian inventor and businessman whose name is linked with Heston through his initial command of the RAF's fledgling PDU (Photographic Development Unit). He and W.G. Antrobus had formed Aeronautical Research & Sales Corporation Ltd with a share capital of £10,000 in June 1939, describing themselves as aeronautical experts and consultants. He was commissioned on 22 September 1939 in the general duties branch of the RAF Volunteer Reserve as a squadron leader and honorary wing commander. He had carried out photographic reconnaissance work in Germany, North Africa and the Middle East on behalf of MI6 just prior to the war. Despite a somewhat unfair reputation as being involved in shady activities, he was put in charge of the PDU (later renamed 1 PDU), which was formed at Heston to undertake photographic reconnaissance work. Cotton was associated with a number of Lockheed 12As with the most well known being G-AFTL, which was registered to Cotton's aeronautical research company and was attached to the PDU but retained its civilian identity. It was equipped with three F24 cameras and a Leica camera was installed in the wing in July 1939 by Airwork. Cotton resigned his commission in mid-1940 but continued his war work with involvement in the aerial target illumination project (see Chapter 3).

The workshops at Heston extended their programme to fitting cameras on to Spitfires and Blenheims, laying the foundations of the RAF's PRU (Photographic Reconnaissance Unit). When war was declared on 3 September 1939, Sidney Cotton and his Lockheed 12A G-AFTL were absorbed by the RAF and formed the nucleus of a unit known as the Heston Flight. They took over the Airwork hangar and offices; the hotel was also commandeered and became the officers' mess. The Air Ministry then took over completely by requisitioning Heston. Airwork were basically left with a very small presence at what had been their founding base. All that remained of Airwork at Heston were the workshops which, in conjunction with the Alan Muntz Company design team, were tasked in 1941 to produce plans for Douglas Bostons to be converted from bombers to airborne searchlight-carrying fighters (see Chapter 3) as well as development work on weapons and other aircraft designs.

Immediate Pre-War Civil Work

Despite the prospect of war looming ever closer in 1939, Airwork continued with one of their principal activities at Heston which was the repair and maintenance of civil aircraft. To give an idea of some of the work carried out leading up to the outbreak of war, the following examples were carried out (note that this is not a comprehensive list).

In January 1939 the following aircraft had their CoA renewed: DH.85 Leopard Moths G-ACKM, G-ACNN, DH.89 Rapide G-ACZE.

The following aircraft had their compasses swung: DH.85 Leopard Moth G-ADBH, DH.89 Rapides G-AFMA, G-AFME, G-AFLY,G-AFLZ, Miles Hawk G-ACDU and BA Eagle G-ACPU.

Other work during the month included the inspection of a Belgian aircraft (Caudron OO-CTI) after a forced landing at Chiswick in fog; the completion of work on crashed Leopard Moth G-ADBH; the modification of ailerons on Vega Gull G-AEZL; and trials of a new Egyptian slotted aircraft. Beechcraft B-17L G-ADLE was brought to Heston for repair work after a crash in Denmark; OK-BET Beneš-Mráz Be-550 for maintenance work; two aircraft were completely dismantled, BA Swallow G-ACUF and Avro Cadet G-ACGY.

In February 1939 the following aircraft had their compasses swung: de Havilland Leopard Moth G-ACTL, DH.89 Rapides G-AFMH, G-AFMG, G-AFMF (swung on 11 February and again on 13 February as well as having an engine upgrade in the engine shop from Gipsy II to Gipsy VI), Stinson Junior G-ACSV.

Other work during the month included the completion of work on Leopard Moth G-ACKM; the completion of windscreen work (which took three days) on Miles M.2F Hawk Major G-ACWW; a test flight of DH.87A Hornet Moth G-ADJV.

In March/April 1939 the following aircraft had their CoA renewed: Leopard Moth G-ACLZ, Leopard Moth PH-ALM, DH.86A G-ADMY. The following aircraft had their compasses swung: Lockheed 12 G-AFKR.

War prize Heinkel He.111 H-20 at Heston shortly before departing to Farnborough on 3 November 1945. (Alan Holloway)

DH.85 Leopard Moth PH-ALM had its CoA renewed on 12 April; Percival Gull Six G-ADMI was given a comprehensive check after a forced landing which took place at Hayes on 11 March 1939; DH.89 Rapide G-ACZF had a generator mounted on board and work was carried out on the instruments; Hornet G-ADKW was serviced; the Airwork Flying School's Cadet G-ACHP was repaired after a crash on 24 April.

In May/June 1939 the following aircraft had their compasses swung: DH.89A Rapide G-AFMJ, DH.80A Puss Moth G-ABMD, Dragonfly OO-JFN, DH.86A G-ADMY, Beechcraft NC19187. Work was carried out on Percival Vega Gull SU-AAX for its CoA. On 17 June 1939, maintenance work was carried out on the flap gear of Percival Vega Gull G-AELS and work was also carried out on Percival Vega Gull G-AEXV from 17 June 1939 to Friday 23 June 1939 in preparation for the CoA. Work was also carried out on DH.87A Hornet Moth G-ADKW and DH.89A Rapide G-AFMH in the same month.

In July/August 1939 the following aircraft had their CoA renewed: DH.87B Hornet Moth G-AEZH, DH.82A Tiger Moth F-AQOX. The following aircraft had their compasses swung: DH.80A Puss Moth G-ABLX, Monospar G-ADLL, DH.80A Puss Moth G-ABUX, Stinson SR-5 Reliant G-ADDG, DH.82A Tiger Moth F-AQOX, Stinson SR-9B Reliant G-AEVX, Percival Q.6 G-AFGX, Stinson SR-9B Reliant G-AFTM, Spartan YI-SOF. Work was carried out on DH.80A Puss Moth G-ABLX; DH.87B Hornet Moth G-AEPV; the tail wheel was changed and work was carried out on the undercarriage of DH.85 Leopard Moth G-ACKM; DH.90 Dragonfly G-AFVJ was checked over after a heavy landing at Heston on Tuesday 25 July 1939; maintenance was carried out on DH.85 Leopard Moth G-ACPF; Spartan YI-SOF; Beechcraft B-17L G-ADLE; BA Eagle II G-AEGO; Fairchild 24C8-C G-AECO; Stinson NC21133; DH.82A Tiger Moth F-AQOX.

Post-War

Airwork had maintained a smaller presence throughout the war at Heston. The airfield itself was in constant use with several squadrons and units either being based there or passing through. Fairey Aviation had intended to make greater use of the airfield after the end of the war but moved to White Waltham in 1947.

Once the war had ended, key Airwork personnel were transferred back from their Renfrew depot and they took up residence in the concrete Jackaman Hangar where they once again started their pre-war civil maintenance work. This was only for a short period as the complete maintenance facility was moved to the Homewood site at Langley.

There was some other commercial activity at Heston with Westminster Airways starting air taxi and charter operations from a hut on the perimeter of the airfield. Westminster Airways operated a holiday charter with an Airspeed Consul on behalf of Airwork from Croydon to St Moritz, which became the first British commercial aircraft to land at Samedan Airport in January 1947.

In a speech in the House of Lords (in response to a question by his predecessor, Lord Swinton) on 10 April 1946, Lord Winster (Minister for Civil Aviation) made it quite clear that Heston would not continue as an airfield. In any event, once the first airline flight had operated from Heathrow on 15 March 1946, there was no future for Heston. After a distinguished civil and military flying record, the airfield officially closed on 15 May 1947.

The M4 motorway now runs though the old airfield site with the Heston services area occupying what was the centre of the airfield. The terminal building and control tower were put on sale in 1978 for redevelopment but were demolished in December 1978. Some of the T2 hangars were used commercially. The only remaining building is the 1929 concrete Jackaman Hangar which has Grade II listed status and, as often happens in these cases, a few of the local roads have aviation-related names.

Despite the official closure, there was flying at Heston: an Auster and DH.84 Dragon G-ACIT flew at the BOAC Sports Festival held on 9 June 1951. The last 'flight' made from Heston was on 6 June 1978 when a helicopter (AB 206B Jet Ranger 2) G-BCWM gave a farewell flight for CAA employees who had been working at Heston.

5

WHITCHURCH

In September 1930 Airwork opened a service depot at Whitchurch, Bristol. At first the facility occupied part of the public hangar as the airport itself had opened only on 31 May 1930 and buildings were still being constructed. Airwork's intention was to have their own premises. The aim was to replicate the same facilities in the west of England as those on offer at Heston, although not on quite so grand a scale. At the official opening of the aerodrome, Airwork erected a temporary hangar in the form of a marquee to cater for any servicing requirements for visiting aircraft on the occasion.

Airwork built and duly moved into their new hangar on 7 April 1931 with a formal handing-over ceremony taking place on 15 May 1931. Present at the ceremony were Nigel Norman and Roderick Denman from Airwork, along with Alderman A.A. Senington of the Airport Consultative Committee and Captain Lea P. Winters, the airport manager and secretary of the Bristol & Wessex Aeroplane Club.

The work carried out at this depot involved repainting of aircraft, repair of crashed aircraft, the overhaul of aircraft for renewal of CoA and complete overhaul of engines.

In October 1932, Richard Muntz was appointed as an outside and service representative at Airwork Whitchurch until he was moved by the company in May 1933 to Barton Aerodrome, where he became manager. Another interesting Airwork employee at Whitchurch was Joan Medlicott, who had a pilot's licence. This was not too strange for a female but what was unusual was the fact that she was employed by Airwork as an engineering apprentice.

By the end of 1933, the number of people employed at Whitchurch Airport had grown to thirty-five and Airwork were the largest employers with fifteen staff. In fact, during the Bristol–Brighton week in the summer of 1933, the Whitchurch branch of Airwork was so busy that it had to call on staff to be sent over from Heston to help cope with the additional work. During the week a daily Westland Wessex service was laid on by Norman Edgar to carry passengers between Bristol and Brighton.

The new Airwork hangar on the south side of Whitchurch was opened on 15 May 1931. The hangar continued in use (as a sports centre) after Whitchurch closed in 1957. (John Penny)

Mr J. Goodban was appointed manager for the depot in July 1935, replacing F. Hinton who transferred to Heston as works manager.

A story concerning Airwork was related by the late Richard Ashley Hall, then chairman of the Bristol & Wessex Aeroplane Club. At the end of 1935, Airwork's managing director Nigel Norman paid a visit to Whitchurch to pursue a long overdue debt from Norman Edgar who had a reputation as a likeable but shrewd operator. Airwork maintained Norman Edgar's Western Airways aircraft and a substantial amount had built up unpaid. After a meeting with Edgar, Nigel Norman came away with the debt still unpaid and having granted Norman Edgar extended credit terms!

In 1936 Airwork's Whitchurch Service Department had a very busy year. This included maintenance of the whole fleet for the Bristol & Wessex Aeroplane Club, along with servicing for the Western Air Transport fleet for most of 1936 plus looking after the servicing of six privately owned aircraft.

An ultra-light aircraft, the Barnwell BSW Mk I G-AFID was built at Whitchurch by the Bristol Aircraft chief designer Captain Frank Barnwell and an Airwork Whitchurch engineer named Cleverley. The aircraft crashed on 2 August 1938 on a road adjacent to the aerodrome and Barnwell was killed.

A new factory building on the airfield commenced construction in 1939 for Airwork so that space could be provided to build wings for the Bristol Blenheim bomber. However, with the start of the war, Airwork were basically forced to find alternative accommodation as the newly formed airline BOAC was relocated to Whitchurch from Croydon and Heston. A search was carried out for an alternative location. In the end it was decided to move to Renfrew Aerodrome near Glasgow in Scotland to undertake Blenheim repairs.

6

BARTON

Barton airfield had been constructed in 1929–30 along with a hangar and was managed by Northern Air Transport. The landing runs were 530yds (485m) north to south, 522yds (477m) north-east to south-west and 738yds (675m) east to west. In January 1933, Northern Air Transport went into receivership after lack of business in the preceding winter months. Operations were run down, with the last commercial flight on 1 April by an Avro 504K and the last club flight the following day. The Northern Air Transport fleet was then sold off.

Airwork were given a seven-year contract by Manchester Corporation to run Barton Aerodrome from 1 May 1933. Airwork's first manager for the aerodrome was Richard Muntz, who moved from Airwork's Bristol depot. Richard Muntz was one of Alan Muntz's brothers and was given a number of positions with the company in various locations. He started as manager of Barton from 1 May 1933 until November 1933 when he was transferred to Misr-Airwork in Cairo. Captain Edward Dundonald 'Don' Ayre was then appointed from managing the workshops at Hanworth to replace him as general manager at Barton from 20 November 1933. A former RFC/RAF pilot in 1917–19, Don Ayre had wide experience of flying including working as a pilot for Imperial Airways, the Henderson School of Flying and Skywork Ltd in South Africa. He left in February 1935 when he took up an appointment to manage Dyce Aerodrome in Aberdeen.

Barton was the third centre owned by Airwork after Heston and Bristol (Whitchurch).

Airwork placed Fox Moth G-ABWF at Barton to be used for air-taxi work. Its first trip was to Stag Lane, followed by trips to other locations such as Belfast. To cover the requirement for flying tuition, Airwork stationed DH.60G Moth G-ABCS at the airfield from April 1933 until it

A general view of Barton in early 1935 showing the control tower and hangar. GAL ST-4 Monospar G-ACFR is parked in front of the tower. (R.A. Scholefield)

was sold in July 1934. After the summer, Percival P.1B Gull Four G-ACHA replaced G-ABWF.

In the spring of 1933, a control tower and wireless station were constructed. Two transmitting masts were placed 1,500yds (1,372m) north-west of the airfield. These facilities were the first at a municipal airport outside London and enabled communication with aircraft in flight over long distances and to give pilots their bearing from the airfield. Meteorological services were located on the first floor with a wireless station on the second floor and flying control officers on the top floor. Teleprinter services were also provided. The intention was to establish Barton as an important centre for air services to and from north-west England. To back this up, Airwork advertised their services at Barton as providing airline servicing, repairs, overhauls, flying training, air taxis and private-owner services, along with meteorological services and the facility of a directional wireless station. By December 1933, a customs officer was available to attend when required.

Ten operators made their first visits to Barton in 1933. These included M&SAF, Blackpool & West Coast Air Services and Hillman Airways.

Despite the work that was put in to establish Barton, Manchester Corporation stated that Barton would not be ready in time in 1934 to enable fast commercial aircraft to use it. Any possible long-term future of Barton as Manchester's future airport was decided in July 1934 with the announcement by the Airport Committee that Ringway had been selected as the most suitable site. They also added that the cost of bringing Barton up to a suitable standard would be £500,000 against £180,000 for Ringway.

Despite the focus on Ringway, Barton had shown promising figures for passengers and movements. In 1936 Airwork's operation at Barton showed a very encouraging trend. From 1 January 1936 to 31 December 1936 there was a 20 per cent increase over the previous year when over 4,500 landings and take-offs were recorded. In addition to this there was a

Initially, Airwork General Trading Company had won a contract to carry out modifications on Armstrong Whitworth Whitley bombers. Both the British Airways Maintenance Unit and Training School along with British Airways had moved from Gatwick to Heston that year. Airwork had asked Airports Ltd for space at Gatwick and eventually took space in the vacated British Airways hangar and started the Whitley modification work. There was a considerable amount of setting up of equipment first which was overseen by the planning manager A.H.A. Bastable, who had been appointed to his post in March 1939 to assist the Airwork works manager R.S. Simpson. The first Whitley to arrive was K7203 on 3 May 1938. The level of work increased to such an extent that a second hangar, funded by the Air Ministry, was started in September 1938. Three special pits were dug on the floor of the first hangar to work on the mid-central turrets on the Whitleys. Other work on the Whitleys involved fitting of navigational equipment, wireless sets, flare chutes and the three gun turrets; up to ten of the aircraft could be accommodated at any one time. A further contract was awarded to Airwork for the repair of damaged Whitleys which was also undertaken at Gatwick. The Whitley work continued into 1942. Prior to the war Airwork also looked to carry out any civil work at Gatwick if it was available. One interesting example was Avro Avian G-ACKE, the fuselage of which arrived for work to be carried out, strapped to the top of a private car in June 1938 and departed Gatwick via the same method.

VICKERS WELLINGTONS & CONSOLIDATED LIBERATORS

The Whitley modification and overhaul work was followed by a contract for repair work to be carried out on Vickers Wellingtons from 1941 to 1945 under contract No. C/Acft/1177/C37b and Consolidated Liberator modifications from October 1945 to February 1946. One example of a Liberator which passed through was FL958 which arrived on 8 October 1945 from Kirkbride. Two examples of Wellingtons which were worked on are ME983 which left Gatwick for Slade Farm on 1 November 1944 and HE446 which arrived on 20 November 1944 from Boscombe Down.

A Vickers Viking in the static area at the Gatwick open day, held on 10 July 1948, with members of the public queuing up to see inside the aircraft. Airwork DH.89A G-AESR and Airspeed Consul G-AIIN gave joy rides during the day. (Royal Aero Club)

POST-WAR

After the war, Gatwick had become the location of Airwork's principal Repair and Maintenance Division, whose work included prototype installations. The Airwork Radio Department was also based there. Contracts were undertaken for British and foreign government work as well as private airline operators. Whilst Gatwick was still a grass aerodrome, serviceable jets were flown into Dunsfold, dismantled in the canvas hangars there and brought over to Gatwick by road with the process being reversed once they had been refurbished. There was considerable civil work carried out in addition to the large military contracts. For instance, Cambrian Airways DH.89As G-ALAT, G-ALZJ and G-AJCL all had new radios installed in April and May 1950.

In 1946 there were thirty-eight overhauls under way for the Ministry of Supply. A group of Sudanese journalists visited Gatwick in July 1946 and were given a demonstration of the DH.104 Dove, which was to constitute the initial aircraft for the Sudanese national airline which was being assisted by Airwork in the Sudan.

Airwork Gatwick also had a contract to maintain the fleet of MCA (Ministry of Civil Aviation) aircraft, which comprised two Austers, two Proctors, two Tiger Moths and six Avro XIXs.

In January 1950 Airwork opened a radio showroom at Gatwick to centralise British equipment in the field at one centre. Collaborating firms included STC, Ekco, Murphy, Cossor, Marconi and Ultra Electric.

Douglas DC-3 Overhauls

Post-war, one of the largest pieces of work undertaken by the Airwork depot at Gatwick was the refurbishment and conversion of ex-military C-47/Douglas DC-3s to civilian use. This included the laborious stripping off of camouflage to the bare metal underneath. Two of the main customers were KLM and BOAC. The work included carrying out the design work to the customer airline's specifications. BEA sent their Douglas DC-3s to Airwork at Gatwick for their CoAs plus any necessary conversion work for passengers or freight. In time BEA took on much of the maintenance and CoA work themselves. The RAF Dakotas were also regular visitors for conversion to VIP standard, paratroop-carrying operations and normal passenger carrying. The UNRRA fleet of DC-3s was also regularly overhauled at Gatwick. In amongst the large batches of airline DC-3 work were odd jobs like the fitting of eight chairs and one settee to a Greek air force DC-3 (ex-USAF 43-49086) which took three days (9 February to 12 February 1949). Another example of a one-off job was American Overseas Airlines DC-3 NC90908 which arrived for three weeks on 11 July 1949 for work on the fuselage door, floor, beam and fuel tanks.

Supermarine Spitfires & Seafires Refurbishment

Refurbishment of Supermarine Spitfires and Seafires constituted a large element of work post-war after a contract was given to Airwork General Trading by the Ministry of Supply in 1950 for refurbishment of these aircraft mainly for transfer to overseas air arms. For example, a number of Supermarine Seafires were transferred from RNAS Anthorn to Airwork General Trading Ltd at Gatwick via Speke in the summer of 1952 and were refurbished for the Burmese Government. The majority of the work was undertaken in 1951 but continued into 1953.

De Havilland Hornets & Sea Hornets

The work for the Hornets and Sea Hornets lasted from 1950 to 1954 and can be split into three separate areas: conversions, repairs and reconditioning. Most of the aircraft arrived by road, although a number arrived by air for repair (e.g. VR850 on 10 June 1953) and reconditioning (e.g. VV434 and VZ680 on 22 July 1953 and 16 June 1953 respectively).

Gatwick *c.* 1952. Spitfire F.22s and a de Havilland Hornet. Most of the 100+ Spitfires and Seafires refurbished by Airwork went overseas. (Tom Pharo via Air Britain)

Gatwick, 15 February 1952. A crowded hangar of de Havilland Sea Hornets including TT207 and VR858. (Royal Aero Club)

A number of RAF de Havilland Hornets received major inspections and were converted from F.3 to F.4s. For example PX291, PX296, PX304, PX329 PX301 and PX334 arrived for conversion in May and June 1952, and PX293, PX299, PX337, PX362 and PX346 arrived for conversion in July 1952.

Supermarine Attacker Refurbishment

The refurbishment of the Hornets and Sea Hornets was followed by another contract to repair and modify Supermarine Attacker jets from 1953 to 1955. The Attackers were flown into and out of Dunsfold Aerodrome and transported between Gatwick and Dunsfold on Queen Mary trailers. A trainee aircraft inspector for Airwork at the time was Barry Flahey who recalled much of his early time at Gatwick labelling all the components from the Attackers. These included items such as non-return valves, accumulators, up locks, jacks and oleo legs etc., which were all labelled using Brown Brothers and other vocabs (terms), all terms in use in the RAF and aircraft industry. Items such as valves with open ends were all sealed using red rubber ends rather like the ends of washing-up gloves and kept in jars of preservative. They were given the nickname of 'Pickled Foreskins'. Once out of the jar the red rubber would dry and shrink, thereby sealing the openings and protecting them from dust and dirt. Any item that was not in the vocab had 'NIV' written on the label. The items would then be sent off to companies like Dowty and Normalair for further testing.

North American F-86 Sabre Refurbishment

The final contract was for the refurbishment of RAF F-86 Sabres in 1954–55 for overseas air arms in which there was a considerable involvement at Dunsfold as the aircraft would arrive at Gatwick on Queen Mary trailers (as with the Attackers) due to the fact that Gatwick was still only a grass aerodrome and could not handle jet aircraft. Once the work was completed in the hangars and workshops at Gatwick, the aircraft were taken by road to Dunsfold to be reassembled, test flown and then delivered to their final destinations.

Airwork moved out of Gatwick in February 1959 and the operations carried out there were moved to Hurn. At its peak of operations Airwork employed up to 550 people at the Gatwick depot.

AIRLINE & ASSOCIATED CIVIL ACTIVITIES

8

622 SQUADRON RAUXAF

The rebirth of the Auxiliary Air Force took place on 2 June 1946 (the prefix 'Royal' was added on 16 December 1946). The two main roles of the RAuxAF were air defence and army co-operation. However, one obvious area where reservist flying could be extended was air transport. Before the war there were few commercial pilots that could be called upon. This situation was to change post-war, particularly with the Berlin Air Lift and a much larger pool of air crew could be tapped into.

The driving forces behind the formation of the unit, described as the Reserve 'Airline', were two senior Airwork men: Sir Archibald Hope (commercial manager of Airwork Ltd) and A.G. Miller. They were also both former group captains in the RAuxAF and they had first put forward the idea of a reserve transport squadron three years before its formation.

The 622 Squadron RAuxAF was reformed as a transport unit on 1 November 1950 and was inaugurated in a ceremony at Blackbushe by Mr Aidan Crawley MP, the Parliamentary Undersecretary for Air, on 15 December 1950. Mr Crawley handed over the log book for the squadron's first Valetta at the ceremony to Wing Commander R.H. McIntosh. Also present at the ceremony were Air Marshal Sir Robert Foster (AOC-in-C., Home Command), Air Marshal Sir Aubrey Ellwood (AOC-in-C Transport Command), Air Marshal Sir Robert Saundby (Ret.) plus Mr M.D.N. Wyatt and Sir Archibald Hope (respectively managing director and commercial manager of Airwork Ltd).

Previously, 622 Squadron had been a Bomber Command unit flying Lancasters and Stirlings from RAF Mildenhall in Suffolk. The squadron's badge and motto did not travel well from the former role of a bomber unit to a reserve transport unit. The badge showed an owl carrying a flash of lightning and the Latin motto *Bellamus Noctu*, which translates as 'We make war by night'.

Blackbushe, 15 December 1950. Handing over of the log books for 622 Squadron's first Valetta. L to R: Air Marshal Sir Robert M. Foster, Air Commodore Finlay Crerar and Airwork managing director Myles Wyatt. (Royal Aero Club)

Blackbushe had been chosen as the base for the squadron. 622 Squadron was the only such unit of its kind to form under an agreement between the Air Ministry and Airwork Ltd. This was to be the first of a number of agreements between the Air Ministry and individual charter airlines to provide air transport squadrons within the RAuxAF. The intention was that 622 Squadron would have a cadre of regular personnel and act in support of RAF operations, although it was entirely under the control of a civilian organisation (Airwork Ltd). The scheme was that the RAF would provide two Vickers Valetta C.1s and suitable officers' and airmen's messes near Airwork's premises at Blackbushe. Airwork, from their existing resources, provided flying personnel, ground staff and all ancillary staff and facilities which were necessary to keep an independent squadron operational.

Blackbushe Aerodrome had been chosen as the base, not only for the support provided by Airwork, but also because the unit would be able to call on the additional support from the air crews operating the numerous Vickers Vikings of the airlines already using Blackbushe (Eagle, Orion, Crewsair and Airwork itself). Should a major emergency have arisen, the idea was that 622 Squadron's Valetta fleet would be swollen by chartered or 'impressed into service' Vikings which were already being flown in and out of Blackbushe by the airlines. Supporting this plan would be Airwork who, with their experience of providing training and contract flying for the armed forces, would be able to assist in the minimal conversion training required.

The full establishment of the squadron was RAF personnel comprising one officer, six airmen and one civilian; and RAuxAF personnel comprising fifty-seven officers and 107 airmen provided by Airwork Ltd. It was commanded by Squadron Leader R.H. McIntosh AFC DFC and was provided with a core of two Vickers Valetta C.1s, VL271 and VX527. A further two Valetta C.1s were used by the squadron at differing times: VW141 and VX542. The squadron came under the command of No. 62 (Southern Group), Home Command. Wing Commander McIntosh was Airwork's chief pilot and instructor and was known by his wartime rank of wing commander but was given the rank of squadron leader in the RAuxAF as commanding officer of the squadron. He had accumulated 18,000 flying hours in thirty-one years and had flown for the RAF in both world wars.

As already mentioned, other than a cadre of regular RAF recruits, the squadron's personnel all came from Airwork. The crews were trained by the regulars in military tasks such as supply, parachute drops, glider towing and snatching as well as service procedures. The Air Ministry had also reserved the right to recruit personnel from outside sources should the need have arisen.

The idea of the military using civil aircraft for transportation was certainly not new. For instance in October 1950, in Exercise Emperor, no fewer than seven charter companies had been used to carry equipment and personnel between RAF stations. The companies included the well-known names of Cambrian Air Services, Skyways and Silver City.

It had been hoped from the outset that if the scheme was a success, then other similar squadrons would be formed using the same idea. By February 1952, an article in *Flight* magazine asked why no further auxiliary transport squadrons had been formed. It had been recommended by the MCA and the Air Council that three further squadrons be formed: Hunting Air Travel at Bovingdon, Scottish Aviation at Prestwick and Eagle Aviation at Luton. However, whilst the concept of the organisation of the squadron looked good on paper, the reality turned out to be different. The airlines were reluctant to let their pilots become reservists, knowing that the call upon the pilots of the RAuxAF would mean the airlines' schedules would be difficult to meet and maintain with constant disruption. The commercial pilots also saw that there were far better financial incentives in civil flying rather than in commitments to 622 Squadron. Unfortunately, as a result of these conflicts, the squadron's life was a fairly short-lived one and it was disbanded at Blackbushe on 30 September 1953.

9

BLACKBUSHE

After the war, the company returned to civil operations. Airwork made strong representations to the MCA for space at Blackbushe. This was prompted by the unsuitability of Croydon for Wayfarer operations. Croydon had been nominated by the MCA for charter operations (state aerodromes) in the London area, but at the time of the decision it had not been envisaged that aircraft of the size of Wayfarers and Lancastrians would be using it. Myles Wyatt expressed concern at the safety aspects of the Airwork Wayfarers operating at full capacity out of Croydon and permission was given for the aircraft to use London Airport until the end of October 1946 as an interim measure. The problem was exacerbated by Airwork's deliveries of Wayfarers to South America and Wing Commander McIntosh paid a visit to the MCA to ask if Airwork could use an RAF aerodrome to train two captains on the Wayfarers as the cost of £6 landing fees at state-owned aerodromes was exorbitant for carrying out practice landings. In the meantime Gatwick, Bovingdon and Stansted were all considered as alternatives to Croydon (Fairlop was also considered for the Wayfarer practice landings), although Wing Commander McIntosh had pointed out that Gatwick was so waterlogged that it was 'useless'. A further concession to Airwork was permission by the MCA to operate Bristol 170 G-AHJD under charter to the SBAC between London Airport and Paris for the period of the Paris Aeronautical Exhibition during 13–15, 18–23, 25, 27–29 November and 2–3 December 1946.

In the end Blackbushe was decided as probably the best option, although there were hurdles to overcome. There was demand from a number of operators for space at Blackbushe and the ministry had informed Myles Wyatt that before space could be allocated the requirements of BEA had to be taken into consideration. In the event BEA were not interested, but a number of other airlines and operators were. It is worth noting that in December 1946 Myles Wyatt had mentioned to the ministry, presumably as an attempt at leverage, that they (Airwork) held 20,000sq. ft of spare hangar space at Scone which they would be prepared to give up should the ministry have a use for it. There was a complaint to the MCA by Sir Archibald Hope at what he felt was favouritism by British Aviation Services having the pick of the hangars at Blackbushe, although this was rebuffed by the ministry.

On 4 January 1947 Airwork were offered half of the T2 hangar in the south-west corner of Blackbushe, along with office accommodation and shared passenger facilities. By 20 January 1947, it was agreed that they could have the whole T2 hangar. The former armoury was given over to use by Airwork engineers with an adjoining Nissen hut being used as a dope store. A number of ex-WAAF huts were given over to use as an air-crew hostel and also for use as dormitories for the engineers.

Airwork started to move into Blackbushe at the end of January 1947 and were officially in place on 10 February 1947. They occupied No. 1 hangar, the only T2 hangar north of the A30 that then ran through the airport. The experience gained by the company in overseas airlines operations such as Misr-Airwork, Indian National Airways and Sudan Airways was put to good use at home. Blackbushe became the home base for Airwork's passenger operations as well as being an aircraft servicing centre. It was the terminal for the East, Central and West African safari services operated jointly with Hunting Clan (which started the safari services as Hunting Air Transport) operating their services initially from Bovingdon.

The ex-BOAC Handley Page Hermes acquired by Airwork put pressure on their facilities at Blackbushe and Airwork, in turn, put pressure on the MCA to do something about improving them. The Hermes could not fit inside their hangar due to the width of its wingspan and the increased passenger capacity of the Hermes, which was double that of a Viking. At the end of 1952, work was started on extending the terminal building by constructing a new 160ft-long two-storey building to the north of the then terminal at a cost of £95,000. The original terminal was refurbished at the same time, which included a new check-in area and restaurant.

DH.84 Dragon G-ACHV at Barton. It operated from Barton for Railway Air Services and had previously been registered to the Anglo-Persian Oil Company and Airwork. It was eventually impressed as X9379 and struck off charge on 7 August 1940. (R.A. Scholefield)

10 per cent increase in passengers handled, with 5,000 passengers recorded. Most of these were carried in the summer by Railway Air Services and Blackpool & West Coast Air Services, the latter of which only operated their services in the summer.

Additionally, two aircraft construction firms operated at Barton. F. Hillson & Sons carried out construction and CoA test flights on Pragas after assembly at Barton. Hillsons also owned the Northern Aviation School & Club Ltd which operated at the aerodrome towards the end of the 1930s with five Hillson Pragas. Fairey also used the aerodrome for the test flying of the Fairey Hendon Mk II.

When Ringway officially opened on 25 June 1938, there was speculation that Barton would be closed and the land used for industrial development. This proved not to be the case but Airwork's management ceased with the outbreak of war, although by that point they were close to the end of their original seven-year contract anyway.

7

GATWICK

The move to Gatwick in 1938 was once again prompted by pressure on facilities at Heston. Airwork eventually took over a total of three hangars giving them 140,000sq. ft of space, a large part of which was eventually taken up with the overhaul of component parts under contract to the Ministry of Supply. Gatwick was not necessarily the best choice of an airfield due to the fact that it was (in 1938) a small grass aerodrome with waterlogging problems.

A covered walkway linked the two buildings. The new building contained an immigration hall, crew rooms and restaurant on the ground floor, with airline offices, a pilot briefing office and a met office on the first floor.

During Airwork's period of occupation at Blackbushe some of their flights operated from and to London Airport/Heathrow with Airwork staff operating from the Field Aircraft Facility, although the Airwork name was never displayed initially. By 1957, London Airport was described as one of the two main operating bases for their airline operations (the other being Blackbushe). After the closure of Blackbushe a number of Airwork staff were transferred to the Field's facility at London Airport/Heathrow.

On 16 December 1953 Airwork opened a town terminal for passengers to and from London at 249 Brompton Road, London, opposite the Oratory. The new terminal was opened as traffic was heavy at the three town terminals belonging to BEA (at Waterloo), BOAC (at Victoria) and KLM (in Sloane Street). The Airwork town terminal was the nearest to London Airport, Northolt and Blackbushe and contained full facilities, including a bar on each of its two floors. The establishment of a dedicated town terminal was also in keeping with Airwork's view that they considered themselves on a par with their state-owned rivals.

In January 1955 Airwork became general sales agents for PIA (Pakistan International Airlines) in the United Kingdom and PIA opened an office within the Airwork town terminal on Brompton Road. The PIA manager sat in with Markham Jackson (the Airwork town terminal manager) in his office until PIA established their own office at Piccadilly close to Airwork's Head Office, just over a year later.

Public relations for the airline was the responsibility of Elisabeth 'Minky' de Stroumillo, who took over from Anne Finnie as Airwork's publicity officer in October 1955. 'Minky' was a colourful character; she was the granddaughter of a Russian émigré and daughter of an Indian tea planter. She later worked for Freddie Laker and became the *Daily Telegraph*'s first full-time travel writer.

Five of the most popular range of aircraft being handled by the Airwork Cessna agency at Blackbushe. (Royal Aero Club)

CESSNA AGENCY

In the summer of 1959, Airwork Services Ltd became the first UK sales agent for Cessna aircraft. Airwork's chief test pilot Joe Tyszko was appointed Cessna sales manager and based at Airwork House in Piccadilly, London.

A number of demonstration aircraft were based at Blackbushe. These included Cessna 150 G-APXY (based from March to April 1960), Cessna 172 G-APYA (arrived 13 March 1960), Cessna 210 N7307E (short visit in April 1960) and Cessna 310 G-APUF (arrived 26 July 1959). All of these aircraft were the first of their type on the UK register.

Joe Tyszko was tragically killed in the crash of Cessna 210D N2313F (operated by Solberg Flyg AB) on 17 January 1965 at Lövsta, Sweden, while trying to make an emergency landing at Bromma as a result of icing. Three were killed in the accident; the passengers were Ernst Svensson and Bengt Rasmussen of Malmö.

RADIO OVERHAULS

Airwork had always looked for areas in aviation where they could carve out a niche for themselves and the introduction of the Air Navigation (Radio) Regulations in 1949 provided such an opportunity. From 1 April 1949, it was a legal requirement for every passenger-carrying aircraft to have its radio equipment checked and the serviceability certificate signed by a licensed aircraft radio engineer. The act also required that at least once a year, usually at the time of an aircraft's CoA overhaul, the radio be removed and overhauled to the manufacturer's specifications. This minimum yearly overhaul was to be carried out either by the manufacturers themselves or an organisation approved by the ARB (Air Registration Board) for such work. Naturally, Airwork set up a new division based at Blackbushe (in July 1949) under D.W. Griffiths to undertake this work. The new division was approved by the ARB and actively sought all types of radio servicing with an emphasis on large maintenance contracts, but no job was too small.

EXPERIMENTAL WORK

A number of Airwork's experimental aircraft were either based at Blackbushe or visited. Among these was the Avro Lincoln II RF342 experimental test bed in which Claude Trusk and Syd Holloway made two short test flights on 2 and 11 April 1951 over from Langley.

Vickers Viking 1B G-AKTU had ILS demonstration equipment fitted between 11 and 13 September 1956. G-AKTU also had a Marconi Doppler AD.2300 navigation system fitted. With an Airwork crew the aircraft left to give a demonstration of the new Marconi Doppler AD.2300 navigation system in Europe to interested airlines, government authorities and representatives of the aircraft industry. With the Doppler's display panel mounted in the Viking's cabin, the various parties could view the operation of the Doppler which was a radically new system. Departing on a ten-day tour on 28 April 1958, the Viking gave demonstrations in Paris, Rome, Zurich, Stockholm, Amsterdam, Cologne and Brussels, before arriving back at Blackbushe to give a series of demonstrations to interested British operators, government departments and service officers. From 30 June 1958 to 11 July 1960 it was fitted with Standard SR31 VOR equipment and ADF Remote Control Unit Type for testing.

Two Airwork Vickers Vikings (G-AKTU and G-AHOP) were used by Marconi as demonstrators or test beds with the aircraft maintained by Airwork. G-AHOP was replaced by Piaggio P.166 G-APWY in 1967. G-AHOP was used for a variety of installations from 1951 and operated from Hurn after the transfer from Blackbushe before it was withdrawn from use at Hurn on 31 July 1967.

Gloster Javelin FAW.9 XH711 was loaned to Airwork for Sperry Mk.12 Autopilot trials from 25 October 1957 and returned to Gloster Aircraft on 27 June 1958. (Robert Belcher)

Two Gloster Javelins were present at Blackbushe in 1957–58. XA634 was loaned to Airwork under a sub-contract from Gloster Aircraft for the continuation of Sperry Mk 12 Autopilot trials (which had begun earlier at Gloster Aircraft). XA634 arrived at Blackbushe on 30 April 1957 and was returned to Gloster on 3 January 1958. Similarly XH711 was loaned to Airwork for Sperry Mk 12 Autopilot trials. The Javelin arrived at some point shortly after 25 October 1957 (authority date) and returned to Gloster on 27 June 1958 prior to trials at A&AEE.

Although not experimental, Airwork also converted a number of Handley Page Hastings at Blackbushe to T.5s during 1959 and 1960.

AIRLINE OPERATIONS

It was quite apparent after the war that the Labour government was going to ensure that the new nationalised airlines were favoured and would get the lion's share of whatever business was available. However, Airwork, along with the newly emerging independent airlines, could see that there would still be commercial possibilities for them. Airwork in particular recognised that many of these opportunities would come from overseas.

Aircraft

With a view to expanding into the fields of passenger and freight charters and contract work, a fleet of DH.89A Dragon Rapides and Vickers 627 Vikings were acquired for the newly established Contract Charter Division.

The first Vikings were delivered in April and May 1947 (G-AIXR and G-AIXS respectively) with a further four delivered in 1947, followed by two Vickers 634 Vikings in February 1948 (G-AKTU and G-AKTV). An ex-BEA/British Nederland Viking G-AHOP was acquired in October 1952.

On 15 August 1954 Vickers Viking G-AIXS took off from Blackbushe with thirty-two passengers on a charter to Nice. Shortly after take-off, the Viking developed a fuel leak and the starboard engine became inoperative. The aircraft tried to return to Blackbushe but crashed 135yds (123m) short of the runway. The aircraft was destroyed by the ensuing fire but there were no serious injuries and half of the passengers elected to continue to Nice by air later the same day. The cause of the engine losing large quantities of oil was due to 'gulping' caused by the breakdown of the oil scavenge system. However, the crash itself was attributed to the captain allowing the aircraft to stall whilst making a single-engine approach to land with a contributory factor being the captain's attention being diverted by the flickering of the red undercarriage lights at a critical stage of the approach.

The first DH.89A Dragon Rapides to be delivered were G-AJDN and G-AKJS in April and December 1947, with a further three delivered in 1948. Both G-AJDN and G-AKJS were transferred to Airwork Services Training at Perth (Scone), along with G-AKRS which had been delivered in April 1948.

The first of seven Douglas DC-3s, G-AGKC, was delivered in October 1949. The next was G-AMBW delivered in June 1950, followed by G-AMRA in April 1952 (still current at the formation of BUA after transfer to Transair in November 1956), G-AMVA and G-AMZD in March 1953, G-AGIS in November 1953 and finally G-AGYZ in April 1954. Two further ex-RAF DC-3s (G-AMZW and G-AMZX) were bought but were sold to Sudan Airways and neither entered service with Airwork. The return of aircraft to Blackbushe for maintenance and servicing brought some unusual problems on occasions. For instance Douglas DC-3 G-AMZD once returned from a charter carrying Danish pigs. The first task was to remove the canvas, which covered the whole of the cabin area including the cabin walls (the seats being removed for the cargo charter), as it was emitting a powerful aroma, before servicing could begin.

The Bristol 170 Freighter was to become the mainstay of Airwork operations in Ecuador and New Zealand and was extensively used in other areas. A Bristol Freighter (G-AHJC) tour of the Middle East was organised between the Bristol Aircraft Company and Airwork in 1947. The intention was to demonstrate the capabilities of the aircraft to the oil companies in Kuwait, Abadan and Haifa (all locations where Airwork had established an interest). A special loading ramp with a hand-operated winch was installed inside the aircraft.

Airwork moved up a stage in equipment when they bought four Handley Page 81 Hermes IVs from BOAC. A total of seven were bought with three being lost in accidents on trooping flights. The Hermes had been bought by Airwork specifically to operate their new trooping contracts to the Suez Canal Zone and Nairobi.

The first four Hermes ordered by Airwork were new aircraft but had been intended for service with BOAC, although as BOAC did not want them they were diverted to Airwork. BOAC seconded staff to Airwork in 1952 for training purposes on the Hermes. The aircraft were

An Airwork HP.81 Hermes on a trooping flight and Vickers Viking IA G-AHOW, which was leased from Eagle Aviation from 11 January 1953 before it was purchased by Airwork two months later. (Royal Aero Club)

returned by BOAC to the manufacturers to have sixty-eight rearward-facing seats (depending on density they could also be fitted with forty, forty-seven or fifty-nine seats as well) fitted for trooping flights carried out by Airwork. These particular aircraft were the first modern, pressurised four-engine aircraft to enter service with a UK independent airline. A difficulty arose with their operation due to the fact that many of the airports used by Airwork had a lack of 115-octane fuel. The engines of these Hermes were adapted to use 100-octane fuel, although as 115-octane fuel became more widely available the engines were converted back. With this modification, the aircraft were given the designation Hermes 4A.

The Hermes aircraft for Airwork were delivered as follows: G-ALDB and G-ALDC in June 1952; G-ALDF in July 1952; G-ALDA in October 1952; G-AKFP in February 1953; and G-ALDG which was purchased from BOAC in 1954. G-ALDB was the first Hermes delivered and undertook tropical trials in Khartoum, returning to Blackbushe on 6 June 1952. It used Hercules 773 instead of 763 engines. G-ALDF was used for crew training with BOAC from 27 February through to March 1952 prior to delivery in July 1952. The training was supervised by the senior BOAC Hermes pilot Captain W.R. Hutcheson with the Airwork operations manager Captain D.A. Woolfe and Airwork chief pilot Captain C.D. Stenner.

In early 1954 there was some trouble with the BOAC engineering staff who threatened not to work on Hermes aircraft sold to independent airlines. The trouble actually concerned the sale of four Hermes to Britavia. Union leaders had said that their staff would only work on the Hermes on condition that any purchasers of the aircraft operated at wages and conditions no less favourable to those pertaining in BOAC and that engines would continue to be overhauled at BOAC's engine overhaul unit at Treforest Works in South Wales. The dispute was eventually resolved amicably by March 1954 and the sales of the Hermes to the independent airlines went ahead.

Despite being a step-up in equipment, Airwork's involvement with the Hermes was not a happy one and there were three accidents. After the first two accidents, Airwork were left with one Hermes pending arrival of G-ALDA in October 1952. An additional Hermes (G-ALDO) was leased from BOAC in 1952 and G-ALDG was not delivered until May 1954 as BOAC workers prevented its movement from Heathrow fearing that independent airlines would take some of their work.

In January 1958 Airwork took delivery of ex-BEA Vickers 736 Viscounts G-AODG and G-AODH, with these aircraft being put to use on the African safari services. These were followed by the delivery of two more Vickers 831 Viscounts (G-APND and G-APNE) in February and March 1959 respectively. Both G-APND and G-APNE were fitted with slipper fuel tanks for the long African routes.

Smaller Charters & Miscellaneous Activities

Sales were still an important function for the company. For example, Wing Commander 'Bats' Page, the Airwork sales manager concluded a sales deal with Aer Lingus whereby Airwork gained the sole selling rights for the seven Aer Lingus Vickers Vikings Mk 1Bs together with a good supply of spares. However, the emphasis was on the new airline and the new Contract Charter Division set about looking for business wherever it could find it. New business was to come from charters for the Crown Agents, the Cameroons Development Corporation and the Ghana Chamber of Mines. The first flight for the Ghana Chamber of Mines charters (flown by Handley Page Hermes) took place on 17 February 1958. When work could not be found for the aircraft they were leased out whenever possible. Examples include DH.89A G-AESR, which was leased in 1949 to Island Air Services to operate its profitable series of pleasure flights at Heathrow, Croydon and Northolt that summer as well as undertaking charter flights to the Continent. Another example was Douglas DC-3 G-AGYZ which was leased to Skyways Coach-Air for two months in the summer of 1956 on its coach-air service between Lympne and Beauvais.

Airwork Douglas DC-3 just arrived from Khartoum at Anvers Aerodrome, Antwerp, in early April 1950, carrying two rare white rhinoceroses plus other animals for Antwerp Zoo. (Royal Aero Club)

In May–June 1950 Airwork completed a charter using Vickers Vikings which made sixteen trips to transport 38 metric tonnes of coins and banknotes to be used for the introduction of a new currency in the Hashemite Kingdom of Transjordan.

In May 1955 Airwork flew three consignments in Vickers Vikings (each consignment containing twenty-five motorcycles) to Entebbe in Uganda. The transport of the motorcycles was organised in conjunction with the Uganda Company and BSA. The goods were for sale in Uganda and East Africa and the more expensive option of transportation by air had been taken because of lengthy delays in shipping them by sea.

Channel Islands Air Services were formed in Guernsey in 1950 and leased Airwork aircraft DH.89A Rapide G-AESR and de Havilland Dove Is G-AKSS and G-AHRJ. Airwork provided technical assistance, but after flying inter-Channel Islands services plus Southampton and Gatwick, and services to Dinard and Cherbourg in France, flying ceased in October 1950. The three aircraft which had operated in the airline's titling were returned to Airwork.

In April 1953, Airwork were granted a licence by the MCA to operate an all-freight service on the route London–Nicosia–Tripoli (Lebanon)–Kirkuk–Baghdad–Basra–Kuwait–Dhahran–Bahrain–Dukhan and/or Jebel Ali with technical stops at Nice, Malta or Rome and Mersa Matruh or Athens. The licence was valid until 31 March 1960.

One significant event took place at Blackbushe on 29 November 1949 when Airwork Viking G-AJFS made the first and only civil use of Blackbushe's FIDO (Fog Investigation & Dispersal System) on a flight to Accra via Gibraltar with urgently needed currency. With visibility at 30yds (27.4m), the system increased visibility to between 600 and 800yds (549–731m). The use of the system on this occasion cost £1,000 due to the fact that the lowest grade of diesel oil was being burned to disperse the fog, but costs could rise as high as £3,500 per hour.

In June 1955, Airwork gained permission from the Ministry of Transport & Civil Aviation for two routes. The first was a Blackbushe–Pisa inclusive tour service to run until 17 September 1955. The other was to operate inclusive tour flights from Blackbushe to Biarritz until 17 September 1955. Also in 1955, newspaper flights with Douglas DC-3s operated from Heathrow to Frankfurt on a daily basis carrying newspapers for the British forces.

For the 1960 summer season the majority of Morton's Channel Island and Rotterdam services were transferred from their Herons and Doves to Airwork's Viscounts, although the Morton Herons and Doves were used when loads were light.

Polytechnic Touring Association & Holiday Flights

A number of charters were flown on behalf of the PTA (Polytechnic Touring Association) to European destinations such as Paris, Dinard and Basle from 1947. The PTA had been founded in 1888 by the Regent Street Polytechnic (now Westminster University) to provide a travel service exclusively for students. The charter flights were popular and the service was extended to the public in the 1950s, with the PTA being renamed Poly Travel Limited before becoming part of Sir Henry Lunn's group (Lunn Poly) in the 1960s and then being acquired by the Thomson Travel Group in 1972.

A number of ski holiday charters were operated in conjunction with Fred Olsen. In January 1953 the Ski Club of Great Britain, in conjunction with the Central Council of Physical Education, awarded a contract to Airwork to fly members of a ski-training expedition to Norway. Airwork operated fourteen flights at weekly intervals between Blackbushe and Sola Airport, Stavanger. The return fare of £38 included refreshments en route, transport, twelve days' board and lodging in Norway, instruction and hire of ski equipment.

There were also ski club flights to Switzerland which continued into 1955–56 with three Hermes and five Vikings being used for the flights from Manchester and Blackbushe.

Airwork aircraft would occasionally divert to bring back an employee from abroad; one example was for engineer Ray Shoebridge in Düsseldorf, when Viking G-AJFT was returning from a Swiss ski charter and called at Düsseldorf to pick him up and return to Blackbushe. During the return flight, the autopilot malfunctioned and Ray had to earn his passage by repairing the equipment en route.

Airwork also provided air transport for George Wenger's Whitehall Travel which represented the British Civil Service.

Suvretta

In January 1947, Airwork advertised a new Swiss service. This was a bi-weekly Douglas DC-3 from Northolt to Samedan Airport in conjunction with the Swiss Suvretta Air Services company to stay at Suvretta House in St Moritz or the Park Hotel in Vitznau. The advertisements caused BEA to complain to the MCA that their statutory monopoly to Switzerland was being infringed. Their impression was that the service was the equivalent of a scheduled service as it was open to all travellers and did not constitute a charter service. The flights were also going to be routed via Zurich which was not mentioned in the advertisements and BEA felt that this would be direct competition for their services.

Investigations revealed that Suvretta House (generally regarded as the best hotel at the time in St Moritz) had formed a company named Suvretta Air Services and had made a number of approaches to Swissair, starting in mid-1946, asking that their passengers be given priority on bookings. Swissair's policy was one of non-co-operation with charter companies and they refused. Suvretta Air Services had appointed Havas International Air Services of 11 Park Street, London SW1, to represent them in the UK. Havas were represented by a Major East who had connections with Scottish Aviation.

Initially, the connection with Airwork was not totally clear, with correspondence between Swissair, BEA and the civil aviation authority in Switzerland and the UK passing back and forth with pieces of information that were either misleading or incorrect. It transpired that Suvretta Air Services had been looking at the possibility of buying a refurbished Douglas DC-3 from Scottish Aviation (possibly an ex-KLM aircraft). There is no doubt that Airwork had been deeply involved and an Airwork representative (Colonel Wharton) had phoned the MCA to discuss the possibility of their operating the service with the intention of carrying other passengers (i.e. non-Suvretta passengers) to ensure full loads. Charles Dodd (the permanent secretary) at the MCA asked for clarification from Sir Archibald Hope of Airwork who eventually responded that they had been approached in December 1946 by C.A. Koelliker, a representative of the hotel's, to act as agents. Airwork agreed and whilst they had no suitable aircraft available to undertake the service they agreed to approach Scottish Aviation for a DC-3 to operate no more than twenty trips, which would be a pure charter operation. In the end, other than a one-off flight to Samedan from Croydon on 23 April 1947 operated by a Westminster Airways Consul under charter to Airwork, the entrenched opposition of BEA put an end to any regular charter service operating.

Berlin Air Lift

The closing of land links to Berlin from West Germany from 6 a.m. on 24 June 1948 led to the massive supply by air of over 4,000 tons a day, which were needed to keep the western sectors of the city going. To ease the strain on military aircraft, numerous civil airlines became involved. Airwork played a small part, and their Bristol 170 Freighters G-AHJD and G-AICT started operating from Hamburg to Gatow corridor on 10 November 1948. Between them they flew only seventy-four sorties but were able to offer greater carrying capacity than other aircraft on some of the larger and more awkward loads. One of them was withdrawn from the air lift to carry a fuselage replacement for a Flight Refuelling Ltd Lancastrian which had broken its back. The Bristol 170 carried the section from Tarrant Rushton to Wünsdorf, Germany. The Bristol 170s were withdrawn on 12 February 1949 after 218 flying hours and uplifting 370.6 tons.

International Refugee Organisation Germany-Canada Contract, 1948/49

At the end of the Second World War there were large numbers of refugees to be processed and moved. Airwork announced on 28 May 1948 that they had gained a contract worth £1.2 million from the IRO (International Refugee Organisation) to move 17,500 refugees from Hamburg in the British Zone in Germany to Montreal in Canada. The cost per person was $260 and was being met by the sponsors and relatives in Canada. Airwork had announced that they would use five Douglas DC-4s on a time charter for the operation. The intention was initially to sub-charter the work to Seaboard and Western Airlines using their Douglas DC-4s, whilst Airwork established their own fleet of DC-4s for the job. Airwork had intended to start the programme of flights in early June 1948, which was extremely optimistic considering the formalities that had to be agreed and set in place; having said that, there was a sense of urgency from the sponsors and relatives in Canada and the refugees themselves who wanted to move to Canada and establish themselves with a minimum of delay. Nevertheless, events proceeded slowly. The attitude of the British Government was ambivalent at best and George Lindgren (the Parliamentary Secretary to the MCA) in particular was hostile. Equally, the attitude of the Canadian Government bordered on hostile towards Airwork and indeed any private charter operators. Canadian Government approval for the whole operation was essential. At first the Canadian Government put forward the view that the work should be undertaken by BOAC. The British Government made their position clear by stating that there was no objection from a commercial point of view to Airwork carrying out the programme of flights.

With the slow pace of progress, Sir Archibald Hope went to Canada to see if he could speed matters along, as up to this point all communication had been between government agencies. The direct approach by Sir Archibald Hope annoyed the British High Commissioner, who felt that, because the proper channels were not being followed (i.e. through themselves), Airwork would only create further problems. It has to be said in Airwork's defence that they were only trying to bring to a close what must have been a very frustrating business. Also Airwork were no strangers themselves when it came to dealing with government officials outside the UK and Europe. Nevertheless, it was all to no avail. The saga rambled on until the Canadian Government finally stated that it would not give its agreement unless the operation was carried out either by BOAC or by Airwork sub-contracted to BOAC. Neither BOAC nor Airwork were prepared to go along with these conditions. Two further proposals also came to nothing when Airwork suggested a partnership with KLM and also the possibility of flying to Buffalo in the USA with the final leg of the journey being made overland into Canada at Niagara. Both were rejected by the Canadians. In the end the IRO had little option but to cancel the contract with Airwork. A final suggestion by the Canadians that Trans-Canada Air Lines be involved gave an indication of the real intention of the Canadian Government, which had been to push the traffic to their airline. In the end this was precisely what happened, with the IRO awarding the contract to Trans-Canada Air Lines who commenced flights in early 1949.

Sudan Government Leave Service

The move to Blackbushe was partly due to Airwork winning a contract to carry British Sudan Government employees taking leave from the Sudan. During the war a considerable backlog of leave had built up for the British expatriate Sudan Government workers. Apart from a few senior officials who travelled via BOAC from Khartoum, the majority had to travel by train to Wadi Halfa, then by River Nile steamer to Luxor, then by train from Luxor to Cairo and complete the final portion of the journey by sea from Egypt to the UK. A further aggravating factor to the time element was that leave for the employees only started when they reached

Mr A.M. Hankin was the 10,000th passenger on the Sudan Leave Service on 4 April 1950. Marking the occasion at Blackbushe were, L to R: Archibald Hope, Mr A.M. Hankin, Mrs Muntz (dark hair), Mrs Hankin, Alan Muntz. (Royal Aero Club)

England. It was Airwork's managing director Archibald Hope who put forward the suggestion that the backlog and the time element could be rapidly reduced with charter flights. The Sudan Government agreed and an initial two-year contract was signed, with the first flight (Bristol Wayfarer G-AHJD), commanded by Captain W.T. Mellor, carrying four crew and twenty passengers, departing on 25 August 1946 to Cairo.

Initially the flights were to Cairo so the state-owned Egyptian steamers and railways and the Sudan Railway traffic were not threatened. The Sudan Government had also chartered a converted Boeing B-17 from the Swedish airline SILA (Svensk Interkontinental Lufttrafik AB) prior to the start of the Airwork service.

Two Vikings (G-AIXR and G-AIXS) were put on the route in April/May 1947. With the introduction of the Airwork Vikings, the service was extended to Wadi Halfa, with the remainder of the service to Khartoum being on Sudan Railways. However, space on the rail service became limited due to the pressure of traffic and at times the Sudan Government requested flights be extended to Khartoum; this was made permanent. At peak periods the flights operated three times a week in each direction.

In 1951 there were 150 round trips carrying 4,000 passengers. After the first two-year contract, the service was put out to tender on an annual basis (except in 1952 which was for two years) and Airwork were the carrier of choice which led to problems with BOAC. BOAC had been initially unable to consider the service because of aircraft shortages and other commitments. However, once the Airwork leave service started to operate from Khartoum and began taking other passengers to fill up seats, BOAC complained to the MCA. Nevertheless, the view of the ministry was that Airwork had bid for and won the contract from the Sudan Government, who were in turn quite entitled to put the work out to tender and pick the most competitive quote. Notwithstanding the fact that BOAC was always shown government favour wherever possible, the Sudan leave service continued to be operated by Airwork.

The service was for the employees and their families, although as well as carrying staff and families going to and from their leave, Sir Robert Howe KCMG, the new governor general of the Sudan, used the service to take up his new appointment in November 1947. Large numbers of children travelled during the holiday periods. For instance over 200 children were taken out to the Sudan for the Christmas holiday in December 1954. On 4 April 1950 one of Airwork's Vikings carried (an oft-quoted statistic) its 10,000th passenger on the leave service (345 round trips, 10,013 passengers and 394 babies).

In October 1947 an Airwork Viking flew what was believed to be the longest flight undertaken by a twin-engine aircraft up to that point. The aircraft flew from Wadi Halfa direct to Blackbushe on the same day touching down at 8.40 p.m. and flown by Captain Norman E. Waugh. The aircraft was not carrying any passengers and was returning to the UK after taking passengers out as part of the Sudan Government's leave service. Norman Waugh had been a transatlantic ferry pilot during the war.

When Airwork started to take delivery of its Hermes, these were used to supplement the Vikings on the leave service where possible, although the layout was more spacious than that used for trooping flights.

Almost exactly one month after the forced landing of Hermes G-ALDB, Hermes G-ALDF was written off near the coast of Sicily on 25 August 1952. With Captain G.S.F. Winsland in command, the Hermes was on a Blackbushe–Malta–Khartoum flight on the Sudan leave service. As the aircraft approached the town of Trapani, on the west coast of Sicily, two of the engines had to be closed down and feathered as the crew were experiencing problems with them. The only remaining electrical power from the batteries soon ran out as emergency signals were sent from the radio equipment. The remaining two engines failed and the aircraft ditched into the sea about 2 miles (3km) off the port of Trapani with seven fatalities.

The subsequent accident report was unable to determine the reason for the failure of the two inner engines. However, the report did outline a number of possible contributory factors, many of which showed the airline and crew in an unfavourable light.

The leave service came to an end with the granting of independence to the Sudan on 1 January 1956.

International Refugee Organisation Europe-Australia Contract 1948/49

In July 1948 Myles Wyatt and Sir Archibald Hope put forward proposals to both the Australian and British Governments for the carriage, by Airwork, of displaced persons to Australia from Europe and in particular Britain. The emigrants would be taken both by air and by air and sea via East Africa and Airwork would operate the service under an associate agreement with BOAC. Prior to any further discussions, Myles Wyatt was concerned that any preliminary publicity would give the initiative to ANA (Australian National Airways) and they could end up with a monopoly. The Airwork proposal was for nine Avro Tudor IVs carrying sixty passengers each. In discussions with the Deputy Undersecretary of State for Air (Safety & General), the latter expressed doubts that sixty-seat Tudors were feasible. Airwork's view was that it could be done in the same seating arrangement as the Skyways Italian emigrant traffic was being carried. The Deputy Undersecretary stated that these Tudor IVs could only be made available with Tudor II conversions and there were no guarantees regarding priority for Airwork. There were ten Tudor IIs which were being built that had been ordered by the government from Avro and these were the aircraft at the centre of Airwork's proposals. Sir Archibald Hope put forward the suggestion that they were a virtually speculative order pending confirmation of the corporation's potential use as freighters and that Airwork would have a definite use for them which would relieve the MCA of the uncertainty.

By November 1948, the contract details had been outlined. This was the movement of 36,000 displaced persons from Europe to Australia over a period of eighteen months for which Airwork would be paid £2.7 million. The plan to use Avro Tudors had been dropped and instead Airwork planned to buy five Douglas DC-4s from the USA for which they sought exchange-control permission. The plan was for the displaced persons to be flown to Eritrea and then, after a transfer to camps formerly used during the war as rest camps by the US navy, they would continue their journey by sea from Massawa to Melbourne. In effect the capacity of the ships was almost doubled as they were covering only 7,000 miles (11,265km) instead of 12,000 miles (19,312km) at a cost not much more than that if the whole passage was covered by sea. It was estimated that the refugees would spend an average of eight days in the camps until there was enough to make a shipload. The cost of the operation was to be met by the Australian Government.

The plan to buy DC-4s from the USA was dropped in favour of leasing KLM Douglas DC-4s. Airwork had started recruiting and training air crews when the whole scheme was abandoned.

Safari Service: East Africa

The colonial coach services were intended as a lower standard of service intended for the lower-fare-paying passenger.

The safari service started on 14 June 1952 with Vickers Viking G-AJFS flying the inaugural service to Nairobi, which was flown in conjunction with Hunting Air Transport. The routing for the Nairobi service was Blackbushe–Nice–Malta–Mersa Matruh–Wadi Halfa–Wadi Seidna–Juba–Entebbe–Nairobi and return. The frequency was once a week with each airline (Hunting and Airwork) operating at two-weekly intervals. The promising initial load factors of over 80 per cent prompted both airlines to apply for increased frequencies and a seven-year licence to operate the service, which was duly granted from 21 February 1953 to 20 February 1960.

An associate agreement was signed with BOAC on 27 March 1953 for the London–Nairobi route. The safari services were operated at a price differential of 15–30 per cent lower than the BOAC fares (the return fare to Nairobi was £180 [£98 single] against BOAC's £252 [£140 single] but with limited frequencies and cabin service). The fares included the cost of coach travel to and from Blackbushe from the airways terminus at Victoria station in London as well as meals and hotel accommodation en route.

Nonetheless, despite not being on a par with BOAC, and the safari service being described as 'C' rate, Airwork had always considered themselves to be a cut above the other private UK airlines. The East African safari service was considered by many travellers who used it to be first-class luxury with silver service provided. The service was also much slower than BOAC as it took two and a half days with night stops in Malta and Sudan in both directions.

An increase in frequencies (from one to two services a week) between Nairobi and London from 28 February 1953 led to a drop in load factors from 85 per cent to 74 per cent.

The introduction of Viscounts on the service in early 1958 led to complaints from BOAC that they were losing traffic on the route. It was, however, a success story for Airwork.

Colonial Coach Service: Central Africa

In their application to operate the new Central Africa service, Airwork stipulated Viking G-AHON would be mainly used with substitutes G-AIXS, G-AIXR, G-AJFS, G-AJFR, G-AJFT, G-AKTU and G-AKTV.

Permission was granted for a service to Salisbury to operate from 1 November 1952 to 31 October 1959. The services were flown every week, Airwork operating the service one week and the next being flown by Hunting Clan so that each airline was operating the route every two weeks. With the introduction of the service to Salisbury (initially the routing applied for was Blackbushe–Nice–Malta–El Adem–Wadi Halfa–Wadi Seidna–Juba–Entebbe–Kasama), Airwork and Hunting Clan were in competition with CAA (Central African Airways) who also ran a colonial coach service (from April 1953). Airwork and Hunting Clan were also allowed to carry passengers between Malta and Central Africa. The year 1953 was good for passenger numbers because of the amount travelling on account of the Coronation and the Rhodes Centenary Exhibition.

At the end of November 1952 Airwork's commercial manager, K.R. Sangster, requested a withdrawal of Malta, Khartoum and Entebbe as stops and the substitution of N'dola and Lusaka. There were a number of stops used at varying times with variations in the technical stops outwards and return. The route was Blackbushe–Nice–Malta–Mersa Matruh–Wadi Halfa–Khartoum–Juba–Entebbe–Tabora–Ndola–Lusaka–Salisbury–Lusaka–Ndola–Tabora–Entebbe–Juba–Khartoum–Wadi Halfa–Luxor (northbound only)–Mersa Matruh–Malta–Nice–Blackbushe. Benina and El Adem were used at differing times as an alternative to Mersa Matruh.

Airwork and Hunting Clan applied to have the frequencies increased from fortnightly to once a week (from 1 April 1954) on the basis that the overheads were costly for a once-fortnightly service and once a week also offered a better service and frequency to the public. The early load factors from London to Salisbury were 85 per cent southbound and 50 per cent northbound. The Airwork load factors for the whole of 1954 were a rather lower 59.5 per cent but improved to 65.6 per cent for 1955. CAA, who were in a tripartite agreement with BOAC and SAA (South African Airways), applied to operate a twice-weekly service. Attempts were made by the two British independent airlines to offer interchangeability of tickets with CAA but they rejected the offer. The request for increased frequencies in 1954/55 was, however, turned down initially, but Airwork were allowed to increase their service to three return flights within twenty-eight days. In February 1955 the ATAC agreed to allow both Hunting Clan and Airwork to substitute Douglas DC-3s on the service in place of Vikings where necessary.

The ATAC gave permission for Viscounts to be used to Salisbury from London and permission for the service was granted for ten years from October 1957, subject to review and Egyptian approval for a stop at Luxor.

West African Safari Service

In April 1954 proving flights were made by Airwork and Hunting Clan Air Transport for a new West African safari service which was due to commence on 10 May 1954. However, there were a number of mainly administrative delays and the service did not start until 14 June 1954, with Airwork Vickers Viking G-AKTU operating the first flight. Both airlines operated the twenty-seven-seat Vickers Vikings on the service. The new route was Blackbushe (Hunting Clan operated their flights from Bovingdon)–Bordeaux (later changed to Biarritz)–Tangier–Agadir–Villa Cisneros–Dakar–Bathurst–Freetown–Robertsfield (or Abidjan)–Takoradi–Accra with night stops at Tangier and Dakar. Rights had been applied for a traffic stop at Takoradi but this had not been granted. Additionally, Royal Mail post was carried on the outward journey to Dakar and in both directions between London (Bovingdon/Blackbushe) and Freetown and London (Bovingdon/Blackbushe) and Bathurst.

The West African safari service was to complement the existing safari services run by both airlines to Rhodesia and East Africa, with the tickets being interchangeable for all services. Each airline ran alternate weekly services which gave a weekly frequency in each direction. The fares were attractively priced at the time, with the cost of a return London–Accra fare set at £144 compared to the standard first-class and tourist air fares of £214 4s and £169 4s respectively.

The unpressurised Vikings operated at a height which gave good views over the countries the aircraft passed over. Lunch was taken at the first stop on the outward route (initially Bordeaux's Mérignac Airport). Tangier was the first night stop with a mid-afternoon arrival allowing time for sightseeing. On some flights Agadir was overflown, with the 1,000-mile (1,609km) journey between Tangier and Villa Cisneros being covered in five hours' flying time. Prior to the building of a proper airport at Villa Cisneros in the Spanish Sahara, the airport there was basically just a marked-out area on hardened sand. The next night stop was Dakar with the onward route from there again following the coastline of West Africa. Freetown was another interesting stop as passengers were transferred from Freetown's Lungi Airport into the town itself by river launch in order to avoid a 117-mile (188km) road trip. There was a rest house for waiting passengers overlooking the beach at Lungi Airport.

In 1958 the Vickers Vikings were replaced by Vickers Viscounts on the colonial coach service by both Airwork and Hunting Clan. This was a major upgrade in service and equipment, and was due to consent being given in June 1957 by Harold Watkins, the Minister of Transport & Civil Aviation, for modern aircraft to be used on the safari routes. The then relatively new Vickers Viscount was an aircraft with passenger appeal and better performance over the post-war Vikings. A fleet of five Viscounts (three Hunting Clan and two Airwork) were allocated to the East, Central and West African safari services which allowed a utilisation of 2,000 hours p.a. on the services with one aircraft in reserve. The Viking required a Check 1 after a single safari service, whilst the Viscount could operate three such services before a Check 1. Additionally, the Viscounts were more economical to operate owing to the introduction of statutory weight, altitude and temperature limitations on the Vikings, which would have seen them having to reduce their passenger loads from twenty-five to twenty passengers – something which would not have made them attractive for the West African service without costly modifications.

The first Viscount service took place on 6 January 1958 when G-AODG of Airwork departed Heathrow for Accra. Among the passengers was E. Asafu Adjaye, the Ghana High Commissioner in London, and some of his staff. Ghana became independent in 1957 which meant the loss of the third-class fare offered to the colonies, so the fares had to move in line with those offered by BOAC. The choice was basically the BOAC Argonaut London to Accra service via Rome, Tripoli and Kano without an overnight stop, or the Airwork/Hunting Clan service via Lisbon, Las Palmas, Bathurst and Freetown with an overnight stop in Las Palmas. In the early stages an engineer travelled with the aircraft in case any problems arose, and later on engineers were stationed at the stops on the route south of Lisbon. A feature of the route was that a high proportion of tickets that were bought were one-way due to the fact that many of the passengers were at the start or finish of their tours of duty. Although the air fares were attractive because the alternative fare by sea travel was so high, it was found that load factors on the last sector between Freetown and Accra tended to be very low and was a matter of concern as the 900 miles (1,448km) between the two points on an overall 4,200-mile (6,759km) journey was a substantial segment operating at a loss.

These West African services routes passed on to BUA.

Trooping Flights

As early as 1949, Airwork had proposed the use of civil aircraft to supplement the use of troop movements by sea. Up to the late 1940s, the vast majority of troop movements were by sea but the attractions of savings in both time and cost became obvious as the independent airlines started looking for business with the potential of supplementing the troopships. An experimental contract for one year was awarded to Airwork in 1950 for the carriage of troops to points in the Mediterranean and West Africa. Roughly 11,000 troops were carried and the experiment was regarded as a success, leading to further contracts being granted to the independents.

The first four Hermes aircraft were allocated with military serials which were used on all trooping flights but particularly with regard to the Suez Canal Zone and Fayid, the main airfield in the zone, as the treaty with the Egyptian Government did not allow civil flights into Fayid. Hermes G-ALDC/WZ840 operated the first trooping flight to Fayid airfield on 17 June 1952.

In addition to the Sudan Government leave contract, Airwork started the first of numerous War Office flights to Cairo and Khartoum on 14 February 1949, carrying wives and families of servicemen from Blackbushe in the company's Douglas DC-3s and Vickers Vikings, and this boosted the numbers travelling considerably.

By 1952, up to 120,000 troops were being moved by air both to and from the UK, but there were also third-country movements within Britain's colonial outposts such as the transfer of Gurkhas between Singapore and Calcutta by Airwork's Handley Page Hermes. Airwork became one of the leading independent airlines involved in troop transportation but their initial involvement got off to an inauspicious start with the problems caused by the withdrawal of three of their Hermes for engine modifications. The shortfall in capacity was taken up by Skyways of London who took over most of the troop movements that Airwork had been undertaking to and from Fayid in Egypt, although they had carried 9,000 passengers on the route themselves. By 1952, Skyways were carrying a yearly total of 50,000 servicemen and their families.

Airwork also gained a small but useful contract for six Hermes flights to Singapore in August 1952 after transit rights had been gained from the Indian Government. Military personnel transiting through Indian airports was an issue to start with, but did not cause as much of a problem as it did in Egypt with arriving and departing military personnel.

The Air Ministry awarded two one-year trooping contracts to Airwork in 1953 for the transport of between 1,500 and 2,000 passengers to West Africa and for a maximum of 1,850 passengers to East Africa using the Hermes in both cases. Air Charter took over the West African trooping from Airwork in May 1954. Airwork themselves had gained the West African contract after Crewsair ceased operations in 1953.

In addition to these smaller trooping contracts to Britain's overseas colonies, Airwork's trooping work was divided into three main areas: the Middle East, Singapore and communications work in the Mediterranean. The Mediterranean communications work involved the transport of 20,000 personnel within the Mediterranean and Middle Eastern area; Airwork based Vikings at both Fayid and Malta to cover this operation. The Vikings had, by 1952, replaced RAF transport aircraft and Royal Navy Corvettes in carrying the personnel. At this stage Airwork were looking for a replacement (beyond 1956) for the Vickers Vikings and considered the Vickers Viscount 700, Bristol Britannia, de Havilland Comet series II and III, and the then projected civil version of the Vickers Valiant. As always, the great cost of new and/or better replacement aircraft was a considerable hurdle to overcome. In terms of trooping, the work paid the independents well. However, whilst a vessel owner could look to ordering a new ship for this type of work and have a ten-year contract which assured continuous business, the independent airlines were granted much shorter contracts by the War Office which were mostly for around two years' duration and in some cases there was no contract in place at all for some of the work, which was conducted on an ad hoc basis.

In 1954 Airwork lost the Canal Zone and the West African trooping contracts to Air Charter but were awarded a new two-and-a-half-year trooping contract by the Air Ministry to carry 7,000 troops a year to and from Singapore and the UK. The contract was worth over £1.25 million p.a. and was the largest single trooping contract placed by the Air Ministry up to that point. The flights were from Blackbushe using Airwork's Hermes aircraft exclusively. They were to keep the contract until it was taken over by Hunting Clan in spring 1959.

The first flight was operated by G-AKFP, which left at 10.30 a.m. on 3 October 1954 from Blackbushe to Rome on the first leg of its journey with sixty-eight troops and their families. The ETA Singapore was 8.35 a.m. on Wednesday 6 October. Prior to their departure, the troops were addressed by Major General A.T. de Rhe-Philipe, the War Office Director of Movements. The crew of the inaugural flight were Captain D.S.F. Winsland (commander), First Officer T.A. Waller, Radio Officer J.R. Carroll, Engineer L.N. Flower, and Stewardesses Hodgson, Ackland and Cooke (a third stewardess was carried on this occasion in addition to the usual two). Crew changes on these trips were carried out at Nicosia and Bangkok. The route varied according to weather but included Brindisi, Istanbul, Baghdad, Karachi, Delhi and Bangkok.

By the time of the inaugural flight, further contracts were gained by Airwork to carry Royal Navy personnel from Blackbushe to Singapore, bringing the total number of military personnel to be carried each year to and from the Far East to 10,000.

In December 1955, the Far East trooping flights were transferred to Farnborough while Blackbushe was out of use.

Also in 1954, Airwork started a Vickers Viking trooping service from Blackbushe to Aden.

There were further changes when Britavia took over the Cyprus and East African trooping contracts from Airwork in July 1955, but Airwork were given a contract in 1955 for twenty-four flights between Singapore and Calcutta for the transport of Gurkha troops to and from jungle training in Malaya, thereby reducing the travelling times from the Gurkhas' homeland in Nepal. The contracts were extended and also involved Skyways, between them making fifty-eight round trips to move 4,500 troops and their families.

The Suez Crisis in 1956 saw considerable involvement from the British civil airlines. British and French forces had begun to assemble in Malta and Cyprus in August 1956. RAF Transport Command aircraft were considerably stretched and, with Airwork acting as co-ordinators, Handley Page Hermes of Airwork, Skyways and Britavia operated sixty flights to Malta and Cyprus. Eagle also operated twenty-one flights to Malta with their Vikings. BOAC had also operated flights to Cyprus using Britannias. Once the fighting in Suez was finished the independent airlines were again involved in assisting with the return of personnel.

By the late 1950s, although trooping flights were on the decline, the business was still an important part of the independent airlines' work. However, the profit margins had been squeezed so much that it was almost negligible. By 1959, Airwork's trooping work had decreased to such an extent that the Hermes were withdrawn and sold that year.

Handley Page Hermes Trooping Accidents

The first accident involved G-ALDB (carrying RAF serial WZ839), which was written off at Pithiviers, near Orléans, France, on 23 July 1952. G-ALDB was on a trooping flight from Blackbushe to RAF Fayid via Malta with six crew and fifty-four passengers. The starboard outer propeller was lost which damaged the starboard inner engine, causing it also to fail. Piloting the aircraft under asymmetric power, Captain Lovelock managed to make a forced landing on a grass airfield at Pithiviers. Despite ground obstacles, the Hermes managed to land and everyone was evacuated before the aircraft burst into flames and was destroyed. There were only three minor injuries and it was felt that the rearward-facing seats had been a factor in the safety of the passengers. The troops were all flown back to London after the accident. Formerly an RAF commanding officer of considerable experience and already a holder of the DFC, Captain R.C.O. Lovelock had joined Airwork as a flight commander with 622 Auxiliary Squadron and was a featured correspondent for *Flight* magazine. For his skilful handling of the aircraft he was awarded the Queen's Commendation for Valuable Service in the Air in December 1952.

The second Hermes accident involved G-AKFP (carrying RAF serial XD632), which was written off on landing at Calcutta's Dum Dum Airport, India, on 1 September 1957 on a trooping flight from Blackbushe to Singapore via Karachi, Delhi and Calcutta with a crew of six and fifty-eight passengers. The aircraft was making an ILS approach to runway 19L when a heavy shower reduced visibility and a decision was made to overshoot. The captain was then offered a radar-assisted approach to runway 01R. Radar control then guided the aircraft and 1 mile (1.6km) from the threshold, G-AKFP was cleared for a visual landing. At this point the aircraft was to the left of the 01R centreline. Once the Hermes had come out of the cloud, the captain turned down the R/T radio and continued a visual approach. In fact they were landing on the wrong runway, 01L. Just ahead was Indian Airlines Douglas DC-3 VT-AUA which was operating a cargo flight and had been given permission to line up on runway 01L and hold. The Hermes struck the DC-3 and although none of the passengers and crew on board G-AKFP were injured, the four occupants of the DC-3 were killed. The cause of the crash was attributed to the captain turning down the R/T at the final stage of the radar-assisted approach and continuing in conditions which did not allow him to identity the correct runway.

There was a kind of grim coincidence in that the aircraft (Douglas DC-3 VT-AUA) struck by G-AKFP was owned by Indian Airlines which had been formed in 1953 from an amalgamation of seven airlines, one of them being Indian National Airways, which itself had been started by Airwork, with Govan Bros.

An Iraq Airways DH.104 Dove being unloaded from the nose of an Airwork Bristol 170. The Dove had been damaged after a heavy landing in Baghdad and was being returned to Blackbushe for repair. (Royal Aero Club)

Freight Service: London to Bahrain

In the first half of 1954, Airwork applied to operate a freight-only service from London to Bahrain under an associate agreement with BOAC. The intention was to carry freight between the Middle East and London but also to try to get involved in carrying inter-Middle East freight. However, there were problems with these proposals, particularly in the Lebanon as the Lebanese air operators did not wish to see any competition to their Middle Eastern air freight business and this was pointed out by the Lebanese Director General of Civil Aviation to the British Middle East Civil Air Attaché in Cairo. The Lebanese eventually agreed to the service but not to any uplift of cargo between the Lebanon and Iraq. The Lebanese would also not agree to any service through Baghdad but did agree to the routing London–Nice–Athens–Rome–Beirut or Tripoli (Lebanon)–Kirkuk–Basra–Kuwait–Dukhan–Bahrain and return. Nice, Athens and Rome were technical stops. With the problems encountered by the proposals, it was decided to abandon the application.

Haj Flights

One area which has long been a staple of many airlines across the world has been the transportation to and from Mecca of Muslim pilgrims for the Haj (pilgrimage).

The Contract Charter Division of Airwork first got involved in this type of traffic in 1947 when the Airwork Ltd representative in East Africa, Colonel B.A. Wilson, held discussions with the leader of the Muslim community in Mombasa to highlight the advantages of transporting pilgrims to Jeddah by air. The result of the talks was five return flights in October 1947 undertaken by Airwork Vikings, from Mombasa to Jeddah each carrying twenty-four pilgrims.

This experience of Haj work caused Airwork to look to other areas for similar charters and found possibilities in Pakistan. In 1950, a series of charters was organised from Karachi to Jeddah. Jeddah was the nearest airport to Mecca being 45 miles (72km) away. The route from Karachi to Jeddah involved a refuelling stop in both directions at Bahrain, with Riyadh as an emergency diversion airfield. Any diversions to Riyadh meant that passengers and crews were confined to the vicinity of the airport with no travel into the city of Riyadh allowed.

The departures from Karachi were usually scheduled around midnight with the pilgrim passengers being shown to their seats and briefed in Urdu by a Pakistani traffic officer. On Airwork's Vikings, the tap in the galley was disconnected in order to provide smaller quantities of water for pilgrims' ablutions before prayer. Additionally, the tap in the toilet was also disconnected and a deep tray fitted to the floor beneath the basin for ablutions for which individual portions of water were provided. A further adaptation was the removal of one complete sanitary fitting to avoid misuse. Prayers were undertaken in the aisle of the aircraft. Arrival at Jeddah was always fixed for late afternoon so that pilgrims could make the onward journey to Mecca by road before sunset. The arrival and departure of Airwork's Vikings at Jeddah (and any other aircraft) would cause a sandstorm. The parking area at Jeddah was very busy during the Haj season and dominated by Saudi Arabian Airlines. In the summer, 'the flies were so numerous that a drink could not be taken in one's hand', one stewardess remarked. An inconvenience not helped by the fact that in the parking area there were no arrangements for the disposal of refuse. All rubbish and rejected food boxes, including the Elsan toilets, were tipped straight on to the sand.

The one aim of the aircraft's agent (from one of Jeddah's mercantile houses) was to pay the Haj fee to the Saudi authorities and turn the aircraft around as quickly as possible.

Airwork & the VLF Controversy

In 1958 Eagle Airways applied to the ATAC for a number of fares which were significantly lower than IATA's international fare structure. These fares were low-fare cabotage services to

Britain's colonies and were known by their acronym VLF (Very Low Fares). The whole concept of VLF threatened both BOAC and the national airlines of the colonial territories in which they were proposed. The suggestion was that the introduction of VLF would draw away traffic from their services to the independent airlines. Part of their argument was that once the air fares were introduced and traffic was drawn away, the independents would then seek higher fares as the original prices were unsustainable, with the losers being BOAC and their peers. BOAC were vehemently opposed to the fares. Apart from the VLF controversy, BOAC were also proposing economy-class tariffs which in their turn would have an adverse effect on the independents.

Following the proposals by Eagle, Hunting Clan and Airwork had come in with their own proposals for VLF. Airwork's main concern was the African colonial coach services which had been operating for seven years. However, their view on the whole VLF controversy differed substantially to that of Eagle and Hunting Clan. Both Eagle and Hunting Clan took the view that VLF symbolised the efforts of the UK independents to overcome what they saw as the obstacles to their expansion and progress. Airwork's Myles Wyatt stated in January 1960 that his concern was about the economics of VLF. He accepted the fact that Airwork would have to withdraw their African colonial coach services when BOAC introduced their proposed economy-class fares. He considered that a fare reduction of around 10 per cent might have been economically feasible with Vickers Viscount 833s, but he did not see much commercial sense in such a service. Hearings had been held in Nairobi with all interested parties invited to submit their views. Airwork's representative at the Nairobi hearings was K.R. Sangster, who made the point that Airwork were not so much cautious about their rights if VLF was introduced, but about the economics of it as already stated by Myles Wyatt. Airwork's general manager for East Africa, Tom Lockhart-Mure, also stated that he did not think VLF would be introduced, but that if it was, then Airwork wanted their full share. He also stated that Airwork had lost traffic on their East African colonial coach services because of the prevarication over VLF.

In 1958, the passenger figures from the UK to Nairobi showed a rough 70/30 per cent split between BOAC/EAA/SAA (6,895 passengers) and Airwork and Hunting Clan (1,661 and 1,763 passengers respectively). A mitigating factor for the independents, however, was that the majority of their VLF applications were based on fortnightly services with the exceptions in Airwork's and Hunting Clan's case of the UK–Nairobi service which was twice weekly (Eagle's proposal was based on a fortnightly service) and UK–Salisbury which was weekly.

The whole VLF saga dragged on into 1960 and in the end a compromise was reached with the independents gaining lower fares (known as Skycoach) at 27 per cent lower on average than the lowest IATA fares. These Skycoach fares became effective from 4 October 1960; however, despite the application of these fares they were nowhere near as low as the original VLF proposals, although it was a step in the right direction from the point of view of the passengers and the independent airlines.

Pre-Merger into BUA

By the time of the BUA formation, the Airwork airline fleet had been whittled down. Handley Page Hermes G-ALDA and G-ALDG (both sold in October 1959) and G-ALDC (June 1959) were sold to Falcon Airways and G-ALDO was withdrawn from use in March 1959. Their four Vikings were sold: G-AIXR and G-AJFT to Tradair in May 1959 and March 1960 respectively, and G-AKTU and G-AKTV in March 1960 and May 1959 respectively, to Air Safaris. Douglas DC-3 G-AMRA was operated by Transair. Their Viscounts continued on the safari services but were transferred to Transair.

At the time of the formation of BUA, Airwork flying crew had to reapply for positions with the new company. This was a source of great resentment as they had been the only flying crew who had to apply for positions in the new set-up. It is worth recording what a senior member of the new airline (but not ex-Airwork) said about the treatment of Airwork staff:

Latterly, in 1960 both companies were part of the merger that formed British United Airways. A salient point sticks in my mind. Whereas Huntings, Lakers and Transair made provision for their aircrews in that merger, Airwork sacked all their personnel when they closed down and they had to re-apply to join the new airline. All lost their seniority. Universally regarded as a shabby and unnecessary operation. I remember flying with ex-senior Airwork captains who were then reduced to working as junior first officers.

10

AIRWORK ATLANTIC

BACKGROUND

In 1955 Airwork attempted to break into the transatlantic cargo market which was dominated by KLM, Pan Am, TWA, Swissair and SAS, who all flew pure cargo services using Douglas DC-4s; the Pan Am service was operated by three Douglas DC-6As after using leased Slick Airways DC-6As. SAS had just suspended their service and this should have been a warning sign to the planned Airwork service. At this time BOAC did not operate a pure cargo service, but cargo was a useful addition to their passenger-carrying Stratocruisers and Constellations.

Douglas DC-6A illustrating the wide variety of loads carried on the Airwork Atlantic service. (Babcock International Group)

Airwork's interest had been stimulated by the British Government's Civil Aviation Policy of 1952 which stated that the non-subsidised UK independent airlines would be granted freedom of opportunity to develop all-freight services. BOAC had undertaken not to extend their freight services for the next twelve months. Two independent airlines, Airwork and Hunting Clan, both applied for licences to operate North Atlantic freight services.

Airwork were assisted in the setting up of the operation by Eric S. Hanks, one of the co-founders of Tradair (Tradair purchased their first two Vickers Vikings from Airwork) and a founder member of the Airbrokers Association at the Baltic Exchange.

Airwork's application was approved in February 1953. Their next step was to apply to the CAB (Civil Aeronautics Board) for a 'Foreign Air Carrier Permit', a formality which took a further fourteen months to complete. At the same time, Airwork had sought and gained approval from the Canadian Government for their freighters to pick up and set down traffic at Montreal. Airwork had always hoped to start the service as quickly as possible using an interim type of aircraft, such as the Avro York, until a suitable aircraft of British manufacture became available. At the end of 1953, Airwork had stated in their CAB application that the use of the Handley Page Hermes on the service would result in an annual £42,000 loss against an annual projected profit of £230,000 using the Douglas DC-6A. The one aircraft that Airwork had a considerable interest in using for this new service was the cargo version of the Bristol Britannia. However, not many were surprised, considering the competitive nature of the market, when Airwork placed an order in August 1954 for two Douglas DC-6A Liftmasters for delivery in early 1956. Contracts were signed shortly after this order for another two DC-6As, with delivery of the first of the four due slightly earlier than originally planned in November 1955. The intention was to have at least two of the DC-6As operating by January 1956.

Airwork saw themselves as a cut above the other UK independent airlines of the time and their foray into the North Atlantic cargo market was not just seeking an area to expand into, but also an attempt to take on the 'Big Boys'. However, it was far from an even contest. There were a number of restrictions placed on them (as on any independent at the time) in addition to the handicap that freight services on any route always stood a better chance of profitability when they were run in conjunction with passenger services, which of course Airwork did not have to North America. One of the most irritating of the restrictions was the stipulation that Airwork could not carry mail, which was an immediate disadvantage as carrying mail has always been a useful source of income for airlines, particularly when starting a new service.

AIRCRAFT & ROUTES

The new venture named Airwork Atlantic, which was a division of Airwork Ltd, started scheduled services on 1 March 1955 with leased American aircraft (from TALOA and Slick Airways) ahead of receiving their own aircraft ordered for the service. Transocean Airlines (TALOA) had provided a Douglas DC-4, N4726V, which flew the inaugural service, and this aircraft operated two week-day return flights between London and New York. Two more TALOA Douglas DC-4s were leased: N5288N was leased from 1 March 1955 and N9894F was leased from 6 October 1955.

The core of the freight service was London–New York (Idlewild, later named JFK) routed London Airport–Manchester–Prestwick–Iceland–Newfoundland–New York, but there was a network in place to feed into this routing in the USA and Canada. Similarly, feeder services from Europe also mirrored the North American side. Airwork's Douglas DC-3s and Vickers Vikings fed in cargo from and to Frankfurt, Düsseldorf, Basle and Zurich.

In addition, Hunting Clan had started their 'Africargo' service to East and Central Africa and reached an agreement with Airwork to feed cargo into the Airwork Atlantic service in London to connect with Airwork's North Atlantic freight flights.

One of the three weekly transatlantic flights went on from London to Frankfurt and Düsseldorf. The Continental freight feeder service also brought cargo into and out of Manchester and Birmingham. The Düsseldorf freight sector was granted permission by the MTCA to run from June 1955 until 31 May 1963.

The Slick Airways Douglas DC-6A N90808 started services on 2 April 1955. In mid-May 1955 the service was increased from two flights a week to three (coincidentally, Pan Am also increased their service from two to three weekly flights at the same time). A Douglas DC-6A, N90809, was also leased from Slick Airways and was operated jointly with a mixed Slick Airways and Airwork crew. The DC-6A operated a weekend flight on Airwork's behalf and each Monday night, after its return from London, the DC-6A would depart from New York on a scheduled Slick Airways service to Chicago, Kansas City, San Francisco and/or Los Angeles, which gave Airwork the opportunity to serve these US inland and west coast destinations on a single waybill without transhipment. The Slick Airways part of the operation involved the aircraft carrying mixed crews so that the Airwork staff worked alongside the Slick Airways and the Transocean crews (captains, engineers and navigators). The fact that British Airwork crews were used in tandem with the American crews meant that Airwork could build up type and route experience ahead of Airwork Atlantic taking over the service completely when their new aircraft were delivered. Airwork crews flying the Slick Airways DC-6As were validated by the US authorities to fly a particular aircraft on a particular journey only.

There were a number of variations to the route both east and westwards. To give some examples (all in 1955): on 4/5 September N90809, commanded by Captain Woolfe with seven crew, flew London Airport–Prestwick–Shannon–Gander–New York (Idlewild) which N90809 repeated on 12 September with Captain Harding and seven crew; on 7 September N4726V, commanded by Captain Nick Bountis plus four crew, flew New York (Idlewild)–Bradley Field (Connecticut)–Prestwick–London Airport. On 14 September N4726V, commanded by Captain Heering and five crew, flew New York (Idlewild)–Prestwick–London Airport, with the return leg on 17–19 September under the command of Captain Ericson plus five crew routing London Airport–Birmingham (Elmdon)–Manchester (Ringway)–Prestwick (crew change with Captain Heering assuming command)–Keflavik–Gander–Montreal–New York (Idlewild).

On 10 October 1955 Captain Harding and six crew flew N90809 London Airport–Keflavik–Toronto (Malton)–Chicago–New York (Idlewild). On 30/31 October N9894F, under the command of Captain Heering and four crew, flew London Airport–Manchester (Ringway)–Prestwick (crew change with Captain Bountis replacing Captain Heering)–Keflavik–Montreal–New York (Idlewild). On 16 October N90809, with Captain Harding and six crew, flew New York (Idlewild)–Sydney (Nova Scotia)–Prestwick–London Airport.

On 2/3 November N9894F, under the command of Captain Kendall and four crew, flew New York (Idlewild)–Stephenville–Torbay (St John's)–Prestwick (crew change with Captain Heering assuming command)–London Airport. On 6/7 November N90809, with Captain Harding and seven crew, flew London Airport–Shannon–New York (Idlewild). On 9 November N9894F, with Captain Dodson and four crew, flew New York (Idlewild)–Gander–Prestwick–London Airport. On 21 November N90809, with Captain Harding and seven crew, flew London Airport–Shannon–Montreal–New York (Idlewild). On 23 November N9894F, under the command of Captain Kyse and four crew, flew New York (Idlewild)–Gander–London Airport. On 29/30 November N9894F, under the command of Captain Bountis and four crew, flew New York (Idlewild)–Sydney (Nova Scotia)–Shannon–Frankfurt–Manchester (Ringway).

On 4/5 December N9894F, under the command of Captain Bountis and four crew, flew London Airport–Manchester (Ringway)–Prestwick–Keflavik–Goose Bay–Montreal–New York (Idlewild). On 6/7 December N9894F, under the command of Captain Kyse and four crew, flew New York (Idlewild)–Gander–Shannon–London Airport.

The Transocean Douglas DC-4 N4726V had an interesting history. After having served in the Second World War it was declared surplus to requirements and sold to the Argentine Government. It was refurbished and became the personal aircraft of the then Argentine President

Juan Perón. After completing its time serving Perón, it was sold to Aircraft broker Lee Mansdorf & Co., who sold it to Transocean. It was given a complete overhaul by Transocean engineering staff and was named *Argentine Queen* during its time with Transocean. Additionally, it was originally believed to have been shown in sequences in the 1954 film *The High and the Mighty* starring Robert Stack. However, close examination of the film shows that the aircraft in the gate sequences at Honolulu is most likely N4665V *African Queen*, although it is quite possible that the taxiing and take-off sequences are N4726V or another aircraft as there were characteristics (a different de-icing boot arrangement) it did not share with N4665V. The eventful career of N4726V continued to the very end. The aircraft was then owned by Facilities Management Corporation, and it was lost en route to Los Angeles from Honolulu on 28 March 1964, with the tragic loss of the three crew and six passengers. The last message from the aircraft reported a serious fire in No. 2 engine and that ditching might be necessary.

The Slick Airways DC-6A had a payload of 24,000lb (10,900kg) but unfortunately the loads carried were relatively small. There was a wide range of goods and destinations, however: from New York there were golf clubs for London, collar buttons for Kuwait, dental resin for Berlin, ham and gaskets for Amsterdam, typewriter parts for Calcutta and coal-tar dyes for Karachi. Goods carried from London westwards included aircraft parts for Winnipeg, machinery and china for New York and clothing for Wellington. One unusual load carried by the DC-6A departing Heathrow on 1 October 1955 was Donald Campbell's *Bluebird* for an attempt on the World Speed Record at Lake Mead. The vehicle was considered a prestige cargo with good publicity for the service. However, *Bluebird* only just managed to fit into the aircraft with inches to spare – something which was not immediately obvious from all the press attention.

Airwork introduced an 'Airwork Cargo Courier' as part of the crew. The cargo courier was responsible for all the cargo (including live cargo) from supervision of loading and would complete import documentation en route, ensure fulfilment of special delivery instructions and also check that pick-ups and transhipments were carried out correctly. The cargo courier was an Airwork innovation and three months into the service it was felt that the post was paying dividends.

Despite the operational restrictions that had been placed upon Airwork Atlantic, the sales organisation backing up the freight service was substantial. The North American side of the division was headed by John Muhlfeld, who had previously been general sales manager for Pan American. In addition, John Muhlfeld had a wealth of experience of the North American air freight scene. He had been involved in discussions and planning which led directly to the growth of air freight between North America and Latin America, and the introduction of transatlantic tourist air fares, and he was also closely involved with the introduction of the extremely successful deferred-payment system which was launched by Pan American and adopted by almost every other major airline. The shipping line Furness Withy, which had acquired a shareholding in Airwork the previous year, used its North American network to act as general sales agents for Airwork Atlantic in Boston, Baltimore, Norfolk, Philadelphia, Chicago, Seattle, Portland, San Francisco, Los Angeles, St John's, Halifax, Montreal, Toronto and Vancouver. With John Muhlfeld looking after the North American side of the sales operation, Ronald Seton-Winton transferred from Furness Withy and was placed in overall charge of the Airwork Atlantic Sales Division.

CLOSURE OF THE OPERATION

After nine months of operation, it was announced on 15 December 1955 that the transatlantic freight service would cease; the last service was flown three days later on 18 December 1955. There had been uncertainties over future US policies which may have affected the service, but the most pressing reason was that a substantial loss of £500,000 had been incurred. The order for the two Douglas DC-6As was cancelled at the suspension of the service and sold ahead of delivery to Slick Airways. The European freight feeder service operated by Airwork continued until 8 March 1956, when it too ceased. An announcement by the company stated: 'Experience since December last has shown conclusively that the Continental services cannot be economically operated separately from the larger North Atlantic Cargo Service.' Ronald Seton-Winton returned to Furness Withy and excess staff were laid off.

In retrospect, the whole concept was doomed to failure. Two former Airwork employees who were both closely involved with the operation described it as 'a shambles', with one stating that the Airwork board were too gentlemanly for the rough and tumble of this type of business and that it needed a Bamberg or Laker type to carry it through. Airwork blamed government policy which prohibited the operation from carrying passengers between the UK and USA, and it was the view of many, even before the operation started, that it would never be profitable unless passengers could be carried. Matters were not helped by Britain's HM Customs & Excise refusing to give permission for a duty-free transhipment zone at London Airport.

Myles Wyatt was very sceptical about the possibilities of the service succeeding. After the service was suspended he commented: 'We discovered that playing in the first league was a very different affair to schoolboy football.' He did, however, manage to sell the DC-6s (which had been allocated registrations G-AOFX and G-AOFY) Airwork had ordered for the service for a good profit, along with three Vickers Viscounts on order (G-AOCA, G-AOCB and G-AOCC).

11

DEUTSCHE FLUGDIENST GMBH

After the war, no German organisation was permitted by treaty either to own aircraft or to train air crew. Lufthansa itself was not revived until 1954 and only started commercial flights on 1 April 1955. The restrictions were finally withdrawn in 1955 and this led to an extraordinary growth in German air transport at a time of general depression and low growth within the aviation sector in the rest of Europe.

Deutsche Flugdienst GmbH (DFG) was established as a charter company on 21 December 1955 with three ex-BEA Vickers Vikings and Airwork providing start-up assistance. The first two Vikings were not registered in Germany until 28 March 1956 and the third on 4 April 1956.

The arrangement with Airwork was a management agreement undertaking to provide training for air crew and maintenance staff for the new airline. A number of Airwork's senior captains went to West Germany for the training and also to undertake the operation of the initial services until the indigenous staff were ready to assume their new roles. Airwork's Captain M.R. Lacey was the senior pilot in charge of training for the air crew. Denis Wareham, the future Airwork Ltd managing director, had a considerable involvement in setting up DFG. He also married one of the air hostesses.

The West German crews also received training with Airwork in the UK, with three of the West German captains coming over to receive training in the UK in early 1955. Lufthansa were responsible for providing certain ground services and flight operations at the outset. The centre of operations for the new airline was the TWA hangar at Frankfurt am Main Airport.

Basically Airwork were providing technical assistance in establishing DFG, building on their experience of other airline start-ups like Misr-Airwork (the forerunner of EgyptAir), Indian National Airways and Sudan Airways. The initial start-up capital was 3 million Deutschmarks split between four shareholders: Norddeutscher Lloyd (27.75 per cent), Hamburg-Amerika Linie (27.75 per cent), Deutsche Lufthansa (26 per cent) and Deutsche Bundesbahn (18 per cent).

In addition to providing training for the maintenance and flying staff, senior Airwork captains were also involved in taking part in operating the new airline's initial services. Operations

D-AFUS c/n 250 Vickers 629 Viking IB G-AJBY BEA *Lord Torrington*, registered to DFG on 4 April 1956.
It was repainted as D-BELA in the TWA hangar at Frankfurt Rhein-Main Airport on 19 April 1958.
(Robert Belcher)

started on 28 March 1956 with a charter flight to Tel Aviv, although the official starting date for operations was 1 May 1956 with the Spanish holiday resorts being the main destinations, primarily Tenerife and Majorca. In addition, starting in November 1956, two scheduled internal West German services were operated on behalf of Lufthansa. The first was Frankfurt to Hamburg and Düsseldorf, and the second was Frankfurt to Nuremberg, making DFG the first German airline to operate into Nuremberg since the war.

Lufthansa did not have the capacity to involve itself in charter operations at the time which was why the decision was taken to be a major shareholder in DFG as this was to be their main area of business, although they operated the two scheduled routes and one of the Vikings was nominally operating the internal routes on behalf of Lufthansa. There were a number of West German travel agents involved with the charter work including Dr Tigges-Fahrten, Touropa, Scharnow and Hummel.

After the completion of Airwork's management agreement, DFG became closely involved with another West German carrier, Condor Luftreederei GmbH, in order to rationalise engineering and operating arrangements. In 1957 Lufthansa increased its shareholding in DFG to 95.5 per cent.

A slump in the charter market led to DFG taking over Condor Luftreederei GmbH on 25 October 1961 and the name of the airline changed to Condor Flugdienst GmbH.

12

FISON-AIRWORK

Fison-Airwork Ltd was formed from merging the crop-spraying operation of Fisons Pest Control Ltd and Airwork Ltd. The two companies formed their new joint enterprise in May 1955 and it was formally incorporated (company No. 00552382) on 22 July 1955.

The real impetus for the formation of the new company had been the awarding of a contract in 1954 by Shell D'Arcy Development Company of Nigeria to Fisons Pest Control to provide two Hiller 360s to assist in oil exploration work in the Niger Delta in Nigeria. This type of work was outside Fisons' usual area of agricultural expertise. Accordingly, they looked for a partner they could work with to provide the additional knowledge in wider commercial operations such as oil exploration. Airwork, of course, had already gained many years of experience in oil-related work in the Middle East and Ecuador by this stage and proved to be the ideal partner for Fisons' requirements.

The Fison-Airwork operation was based at Bourn airfield near Cambridge and was one of the world's largest and most experienced industrial helicopter users (outside the USA and Australia).

The Board of Directors was composed of personnel from both organisations and consisted of Myles D.N. Wyatt, W.J. McEwan, James Edgar Harper, Dr W.E. Ripper and Major General G.E. Wildman-Lushington. Bourn was already the headquarters for the Hiller 360s and it was decided to continue using it as the main base and head office with the option later to move to one of Airwork's centres of operation. However, despite this intention, Bourn remained as the main base until the formation of Air Holdings in 1961.

Prior to the formation of the new company, Fisons Pest Control Ltd had been operating passenger and freight charter services as the company had also operated seven Auster Autocars and one Auster Aiglet. The main source of work, however, were contracts involving agricultural and forest spraying in the UK, rubber plantation spraying in Ceylon, cotton spraying in the Sudan, locust control in East Africa and the Sudan, and oil exploration work in Nigeria.

The intention of the new company was for Fisons to continue to pursue agricultural-based contracts and developing the equipment to be used in this work, which was their area of expertise, and for Airwork to seek new helicopter-based business. This new business was to come from charter, survey and construction work.

Two key members of the Fison-Airwork team were David Bond and Victor King. David Bond was the operations manager and Victor King was the chief engineer. Both played important roles in the company's operations, especially overseas, and the two went on to form Management Aviation Ltd, which eventually became Bond Helicopters (as, in January 2012, run by Stephen Bond, David Bond's youngest son).

At the time of the merger Fisons owned eight Hiller 360s. By November 1956, they were operating a mixed fleet of two Westland Whirlwind S.55s and eight Hiller 360s. By 1958, the fleet comprised nineteen Hiller 360s and five Westland Whirlwind S.55s. By this time most of the Fison-Airwork contracts were based on crop spraying and power-line inspection undertaken overseas with associated companies in East and South Africa and Australia. The main contracts were for oil and gas work in Pakistan and Nigeria.

By 1959, the fleet had grown further to twenty-eight Hiller 360s and five Westland Whirlwind S.55s, plus a total of three Scottish Aviation Twin Pioneers.

The first passenger service to be operated by the new joint venture was on 13 May 1955 when a Hiller 360 was chartered by the holiday camp owner Billy Butlin, to take him from the South Bank in London to Bolton in Lancashire to open a new sports pavilion there. In July 1955 Hiller 360 G-ANOC paid a visit to Manchester Airport and gave demonstrations and pleasure flights. One of these involved taking the Lord Mayor of Manchester to Platt Fields on 9 July 1955. A further trip was made to Bradford from Manchester Airport by G-ANOC. The bulk of the company's work, however, was in large-scale crop spraying and industrial contracts from the oil and gas sectors.

FISON-AIRWORK HELICOPTER TRAINING SCHOOL

The company operated its own training facility at Bourn where pilots were brought up to standard on Hillers. Among some of the Fison-Airwork pilots who trained at this facility were John Odlin, Bob Brewster, John Millward, Peter Gray, Dave Harrison and John Waddington. The training was paid for by a period of reduced salary and allowances after the pilots had qualified. For instance, on an overseas contract in the late 1950s, a Hiller pilot would be paid £800 p.a. plus 50 per cent overseas allowance, as well as receiving free messing and accommodation. When Alan Bristow took over the management of the company after it became Airwork (Helicopters) Ltd, he increased the salaries of these pilots, although it was said that he could afford to as another company had already paid for the training.

BACKGROUND TO CROP SPRAYING

Helicopters

The core of the business was crop spraying. Using aircraft for crop spraying was first carried out in the UK in 1947 on an experimental basis. The cost of using helicopters as opposed to fixed-wing aircraft in aerial crop spraying was considerably more in monetary terms. In Britain the cost was usually double (in 1956 this was up to £40 an hour for a helicopter) and sometimes as much as treble the cost of a dedicated crop-spraying fixed-wing aircraft such as the Auster Agricola or Edgar Percival P.9. However, there were many advantages. In particular a helicopter could operate in a restricted environment where a fixed-wing aircraft could not, particularly if obstructions and hazards were present. Additionally, sometimes there are no landing areas available for fixed-wing aircraft and finally the application of some pesticides demanded a very close control of the actual spraying operation which would be far easier to carry out in a helicopter than a fixed-wing aircraft. Overall, the big selling point for a helicopter in crop spraying was its manoeuvrability.

Aerial crop spraying was arduous work for both pilot and machine. James Harper, one of the directors of Fison-Airwork and a helicopter pilot himself, stated that 85 per cent of aerial crop spraying was carried out a few feet from the ground, which required intense concentration. The continuous strain meant that at best only four hours of continuous flying could be safely achieved in most circumstances due to the constant landings and take-offs, manoeuvring, avoiding obstacles and constant turns. For short periods some pilots could achieve eight hours of flying, but this was unusual. After the merger, Fison-Airwork considered what type of helicopter would be the most suitable and economic to use in this type of operation.

The suggestions were that ideally the helicopter would be sturdy and basic with quick change components, including the easy removal of the engine, transmission and rotor head, and would cost in the region of £5,000 at 1956 prices. The fuselage should be open and of tubular construction, without superfluous parts, and the undercarriage should be interchangeable with wheels and skids; the rotor blades should be metal and there should be enough ground clearance from the blades to allow the fitting of the insecticide tank. Seating for the pilot should be in the centre and if this could not be achieved he should sit on the left. Trimming should be electrical and the controls should be light, while cockpit canopies should be detachable and convertible to either completely open or closed with doors separately removable. The machine should be as small as possible and an engine of 250–300hp would be preferred; the payload should be a minimum of 900lb (408kg) with a 5,000ft (1,524m) hovering ceiling at full load and a cruising speed of 100mph (160.9km/h), and an endurance of two and a half hours.

The first Westland Whirlwind S.55 came into use with the company in March 1956. It had a greater carrying capability than the Hillers, with a 200-gallon (909-litre) tank for chemical spraying or, alternatively, a 2,000lb (907kg) load.

Fixed-Wing Aircraft: Agricultural Spraying

As with crop spraying by helicopter, the same demands were also placed on the pilot of a fixed-wing aircraft. It was said that it took one season's work to make a good pilot into a good crop-spraying pilot.

Fison-Airwork and de Havilland collaborated to produce a crop-spraying conversion of Chipmunk G-APMN (ex-RAF WB680) to a Mk 23. The changes involved removing the front cockpit and replacing it with a tank-hopper; relocating the pilot's seat in the rear cockpit to a higher position for a better view; adding fixed leading-edge slats on the outer wings; and redesigning the wing-root leading-edge spoilers. De Havilland was responsible for the air-frame modifications and Fison-Airwork designed and installed the dispensing equipment and controls.

G-APMN crashed on 6 August 1958, only a very short period of time after its conversion, and was replaced by Auster J1N G-APOA.

The economics of ground and fixed-wing aerial spraying could be difficult to compare precisely. The amount of chemicals used per hour in agricultural spraying by air compared to ground application was roughly ten times more in the 1950s. However, an aerial contract sprayer could negotiate a better price on account of the larger quantities used. Yet as a general rule contract prices for fixed-wing aircraft spraying were about 50 per cent higher than for ground spraying. A sliding scale of charges would be offered so that an area under 10 acres could end up costing more than an area of 200 acres. Reductions would be made when two or three treatments were necessary.

For each pilot there would have to be two men on the ground. If markers and tanker drivers were included the figure would need to be three to four ground personnel. Spraying within the UK was a highly seasonal operation but overseas it was a year-round activity, with the nature of the work encompassing fertiliser top-dressing, anti-mosquito and locust spraying, locust swarm spotting, survey work and carrying oil-drilling equipment, along with other work which would not normally be found in the UK. The work within the UK was generally crop spraying but other areas of work were starting to be undertaken, including fertiliser application, slug baiting, seed sowing and more haulage-type work (e.g. delivering fencing posts to inaccessible areas).

CONTRACTS

UK

There was a considerable amount of work within the UK for crop spraying, which had grown since the end of the war due to the development of improved pesticides and weed-killers, the development of the helicopter, greater awareness by farmers of the possibilities of crop spraying and damage done to crops and soil by heavy farm machinery, and the availability of large numbers of suitable surplus aircraft after the war which could be converted.

The years 1958 and 1959 saw the worst outbreaks of potato blight of the twentieth century which coincided with exceptionally wet soil conditions. The potatoes had to be sprayed with copper fungicide without delay. However, the exceptionally wet soil would not allow the use of a tractor and sprayer so the situation was ideal for aerial crop spraying. It is estimated that over 100,000 acres were sprayed from the air alone in 1958. Due to the intensive effort that was put in, the damage to the potato crop was far less than expected.

Caribbean, Central & South America

Aerial spraying against leaf spot on banana plantations in Jamaica, Panama and Costa Rica comprised other projects undertaken by the company. The Panama contract was on behalf of the United Fruit Company of Central America. Fison-Airwork established two bases in Panama.

These were at Puerto Armuelles (the United Fruit banana port on the west coast near the Costa Rican border) and Changuinola Base Line, a grass airfield with a small hangar for helicopters, near Almirante (on the east coast). Two Hillers, G-APDU and G-APDV, were based at Changuinola but only one pilot was based there. John Waddington took over from the original pilot (Roger Spain) at Changuinola and Chas House took over from the original engineer, Johnny Truslove.

There were up to five Hillers based at Puerto Armuelles at any time and these included G-APKX, G-APRD, G-APNI, G-APJN, G-APMP and G-APSH. All these Hillers used 178hp Franklin engines which were upgraded to 200hp and then 210hp.

Among the pilots who worked out of Puerto Armuelles were 'Taffy' Evans (chief pilot), John Odlin, John Waddington, Gary Tarrant, Kevin Keegan, Roger Spain, John Millward, John Pridie, Sid Bignall, Dave Harrison and Peter Piggot (a Rhodesian). Some of the engineers were Tommy Bayden (chief engineer and replaced by Don Strange), Jack Peabody, Graham Conway and Chas House. Both Chas House and John Waddington transferred to Almirante.

Spraying work from Panama was also conducted over the Costa Rican border close to Golfito. There was, however, a permanent banana-spraying base in Costa Rica at Palmar Sur, north of Golfito. The Costa Rica pilots were Barry Newman and Andy Neale. The engineers were Jack Willis, Graham Conway, John 'Fred' Hughes and Johnny Truslove.

The Panama contracts ended in spring 1960.

Jamaica was the HQ for the Fison-Airwork Caribbean operations before it moved to San Jose, Costa Rica. The area manager was Dicky Henderson and the area engineer was Vic King.

The contract for Jamaica was to spray over 6,000 acres seventeen times over the course of a year using Orchard Oil to combat the leaf spot. This was believed to be the first time that banana crops had been extensively sprayed from the air. Two new Hiller UH-12C helicopters and a Piper Super Cub were ordered for the Jamaican work. During the period of the Jamaica contract tragedy occurred when one of the Fison-Airwork Hiller pilots, Bill Andon, was killed in an accident after being hit by the tail rotor of a Hiller being manoeuvred.

Hiller 360 12A at Valverde Mao, Dominican Republic, in March 1960. Pilot John Odlin (standing on oil drum) is washing G-APKX down after a morning spraying banana plantations. On the left is Prospero Amaro, a local who was trained up as a fitter. (John Odlin)

In this region there were also contracts awarded by both the United Fruit and the Standard Fruit companies for spraying banana plantations in the Dominican Republic, Honduras and Ecuador. The chief pilot on the Honduras contract was Willie Dosset. Other pilots were Barry Newman (took over from Willie Dosset), Bob Brewster and Peter Gray. The engineers were Johnny Truslove, John (Fred) Hughes and Stan Chapman. Prior to his departure to Honduras Peter Gray was dispatched to Sudan to fly back Auster ST-ABD (which became G-AIGM) in order to bring up his fixed-wing flying hours. The Hillers used in Honduras were G-ANZM, G-ANMR and G-ANMS.

The main Dominican Republic base was at Walterio on the north coast, with a smaller base at Valverde Mao, nearer to Santiago de los Caballeros. The Hillers used in the Dominican Republic were G-AMDN, G-ANOA, G-APSL, G-APKX, G-APDU, G-APOA and G-APDN. The pilots on this contract were John Odlin, Dave Auty, Bob Brewster, Peter Gray, John Waddington, John Pridie and John Millward. The engineers were Tommy Bayden (chief engineer) and Graham Conway (both ex-Panama).

A contract in Ecuador was based in Guayaquil with Hillers G-APJN and G-APNT. The pilots were Alan (Jim) Mackie and Johnny Kirk, and the engineers were Peter Durrant and Frank Lee. The contract in Ecuador effectively ended with legal problems caused by the death of a local employed on the operation who was killed when he walked into the tail rotor of a Hiller.

In addition to the Caribbean banana-spraying work, Fison-Airwork gained a contract in Trinidad (from the local Texaco Company, TRINMAR) for CASEVAC/emergency and supervisor transportation to fixed production platforms and a drilling barge in the Soldado oilfield in the Gulf of Paria. The ex-Panama Hiller 360 12C G-APDV was used for this work. The registration was later changed to the Trinidadian VP-TCE in April 1961.

Nigeria

In 1954, the year before the formation of Fison-Airwork, Fisons Pest Control had initially gained a contract to provide helicopter services under charter to the Shell D'Arcy Development Co. of Nigeria, later renamed the Shell-BP Development Co. of Nigeria, which was prospecting for oil in the Niger Delta coastal region at the time. This was a new area of work for Fisons Pest Control and the work, which was geophysical surveying, soon expanded as oil was discovered in commercial quantities. As mentioned, this expanding contract was the catalyst for the formation of Fison-Airwork.

Due to the increasing nature of the work, it was decided to add two Westland Whirlwind S.55s (G-AODO and G-AODP) to the contract, which was being operated by two Nigeria-based Hiller 360s. To add to these two Whirlwinds, a third was ordered in January 1957 and a fourth Whirlwind was ordered in March 1957, both being shipped to Nigeria on delivery; the third Whirlwind, G-AOYB, was delivered in April 1957, and the fourth, G-AOZK, in January 1958. The two additional Whirlwinds joined the two Hiller 360s and two Whirlwinds already in Nigeria at this stage.

The work now involved transporting personnel, supplies and equipment. By May 1959, four of the company's five Whirlwinds and two Hiller 360s were employed on the contract for oil exploration between both Nigeria and the Caribbean.

In order to provide some fixed-wing heavier-lift capacity in Nigeria, Fison-Airwork ordered two SAL Twin Pioneers. The aircraft (both of which had been ordered but not taken up by Trabajos Aéros y Enlaces) were G-APLM and G-APLN. The rugged aircraft, with its STOL capabilities, was ideal for work in the Nigerian oil delta.

G-APLN was delivered on 26 June 1958 and G-APLM on 22 August 1958. Both were based in Port Harcourt, Nigeria, and both aircraft followed similar histories. In addition, a third Twin Pioneer G-APRS was leased from Scottish Aviation from 17 September 1959 to 17 May 1960.

Fison-Airwork also operated a Piper Apache PA-23 G-APLJ on behalf of UAC (United Africa Company) which regularly flew between Kano and Lagos for Kingsway Stores. This aircraft arrived in Nigeria on 11 March 1960 and was generally flown by Paddy O'Hagen.

Westland S.55 Whirlwind G-AOYB, damaged after a heavy landing where the blades have sheared through the rotor boom. The S.55 was repaired and returned to service. (Helen King)

West Pakistan: Sui Pipeline

In 1955 Fison-Airwork gained a contract in West Pakistan (this was before East Pakistan split away to become Bangladesh in 1971) for pipeline inspection work of the 350-mile (563km) Sui to Karachi pipeline which carried natural gas. Sui is a small town north-east of Jacobabad in the province of Balouchistan. In 1950–51 one of the world's largest deposits of natural gas was found there at 10,000ft (3,048m) below the surface by the Burmah Oil Company who had been drilling for oil. The Sui-Gas Transmission Company was established. Operations started in 1955 to tap this resource and a pipeline was laid in 1955 to provide the natural gas as a source of power to industries in Hyderabad, Karachi and Sukkur initially, with an extension in 1958 to Multan. The Sui gas was also used as a source of fertiliser and in Pakistan's growing petrochemical industry. The first gas arrived in Karachi in September 1955.

The conditions, as on so many overseas Airwork contracts, were arduous. The pipeline itself, which was 16in (40.6cm) in diameter, lay 4ft (1.2m) beneath the ground of the Sind Desert, except where it crossed the River Indus and drainage canals where it was carried over on metal bridges or established dams. The pipeline also crossed swampland and heavily irrigated rice paddies. To add to the difficult physical conditions, the summer heat made the area one of the hottest places on earth. The summer temperatures were regularly recorded at over 130°F (54.5°C) and one Fison-Airwork pilot, Captain R. Bradbury, recalled that the cockpit canopy of the Hiller once warped like a tulip leaf in the extreme heat.

Considering the gas was highly combustible (it was 90 per cent methane) and loaded in the pipe at 800psi, great care had to be taken in patrolling the line and carrying out any repairs.

The Sui-Gas Company negotiated a contract with Fison-Airwork to provide one Hiller 360 to patrol the pipeline as a helicopter was considered the best option for the task.

The Hiller would patrol the line at a height of 50ft (15.2m) or less and at a constant speed of 60mph (96.6km/h), which was the optimum for close observation. If any problem was found, the Hiller 360 could transport an engineer quickly to the spot to make an adjustment, effect a repair or just to check the line. Along the route there were regulating and radio booster stations which would be visited by the helicopter to check conditions, deliver mail and supplies, and transport engineers on constant observation tours. The stations themselves were very remote. Guards known as *Choukedars* were employed along sections of the route.

Despite the inhospitable terrain on the pipeline patrols, there was a considerable amount of human activity. On one occasion when Captain Bradbury was patrolling the line in a remote part of the Sind Desert, he stated that there was nothing but wind, sand and sun. However, on landing for an inspection, he was surrounded within five minutes by thirty Bugti tribesmen who were curious about the sudden appearance of the helicopter.

The Hiller 360 also played another role in the monsoon season. The monsoon lasted only about two weeks but caused severe flooding from the River Indus, causing a great deal of damage and costing a number of lives. The Hiller would often fly mercy missions carrying plasma, medicines and supplies.

The extension of the Sui-Gas pipeline north from Sui to Multan in the Punjab in 1958 involved the Hiller in different work to the normal pipeline patrol work to Karachi. This consisted mainly of being involved in the survey work for the new pipeline and carrying the engineers between base camps. Additional to this work was the ever-present requirement to undertake emergency medical flights for staff and locals alike as medical facilities in these areas were primitive.

Although it was perhaps a fairly basic helicopter, the Hiller 360 performed its task exceedingly well under the difficult conditions in West Pakistan.

Captain Bradbury later became a senior instructor at Bourn.

West Pakistan: Shell Oil

A contract was started in April 1958 to operate services for Shell Oil in the north-west frontier area at Giandari from where staff and supplies were moved to an airstrip at Kashmor by the River Indus. The terrain was some of the most terrifying the pilots had ever flown over, one christening it the 'Jaws of Death'. Whirlwind S.55 G-APKC was shipped out to Karachi by sea and assembled on the dockside in the open after arrival by engineers Cliff Saffron and Mickey Mann.

Spanish Sahara

A small contract for an oil company started in May 1959. Centred on Al Aiun in the Spanish Sahara, the work was a local geological survey which involved flying as far east as the town of Semara. Hiller G-APOF was flown out to Al Aiun in a Britavia Douglas DC-3 and assembled in the open by a Fison-Airwork fitter. The whole area was under martial law at the time. The airstrip at Al Aiun was a single sand strip and was the base for the Spanish Legion (French Foreign Legion equivalent) which was supplied by a Spanish air force Ju.52.

No oil was discovered and the contract was finished in August 1959.

Air Holdings Formation

Fisons had declined Airwork's offer to participate in the purchase of Bristow as it was too far removed from their chemical interests. Airwork purchased and wholly owned Bristow Helicopters (Eastern) Ltd (previously Air Whaling Ltd), Bristow Helicopters Ltd, Bristow

Westland S.55 Whirlwind G-APKC was on exclusive charter to the Shell Oil Company of Pakistan. It also transported military personnel to observe the devastation caused by the Indus River flooding. Mark Vardy, pilot of Fison-Airwork, on the right. (Helen King)

Helicopters (Bermuda) Ltd and Helicopter Rentals Ltd (also incorporated in Bermuda). In May 1960 Fisons sold their 50 per cent shareholding to Airwork and the company was renamed Airwork (Helicopters) Ltd on 16 June 1960, with the management of the company coming under re-appointed directors Alan Bristow, George Fry, Alan Green and Jack Wooley. The headquarters moved from Bourn to Redhill.

Airwork (Helicopters) Ltd later became Airwork International Ltd and subsequently United Helicopters Ltd under which it is still (at February 2012) registered.

There were a number of most able staff from Fison-Airwork who were later given positions within Bristow Helicopters, some of them rising to senior posts, including Bryan Collins (managing director), John Odlin (director), Bryan Shaw (director) and senior pilots Peter Gray, Bob Brewster and John Waddington. Senior engineers within Bristow included Jim MacKaskill, Don Strange and Cliff Saffron.

OVERSEAS

13

ADEN & YEMEN

Airwork enjoyed a long on-and-off involvement with Aden and South Yemen. In early 1954 two Airwork Douglas DC-3s, G-AMRA and G-AMZD, were prepared at Blackbushe for a year's charter to the Aden Petroleum Refining Co. Ltd. G-AMRA transited through Malta on its way to Aden on 22 April 1954 with G-AMZD delivered in May 1954. G-AMBW also spent some time in Aden. All three aircraft were painted in the colours of Aden Petroleum Refining Co.

The British left Aden on 29 November 1967 after 128 years, and independence was declared the following day. In May 1967 there was a large air lift of families and personnel from Aden by BUA, supported by Airwork ground staff. In the final years leading up to the British departure, the level of terrorism had increased dramatically. The two protagonists, the NLF and FLOSY (respectively National Liberation Front and Front for the Liberation of Occupied South Yemen) carried out several attacks on British forces and murdered over 1,250 Yemenis who were considered to be stooges of the British. Prior to the departure of the British, Wing Commander John Severne had arrived in 1966 at Headquarters Middle East and was appointed as air adviser to the South Arabian Government (additional to his primary role of commanding the British fighter, maritime and helicopter force). He was given a budget of £2 million to form a South Arabian air force. At this time, the British Ministry of Defence had contracted Airwork Services Ltd to source and provide the aircraft for the new air force. Airwork were also responsible for recruiting the pilots and engineers. The new air force comprised four Douglas DC-3s (refurbished at a cost of £25,000 each and actually provided by the Crown Agents on behalf of the British Government); four ex-RAF Hunting Jet Provosts Mk 4 (refurbished and modified to Mk 52 standard); six Westland-built Agusta-Bell 47G.3B-1 Sioux; and six DHC Beavers. The DHC Beavers, which were brand new, had radios fitted at Hurn by Airwork. Wing Commander Barry Atkinson MBE DFC was seconded from the RAF to act as commanding officer.

A maintenance contract for the new South Arabian air force was awarded to Airwork Services. The Airwork staff were using old RAF accommodation to support the small air force.

BAC Jet Provost T.4 101: one of four Jet Provosts for the South Arabian air force. (Via Sir John Severne)

The initial Airwork contract was for three years starting in 1967 and ending in 1970. Airwork sent out technicians and engineers basically to take over as the British forces left. This included the small naval operation as well as the air operation. Shortly after his arrival in Aden, Ray Shoebridge of Airwork was tasked with compiling a report on the condition of the two patrol vessels and then streamlining the three air force engineering workshops into one large one. Much of the equipment was damaged and many items such as lathes had to be completely replaced. The eighteen members of the flying crew were mainly ex-RAF apart from a Belgian, a German and a Czech, and were commanded by Squadron Leader 'Rags' Barlow, an RAF navigator who had taken early retirement from the RAF (he was also the operations/ intelligence officer as well as adjutant to the commanding officer). The new government had been given £5 million towards the running of the new air force and 'Rags' Barlow, and the new air crew, were under contract to the South Arabian Government. After independence was declared on 30 November 1967, the Federation of South Arabia was immediately renamed the People's Democratic Republic of Yemen (more usually known as South Yemen) and the new air force was renamed the People's Democratic Republic of Yemen Air Force (PDRYAF). The South Arabian markings on the aircraft and helicopters were removed and replaced.

However, barely three months into the official life of the new air force, the South Yemen Minister of Defence took a trip to Moscow and made an anti-British broadcast in which he stated that members of the South Yemen air force were basically acting as spies and informing the British Embassy of what the new government was doing.

The British Government had originally instructed the South Yemen Government that its aircraft were to keep within its borders as the British were concerned of possible conflict between British nationals flying combat missions for South Yemen against British pilots flying combat missions for Saudi Arabia. The South Yemen Government was incensed at what they regarded as interference in their internal affairs. On his return, the Defence Minister called all the British personnel together for a meeting on 27 February 1968. Under armed guard they were informed that their services were no longer required. They and their families were given one hour to collect their belongings under guard and had to leave the country. The Airwork staff under contract to the South Yemen air force were not affected by this turn of events. New staff were then recruited to make up the loss of flying personnel. The new crews were a mixture of different nationalities including Yugoslav, Bulgarian and Dutch pilots.

In 1970, when the Airwork contract had run its course, the firm was not asked to tender again for the contract and thereafter the work previously carried out by Airwork employees was taken over by the Soviet Union and Eastern Bloc personnel.

During the period of the contract, staffing never exceeded twenty Airwork personnel at any one time, and Peter French was general manager throughout.

A contract to carry out aircraft engineering support in Yemen still continued as late as 1984 on an ad hoc basis.

PETER BALKWILL

A most unusual event occurred during the period of the Airwork contract in Aden. Peter Balkwill was employed by Airwork as a ground equipment engineer. He had previously been flying Agri aircraft on crop-spraying tasks in Sudan after finishing National Service in the RAF. After he had been in Aden for almost two years, his family had returned to the UK and he was one month away from the completion of his Airwork contract to return to the UK for good. However, he did not live long enough to return. The supposed circumstances of his death are these: on the night of 21 December 1969 he was crossing the road near the cold store in the Ma'ala area of Aden when he was hit by a car. Nobody who knew him could understand why he was in this area as it was several miles away from his home. At the time he was taken to Gumhouria Hospital (then Queen Elizabeth Hospital) in Crater where he died, and a death certificate was issued which stated that he was buried in the Christian cemetery at Ma'ala. His family in the UK were informed of his death but did not attend the funeral which was held in Aden. Subsequent enquiries and several visits to Aden by the family to visit his grave years later have found that not only was there no grave, but there is no proper record of his death. Also, although there was supposedly a funeral, there is no record of it. His friends and colleagues had assumed that his body was repatriated for burial and therefore did not attend the supposed funeral in Aden. Equally, officials who may have been expected to attend the funeral or had some involvement in it have no recollection or knowledge of the events and, apart from a one-line entry record in the British Embassy, neither are there any records with any related organisations. There are also numerous inconsistencies relating to the whole episode. Furthermore, no trace of his car was ever found.

The circumstances of his death and the whereabouts of his body remain a mystery to this day. To all intents and purposes, Peter Balkwill disappeared off the face of the earth on the night of 21 December 1969.

14

EAST AFRICA

Airwork (East Africa) Ltd was formed in August 1948 with its headquarters at Nairobi. The new company was formed to take over Airwork's existing interests at the time in East Africa and simultaneously also took over the aircraft interests of the Uganda Company, which had imported Austers. Airwork took a large shareholding in Noon & Pearce Air Charters Ltd, a local air charter company with a fleet of two DH.89A Dominies, three Austers, six Miles Geminis, one de Havilland Fox Moth, three Stinson Reliants and one de Havilland Moth Minor.

Although the new company was controlled by Airwork, the other companies were represented on the Board of Directors. The chairman was Sir Alfred Vincent and the managing director was Lieutenant Colonel B.A. Wilson. Also on the Board of Directors were Myles Wyatt, Alexander M.T.B. Noon, Joseph T. Simpson and D. Elphick. S.H.J. Hammond was general manager.

The aim of Airwork (East Africa) Ltd in combining and amalgamating with local air operators was to provide an effective freight and passenger charter organisation to operate anywhere between Cairo and Johannesburg, as well as providing first-class maintenance facilities and a sales organisation in the region. The intention was to sell off the smaller aircraft and use those that had a seating capacity for seven or more passengers. The company was based at Nairobi West Airport. Noon & Pearce acted as a handling unit for the booking organisation of Airwork's regular East African Viking charters. The company also acted as East African agents for British manufacturers such as Dunlop, Cellon, Blackburn and Auster.

By 1951, Noon & Pearce were in the process of replacing their Gemini fleet with single-engine Beech Bonanzas.

The Bristol 170s G-AHJD, G-AICS and G-AICT were used mainly in Tanganyika (but also flew out of Nairobi). Large quantities of food were flown into Dar es Salaam and there was considerable demand for supplying inaccessible outlying regions of Tanganyika. Where landing was impossible, Airwork looked to use parachutes to supply these points. The use of supply by parachute from the Bristol 170s was something Airwork had already gained experience of in their operation to supply Shell bases in Ecuador at this time.

In October 1953, Alec Noon of Noon & Pearce Air Charters Ltd took delivery of their DH.89A Rapide VP-KLL, which had been converted by Flightways at Southampton's Eastleigh Airport to a series 4 model. Alec Noon also purchased a set of drawings from V.H. Bellamy of Flightways in order for Noon & Pearce to carry out similar conversions on other Rapides flying

Bristol 170 G-AICT. In East Africa one of the tasks undertaken was the transport of labourers and their tools on the ill-fated Groundnut Scheme. (Royal Aero Club)

in Africa at their Nairobi West facilities. This Rapide VP-KLL was one of two converted Rapides with de Havilland Gipsy Queen 2 engines, which gave the aircraft a much better and livelier performance. In Africa, much of the country over which the Rapides flew was unsettled and the ability to hold height at 6,000ft (1,828.8m) at an all-up weight of 6,000lb (2,721.5kg) was reassuring. Additionally, the new engines also gave increased speed and range to the aircraft. One of Noon & Pearce's main routes was Nairobi to Dar es Salaam. The distance between the two cities was 418 miles (672.7km) and their Rapides were unable to make the full journey without an intermediate stop. The converted Rapide was able to make the journey non-stop even with a head wind.

From 1954 to the beginning of 1956, both Airwork (East Africa) and Noon & Pearce Air Charters became involved with and helped to provide financial backing for an unusual aviation project. DH.51 VP-KAA, named *Miss Kenya*, was a thirty-year-old aircraft (one of only three built) that was not expected to fly again as it was lying in a dilapidated condition in the hangar at RAF Eastleigh (Nairobi), its fuel tanks filled with beer by RAF personnel sympathetic to its condition. This particular aircraft had been test flown by Sir Geoffrey de Havilland in 1925 before being sold to Mr J.E. Carberry, who brought it out to Kenya as the first aircraft to be imported into the country. The aircraft was originally registered as G-KAA before being re-registered VP-KAA on 3 January 1929 (the first aircraft on the Kenya register). Various owners followed and it was involved in a crash at Kisumu followed by a heavy landing on its eventual delivery to RAF Eastleigh in 1951.

In 1954 the RAF agreed to give *Miss Kenya* to Mr J.A. Johnstone of the ARB (Air Registration Board) and Mr J.S. (Jack) le Poer Trench of Noon & Pearce Air Charters in order for it to be restored to flying condition. Jack Trench registered *Miss Kenya* in his name and, with the aforementioned material and financial assistance, the vintage aircraft took to the skies over Kenya again. *Miss Kenya* is with the Shuttleworth Collection at Old Warden as of January 2012.

An Airwork Bristol 170 and a Miles M.57 Aerovan were used to carry labour and produce between Mombasa and Arusha for the ill-fated Tanganyikan Groundnut scheme which began in 1946 and was cancelled in January 1951. The Aerovan was G-AJKO, which was re-registered to Airwork (East Africa) Ltd as VP-KEN in September 1947. It crashed in the Kenya Rift Valley on 31 December 1949.

TSETSE FLY EXPERIMENTAL SPRAYING CONTRACTS, 1948–52

An experiment was undertaken by the Colonial Office Insecticide Committee on behalf of the Institute of Tropical Medicine in conjunction with the government of Uganda in aerial spraying against the tsetse fly. Two Avro 652A Ansons (G-AKMV and G-AIRW), with crews, were based on four islands on Lake Victoria with the headquarters of the operation in Entebbe. Both G-AKMV and G-AIRW were registered to Airwork Ltd on 1 July 1948 and 9 August 1948 respectively. At the end of their work in Uganda, they were moved to Kenya and re-registered with Airwork (East Africa) Ltd as VP-KHT and VP-KHS respectively.

Two further contracts were negotiated. The first contract ran from 11 July 1950 to 10 July 1951, and the work continued without pause past the 11 July 1951 expiry date before the second contract was signed in September 1951. The second contract officially started on 11 July 1951, again for one year, and although the spraying work was on behalf of the Colonial Office Insecticide Committee, the contract was actually between Airwork and the MCA.

Aircraft

The basic sturdiness of the Avro Anson airframe was ideally suited to the rugged conditions in East Africa. The Airwork Avro 652A Ansons (VP-KHS and VP-KHT) were allocated to the experimental spraying contracts and were based principally in Arusha. Initially provision was made for up to four members of the Colonial Insecticide Research Unit to be carried in VP-KHT and up to two members of the unit in VP-KHS. After the crash of VP-KHT in August 1951, this was altered to up to four passengers in VP-KHS and two in VP-KJK (which replaced VP-KHT).

At a meeting (see below) held between the Airwork representatives (chief pilot on the contract Mr E.C. Jaques and technical manager Mr I.J. Rees) and the Colonial Office in London on 17 April 1952, one issue raised was Avro Anson G-AKDU, which had been delivered to Arusha by the RAF in April 1952. The aircraft needed repairs and it was suggested by Mr Rees of Airwork that, provided spares could be obtained, Airwork could repair the aircraft if the RAF would reimburse them via the Air Ministry. With a full programme of spraying being undertaken with two Ansons, it was felt that G-AKDU would have been a back-up aircraft. However, apart from the repairs, G-AKDU would have had to have been flown back to the UK for a spraying boom to be fitted; as such, the proposal appears to have been dropped.

The date of 30 April 1952 was taken as the delivery date to Arusha of G-AIRX, the replacement Anson for VP-KHT. G-AIRX had undertaken spraying tests at A&AEE Boscombe Down from 24 April 1952 after the equipment had been fitted by Airwork in their workshops. The Boscombe Down tests delayed the delivery to Arusha until May 1952. It was registered to Airwork (East Africa) Ltd as VP-KJK. This aircraft met a tragic end four years after the spraying contract had finished. It crashed on 1 October 1956 when the port wing broke off on take-off from Kitale, killing the three occupants.

Operations

The day-to-day work of the two Ansons was under the direction of the officer in charge of the Colonial Insecticide Research Unit in Arusha, Tanganyika. This was the third phase of experiments conducted by the Colonial Insecticide Research Unit with four separate experiments, two of which used the Ansons for a total of 350 hours' flying time. In one experiment, seven aircraft applications were made over an area of bush infested with three different species of tsetse fly. A quarter of a pound (113.4g) of DDT insecticide in oil solution per acre was used over 15sq. miles. The final results, after one year, showed reductions of 99.1 per cent, 95.6 per cent and 99.9 per cent in respect of each species.

Another experiment with BHC pesticide concerned an area of 9sq. miles which had been treated in 1949. The infested area had previously been treated during the rainy season with eight fortnightly applications of smoke-produced BHC by injecting 10 per cent solution of BHC in kerosene and furnace oil into the exhausts of aircraft which had the effect of reducing the infestation by 93 per cent. Since the first series of experiments in 1949, the tsetse flies had increased and a further series of applications was carried out during the rainy season while the bush was in full leaf. The second series of applications involved using a solution of 20 per cent BHC with a greater swathe-width. During the wet weather, heavy rain (40in [1m] in two months) hampered operations and reduction of infestation was usually found to be only 90 per cent.

During spraying it was necessary to eradicate the tsetse fly completely. Killing 98.5 per cent of the tsetse fly population in any area was a fairly simple matter but to eliminate the remaining 1.5 per cent was always difficult. The remainder would always have to be eradicated as the flies would merely start to re-infest the area that had just been cleared. In this respect the direction of spraying runs was important as the tsetse flies moved from one area to another between spraying. It was important to overlap spraying runs widely to allow for this movement, but a long spray run to cover the area completely could sometimes be longer than the capacity of an Anson in one run.

Among areas sprayed were Kikore, Atta Island (near Kikore), Musoma, the Urambo area and Dar es Salaam. Atta Island was actually an area of bush on raised ground rather than an island surrounded by water.

As part of the spraying programme, it was necessary for the Airwork crews and government employees to develop aerial photographic, map-making and processing techniques to assist in flying over and working on remote bush areas on which no previous detailed survey work had been undertaken. The aerial photographs enabled a plan to be set out along with markers to aid the control of spraying. One of the Airwork employees on the contract, Mr Alkin, using a borrowed aerial camera, had constructed photographic mosaics of Atta Island, Ukara Island, the Pallidipes ravine area and the Musoma area.

The second contract was marred by the crash, on 1 August 1951, of Avro Anson VP-KHT. The aircraft had force landed during a rainstorm but hit a tree and was burnt out 5 miles (8km) from Arusha. The Anson had been spraying a thicketed ravine under the direction of the provincial tsetse officer when the accident occurred, fortunately with no loss of life. The programme of spraying operations was revised after the crash of VP-KHT and the expiry of the first contract on 10 July 1952. The spraying flights tended to be early in the morning, just before dawn, and were undertaken after extensive ground work was carried out. A 100sq.-mile area near the town of Musoma by the south-eastern shore of Lake Victoria was designated to be cleared of tsetse flies.

Contract Problems & Living Conditions

There were two sources of contention for the Airwork staff in East Africa on the tsetse fly-spraying contract. The first was the provision of ground transport which the government were duty bound to provide, and the second was the standard of accommodation which the colonial authorities provided. A meeting between the Airwork representatives (chief pilot on the contract Mr E.C. Jaques and technical manager Mr I.J. Rees) and the Colonial Office was held in London on 17 April 1952 to iron out the problems.

Whilst accommodation was considered to be inadequate, conditions varied as the spraying teams moved to different areas from the Arusha base. For instance, the Airwork crew spraying from the private airstrip at Kikore were housed 'in some style', as stated by Chief Pilot E.C. Jaques. They stayed in 'Rhino Hall' – two houses built in the early 1920s by Sir Frank Swynnerton, who was regarded as the father of tsetse fly research in East Africa. One of the drawbacks of working in the bush was the presence of dangerous animals such as lions, leopards and rhinos.

Low-flying spraying work has always been a hazardous activity. Although flying hours were comparatively low, the ratio of take-offs and landings to flying times is far greater than normal (between five and ten times in the case of the Ansons). In addition, due to the dangerous nature of low-flying spraying work, a matter of great concern was the issue of insurance liability. In long-drawn-out negotiations between Airwork and the Colonial Office in 1952 prior to the agreement of a new contract, a sum of £3,000 per passenger seat was covered by legislation (both the Warsaw Convention and the UK 1952 Carriage of Air Act for non-international passengers) but as their liability was in theory unlimited Airwork sought further reassurance that a higher figure of liability would in some way be covered by either the British Government or the colonial government they were working for. The possibility of a disclaimer for a sum in excess of £3,000 per passenger was rejected and Airwork suggested the payment of an additional premium covering liability up to £50,000. The passengers affected were employees of the Tanganyika Government and the discussions were not merely procedural or contractual matters, as the crashes of two Avro Ansons were to show.

Conclusions

The aerial spraying activities in East Africa were closely analysed by the Colonial Insecticide Research Unit at Porton, Wiltshire, and a modified type of boom and apparatus (from the equipment on the Airwork Ansons) was designed and manufactured as a result of the experience gained. Further trials were also carried out using an Avro XIX with smoke-producing apparatus fitted to the exhausts.

Meteorology was also closely studied; in particular the effects of atmospheric turbulence on the distribution of finer droplets. Investigations were also carried out on the effects of turbulence in acacia woodland.

15

ECUADOR

SHELL OIL CONTRACT

In 1937 the Shell Oil Co. was granted a concession by the government of Ecuador to prospect for oil. Although it is a cliché, the expression 'some of the most inhospitable conditions on earth' adequately describes the region of Oriente where Shell was allowed to prospect for oil. Set in the rainforests of the Andes, Mera was a small village in the centre of the Ecuador hinterland, actually in the foothills of the Andes, which the Shell Oil Co. of Ecuador used as their centre of operations while they prospected for oil. The village came to be known as 'Shell Mera' and an airstrip, roughly 750yds (686m) long, was laid out on the banks of the Pastaza River in 1937. The airstrip was actually approximately 3 miles (5km) from Mera but the two came to be known collectively as Shell Mera. The village itself was not considered to be a very pleasant place either. Surrounded by native tribes (one particularly hostile), there was only one way the village was accessible, through a pass to the east. The weather could change in a matter of minutes and this could happen a number of times a day, when the weather would close in and there was very little room for aircraft to manoeuvre between the surrounding mountains. The hostility of the Huaorani (also known as Auca) tribe to outsiders was not to be underestimated. They frequently ambushed groups of prospectors and in 1956, after Shell and Airwork had departed, they were responsible for killing five American missionaries who had established themselves in Shell Mera. To add to the problems, the region in the 1930s had been barely mapped. Once Shell had been granted the concession, they enlisted the services of Fairchild Aerial Surveys (one of the principal photo-mapping companies of the time, founded by Sherman Fairchild of Fairchild Aircraft fame) to start photo-mapping the area using a Ford Tri-Motor NC9606 (later used by Shell in Ecuador as HC-SBQ) and later Fairchild 71s and a Lockheed 12A (possibly Shell's YV-VOD). Fairchild Aerial Surveys had previously worked for Shell, photo-mapping in Venezuela. A taste of events to come occurred when the Lockheed 12A started its mapping and the aircraft was negotiating its way through mountain peaks; it encountered severe turbulence and fell 13,000ft (3,962m) before the pilot was able to regain control. The very basic nature of flying in this region meant that there were few aids to flying other than VHF radio links with radio beacons and a VHF DF Homer at Shell Mera.

The inaccessibility of the region meant that from the capital Quito, supplies had to be taken by train to the mountain railhead at Ambato. From there they were trucked down a highway through the Baños Pass to Mera. Once the airstrip was established, Shell had to bring in as many aircraft as possible as everything, including equipment, food and personnel, had to be carried by air out to the prospecting locations. There was a shortage of suitable aircraft during the war years and shortly afterwards. Shell had used contracted American Grace DC-2s and DC-3s, Ford Tri-Motors and four Budd RB-1 Conestogas along with Grumman Goose Amphibians which had previously been used by Shell in Venezuela. Aircraft availability eased as time went on, although just prior to Airwork assuming control a shortage of capacity had forced Shell to use freight capacity from local carrier ANDESA (Aeronavias Nacionales del Ecuador SA). Formed in 1945, initially as West Indies Flying Services Inc., ANDESA used its Curtiss C-46 Commandos and UC-64A Norseman aircraft to supplement the Shell freight operation from October 1946 to 24 April 1947.

The arrival of Airwork to take over the Shell operation had a serious impact on ANDESA as 60 per cent of their revenue came from the Shell business. By October of 1947, all their assets were seized by the Ecuadorian Government for non-payment of taxes.

AIRWORK TAKE OVER THE SHELL AVIATION OPERATION

At the beginning of 1947, Shell reached an agreement with Airwork to take over the running of the Air Transport Division of Shell's Ecuador operation. Airwork had been chosen for the management of the Air Division because of their oil industry experience gained in Iraq and Iran. The ownership of the aircraft remained with the Shell Oil Co. of Ecuador and Airwork were responsible for maintaining and operating the small fleet of aircraft on behalf of Shell. The number of expatriate staff employed by Airwork would average a total of twenty plus local labour. The aircraft were used to fly food, machinery and other supplies into established airstrips in support of survey parties prospecting for oil. By the time Airwork entered the scene in early 1947, the runway at Shell Mera was a 4,200ft (1,280m) gravel strip with a large hangar and engineering workshop at one end. Also present at the airstrip was the hulk of one of the Budd RB-1 Conestogas (HC-SBE) which had made a wheels-up landing within five months of arrival on 15 May 1946 and had been written off. It had been cannibalised for spares and the hull was used as a bar known as 'The Budd Club'.

Aircraft movements at Shell Mera were up to four per hour on average, due to the intensity of the air operation supporting the outlying wildcat drilling sites. Five drilling sites had been established in the rainforest surrounding the base. Four of these had been named after local tribal chiefs: Arajuno, Ayuy, Taisha and Tiputini. Villano was the fifth site. Arajuno had been the first to be established, 35 miles (56km) north-east of Shell Mera. The method of establishing the sites involved firstly identifying the site by surveyors; using jungle trails to the site with pack-mules carrying the equipment and stores; clearing and establishing the site using friendly Yumbo natives; and air drops by parachute of supplies to the site whilst it was being cleared for operation (sometimes using the Grumman Goose to retrieve the supplies if they landed in one of the many rivers in the region). Finally, once an airstrip had been cleared aircraft could land with heavy earthmoving and drilling equipment. All the while, the living conditions at these sites were even more unpleasant than Shell Mera due to the closer proximity of the Huaorani, poisonous snakes and spiders, vampire bats and the rainfall measured in feet rather than inches which turned the ground into a quagmire.

By the time of Airwork's arrival, the four ex-US navy Budd RB-1 Conestogas were no longer being used (excluding HC-SBE which was being used as The Budd Club). The Ford Tri-Motors were superseded by the introduction of two Douglas DC-3s (HC-SBR and HC-SBS in April and July 1947) and two Bristol 170 Freighters (HC-SBM and HC-SBN in March and April 1947). Three Grumman G-21A Grumman Goose Amphibians (HC-SBA, HC-SBB and HC-SBT) supplemented the operation. The introduction of the second Douglas DC-3 HC-SBS involved an unusual coincidence. This particular DC-3 was an ex-RAF example, KG731 of 525 Squadron, which had been completely reconditioned by Airwork for use in Ecuador. The pilot who originally collected it from the maintenance unit in Doncaster in 1944 was V.R.H. Ferguson, who flew the aircraft collecting stretcher cases from Normandy after D-Day. After this, he flew this same aircraft on runs to India and Copenhagen for 525 Squadron. After its reconditioning for Ecuador ten years later, Ferguson was reunited with his old aircraft as he was now Airwork's chief pilot in Ecuador. Ferguson was an ex-RAF squadron leader and holder of the DFC.

Despite their age, the Ford Tri-Motors had proved their worth with their ability to operate into a rough 1,312ft (400m) strip carrying a 1½-ton freight load. In 1946 they had carried a total of 9,000 passengers and 2,150 tonnes of freight to the drilling locations. The three remaining Tri-Motors HC-SBJ, HC-SBK and HC-SBQ were phased out by 1948. HC-SBJ and HC-SBK were both AT-5 models powered by the more powerful Pratt & Whitney Wasp C radial engines of 425hp and had been acquired from the Venezuelan carrier AVENSA. HC-SBQ had been acquired from Dominicana in December 1946. Despite no longer participating in operations, two of these three Ford Tri-Motors were at Shell Mera for the duration of the Airwork contract. Although it is not certain, it is believed the two at Shell Mera were HC-SBJ and HC-SBK as HC-SBQ was reportedly based at Caracas by 1948 and was no longer with Shell.

The Tri-Motors had given excellent service, but the arrival of the Bristol 170s HC-SBM and HC-SBN in 1947 gave a major boost to the freight capacity of the supply operation. In December 1948 they claimed two world records. The first was the heaviest load carried by a twin-engine aircraft and the second was the transportation of the heaviest single piece of machinery yet transported by air. Drilling equipment is large and heavy. The first item mentioned was an

HC-SBZ was originally with the Shell contract as HC-SBN. It returned to Ecuador on 14 October 1949 to replace HC-SBU and was given a new registration HC-SBZ. (MAP)

EMSCO Drawworks stripped down to 9,000lb (4,082kg) plus 3,000lb (1,361kg) of accessories, which was flown the relatively short distance from Arajuno to Villano. The other item, the heaviest single piece of machinery yet carried, was an EMSCO block.

During the transfer of heavy equipment from Arajuno to Villano, just prior to the preparation of the Villano strip, part of the heavy equipment was moved to its destination by land through hostile Auca territory. The convoy of heavy equipment, led by F.R. Callender, accomplished the transfer between the drilling locations in ten days, fortunately without any confrontation or incident.

Another heavy item transported by the Bristol 170s was the Allis Chalmers HD7W tractor, which was transported without its bulldozer blades, power control units, batteries and radiators. Caterpillar D6s also had to be stripped down for transport to the sites and reassembled on arrival. Tony Lane, the head of transport at Shell Mera, was a former army cargo specialist who understood very well what was required in the supply operation. He organised his teams to start loading the aircraft before sunrise so that the pilots could make the maximum use of daylight hours.

Just prior to the takeover by Airwork, Sir Richard Barlow (Airwork's South American manager) had travelled to Ecuador to make a survey of the whole operation. Once he had completed his task, he took off from Shell Mera on 3 December 1946 for Quito in Grumman Goose HC-SBL, flown by Pilot Gene Gates and accompanied by two sick workers and a male nurse. Once the Amphibian had gained enough height after taking off in an easterly direction, Gates turned back to fly westwards through the Baños Pass. However, visibility was very poor and rain clouds were being funnelled up through the pass. Flying on instruments, the Amphibian struck one of the mountains bordering the pass a couple of hundred feet from the summit. All on board were killed and it took three days of searches to find the wreckage, which was spotted from the air 14,000ft (4,266m) up the Llanganate range of mountains. This tragic accident involving a senior pilot and a senior member of Airwork brought home to everyone the extremely hazardous nature of flying in the area.

There were no more accidents until June 1948, when an Ecuadorian air force C-47, serial 02, was practising take-offs and landings at Shell Mera. On taking off with the engines at full power, the aircraft swung to the right was then overcorrected, swinging violently to the left and running along a ditch for 200m, losing parts of the port wing on the way. The C-47 then mounted a bank on the far side of the ditch it was running along, hit a tree stump, losing one engine in the process, and then swung around, demolishing the Shell Accounts Department in Shell's administration building. Despite being fully occupied, only one man was killed (by being hit on the back of the head by a flying typewriter). Courageous and quick thinking by Airwork's chief pilot, V.R.H. Ferguson, stopped a larger fire from breaking out when he grabbed a foam fire extinguisher and put out a small fire which had started and threatened the aircraft's fuel tanks.

The average aircraft establishment while Airwork ran the operation was usually two Bristol 170 Freighters, two Douglas DC-3s and three Grumman Goose Amphibians.

PARACHUTE OPERATIONS

One element of the Airwork operation in Ecuador which gave it a unique aspect was the use of supply by parachute. This method of supply had been used prior to the airstrips being cleared at the drilling camps but continued to be used for survey parties in the field (a seismic team needed up to seventy parachute loads a week) and also at Tiputini airstrip, which was not an all-weather strip due to a lack of paving material. Drops to survey parties were the most challenging and would usually involve parachuting supplies into a rough rectangle of around 650ft x 500ft (approximately 200m x 150m), the rectangle having been cleared from the jungle beforehand and its location roughly described and sent with a runner. Before a drop took place, the Air Transport Division would check off the materials required (spares, fresh vegetables, sacks of rice, drums of oil, mail, dynamite and sometimes live sheep and pigs) and prepare them in packages of 154lb (70kg) (the capacity of the parachute being 132–176lb [60–80kg]) with the parachute on top. The loads would then be laid in two lines down the centre of the aircraft cabin. With a dropping speed of 23ft (7m) per second, soft ground was preferred for the drops to minimise breakages. Food was packed in 5- or 10-gallon (23 or 45 litres) tins and, with other commodities in boxes, two of them (measuring roughly 25cm x 35cm x 50cm [10in x 14in x 20in]) would be the load for one parachute. The dropping height had to be low (60–100m [200–300ft]) in order to avoid drift of the parachutes into the surrounding jungle.

The parachute crew was usually formed of four local staff. Two dispatchers would be harnessed by the door and the other two were stackers responsible for keeping the supplies moving aft to the dispatchers. The use of parachutes started in late 1945, not long before Airwork took over. However, in 1949 Airwork staff (by suggestion of one of the mechanics) changed the system of dropping the parachutes from basically pushing the loads individually out of the aircraft door to placing up to six packages at a time on a hinged and greased metal tray by the door. The tray was hinged on to a recess at the base of the door of the aircraft. Once loaded, the aircraft would fly in at a low speed (a DC-3 would fly at around 85mph [137km/h] at 300ft [100m]), and would then tip the tray over the drop zone and the packages would fall out, to be quickly replaced by the next batch on its return flight over the zone.

Livestock was also dropped individually by parachute. One Airwork pilot described dropping live pigs and sheep by parachute, with the sheep seemingly taking a great interest in all around them and, once they landed, immediately starting to eat weeds as if arriving from the sky was the most natural thing in the world. Aircraft would also carry a locally recruited aircrew assistant who looked after cargo security, operated doors and handled the mooring lines of the Grumman Goose Amphibians.

Once the drop had been completed, the parachutes would be returned to Shell Mera to be repacked and used again. In most cases, the parachutes would be taken by labourers to a base camp by a river where a Grumman Goose would land and take the parachutes back to Shell Mera. The distance from a drop zone to a riverside base camp could be anything up to 50 miles (80km). With a large survey party, such as a seismic survey party, receiving up to seventy parachute loads a week and a labourer able to carry only two or three parachutes at one time to the base camps, it can be seen that this was a highly labour-intensive operation. The parachutes would last for approximately twenty-five drops before they had to be replaced. The humid climate also made them difficult to dry out when they got wet. Swedish paper parachutes, which were a quarter of the cost of the normal cotton ones, were introduced, although these could generally be used for only one drop. Some of them were returned to Shell Mera for drying in the sun but this could take up to a week for the parachute to be completely dry for reuse. It was generally reckoned that the most economical use of parachutes was when the drop zone was within 12 miles (20km) of a point where they could be picked up by a Grumman Goose. In all, it was estimated that around 1,650 tonnes of supplies were dropped by parachute through the course of their operation. The use of helicopters was looked at with regard to the whole supply operation but the remoteness of the locations, the cost and the lack of cargo capacity of the helicopters then in use ruled out their use in the Oriente.

The Grumman Goose Amphibian, despite not being able to carry as much cargo as the DC-3, Tri-Motor or Bristol 170, was very useful for delivering supplies to survey teams near rivers. It carried two crew and enough fuel for two hours' flying and, stripped of non-essential fittings, the Goose could carry 1,000lb (455kg) of food, fuel and equipment to the teams and return to Shell Mera with rock specimens and geophysical records for analysis, plus air-lifting the occasional medical case. The Goose supported teams of up to sixty surveyors and attendant staff who were mapping the area of Ecuador bordering Peru, primarily by carrying their equipment from one riverside location to the next, which saved a considerable amount of time and trouble by avoiding the need to carry items like concrete posts and theodolites through the jungle. Landing on these jungle rivers was no straightforward matter for the Goose. The pilot would make a dummy run first to view the general situation. The depth of the water would have to be checked by the surveyors in motorised canoes. Any overhanging branches or trees also had to be removed (particularly on the approach) and underwater obstructions had to be removed by blasting with dynamite. The Goose required a landing area 3,000ft (914m) long, 240ft (73m) wide and 5ft (1.5m) deep. After landing the Goose would taxi up to a balsa wood docking ramp at the riverbank and unload its supplies.

MISHAPS IN 1949 & 'BLACK AUGUST'

Despite the quality of airmanship and maintenance provided by Airwork in this most demanding of conditions, 1949 was a bad year. On 17 February 1949, Goose HC-SBB landed on the Rio Curaray next to a base camp in the Pavacachi region. Ironically, Shell had named HC-SBB *Curaray*, after the river, on its arrival on 2 January 1945. Once the Goose had discharged its supplies it took off and the right undercarriage fell down out of its well. The pilot had already requested advice by radio when he decided to try a water landing to see if the water would drive the undercarriage back up into the well. However, the leg had locked into position and once it hit the water, it caused the aircraft to flip over on to its back and was written off. Shell Mera had radioed back via relay at the base camp to tell the pilot to select gear down and return to Shell Mera, but this information had not been received in time. Fortunately, both the pilot and mechanic survived.

The operation was now left with one Goose out of a fleet of three. The other Goose, HC-SBT, had been sold to Shell in Venezuela in early 1949 and was registered YV-C-AEP. Shell Venezuela (the Shell Caribbean Petroleum Co.) was unable to return the Goose at this point as they were short of capacity themselves, having just sold their Sea Otter Amphibian YV-P-AEN. A new Goose, HC-SBV, was provided and it arrived at Shell Mera on 28 April 1949. Shortly after its arrival, it was being tested for single-engine performance at a height of 1,500ft (500m) near Shell Mera when the live engine stopped without warning. With insufficient height to make the River Pastaza, the Goose hit the trees at the river's edge. Whilst the earlier crash of Goose HC-SBB had been without loss of life, HC-SBV had made a violent impact which tragically resulted in the deaths of Bob Ferguson, Airwork's chief pilot, and Harry Riggs, Airwork's chief engineer. Both had suffered severe head injuries in the crash and died instantly. It was a heavy loss for the operation. Both Ferguson and Riggs were buried in a cemetery on the slopes of the Andes near Quito.

An order was placed for another Grumman Goose G-21A immediately, which arrived in August 1949 as HC-SBX. HC-SBA had continued to soldier on in the intervening period with a considerable burden being placed on the aircraft to fulfil all operational requirements normally carried out by three aircraft. On 2 August 1949 HC-SBA had completed twenty consecutive trips when it made a wheels-up landing at Villano airstrip. The aircraft was capable still of flying but could not land on water, which made it useless for the supply of seismic parties, so it had to be sent back to the USA for repairs.

Unfortunately, ill luck continued to dog the operation. A severe earthquake took place on 5 August 1949 with the epicentre between Ambato and Baños. The small village of Pelileo, on the road to Shell Mera, was almost destroyed by the tremors, with only one-tenth of the population surviving. Most of the small villages in the surrounding area suffered the same fate, but most of the facilities used by Shell and Airwork escaped with only light damage (there was a transportation and materials yard in Ambato). The following day, Bristol 170 HC-SBU took off from Shell Mera to Ambato with relief teams and supplies for the earthquake victims. However, the Baños Pass was to claim another victim when the Bristol Freighter crashed near Salasca Hill. The Airwork captain, Patrick Billington, was sadly killed along with thirty-four others on board. Another earthquake and a volcanic eruption caused clouds of dust to rise thousands of feet into the air and, with disturbances to the magnetic field, communications were affected. Captain Billington had attempted to turn back 180 degrees and return to Shell Mera. The wreckage was found by one of the DC-3s from Shell Mera, 600ft (183m) from the top of Salasca Hill at the mouth of the Baños Pass, and it had been engulfed in a mud landslide.

This further blow to Airwork's operation left the Air Transport Division with a serious capacity shortage which was made worse by the need to transport relief supplies on account of the earthquake. The operation was left with one Douglas DC-3 and one Grumman Goose Amphibian which was incapable of alighting on water. With the road closed between Ambato and Shell Mera on account of the devastation caused by the earthquake, there was an urgent requirement for further aircraft to move the 400–500 tons of supplies needed every month to keep the Shell operation going. A request was made for the immediate return of Douglas DC-3 HC-SBR from Curaçao, where it was receiving a major check with KLM; Shell Venezuela also loaned their Grumman Goose YV-C-AEP which was then repurchased by Shell Ecuador and registered HC-SBY. This Goose had originally gone to Shell Venezuela from Shell Ecuador as HC-SBT before being registered in Venezuela. In addition, aircraft were chartered in from regional carriers, such as DC-3s from Panagra and Avianca, and a Curtiss C-46 from local company AREA. These were required to bring in supplies from Ambato which would normally have been brought by road.

Even then, the bad luck continued as Douglas DC-3 HC-SBR taxied out at Hato Field, Curaçao, on 22 August 1949 for its return flight to Shell Mera. Due to a misunderstanding of ground signals, the DC-3's right wingtip collided with another aircraft. The wingtip had had to be replaced, delaying the return of the aircraft.

Still in 'Black August', the chartered Curtiss Commando of AREA had a minor accident on the runway at Shell Mera which required the replacement of a propeller, putting the aircraft out of action for a week.

Last but not least, there was yet another accident, this time involving the Grumman Goose returned from Shell Venezuela (now registered HC-SBY). After arriving at Shell Mera on 19 August 1949, it was given a 100-hour inspection which was followed by a test flight on 25 August 1949, and was found to be in good working order. It entered normal service on the following day with Pilot G. Howden. The aircraft was scheduled to depart Shell Mera at 8.24 a.m. and fly to Marasumu, then refuel at Villano before flying to Lorocachi and Marasumu before commencing a series of shuttles between Marasumu and Villano. After departure with a co-pilot and passenger Howden found the weather rapidly deteriorating and elected to return to Shell Mera. On landing, the aircraft started slewing to the left which was corrected with right rudder, but then the aircraft went nose down and the keel of the Amphibian scraped along the runway, coming to a halt whilst slewing to the right before settling back on its tail. The occupants were unhurt but the Amphibian was put out of commission until parts could be rushed from the USA. This left the Shell operation without any amphibious capability and once again the seismic parties were reliant on parachute supply only as the other Goose, HC-SBA, was already being repaired in the USA. It was to be one month until Goose HC-SBX arrived to get things back to normal.

The road to Ambato was finally reopened in October 1949, although the contract with AREA for the use of the Curtiss C-46 to fly in supplies to Shell Mera from Ambato, which was due to expire on 10 October 1949, was extended for two weeks to ensure continuity of supplies.

CONCLUSIONS

By the end of 1949 it was becoming apparent that the search for oil was not producing any results and the operation was starting to wind down. One of the last operations undertaken by Bristol 170 HC-SBZ and one of the DC-3s was the removal of the EMSCO drilling rig from

Villano to Shell Mera for final evacuation. The sixth and last well to be drilled was dry and this led Shell to start winding down the whole operation. When Douglas DC-3 HC-SBS returned to England for overhaul at the end of 1949, Shell Ecuador were asked by their Head Office if they could manage without this aircraft, to which they agreed. The decision to call a halt and start evacuating was eventually taken in March 1950. HC-SBZ did not leave until September 1950.

Airwork's time with Shell in Ecuador was relatively brief but it was an operation to which the company was ideally suited with its expertise of operating and maintaining aircraft in the most arduous of conditions. Despite the extremely difficult conditions experienced by Airwork staff, they continued to perform their duties without regard to the circumstances they found themselves in. For example, on the maintenance side, from July to December 1947 over 1,500 daily inspections of aircraft were carried out. Many Airwork staff were ex-servicemen who were used to giving of their best in the most trying of circumstances and the statistics give some idea of the scale of the operation: 38,000 tonnes of freight and 71,000 passengers carried in approximately 26,000 flights.[1] In a busy month there could be up to 700 flights and 100 tons of supplies carried. The high rate of accidents was more down to the difficult and hazardous operating conditions than any shortcomings in Airwork pilots and staff. Pilots would generally fly for only three hours a day to ensure they had enough rest and the service contract had been reduced from three to two years. Annual leave had also been extended from fifteen days per annum to twenty-one days. On top of this, pilots were given four days' rest every six weeks away from the Oriente region in addition to their normal rest days.

Despite the long search for oil, none was found and, as previously stated, in the latter part of 1949 and into 1950, Shell scaled the operation down and eventually pulled out completely in 1950.

However, oil was discovered later in the same region by a Texaco-Gulf oil partnership in 1963, long after Shell had pulled out. This was at Orito, on the border between Ecuador and Peru. A pipeline was then built from the area down to Esmeralda on the Pacific coastline of Ecuador. The discovery proved that the Shell geologists were on the right track. A further exploration by other companies went into the Oriente and oil was discovered between Orito and Tiputini, which had formed part of the original Shell concession.

16

INDIAN NATIONAL AIRWAYS

Indian National Airways (INA) was the second domestic airline to be established in India. The airline was formed in May 1933 with a capital of 3 million rupees, principally to serve as a shareholder in Indian Trans-Continental Airways (ITCA), but also as an agent to develop internal services in northern India as well as to provide feeder services for the proposed Imperial Airways service across India to Singapore. ITCA itself was intended to concentrate on airline operations to the east of Calcutta in conjunction with Imperial Airways. The formation of ITCA was due to pressure for Indian participation in the extension of the Imperial Airways route from Karachi to Singapore, which was planned to be in place by 1935. There was to be considerable competition from Tata Air Lines in the race to establish Indian air services, but the Indian Government had given assurances to INA that, other than the ITCA feeder services for Imperial Airways, INA would be given the areas to the north and east of the empire air route to develop its services without consideration to other possible operators.

---

1   Over the total period of the operation including Shell's period of operation prior to the takeover by Airwork.

The Board of Directors of INA consisted of the managing director Raymond Eustace Grant Govan and directors Sir Phiroze Sethna, F.P. Raynham, Sir H.M. Mehta and the Hon. B.K. Basu. Raymond Grant Govan was also a director of ITCA.

Govan Brothers was a trading house based in Delhi, and Raymond Grant Govan had visited Heston and owned his own aircraft (DH.80A Puss Moth VT-ABZ and later DH.90 Dragonfly VT-AHW). He also held Indian Aviators Certificate No. 7 (the Indian 'A' licence).

Airwork Ltd provided technical assistance to INA under contract, although their involvement was not as extensive as it was with Misr-Airwork in Egypt, which had been formed the previous year (1932). For instance, neither Alan Muntz nor Nigel Norman was on the Board of Directors as they were with Misr-Airwork. Govan Brothers owned the controlling interest in INA with 60 per cent of that holding being non-Indian. On 7 July 1933 INA acquired a 25 per cent stake in ITCA and immediately began marketing their services and that of the Imperial Airways service. The major shareholder in ITCA was Imperial Airways with 51 per cent; the balance was held (besides INA's 25 per cent) by the Indian Government at 24 per cent. However, a key role was played by Robert Maxwell who joined Airwork from Blackburn Aircraft and took control of day-to-day operations. He performed exceptionally well during the time he was with INA, from 1934 to 1936, before being moved over to perform the same task at Misr-Airwork in 1936.

AIRCRAFT

The first aircraft used by the new airline was DH.83 Fox Moth VT-AEB which was actually registered on 1 June 1933 to the government of Bengal but was operated by INA and based at Dum Dum Airport, Calcutta. In October 1934 two DH.84 Dragons VT-AEK and VT-AEL joined the airline to give a boost to capacity. In December 1933, the end of the first year of operation, another DH.83 Fox Moth, VT-AEM, was registered to the airline and was also based at Dum Dum Airport.

In 1934 INA took delivery of a further eight aircraft: a DH.84 Dragon (VT-AES); a DH.83 Fox Moth (VT-AFB); three DH.60G Moths (VT-AFG, VT-AFH, VT-AFJ); two Percival Gulls (VT-AFU, VT-AFV); and an Avro 628 Ten (VT-AFX), which had been delivered from the Egyptian air force (ex-F201).

At the end of 1935 an agreement was reached between the government of India and Indian National Airways, under which the airline would be responsible for the maintenance and

Vickers 604 Viking IB VT-AZA at Heston. On 8 August 1946, in a ceremony organised by Airwork, VT-AZA was named *Jumna* by the wife of the Indian high commissioner. (Alan Holloway)

operation of the viceroy's Avro 642 *Star of India* VT-AFM. Under the same agreement, the airline agreed to continue the maintenance and operation of the Indian Government's Avro Ten VT-ACT.

DEVELOPMENT OF SERVICES & SUBSIDY PROBLEMS

Initially, the first INA services were passenger only. There was no formal contract from the Indian Government to carry mail until the end of 1934, although ad hoc requests made to the government to carry mail on particular services for short periods were made and granted.

DH.84 Dragons started a weekly Calcutta–Rangoon service via Chittagong, Akyab and Bassein on 1 December 1933. The service was increased to twice weekly and mail was carried for a short period. The saving in transit time (nine and a half hours by air) was considerable as the normal journey by steamer took three days and two nights. However, passenger figures were low, with forty-two in December 1933, 242 in 1934 and 232 in the first seven and a half months of 1935.

On the same date, INA DH.83 Fox Moth VT-AEB (followed shortly after by VT-AEM) commenced a daily Calcutta–Dacca service which was intended to supplement ITCA operations to the east of Calcutta. Again mail was carried briefly on this service but there was no formal contract as such. Also the saving in travel time was considerable (one and a half hours by air as opposed to sixteen and a half hours by combined steamer and rail). Passenger traffic and freight failed to develop, however, with 501 passengers carried in total in 1934 and 268 for the first five and a half months of 1935 before the service was withdrawn.

INA were also responsible for the formation of the Rangoon Aero Club with two DH.60G Moths.

In 1934 INA were extensively involved in relief and survey operations after the Bihar earthquake.

An important step for INA was the granting of a contract (worth 70,000 rupees) by the Indian Government for a mail service in north-west India from Karachi to Lahore. At the same time the government granted INA 31,800 rupees to operate and maintain Indian Government aircraft. There was not enough passenger and freight demand to make the Karachi–Lahore route a viable service. One of the stipulations for the contract was that aircraft used should have a minimum speed of 130mph (210km/h). A similar government contract mail service, granted to Tata Air Lines for ten years to operate a Karachi–Madras mail service, had a stipulation that the aircraft used must have a minimum speed of 105mph (170km/h). The INA mail service from Lahore to Karachi was routed via Sukkur and started on 4 December 1934 using the Percival Gulls, with the first return two days later, although Sukkur was dropped on 13 June 1935.

The dropping of the Sukkur call was an indication of the financial viability of the fledgling airline's operations. Alan Muntz commented on more than one occasion that without government help in the form of subsidies it was extremely difficult to operate profitable airline services. After a year and a half of operations, and two days after the dropping of Sukkur from the Lahore–Karachi mail run, the daily Calcutta–Dacca service was withdrawn on 15 June 1935, again due to lack of finance. In addition, on the same date Chittagong was dropped from the Calcutta–Rangoon route (run by Indian Trans-Continental Airways with IAL using two Armstrong Whitworth Atalantas); the whole service was withdrawn on 9 August 1935. This was also partly due to the operation of a Calcutta–Singapore route which virtually duplicated the INA service.

The losses to INA on the Calcutta–Rangoon and Calcutta–Dacca routes were considerable, amounting to a total on both routes of 5 million rupees.

This state of affairs led to only one service being offered by INA in 1936, which was the previously mentioned Karachi–Lahore mail route. INA applied for an Indian Government subsidy equivalent to £8,300 in February 1936, but the application was rejected by the Finance Committee of the Legislative Assembly. The airline needed the money to maintain the existing twice-weekly Lahore–Karachi mail service. In addition, extra finance was needed at their Head

Office and also to develop new services to tie in with the new Empire Mail Scheme which was coming into service at the beginning of 1937. The chairman of INA stated at the airline's annual general meeting in 1936 that they were pleading for government help in the form of subsidies for their domestic services to continue. Surprisingly, perhaps, it was a view shared by the director of Civil Aviation for India, Frederick Tyms (later Sir Frederick Tyms), who had stated in the *Times of India* in October 1934 that 'scarcely anywhere else in the world was there an air service operating without support from the government'.

Although the Indian Government had rejected the request for a subsidy in 1936, in November and December 1937, INA used an Indian Government Avro Ten (VT-AFX) to survey the southern China Shan states for a possible INA route to China. The survey was carried out under charter to the British Air Ministry.

On 1 July 1939 a thrice-weekly service was begun to Kalka from both Delhi and Lahore.

The mail route was not without its problems, as Percival Gull VT-AGO crashed near Jacobabad on 26 January 1937 whilst en route from Karachi to Lahore, and the pilot, R.N. Batra, was killed. This was followed by another serious crash just over two and a half years later, when DH.84 Dragon VT-AEL crashed 40 miles (64km) from Lahore on 26 August 1939, again on the mail flight, with two killed.

In total, between the airline's formation in May 1933 and the outbreak of war, of the eighteen aircraft flown by INA, there were seven crashes and write-offs, including a mid-air collision between two of the company's aircraft: Percival Vega Gull VT-AJD and Beech E17B VT-AKJ, in which INA's chief pilot, P.D. Sharma, lost his life 30 miles (48km) north of Karachi on 23 February 1939.

EMPIRE AIR MAIL SCHEME

Some financial relief was to come for INA in 1938. Under the terms of the Empire Air Mail Programme, the government placed a contract with INA on 28 February 1938 for the transport of first-class un-surcharged mail over the Lahore–Karachi route, with Jacobabad and Multan added as stops. Beech 17s commenced the service the following day. The Lahore end of the service was extended to Delhi in November 1938 and was further extended to Calcutta on 27 June 1940. The Beech 17s were still used and by now Cawnpore and Allahabad were also served; the frequency was doubled on 8 December 1940. Between 30 March 1940 and 25 August 1941, Patna replaced Allahabad on the Delhi–Cawnpore–Calcutta segment of the route before Allahabad supplanted Patna.

SECOND WORLD WAR & A NEW OWNER

With the advent of the Second World War, INA operated several additional routes, a number of which were contractual obligations for the RAF for the carriage of freight, military personnel, mails and priority civil passengers. Among the numerous services operated were a weekly Delhi–Bhopal–Hyderabad–Bangalore–Trichinopoly–Colombo service which started on 27 May 1942 with Beech 18s; a daily Lahore–Multan–Jacobabad–Quetta service operated throughout the summer of 1942; a thrice-weekly Delhi–Karachi via Jodhpur route initiated on 17 January 1943 with Douglas DC-2s; Calcutta–Tezpur–Dinjan in 1942/43, with Jorhat replacing Dinjan on 20 January 1943; and a thrice-weekly Delhi–Lahore–Peshawar service started using DH.89As and Beech 18s on 19 August 1943, with Rawalpindi as an optional stop.

Much-needed additional capability was provided with the arrival of two Douglas DC-2s (VT-ARA and VT-ARB), which were delivered in October 1942 and placed on the Delhi–Colombo route. The first Douglas DC-3 (VT-ARI) was introduced on the Delhi–Colombo route in March 1944.

INA played a conspicuous part in the evacuation from Burma after the Japanese attack, with the evacuation flights being conducted on a daily basis for a month from Rangoon, the aircraft returning to Calcutta via Chittagong and Akyab. Turnaround times at Rangoon during these flights were limited to twenty minutes due to the threat of attack from Japanese forces.

In July 1946 INA were acquired by the Dalmia-Jain Group but continued to operate under their own name. After the Dalmia-Jain takeover, Govan Brothers acted as managing agents for the airline. Airwork continued as European agents for INA up to the nationalisation of Indian airlines, which took place in 1953, with Dalmia-Jain and INA becoming part of Indian Airlines Corporation (IAC). IAC was rebranded as 'Indian' on 7 December 2005, and on 27 February 2011 Indian Airlines Corporation and Air India merged.

17

MIDDLE EAST OIL WORK

ANGLO-PERSIAN OIL/IRAQ PETROLEUM CO./KUWAIT OIL CO.

IRAQ

IPC (Iraq Petroleum Co.)

Prior to Airwork's arrival, the IPC requirements were operated by Imperial Airways aircraft on charter.

On 12 July 1933, Captain Neville Stack had flown a DH.84 Dragon out from Heston to be used by Airwork for special charter work on behalf of the IPC in Iraq and the Middle East. He covered the 1,100 miles (1,770km) from Heston to Rome in a day. On board was P.H. Baker who was travelling to Cyprus, where he left the aircraft to continue his journey by sea to Egypt to take up his duties as general manager of Misr-Airwork. Stack's arrival at Larnaca on 17 July 1933 was greeted by a large crowd, including the mayor, the district commissioner and chief of police. Stack then made a series of ten-minute flights carrying a total of fifty-six passengers.

By 1935, Airwork started providing contract air services to the IPC with DH.84 and DH.89As. Three DH.89A Dragon Rapides, G-ADNG, G-ADNH and G-ADNI, were registered to the Iraq Petroleum Transport Co. on 15 August 1935 and based at Haifa for operations. DH.89A G-AEGS was also registered on 15 May 1936 and G-AESR was registered on 18 March 1937.

Two further DH.89As, G-AFFB and G-AFFC, were registered to the Iraq Petroleum Transport Co. on 12 April 1938 and also based at Haifa.

Cyprus continued as a staging post and a destination for Middle East IPC staff on rest and recreation.

Post-war there was still a major requirement for air transport by the IPC and other airlines had been involved in transport work for them (besides Airwork), including Hunting Air Transport, Lancashire Aircraft Corporation, Scottish Airlines and Silver City.

The centre of operations for the IPC and its associates was at Kirkuk in northern Iraq. The oil pipelines extended from Kirkuk westwards to the Mediterranean and south-east to the Persian Gulf. IPC relied heavily on air communications both internally and for overseas work. DH.89A Rapides continued in operation for several years and supplemented the DH.104 Doves after their introduction to the shorter internal operations. The first Dove, G-AHRI, was handed over on 31 December 1946, followed by G-AICY on 11 April 1947, G-AJJF on 21 August 1947 and G-ALBF on 22 July 1948. This was followed by further deliveries in 1951.

DH.104 Dove I G-AHRI of the Iraq Petroleum Transport Co. at Heston. (Alan Holloway)

For the post-war longer routes, Vickers Vikings and Douglas DC-3s were chartered from Airwork.

From Kirkuk, the westward oil pipelines crossed the Syrian Desert and originally separated to go to the ports at Haifa and Tripoli. Pumping stations were established along the pipeline, each one with its own water plant, air-conditioned accommodation, radio station and telegraph. Landing strips were established at each of these pumping stations in addition to landing strips on the oilfields themselves. Much of the landscape over which the pipelines were laid was composed of desert and mountain ranges, with the attendant climatic problems which made flying difficult.

The political problems between Israel and the Arab League resulted in the closure of the Haifa sector and its refinery. With additional piping, the line to Tripoli took over the capacity which had formerly been handled by Haifa.

The base airport for the Airwork operation for the IPC was at Tripoli's Kleiat Airport. As well as being the base for the pipeline flying work, Tripoli was also the base for charter crews when stopping overnight after flying out from the UK. Kleiat Airport lay between the Tripoli–Homs coastal gap at the extremity of the 10,000ft (3,048m) Lebanese mountain range. Landing at Kleiat Aiport, particularly westbound in winter, was a tricky operation on occasion due to the weather. In the north of the Levant coast, there are strong winter depressions which force their way through the mountains in order to traverse Mesopotamia. These weather systems would cause heavy rain or hailstones and at times snowfall. The other aspect of the funnel effect of the gap in the mountains is high wind speeds, which reach up to 100mph (161km/h). There was also a build-up of static electricity and the turbulence created by the combination of the weather systems and mountains was hazardous. A high degree of skill was required to fly aircraft in these conditions.

In order to aid flying along the pipeline route from Kirkuk to Tripoli, four radio stations with medium-frequency beacons were placed at Haditha, Homs, Palmyra and Kleiat. In bad weather, aircraft bound for Kleiat Airport from an easterly direction could join the track of the pipeline by homing successively on to the beacon at Homs and Nicosia at a quadrantal height of 6,500ft (1,980m). Once Kleiat was abeam to port then a descent could be made safely out over the sea before homing on to Kleiat Airport.

From Kirkuk, Airwork aircraft would fly south via Basra to a new exploration area at Dukhan in Qatar and further on to the Trucial State of Abu Dhabi, where drilling for oil was being undertaken. For some of the flights to provide support for the drilling operations in Abu Dhabi, Airwork Vikings would fly direct from Kleiat Airport into Taif. At some of the drilling locations, a grader would clear a landing strip which would then have a hard layer of gypsum underneath the sand. If a drilling location struck oil more permanent facilities would be built. These drilling locations were equipped with radios but they were always close to the rig itself rather than the landing strip, and, once a drilling location was found by an aircraft delivering supplies, quite often a fresh search would have to be made for the strip itself before landing. Flying in the Gulf region also brought weather problems with the *Shamal* wind. The *Shamal* would blow at 30 knots, raising dust up to 10,000ft (3,048m) and reducing visibility to almost zero. The dust and sand would stay in the atmosphere for up to two days after the wind had dropped.

Trucial States Support

Fisons Pest Control had a contract to carry surveyors for seismic surveys. Based in Tarif, the surveys were carried out on the Trucial States/Saudi Arabian border. The Hiller 360s carried gravity meters used by the surveyors when searching for oil. The operation was reliant on Airwork providing supplies to them. An IPC (Airwork) Vickers Viking G-AJFR flew in larger supplies direct from Tripoli, Lebanon. The Viking also carried an air hostess. Jim Hawkin, who was working on the contract, said that it was the one time everyone would be spruced up and on their best behaviour as it was the only female they would see for months. The Airwork crew would use the mess facilities during their turnaround at Tarif. More regular supplies arrived from Bahrain in an Airwork/IPC DH.89A Rapide, which also brought in a barber and a chaplain. When space was tight the barber would take precedence over the chaplain. The Rapide had variable pitch airscrews. Unfortunately one of the DH.89A Rapide flights came to grief when the carburettor set fire to the fabric on G-AGUV on 26 August 1954, although the aircraft was evacuated without any serious injuries.

One of the Hiller 360s also crashed with some injuries. The very high temperatures in the summer meant the Hillers were almost having to make rolling take-offs to get airborne.

The seven de Havilland Doves (G-AHRI, G-AICY, G-ALBF, G-AJJF, G-AKJP, G-AMUZ, G-AMVV) of the IPC were all given major overhauls at the Airwork facility at Liverpool's Speke Airport in 1956/57. G-AHRI, G-AICY and G-AMVV arrived in late 1956–early 1957 and were sold on after their overhaul.

Iraq-Airwork Ltd

Iraq Airwork Ltd was formed in 1933 by Alan Muntz with the full personal support of the Iraqi Prime Minister Nuri Pasha and the British ambassador Sir Francis Humphrys. The general manager was Colonel E. Dwyer and the registered office was Willingdon House, Al Rashid Street, Baghdad. It was intended that the new Iraq airline would be developed along the same lines as Misr-Airwork, which was then starting to establish itself.

Two routes were proposed from 1 March 1933 (a date which proved to be over-optimistic): a once-weekly Baghdad–Tehran service and a twice-weekly Baghdad–Aleppo–Larnaca service. The latter was central to the new airline's ambitions. It was intended to connect with liner services operated by Lloyd Triestino vessels calling at Cyprus from Trieste and Brindisi, and passengers would connect with these vessels thus saving themselves a further sea journey to Palestine and Syrian ports and an overland journey to and from Baghdad. The authorities in Palestine were also keen to promote a possible summertime service to and from Haifa to be operated by Iraq-Airwork. It was also intended to have the Iraq-Airwork flights connect in Cyprus with Misr-Airwork flights from Cairo and Alexandria.

The Baghdad–Aleppo–Larnaca flights were also intended to connect in Aleppo with the Taurus Railway Express to and from Constantinople to save three days on the rail journey between Aleppo and Baghdad.

Protracted negotiations followed with the authorities for the lease of the aerodrome in Larnaca and were not concluded until 1935. While negotiations carried on, a Spartan Cruiser

2 YI-AAA, flown by Neville Stack, was sent out from Heston on 23 February 1933 to begin airline operations. Neville Stack had been appointed chief pilot/air superintendent of Iraq-Airwork Ltd. The Spartan Cruiser went to Almaza in Cairo first, where Alan Muntz and his secretary (Miss Bentham) joined the flight for the journey to Baghdad, departing on 1 March 1933. A welcoming committee at Baghdad composed of King Faisal, Nuri Pasha and the British ambassador awaited the arrival of Iraq's first airliner. After refuelling at Rutbah, the aircraft took off only to have all three engines fail, one after another. The aircraft crash-landed, coming to a halt across old First World War Turkish trenches on the aerodrome. Fortunately only minor injuries were sustained, but Alan Muntz stated later that 'the accident put paid to Iraq Airways'. YI-AAA was repaired in Baghdad and although it would have been possible to get around this initial bad start, there appeared to have been a lack of will to do so. In 1936/37 the name 'Iraq Airwork' appeared in *Jane's*, which reported 'no services at present'. Airwork Ltd of Heston was granted a yearly lease on Larnaca Aerodrome from 8 April 1935. There were British Government objections to Misr-Airwork, who had conducted the negotiations for the aerodrome, as it was felt the Egyptians could push Airwork out of the partnership at any time. Despite the seeming failure of Iraq-Airwork to start operations, Cyprus was to play an important role in future Misr-Airwork and Middle East operations. On 26 July 1938 Cyprus Airwork Ltd was formed to co-ordinate Middle East operations and operate Cyprus-based services to Baghdad and Egypt, but the war interrupted these plans.

PERSIA (IRAN)

Anglo-Persian Oil Co.

Alan Muntz had a number of contacts from his time with the Anglo-Persian Oil Co. (which later became the Anglo-Iranian Oil Co.) and he was asked if Airwork would provide aircraft for the transportation of personnel and equipment within Persia from the end of 1934 onwards. This work had been carried out by German-operated Junkers aircraft up to this point.

On 19 December 1934, an Airwork DH.89A, G-ACZE, left Heston to undertake work on behalf of the Anglo-Persian Oil Co. It was flown by Airwork's then technical manager at Heston, Mr John J. Parkes, who was accompanied by his wife and other passengers. In 1935–36 Airwork started providing full contract air services to the now renamed Anglo-Iranian Oil Co. with DH.84 G-ACHV and DH.89As G-ACZE and G-ACZF operating out of Abadan. Airwork's chief pilot for the operation was Captain E.D. Cummings.

By 3 September 1936, Airwork operated two DH.89A Rapides which were being operated on behalf of the Anglo-Iranian Oil Co., when they placed an order for a third DH.89A (G-AEMM). This was followed by G-AFHY, G-AFHZ and G-AFIA, which were all registered on 1 July 1938 and arrived in Abadan on 19 October 1938.

Also in 1936, Larry Lafone (Airwork's technical superintendent to the Anglo-Iranian Oil Co.'s flying operation) paid a visit to the base at Abadan, which was staffed by Airwork personnel. At the end of 1935 and beginning of 1936, John J. Parkes made another tour of the Airwork operation in Abadan and the oilfields. By this stage Airwork were fully engaged in providing support to Anglo-Iranian Oil Co.'s operations in the oilfields. At the time of his visit, the area had been subjected to incessant heavy rains which had left the Airwork DH.89A Rapides as the only suitable method of speedy communication with the oilfields. The alternative to the flights was a three-day trip by river steamer. The flight from Abadan to the principal oilfield aerodromes took forty-five minutes by Rapide. The desert around Abadan at the time of Parkes' visit was completely covered by water owing to the rains, and the raised tarmac runways of the various aerodromes had the effect of looking like aircraft carrier decks in the sea.

Up to five DH.89A Rapides were based at Abadan at any one time for the Anglo-Iranian Oil Co.'s requirements and these were supplemented by two DH.104 Doves (G-AHYX and G-AJHX)

The first DH.89A Dragon Rapide G-ACZE for the Anglo-Iranian Oil Co. prior to delivery, outside the Jackaman Hangar at Heston in 1935. John Parkes is on the left with his wife. He joined Airwork in 1929 as technical manager and test pilot. (Royal Aero Club)

after the war. DH.89A G-AFIA was destroyed by fire at Abadan on 20 August 1942. One of the Doves, G-AHYX, crashed on take-off at Isfahan on 24 September 1949.

As with the Iraq Petroleum Company, other post-war British airlines had been involved in transport work for the Anglo-Iranian Oil Co., such as William Dempster with Avro Tudor Vs, and from May 1946 Skyways held a contract to carry all passengers and freight for the Anglo-Iranian Oil Co. to Basra from the UK using mainly Avro Yorks and occasionally Avro Lancastrians.

KUWAIT

Kuwait Oil Company

After the war, Airwork based a DH.89A Rapide (possibly G-AJFJ) at Kuwait for the use of the Kuwait Oil Co. To augment the Rapide's work, on 17 October 1947 a Vickers Viking of the Airwork Contract Charter Division left Blackbushe for Kuwait. It was the first large aircraft to be based at Kuwait, where it was on charter to the Kuwait Oil Co. for passenger and freight movements. Periodic checks of the Viking were made in Baghdad but the Viking returned to Blackbushe for major overhauls.

In addition to Airwork, Skyways (in 1948) had two DH.89A Dragon Rapides (one was G-AHIA) and two Douglas DC-3s (at various times G-AGBD, G-AIWC, G-AIWD and G-AIWE) based in the Middle East, under contract to the Kuwait Oil Co., to carry freight and passengers in the region and also to and from the UK. The contract continued until 1951.

18

MISR-AIRWORK[1]

FORMATION OF A NATIONAL AIRLINE

There were two main reasons that led to the formation of Misr-Airwork. The first was the great interest in the establishment of commercial aviation in Egypt from around 1924. In the spring of that year, a committee was formed by the Ministry of Transportation to examine the possibilities for commercial aviation activities. The committee members were taken from the Ministry of Transportation and customs officials. *Al-Ahram* newspaper described the committee and its work as 'The Great Project'. In August 1925 the first civil aviation mission to Europe was dispatched and a company was formed in October 1925 by entrepreneur Hassan Anis Pasha for the 'advancement of commercial aviation in Egypt'.

However, the real impetus behind the establishment of commercial aviation in Egypt was Mohammed Talaat Harb Bek (hereafter shortened to Talaat Harb), the renowned Egyptian economist and industrialist. There were favourable factors which aided Talaat Harb in his vision of an Egyptian airline. At the time, Egypt was a British protectorate and Cairo had become an important crossroads on the Imperial Airways routes. From 1925 onwards Imperial Airways took over from the RAF, who had been operating regular services through Cairo. Talaat Harb was also an Egyptian nationalist who had been responsible for establishing many organisations with an Egyptian identity under the Misr Group of companies through the auspices of Banque Misr, a bank he was instrumental in forming. From 1930 to 1936, seven firms were established, including the airline. There were a number of prominent Egyptians who had developed links with British interests. Among them was Ahmad Abd Al Wahab, who not only had studied in the UK but was closely involved with Banque Misr as well as being Undersecretary at the Ministry of Finance in the 1920s and Finance Minister in the 1930s. He persuaded Talaat Harb to look to form joint ventures with British companies and Banque Misr.

The second main reason for the involvement of Airwork resulted from a request in the summer of 1930 from Sir Sefton Brancker (the director general of Civil Aviation) to Alan Muntz to come to see him to discuss ways of forestalling an attempt by Mussolini, the Italian dictator, to establish a joint Egyptian/Italian airline. Earlier attempts by Imperial Airways and National Flying Services proved fruitless and it was felt that Airwork, which was independent and untainted by imperial overtones or British Government involvement, stood a good chance of succeeding.

Alan Muntz duly departed Heston on 8 December 1930, flying DH.60 Puss Moth G-AAVB and carrying Dame Ethel Locke-King as a passenger. Muntz met Talaat Harb and started to make the necessary contacts in Egypt whilst putting forward his proposals to establish an airline and also to train pilots and provide aviation services similar to their Heston operation.

Whilst conducting negotiations with Alan Muntz, Talaat Harb continued to push the Egyptian authorities to approve his proposals. A Ministry of Transportation report in 1930 had

1 *Misr* is Arabic for Egypt.

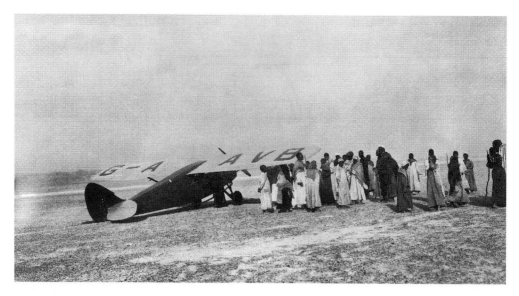

Alan Muntz toured Egypt and Sudan in DH.80A G-AAVB, seen here at Lake Kairoun, near Fayoum. On a visit to Khartoum, he fell foul of Sholto Douglas (the senior RAF officer), who berated him for taking off on a local trip without permission. (Mrs Nicolette Baring)

recommended the building of two civil airports with full facilities in Cairo and Alexandria. The Cairo airport was built at Almaza, 1.2 miles (2km) east of Heliopolis, on land the government obtained from the Ain Shams Oasis Co. in exchange for a tract of land on the Cairo–Suez road. The airport for Alexandria (named Dakheila) was located 2 miles (3km) from Al Meks. The report also stressed the importance of creating an Egyptian airline with help from 'foreign experts', i.e. Airwork.

On 12 January 1931 *Al-Ahram* reported under the headline 'In Almaza Airport: Minister of Transportation and Talaat Harb Bek take to the air in small aircraft'. This event was part of the celebrations accompanying the decision to form an Egyptian airline. Present at the ceremony was the Deputy Minister for Foreign Affairs, the first secretary of the king, the project director of Banque Misr, the British commercial attaché in Cairo and the director of the Aviation Department at the Ministry of Transportation. The report stated that the onlookers watched as 'The Director of an Airport in Britain circled overhead in a three-seater model', this being Alan Muntz. Following a brief display, Muntz landed and Talaat Harb got on board for the first flight of his life. After twenty minutes of flying over Heliopolis, the aircraft landed and Talaat Harb disembarked, stating that he was not in the least tired and found flying to be similar to being in an automobile with the difference being that movement was not restricted by traffic and attendant nuisances.

On 17 December 1931, the Egyptian Parliament opened and at the same time announced that approval had been given for the formation of an Anglo-Egyptian company to undertake civil aviation enterprises in Egypt. The new company was to be known as Société Anonyme Misr-Airwork with the capital to be subscribed jointly by Airwork Ltd and Banque Misr, although the bank was putting up most of the capital. The new company was given a wide mandate of operations, to undertake the establishment and operations within Egyptian territorial limits of civil flying training schools; local passenger-carrying flights; service stations; housing; provisioning; maintenance and repair of civil aircraft; aerial photography and survey; and occasional civil air transport services for carrying passengers, mails and goods.

Alan Muntz's second trip to Egypt was in April 1931, when he was asked by Dame Ethel Locke-King to help her family get Lord Lovelace's Ford 5 G-ABHO back in the air after overrunning the landing ground at Tripoli in Libya. He accomplished this with Aubrey Burke, who carried out the repairs and accompanied Alan Muntz to Cairo in the aircraft. Muntz was impressed by Burke's skills and offered him the post of engineer-in-charge of hangaring and repairs with Airwork at Heston on their return, which Burke accepted.

Airwork obviously did not neglect any other opportunities that might come their way in Egypt. On Alan Muntz's various trips to Cairo in 1931 and 1932, he looked for military business as well as civil. In January 1932, shortly before he was due to travel to Cairo to finalise the agreement with Banque Misr, two Avro 618 Tens arrived in Abukir. They were both originally intended for the Indian Government but were sold by Airwork to the Royal Egyptian Air Force. Originally given the British registrations G-ABSP and G-ABSR and registered to Airwork, they had wireless equipment fitted at Woodford Aerodrome and left Heston at 8.30 a.m. on 12 January 1932, arriving on 18 January, flown by Flight Lieutenant Christopher Clarkson and Captain Dan Cameron. One of the passengers was a Captain Stocks who was flying out to assist Air Commodore A.G. Board, the technical adviser of aviation to the Egyptian Government.

The Avro 618 Tens were given the Egyptian air force serials F-200 and F-201.

Despite the approval of the Ministry of Transportation and the endorsement of the Council of Ministers for the establishment of the Misr-Airwork airline, officials at Banque Misr felt that in return for the financial assistance provided by the government, their control was too restrictive. Further negotiations then followed to ease the restrictions and reach a compromise which satisfied both sides. One concession which Alan Muntz obtained was that, under the agreement with Banque Misr, preference would be given to British aircraft, which would be supplied by Airwork.

On 7 May 1932 Misr-Airwork was formed, with Banque Misr putting up 85 per cent of the 20,000 Egyptian pounds capital, Airwork providing 10 per cent and Harb, with Egyptian colleagues, contributing the remaining 5 per cent.

The Board of Directors consisted of both Egyptian nationals and British nationals. The Egyptian directors comprised two Banque Misr representatives, Talaat Harb himself and Medhat Yakan Pasha, who became the first chairman of Misr-Airwork; the deputy chairman, Mohamed Taher Pasha (who was also chairman of the Egyptian Aviation Club); two Egyptian Government representatives, Mohamed Mazloum Pasha (formerly the director of the Postal Authority) and Saleh Enan Pasha (former Undersecretary at the Ministry of Domestic Works). Finally there was Kamal Elawi Bey who was Misr-Airwork's managing director, responsible for day-to-day operations. Kamal Elawi Bey was later granted his Aviator's Certificate by the Royal Aero Club of the United Kingdom on 5 September 1939 (through the Hanworth Club).

The British directors were represented by Nigel Norman and Alan Muntz from Airwork, plus James Lister Shand (an associate of the two Airwork directors) and Mr R.C. Martin, who was the director general for Shell in Egypt. The inclusion of Martin was at the request of Nigel Norman and Alan Muntz, due to his in-depth knowledge of Egypt, and required approval from Shell in the UK, which was granted.

James Shand had originally arrived in Cairo at the end of September 1931 and made a statement outlining the problems faced by the airline due to the economic crisis around the world, but that the airline had aircraft ready to come out from Heston and would proceed cautiously.

Captain Tony Spooner had already left Heston on 26 April 1932 (just prior to the official formation of the company) to travel to Almaza to take up his position as chief instructor to the new airline. Misr-Airwork was granted a thirty-year concession from the Egyptian Government, along with the promise of a government subsidy for the first fifteen years of operation and a monopoly on certain domestic routes after that time. One stipulation was that government officials using the airline be given a 15 per cent discount when going on leave.

Just prior to the formal establishment of the new company and in order to help promote Misr-Airwork, a number of journalists and government officials were invited to a tea party at Almaza Aerodrome on 27 April 1932, after which they were flown over Cairo and its suburbs.

Part of the intention in the public relations exercise was to introduce and advertise the proposed new twice-daily service Misr-Airwork were going to operate between Cairo and Alexandria, departing Cairo at 8 a.m. and 4 p.m. each day. The proposed cost of tickets, at 195 piasters one way and 351 piasters for the return trip, was considered by some to be exorbitant for the time, particularly in view of government assistance being provided to the airline. However, at this point the new service was a year away from starting.

RELATIONSHIP BETWEEN BANQUE MISR, MISR GROUP & THE EGYPTIAN GOVERNMENT

From its foundation in 1920, Banque Misr was used to establish the Misr Group of companies, which all had an Egyptian identity. Laws passed in 1928 and the early 1930s required companies registered in Egypt to have at least two Egyptians as directors and at least 50 per cent of the employees to be Egyptian nationals. Whilst the bank tried to keep out of politics, it was inevitable the two would become entwined as members of the government were given directorships in the Misr companies. Serving ministers would be expected to show favour towards the less profitable companies, particularly so in the case of Misr-Airwork which relied heavily on yearly government subsidies. In return, on leaving their government posts, ex-government ministers and senior officials could expect to be given directorships within the Misr Group of companies. One minister in particular, Tawfiq Duss Pasha as Minister of Transportation, enabled Banque Misr to secure the right to establish the airline with exclusive rights of carriage within Egypt. Equally as important, Tawfiq Duss Pasha made sure that Misr-Airwork was given a government subsidy. Later he was to be appointed to directorships of two Misr Group companies.

The nature of Egyptian politics caused many problems with this arrangement. The Ismail Sidqi government, which fell in 1933 and had been pro-Misr-Airwork, was replaced by a government which was anti-Misr-Airwork. An unsuccessful attempt was made in 1936 by an Egyptian industrialist, Mohammed Ahmad Abboud, to block Misr-Airwork's subsidy completely, as he felt the Egyptian Government unfairly favoured Banque Misr and the Misr Group over other business interests, notably his own. The payment of the government subsidy in 1934, 1935 and 1938 was severely delayed due to political intrigue.

Whilst it was felt in certain quarters that subsidies were wasted on Misr-Airwork, the airline was viewed as a 'prestige' company which projected the status of Egypt beyond its borders.

Many loans from the bank to Misr Group companies were made on terms which would not have been made by other banks. A loan to Misr-Airwork in 1938 for 81,984 Egyptian pounds was made without any government support or backing, although during that year five other Misr Group companies were given loans which had government support.

The constant factionalism and infighting was one of the reasons for the collapse of Banque Misr in 1939, along with both the unsound financial decisions made as a result of the foregoing and economic factors in the wider world.

EXPANSION OF ROUTES & COMMERCIAL ACTIVITIES

At the same time as Misr-Airwork was being established, work was proceeding on Almaza Aerodrome in Cairo and Dakheila Airport in Alexandria to bring them up to acceptable standards for commercial operations. From October 1932, Dakheila Airport was fitted with first-aid and fire-fighting equipment, along with a telephone connection to a wireless station at Ras Ettine to facilitate the sending and receiving of signals related to aircraft arrivals and departures. Almaza Aerodrome, which was more established, had wireless facilities installed and improvements were made to the lighting. An extension to the main Heliopolis road to run

Spartan Cruiser II G-ACDW was originally delivered to Spartan Air Lines on 12 May 1933 and was leased to Misr-Airwork from 28 April 1934. It was bought by Misr-Airwork in August 1934 and registered SU-ABL. (Babcock International Group)

close to the north of the aerodrome was also proposed with the deadline for all work to be complete by the end of 1933.

Under Airwork's management and technical expertise, the new airline's base was established at the rapidly developing Almaza Aerodrome. Prior to the starting up of airline operations, a flying school was established at Almaza which started operations in June 1932, with the encouragement of Talaat Harb who felt that a flying school would generate interest within Egypt. De Havilland Gipsy Moths were initially used for flying training by the school. The first aircraft to arrive was actually in 1931, when DH.80A Puss Moth (ex-G-AAVB) was flown out on Alan Muntz's first trip and given the Egyptian registration SU-AAB. A further six aircraft arrived in 1932 (DH.80A Puss Moth SU-ABE in March, DH.60G IIIs SU-ABB and SU-ABC in May, DH.80A Puss Moth SU-AAC and DH.60G SU-ABD in June, followed by DH.83 Puss Moth SU-ABG in November). The cost of learning to fly at the school was quoted by *Al-Ahram* newspaper as 'not cheap' at 5 Egyptian pounds per hour. The twelve hours necessary to gain an 'A' licence therefore cost 60 Egyptian pounds. Misr-Airwork looked to the Egyptian Government to cover as many tuition costs as possible with respect to training future pilots for the national airline.

Two more flying schools were opened in the following years: Alexandria in July 1933 and Port Said in 1934. By 1945, over 450 pilots had obtained 'A' and 'B' licences spread across the three schools – quite an achievement considering the difficulties during the war years. Although the schools had been established to train Egyptian pilots primarily, pupils were also accepted from neighbouring Arab countries, including Syria, Lebanon, the Hejaz, Palestine and Iraq. In 1939 a ground engineering school was established at Cairo and by March 1945 over thirty students had obtained their 'A' and 'C' licences. In June 1944, a radio school was established to prepare candidates for obtaining the Egyptian Government's radio licence after examinations set by the Telegraphs and Telephones Department.

One aspect of the Misr-Airwork operation was the social life provided at Almaza Aerodrome, which was very similar to the upper-class ambience created at Heston by Alan Muntz and Nigel Norman. For instance, on the evening of 6 September 1933, Misr-Airwork entertained some 300 guests in the club enclosure, with a further 1,000 guests in the public park. The club was brilliantly lit by floodlights and sixty-nine joy riders were taken by air over Cairo and the pyramids during the course of the night beneath a full moon. Instructional work, including night flying, was also carried out from 8 p.m. until midnight. Those who tired of the aviation activities were able to dance in the clubhouse to music provided by a military band. During the course of that day, Swiss millionaire and aviation enthusiast Willy Seitz had arrived at Almaza Aerodrome in his Fokker monoplane en route to Nairobi for big game shooting. The reason for his arrival was trouble with the engine of his aircraft, and this was soon put right by Misr-Airwork maintenance staff. The following day a Wilson Airways DH.84 Dragon arrived at Almaza on its way to operate for the airline in Kenya and this was also serviced by the Misr-Airwork maintenance staff.

In July 1933 Misr-Airwork started airline operations. The first route to be operated was a once-weekly Cairo–Alexandria–Mersa Matruh service. On 1 August 1933 a new twice-daily service was started between Cairo and Alexandria which was increased to three times a day in 1935 and four times a day in June 1944. In December 1933 a new Cairo–Assiut–Luxor–Aswan twice-weekly service was started which was aimed at winter tourists travelling to these destinations. In the summer of 1933 the vice president of Misr-Airwork, Taher Pasha, had travelled to London and, whilst staying at the Heston Airport Hotel, watched the departure of DH.84 Dragons SU-ABH and SU-ABI on their delivery flights from Heston. Both were intended for use on the Cairo–Alexandria route and they left on 26 June 1933, flown by Captain Spooner and B.W. Figgins and carrying three wives of Misr-Airwork staff as passengers. Cannes was the first overnight stop for both aircraft.

Commander P.H. Baker had arrived by sea from Cyprus in July 1933 to take up his duties as general manager, having been flown to Cyprus in an Iraq-Airwork DH.84 Dragon from Heston.

In the summer of 1933 Misr-Airwork began to use specially adapted Leyland Cub coaches to transfer passengers from Alexandria to Cairo. The insides of the coaches were designed to resemble the layout of the passenger cabins of the DH.84 Dragons from which the passengers were transferred.

In April 1934 a Spartan Cruiser 2 (G-ACDW, re-registered SU-ABL) was leased by Misr-Airwork from Sparton Air Lines at Heston.

In July 1934 the airline's first international service was started from Cairo to Lydda and Haifa in Palestine. It should be mentioned that as early as January 1933, Misr-Airwork (and Iraq-Airwork) had sought permission to land at other aerodromes for customs purposes apart from Gaza, Samakh and Ma'an on journeys to and from Palestine and Transjordan. It was later found that as Iraq was a party to the Air Navigation Convention of 1927, Iraq-Airwork did not need permission, but Egypt was not a party to the convention, which meant Misr-Airwork had to seek permission.

Gaza Aerodrome was leased to Imperial Airways at the time. Misr-Airwork were unhappy at the charges levied by Imperial Airways at Gaza and there was concern by the Air Ministry in London that the authorities in Palestine did not fully understand how the scale of charges were to be applied to all aircraft using aerodromes in Palestine, principally Gaza. The set charge of 1 Palestinian pound, which Misr-Airwork particularly objected to, was for services rendered – provision of mechanics, petrol pumps, rest rooms, etc. This charge was levied at the set rate by Imperial Airways in agreement with the Air Ministry, but it was felt that Misr-Airwork had legitimate cause for complaint and that steps would be taken to charge only for services actually used or for the charge to be waived altogether. A further complaint by Misr-Airwork was the insistence by Imperial Airways that all aircraft entering Palestine from the south had to land first at Gaza. It was felt by the Foreign Office and Air Ministry that unless something was done to ameliorate Misr-Airwork's complaints, there was the possibility that Misr-Airwork could use its influence with the Egyptian Government to retaliate against Imperial Airways in Egypt. By September 1933, it was agreed that Misr-Airwork, in addition to Gaza and Samakh, could use RAF aerodromes and landing grounds at Jericho, Gidru, Haifa Bay and Lake Tiberias for customs clearance purposes. It was also indicated to Misr-Airwork that they could use landing grounds at Ramleh and Ziza, which were again under the control of the RAF.

The new Cairo–Lydda service was twice weekly which was increased to a daily service in 1935. By 1936/37, the flights to Lydda were not without problems due to the deterioration in the relationship between Arabs and Jews in Palestine. Flights had to stay above 2,000ft (610m) until the descent for landing due to small arms fire from snipers on the ground taking 'pot-shots' at the aircraft. After landing, the aircraft were guarded and also searched for bombs before departure. A number of Christian Arab police guarding Lydda Airport were murdered and an attempt was made by the Arabs to burn down the airport buildings at Lydda during this period, which resulted in the loss of a wooden building containing several thousand pounds' worth of radio equipment and passengers' passports. Misr-Airwork air crew tended to stay and sleep at the airport rather than risk the journey into town.

Another international service was started in 1935 from Cairo and Port Said to Cyprus. Initially this was a trial summer service but it proved to be successful and it became a regular daily service from May 1940, although by this time it was used mainly by military personnel. A boost was added by the signing of a mail contract with the government of Cyprus. Further international expansion had taken place in September 1936 with the start of a twice-weekly service to Baghdad from Cairo via Cyprus and Haifa, with one of the services operating direct to Baghdad from Cairo. One flight from Baghdad, which had departed Haifa, disappeared for twenty-four hours. The DH.86, flown by Captain T. St J. Arbuthnot had to make a forced landing due to heavy rainstorms leading to a fuel shortage. The aircraft was undamaged and occupants unharmed when it was found on 24 November 1936 near Magdhaba by Bedouin tribesmen.

A forerunner of the part aviation was to play in pilgrimage flights in decades to come was the operation of Haj flights in 1937 to Jeddah and Medina.

By October 1936, Misr-Airwork operated three daily services between Alexandria and Cairo; a daily service southwards from Port Said to Cairo and along the Nile to Minia, Assyut, Luxor and Aswan; a daily service to Haifa from Port Said via Ramleh; and twice-weekly services to Baghdad (once direct and once via Cyprus). The service to Haifa had connecting road services to Jerusalem, Jaffa, Tel Aviv and Beirut.

Although military personnel made use of the airline's services, the majority of the civilian passengers on international flights were British, followed by Palestinians, as Egyptian nationals did not travel by air outside Egypt in any great numbers. The Palestinian passengers were actually mainly Jews. Jewish passengers also covered the bulk of passengers from other nationalities, including, for example, Chileans, Mexicans, Danish, Norwegians, Chinese and Japanese.

Misr-Airwork were commonly known as Misr Airlines (or Misrair) and the Misr Airlines title was on their aircraft from the first DH.84 delivery in June 1933.

The year 1935 saw a large number of deliveries. DH.86 SU-ABN arrived at Almaza on 12 June 1935 and was put to work immediately on the daily Cairo–Alexandria service. Later that same month, on 23 June, the summer service to the resort of Mersa Matruh was reopened with a weekly flight (on Sundays) calling at Alexandria. To cope with the increasing demand DH.89A Dragon Rapide SU-ABP arrived in August 1935, followed by the arrival in September 1935 of three DH.89A Dragon Rapides, SU-ABQ, SU-ABR and SU-ABS, DH.86 Express SU-ABO and DH.87B Hornet Moth SU-ABT. A further DH.89A Dragon Rapide SU-ABU joined the fleet in December 1935.

In January 1937 DH.86B SU-ABV was delivered from Heston to Almaza by Captain R.W. Hall with Mahomet Hazek Effendi as second pilot and Mahomet Fawzi Effendi as ground engineer. Mr T.H. Fox served as radio officer for the flight and there were two passengers.

The Greek Airline Elliniki Etaireia Enaereon Synhinoion AE (EEES AE) signed a pool agreement with Misr-Airwork in January 1938, for the route Thessaloniki–Athens–Crete–Alexandria to be flown weekly. The intention was for the two airlines to tie in their services to meet in Crete and continue in their respective directions to Greece and Egypt, with the Greek side covered by EEES AE and the Egyptian side covered by Misr-Airwork. The actual service did not start operating until mid-April 1939, when Misr-Airwork opened the service between Alexandria and Megalokastron on Crete. This service tied up with the Ju.52s of EEES AE and thus became the first international service operated by the Greek airline. The service was operated three days a week despite the initial agreement being for a weekly service. Unfortunately the war intervened and Greece was invaded by Italy in November 1940.

Passenger figures grew by over 100 per cent from 1935 to 1936, from 7,015 to 15,710, before settling down to 17–18,000 p.a. until 1941, when the figures grew again to 22,872.

By 1938, the airline was commonly known as Misrair.

AIRWORK PERSONNEL & MISR-AIRWORK

Several well-known Airwork employees either worked for the airline or paid regular visits. Alan Muntz made a yearly tour of Airwork operations in the Near and Middle East of which Misr-Airwork was the centrepiece. Richard Muntz (the brother of Alan Muntz) flew out to Almaza on secondment in an Airwork DH.84 Dragon in mid-December 1933.

Larry Lafone, later a director of Airwork, was superintendent of aircraft operations for Misr-Airwork prior to his return to Heston in early 1936.

Technical manager John J. Parkes inspected the Misr-Airwork workshops as part of his Middle East tour returning on 6 January 1936, prior to his departure to join de Havilland that same month.

Robert Maxwell joined Misr-Airwork as controller of operations at Almaza in 1936 and stayed in the post for two years before joining British Airways back in the UK in 1938. He joined Misr-Airwork from Airwork associate company Indian National Airways where he performed exceedingly well.

Another significant member of the British Misr-Airwork team was E.G. Parsons, who was on the airline staff from the beginning as a pilot as well as being an instructor. He flew the final pre-war DH.89A Rapide, SU-ABU, out from Heston on 13 December 1935 to Cairo with two new Misr-Airwork employees: Flying Officer N. Samuels, who was starting with the airline as a pilot, and a Mr Kimberley, who was joining the airline as a ground engineer having just gained his licences at Heston.

Flying Officer D.L. Dustin was seconded to the airline for three months from 6 February 1936 to join the piloting staff.

Conditions for British pilots working for Misr-Airwork were good. Guy 'Flip' Fleming, a former Hillman Airways pilot, joined the airline in Cairo on 24 July 1936. By this time (early 1936), roughly a dozen British pilots were employed by the company, along with British and Egyptian engineers. There were also several Egyptian pilots in training for the company at this point.

'Flip' Fleming described the weather in the region (particularly around Cyprus in winter) as some of the worst he had experienced after flying in thirty-four countries. He described flying to Baghdad in a thunderstorm over the Jordan Valley in DH.86 SU-ABN on 13 January 1937, when they were struck by lightning which knocked the three crew 'out cold'. Fleming recovered to find the aircraft in a steep dive from which he managed to recover the DH.86. The shaken passengers elected to carry on to Baghdad with a hole in the roof of the cabin and one passenger holding the door of the aircraft in place with his feet. Due to the instruments being unserviceable from the lightning strike, they followed the Iraq Petroleum Co. pipeline for most of the remaining 640 miles (1,030km).

On another journey from Baghdad to Lydda in DH.86 SU-ABO in winter, before departure, Fleming had to pour hot water over the brake drums as they were locked frozen. After take-off, he then ran into one of the worst snowstorms he had ever encountered, forcing him to land at the oil-pumping station at Rutbah in a foot of snow which obscured the runway markings.

Despite the extreme conditions, the maintenance and servicing was of a high standard. Engines were maintained by Charles Hedges and Pat Coyle, plus a team of other British engineers.

SAUDI ARABIA

The first flight by Misr-Airwork into the Hejaz left Suez on 2 December 1933. This was a DH.84 Dragon piloted by J. Mahoney, which arrived in Jeddah on 3 December via Tor (overnight stop), Wedj and Yanbu (both refuelling stops) carrying Talaat Harb accompanied by a small party. Apart from being the first flight into the Hejaz by a Misr-Airwork aircraft, it was also the first flight by a civil aircraft into that region. At Jeddah short flights were organised for locals and Europeans.

Just over a year later, in December 1934, two further flights were made by the airline on the same route to Jeddah from Almaza. The first aircraft was a DH.84 Dragon flown by G.S. Brown and the second aircraft was a de Havilland Fox Moth piloted by Sidki Effendi. At the beginning of 1936, Talaat Harb and a party again flew from Almaza on Thursday 9 January 1936, in a DH.89 Rapide to Jeddah, arriving the same day after a journey of six hours and thirty-three minutes with stops at Tor and Yanbu. Just after a week later, on Saturday 18 January 1936, Talaat Harb and his party left Jeddah in their Rapide to fly to Medina. This was the first flight of a civil aircraft into the holy city of Medina.

They left Jeddah two days later on 20 January to return to Almaza via Yanbu in a journey which took five hours and forty minutes. On 8 February 1937 the first seasonal air service in Saudi Arabia was started when Misr-Airwork DH.89A SU-ABS *Helwan* took off for Medina with five pilgrims and mail. The service was once daily in each direction during the peak pilgrim season. Among the passengers was the Khan of Kalat.

A picturesque view of DH.84 Dragon SU-ABJ over the pyramids. SU-ABJ was destroyed in a fire at Almaza Aerodrome in 1934. (Babcock International Group)

HORUS

Taher Pasha (the Misr-Airwork vice president) was a member of the Egyptian royal family and businessman who maintained strong links with German political and business interests from the mid-1930s. For this reason, he alarmed the British, although Talaat Harb had also developed links with German business organisations. Despite Taher Pasha's involvement with Misr-Airwork, he had an interest in establishing airline services between Egypt and Central Europe with the assistance of German business interests, notably Lufthansa. Taher Pasha was supported in his idea of forming an airline with German backing by Tawfiq Duss Pasha, who was also connected with Misr-Airwork and, as mentioned earlier, had greatly helped in its establishment. Such was the nature of the intriguing and infighting at the time. The proposed airline was to be called Horus and was a matter of great concern to Misr-Airwork as it was felt the new airline would try to compete on their established routes. In April 1936 Alan Muntz found himself staying, by coincidence, in the same hotel in Budapest with Taher Pasha and they had two meetings to discuss the issues (in particular Horus) which affected Misr-Airwork. Taher Pasha displayed great antipathy towards Talaat Harb and Banque Misr, who he felt interfered too much in the running of Misr-Airwork. Alan Muntz concluded that although Taher Pasha still considered routes to Central Europe to be necessary for Egypt, he felt that the establishment of Horus was unlikely and this proved to be the case.

LOTFIA EL NADI

One remarkable employee of the company was Misr-Airwork's telephone operator and receptionist at Almaza, Lotfia El Nadi. She became Egypt's first female pilot to fly solo in 1933. The nature of the conservative society in which she lived made her achievement all the more noteworthy.

She had obtained her first flight in an aeroplane by hiding in an aircraft at Almaza, just so she could experience what it was like to fly. After this she informed her father that she was attending a study group twice a week when in fact she was taking flying lessons at Almaza. Her mother assisted her in her dream of becoming a pilot. In addition, she met and became friends with Amelia Earhart, the two keeping a regular correspondence.

At the International Oasis Meeting held on 18–24 December 1933, Lotfia El Nadi flew Gipsy II Moth SU-ABB.

Madame Mimi di Castro, who immigrated to Canada, was a close neighbour (as a young girl) of Lotfia in Cairo. She remembered her as a very amusing, independent and determined woman. Born in 1907 in Cairo, Lotfia spent her later years in Lausanne in Switzerland and Canada before returning to Cairo. She died in 2002 at the age of 95. A sixty-minute documentary of her life was made in 1996 entitled *Take Off From the Sand*.

PRE-WAR & THE WAR YEARS

The approaching war affected Misr-Airwork in a number of ways. On one occasion, on 2 April 1938, DH.89 Dragon Rapide SU-ABP was believed to have been sabotaged when engine cowlings came undone on a flight to Aswan from Almaza, forcing a landing at Assiut. The flight then continued to Aswan for the night. However, on the return journey the port engine vibrated so badly it was turned off and the aircraft returned to Aswan, where an inspection showed that the No. 2 cylinder had almost completely worked loose and three of the nuts were missing.

In 1938 the Egyptian army had purchased searchlights and, for practice, Misr Airlines aircraft were detailed to fly their DH.89 Rapides on twice-weekly searchlight training sessions. On the basis of being a former Bomber Command pilot, 'Flip' Fleming flew most of these training sessions. This would involve the Rapide flying a triangular course from 10 p.m. until midnight. It was tedious work and once caught in a 'cone' of searchlights, the effect was blinding. Fleming found that side curtains did not stop the glare, so he devised a mask using a tube made from a piece of black cardboard with an elastic band to keep it on his head. Once caught in the lights, he pulled the tube down over his face so he could fly using his instruments. He had no oxygen at that height and one night he passed out, coming round in time to pull out of the dive. After being put in a crude decompression chamber set to 18,000ft (5,486m), he again passed out and was cleared to fly without oxygen only at heights up to 10,000ft (3,048m). As he stated, he was not sorry to have to stop the searchlight work, and this was in addition to his normal airline duties. Illness also affected Fleming during the same year when, on 4 October 1938, he almost passed out in command of DH.89 Dragon Rapide SU-ABR from Assiut to Almaza. An ambulance met him on arrival to take him to hospital. He had passed out after turning the engines off immediately after landing on the runway and was later diagnosed as having sand fly fever.

Not all the flying jobs given to Fleming were onerous. In November 1938, he was selected to fly VIPs (including Prince Ali Khan and his family on a number of occasions and General Wavell along with other senior military officers) on charter flights and also to act as personal pilot to the British ambassador, Sir Miles Lampson. Once a week, Fleming would fly Sir Miles Lampson to Ikiad to go duck shooting as well as ferrying him on official duties.

After war was declared, one main effect on the airline was the departure of all British employees. Most returned to the UK for service in the armed forces. 'Flip' Fleming was one of these and after volunteering for service in the UK he was sent back out to Egypt to serve with Misr-Airlines on RAF duties, where he was informed he would be of the greatest use! On his arrival back in Cairo, he found that the remaining Egyptian staff of Misr-Airwork were still on pay terms and conditions that were still well below what had been given to the British staff and was surprised that they had not used the departure of the British as a bargaining lever. However, most had a fatalistic attitude that to create trouble would result in the loss of their livelihoods. In fact, some of them did make their feelings known to Rushdi Pasha, the Egyptian Air Minister, but he threatened them with the sack.

The salary of a British pilot at the time (leading up to the war) was a basic £350 plus £450 overseas allowance with a further £100 paid if the pilot held a second-class navigators' licence and was a captain of one of the larger aircraft. A flying allowance was also paid, which worked out at around 8s per flying hour, adding a further £400 p.a. to the salary making a total of £1,300 p.a. less 7 per cent Egyptian income tax. In addition, free telephones were installed in their accommodation, all expenses were paid away from base and transport was provided to every aerodrome and stopping place. Egyptian pilots received the same basic salary of £350 p.a. plus a lower rate per flying mile. Only two Egyptian pilots held the second-class navigators' certificate so most did not receive the additional allowance, and they did not receive the overseas allowance, so of course their pay by comparison was much reduced. On average an Egyptian pilot earned £500 p.a. while the junior pilots were paid £300 p.a. Egyptian radio officers were also fairly badly paid. For instance, an Egyptian radio officer flying 700 hours a year received only £12 to £15 a month.

The early 1940s saw further Middle East expansion with a new, once-weekly service from Egypt to Adana in Turkey in 1941 (although this routing varied considerably), followed by two new routes in 1942; a twice-weekly Cairo–Beirut service; and a once-weekly Cairo–Khartoum service. With the introduction of a twice-weekly Cairo–Damascus service in June 1944, Misr-Airwork had achieved comprehensive airline coverage of the Levant region, despite difficulties caused by the war. Many of the passengers were high-ranking military personnel. As mentioned previously, 'Flip' Fleming had returned to Cairo and his description of his flying activities gives a good idea of the wartime work Misr-Airwork was involved in. As with his pre-war VIP work with Misr-Airwork, Fleming's duties consisted of ferrying senior military personnel from all three services and diplomats around the Levant region and down to the Sudan. All military personnel flying in Misr-Airwork aircraft had to travel in civilian clothes regardless of rank.

Fleming made eighty-nine trips to Cyprus and Turkey (Adana and Ankara) during the early stages of the war. The flights to Turkey were primarily to carry diplomatic mails which had previously travelled via France (and southern Europe) until that country's collapse. The Adana and Ankara flights were initially intended to carry diplomatic mail for onward transmission to Russia and the Balkans. The routes were decided by the military authorities and could be Port Said to Cyprus and Adana or Port Said to Ankara direct, with a return via Cypus or Port Said direct to Adana, Lydda to Cyprus and Adana or Lydda to Cyprus and Ankara. Flights to Turkey during this period were hazardous as they were exposed to attack from German fighters operating from Rhodes. On one occasion, on 9 July 1941, flying DH.86 SU-ABV from Lydda to Cyprus, Fleming had to turn back from Cyprus as the area was being bombed by Ju.87 Stukas only to get a message that Lydda was also being attacked by the Germans. He changed course for Cairo with a refuelling stop at Port Said. Eventually the stop at Cyprus was dropped completely, with the flights being made direct to Turkey but with the added stress of a much longer flying time. The flights to Adana and Ankara were discontinued after the end of the Syrian campaign as mail and diplomats went by rail from Cairo through to Syria and Turkey.

Fleming also flew General Catroux (a close confidant of General de Gaulle) to Khartoum on 15 October 1940 and also acted as General Platt's personal pilot on flights to the Sudan during the early part of the war. General Blamey (the Australian GOC) was another of Fleming's regular passengers during the Syrian campaign. On 19 June 1941 they flew from Beirut in DH.86 SU-ABQ. Prior to take-off, a major arrived for the flight with a large amount of luggage which dangerously overloaded the aircraft. Fleming realised the aircraft was having difficulty getting airborne, so relying on the 200ft (60m) cliff drop at the end of the short runway, he bounced the aircraft; it went over the cliff edge and down towards the sea, which gave the DH.86 enough airspeed to get sufficiently airborne.

One of the main problems faced by the airline during the war period was a lack of more modern and larger-capacity aircraft. By March 1945, the Misr Airlines fleet was fourteen strong, consisting of three DH.89A Rapides, two DH.89A Dominies, four DH.86 Expresses, three Avro Ansons, one DH.84 Dragon and one DH.90 Dragonfly. The flying school's fleet was made up of two de Havilland Gipsy Moths, one de Havilland Leopard Moth, five de Havilland Tiger Moths and two Miles Magisters.

LODESTAR REPLACEMENTS THROUGH US LEGATION IN CAIRO, 1942/43

Two DH.89A Dragon Rapides ordered from the UK by Misr-Airwork in 1941 were sunk in transit to Egypt in November 1942. These were SU-ACS and SU-ACT, which were originally intended for RAF use as DH.89A Dominies X7524 and X7525, but were diverted to Misr-Airwork due to their urgent requirement in Egypt. They were replaced by DH.89A Dominies X7384 and X7391, which took the civil Egyptian registrations originally reserved for the two lost aircraft.

After the loss of the two Dragon Rapides at sea, a request was made by Misr-Airwork for two Lockheed Lodestar replacements from the USA. The request was made by the Egyptian Government to General Frank M. Andrews, commanding general of the US army forces in the Near East at the US Legation in Cairo. Despite objections from the British, General Andrews supported the request as he viewed the provision of the aircraft (to be paid for in cash and include the cost of flying out to Cairo by the manufacturer of Pan Air) as a contribution to the successful conclusion of negotiations then being carried out regarding military jurisdictional rights. At this point Misr-Airwork's fleet consisted of eight aircraft, the majority of which had over 7,000 hours of flying time, and their safety was becoming harder to maintain. This argument regarding the age of the fleet was used as a lever to persuade the Americans to provide the Lodestars. However, despite a number of exchanges of cables between the legation in Cairo and the Secretary of State in Washington, the request was turned down due to the great requirement by the US military for these types of aircraft and, more importantly, Washington did not want to deviate from protocol. All requests from the Egyptian Government for 'Warlike and other stores' were supposed to be placed through the British Military Mission. Whilst there was the argument that Misr-Airwork was a civil concern, Washington was not keen to get involved in any transactions which would cause conflict with the British in Egypt. Eventually Avro Ansons were bought.

POST-WAR

The airline had expanded its operations greatly during the war years; for instance, 30 per cent of the traffic carried in 1944 was Allied military personnel. Misr-Airwork emerged from the war with Alan Muntz still on the Board of Directors and the Airwork shareholding still at 10 per cent (2,000 shares). The other shareholding of 17,000 shares for Banque Misr and 1,000 shares to private Egyptian nationals still had the same proportions as at the formation (although Talaat Harb had died in 1941). The former director of Egyptian Civil Aviation, Mohamed Roushdy Bey, had become managing director.

However, three accidents in 1945 led to a strike by pilots and engineers, which started on 6 February 1946. The strike was over poor and ageing equipment, along with pay and conditions. Operations were suspended for two months but the company promised improvements in equipment and better pay. Once the improvements were agreed, services were then resumed in May 1946. By September 1947, the fleet consisted of sixteen aircraft: four Avro Ansons, eight Beechcraft and four DH.89A Dragon Rapides.

In 1948 discussions were held between BOAC, Airwork and Egyptian shareholders in which Misr-Airwork would be reorganised and each party would have a shareholding. These discussions had taken place intermittently since the start of the war; however, in 1949, the name of the airline was changed to Misrair SAE and it became wholly Egyptian owned, with the Egyptian Government taking control of all the airline's capital and equipment. Airwork had had little influence within the airline for some years by this point. This was not entirely unexpected. Although Talaat Harb had died in August 1941, his original vision coupled with the surging nationalist fever spreading throughout Egypt during this period ensured that the airline would be run purely as a national concern with as little foreign influence as possible. In fact, it was due to the professionalism of the crews and ground-support staff along with Alan Muntz's influence that Airwork retained an interest in the airline as long as they did.

19

NEW ZEALAND

SAFE (STRAITS AIR FREIGHT EXPRESS)

In the late 1940s New Zealand Railways was having increasing difficulties with the transfer of its freight between the rail systems on the two main islands. The privately owned shipping service which carried the freight between the two islands was not adequate.

Some experimental services were operated by Royal New Zealand Air Force (RNZAF) DC-3s in conjunction with the domestic airline NZNAC. However, the type of freight carried by the railways was unsuitable for the Douglas DC-3. The experiments were observed by a New Zealand air force movements officer, Tom O'Connell. After watching the loading and unloading process,

Inauguration of the Wellington–Nelson freight service, 10 November 1952. (Royal Aero Club)

he came up with the idea of mechanising the whole process using what he called 'Cargons', which he was convinced would work but only with the right type of aircraft. He approached both Airwork and Bristol with his idea.

SAFE was incorporated as Straits Air Freight Express Ltd in November 1950. Airwork Ltd were not the sole founder of SAFE as is sometimes mentioned, but had become the majority shareholders by August 1951. Shares had originally been offered to the public, but the reaction and take-up of these shares was very disappointing. One year after the formation of the airline, Airwork were invited to join the company and become a shareholder, which they did, contributing £1,050 of the £2,050 share capital, thus becoming the major shareholder in the new company. Airwork increased their shareholding until they owned 93.5 per cent of Safe Air Ltd (having changed its name in 1967) in August 1971.

Prior to the takeover of the Cook Strait operation by SAFE, they leased three Curtiss C-46 Commandos owned by American company Civil Air Transport. This company had been working in the Far East to assist in the upsurge of traffic over the Cook Strait in May 1951, prior to the introduction of the Bristol 170s on 1 June 1951, which was also the official start date of SAFE. This same date was the official takeover date of the operation from the New Zealand Railways Department.

COMMERCIAL OPERATIONS

On 6 May 1951 two Bristol 170s (ZK-AYG and ZK-AYH) left Blackbushe to fly to New Zealand to start operating the new service across the Cook Strait, during which time the freight was being carried by the aforementioned C-46 Commandos.

The principal route served by the Bristol 170s over the Cook Strait was between New Zealand's North and South Islands, flying from Woodbourne near Blenheim in the South Island and Paraparaumu near Wellington in the North Island, in order to link the railheads of the two islands. The distance between the two points is 72 miles (115.8km). The two newly arrived Bristol 170s started to ply the route. For 1953, ZK-AYG and ZK-AYH achieved notable results carrying racehorses, sheep, cattle, fruit and 700 cars at an average load factor of 78 per cent and carrying a record 110 tons in one day. This record was improved in July 1958 when 201.8 tons of freight was carried in one day.

With two Bristol 170s, the requirement to move an annual tonnage of 14,000 tons of mixed cargo required intensive use of the aircraft. The key to improving the operation was found in shortening the amount of time spent on the ground at each terminal. Initially loading of the aircraft was done using fork-lift trucks and manual labour with trucks backed up to the level of the wide opening cargo doors at the nose of the aircraft. Mobile cargo such as cars and tractors could be driven on ramps into and out of the aircraft. SAFE drove the cars on to truck decks first then into the aircraft from the truck. On average, this operation took sixty minutes to unload the freighter and reload it for the return trip. The flying time between the two terminals was only thirty minutes. Engineers from New Zealand Government Railways then worked with SAFE to create the cargon system, a pallet and transfer system to speed up the loading and unloading process. A unique mechanical loading platform was devised which dispensed with the manual requirement for bulk handling of cargo on the aircraft itself.

The loading platform consisted of two suitably spaced sets of railway lines laid parallel to each other and laid horizontally in front of the aircraft from left to right. Two trolleys, known as 'traversers' were then placed on the railway lines to run along at right angles to the aircraft. The trolleys supported flat platforms on top of which the metal containers, the cargons, would be placed. The cargons were built to dimensions which fitted exactly between captive side rails and stops at the front and in the doors of the aircraft, end to end, inside each Bristol 170.

Upon the arrival of an aircraft at each point, the Bristol 170 would taxi up to the loading platform and stop hard up against chocks and the empty traverser. With the nose doors open, the traverser would be driven under the open doors and adjusted to exactly the level of the aircraft hold floor and then the four cargons inside would be winched on to the traverser, which would then be moved down and to the side for the cargons to be loaded on to a truck. The other traverser, holding four cargons loaded with lashed-down freight, would be moved into place for immediate loading on board. The use of these metal pallets enabled the freight to be pre-stowed, weighed and trimmed.

The introduction of this mechanical loading method reduced the time spent on the ground by the Bristol 170s from sixty minutes to ten minutes (best time was six minutes without the crew leaving the cockpit) and was obviously a vast improvement. The record movement by SAFE of 163.5 tons of freight in one day occurred on 1 March 1955, between the North and South Islands, providing proof of the worth of the method. Tom O'Connell, who had first conceived the idea of the cargons, was to be tragically killed in the crash of ZK-AYH (see below).

The cargon and associated loading system, the 'traversers', was the brainchild of Tom O'Connell. The build and final design were carried out by New Zealand Railways workshops and were solid and extremely reliable. (Royal Aero Club)

As mentioned below, Bristol 170 Mk 31M serial NZ5904 was loaned by the RNZAF to SAFE for top dressing trials. Aerial top dressing was an important activity with almost half of the approximately 400 aircraft on the New Zealand civil register in the mid-1950s devoted to it. In the case of New Zealand, aerial top dressing was the dispersion of fertiliser and grass seed by air over primarily rolling hill country that was better suited to aerial operations as it was difficult and expensive to carry this activity out with horses and sleds. The bulk of the work was carried out by de Havilland Tiger Moths and, whilst there was additional expense involved in operating larger aircraft, this was offset by the greater load-carrying capabilities. For instance, the Bristol 170s ordered for 41 Squadron RNZAF were delivered with the floors ready adapted to match the Tom O'Connell-designed hoppers containing seed or lime and superphosphate fertiliser; a Bristol 170 could discharge the full load of 6 tons in forty seconds or less.

In December 1967 SAFE was granted a licence to operate a passenger service between the capital Wellington and the Chatham Islands.

The company name was changed on 31 October 1967 from Straits Air Freight Express to SAFE Air Ltd.

BRISTOL 170

The Bristol 170 freighter is strongly associated with the Cook Strait operation and, for the time, it was probably the ideal aircraft for the service. Part of Airwork's interest in the SAFE operation was no doubt helped by the cargo-carrying capacity of the Bristol 170, which had been used to great effect by Airwork in their Shell operations in Ecuador.

The first visit of a Bristol 170 was in 1947 when G-AIMC arrived in New Zealand on 23 July 1947 as part of a Bristol demonstration tour to Australia and New Zealand. Flown by a Bristol crew plus a Qantas navigation officer and Marconi radio officer, G-AIMC visited ten New Zealand airports and airfields. On 29 July 1947 G-AIMC was loaned to New Zealand Railways for trials to carry freight across the Cook Strait. The first flight was made from Paraparaumu to Woodbourne carrying port wine and household effects. The following day a car was carried. The trials were a success and G-AIMC departed New Zealand on 9 August 1947.

The demonstrations given by G-AIMC were not without mishap as it hit and removed part of the boundary fence at Woodbourne on one flight.

One of the two Bristol 170s first ordered by SAFE, ZK-AYG, arrived at Woodbourne on 19 May 1951. ZK-AYG was flown out from the UK by H. Boyes from SAFE and D. Woolf, the chief pilot for Airwork. It was named *Captain Cook* and entered service on 31 May 1951. The other Bristol 170, ZK-AYH, also arrived at Woodbourne on the same day, flown by R. Hamilton and D. Marson. ZK-AYH was named *Endeavour* and entered commercial service on the same day as ZK-AYG, 31 May 1951. Both of these two aircraft had their share of problems (ZK-AYG as G-AINK had already crashed at Filton on take-off in October 1950 and was rebuilt as a Mk 31).

Barely two months into commercial service, on 27 July 1951, ZK-AYG was landing at Paraparaumu when the aircraft suffered a brake failure and overran the runway ending up in a ditch. The aircraft was repaired and the port wing was replaced, allowing it to re-enter service on 14 November 1951. Whilst ZK-AYG was in the CAA hangar and ready to go back into service a storm blew in the four hangar doors on to the aircraft. In early 1954, the aircraft received spar modifications but suffered more damage on 3 February 1954 when it ran into a ditch after an aborted take-off at Woodbourne. The aircraft was returned to Weston-super-Mare in the UK for repair. It was rebuilt without windows and returned to New Zealand on 13 March 1955 before once again re-entering commercial service on 31 March 1955. However, bad luck was to strike again on 21 August 1955 when ZK-AYG was performing at the Omaka Air Show. The pilot feathered a propeller then feathered the second propeller before the other was up to speed. The aircraft crashed and sank into a riverbed. After being rebuilt at Woodbourne with a new floor, nose doors and undercarriage, ZK-AYG returned to service on 20 July 1956.

This rebuild work was carried out by SAFE engineers and was the largest and most comprehensive rebuild in New Zealand to that time, and was followed by SAFE carrying out major rebuilds of its fleet of Bristol 170s. It was a comprehensive and thorough approach to engineering which is carried on to this day.

ZK-AYH, the second Bristol 170 delivered, also encountered serious problems. In its first year of operation with SAFE in 1951, the nose doors opened during take-off at Paraparaumu. The nose doors were replaced and three years later the aircraft received modifications to the spars. However, tragedy struck on 21 November 1957 when ZK-AYH crashed and the founders of SAFE were tragically killed. The crew of R. Hamilton (operations manager) and H. Torgerson, along with passengers Tom O'Connell (general manager) and J. McLaggen, all perished when the starboard outer wing folded up and back before separating from the aircraft at 3,000ft (915m); the aircraft came down on Russley golf course close to Christchurch Airport. To fill the management vacuum, Larry Lafone (Airwork's overseas manager) went out to New Zealand to keep the airline running until a new manager could be found. The replacement was a New Zealander, Mr D.P. Lynskey. A Bristol 170, ZK-BVM, was flown out from the UK by an Airwork crew as a replacement for ZK-AYH.

Due to a lack of capacity, a Bristol 170 Mk 31M serial NZ5904 was loaned by the RNZAF to SAFE for sixty hours of aerial top dressing trials. The aircraft was given the civilian registration of ZK-BEV for these trials, which lasted from March 1954 to 27 June 1954, before the aircraft was returned the following day, 28 June 1954.

While ZK-AYH was being rebuilt in 1954, a further shortage of capacity led to SAFE requiring the use of another Bristol 170. On 2 February 1954 SAFE borrowed a Bristol 170 Mk 31M from the RNZAF. This aircraft (RNZAF serial NZ5905) was given the civilian registration ZK-BEO and entered service with the airline on 31 May 1954, being given the name *Resolution*. The Bristol 170 served with SAFE for a year before it was bought by the airline on 12 May 1955. ZK-BEO served until 27 May 1967 (almost exactly thirteen years) before it was withdrawn from use. The aircraft was then parked up at Woodbourne before being scrapped.

The next Bristol 170 to arrive was ZK-BMA (sold to Airwork by Aer Lingus), which arrived on 22 November 1955. ZK-BMA soldiered on until 10 July 1967, when it was withdrawn from service and the fuselage used to build ZK-CVY. The wings of ZK-BMA went to rebuilding ZK-CRM.

The last Mk 31 Bristol 170 to be built was ordered by SAFE on 28 November 1957 and registered ZK-BVM on 23 January 1958. Airwork delivered the aircraft over a two-week period, arriving in New Zealand on 18 March 1958 and was named *Blenheim*. The name was changed immediately, however, to *Merchant Carrier*, and it entered commercial service the same day with the CoA being issued the following day on 19 March 1958.

EX-RPAF AIRCRAFT

SAFE bought nine ex-RPAF (Royal Pakistan Air Force, becoming PAF in 1956) Bristol 170s (one was an ex-Pakistan Government aircraft), the first two being sold to SAFE in 1961. The first was registered ZK-CAL on 7 June 1961 and the aircraft was delivered to Woodbourne on 9 December 1961 by its crew, A. Forbes, J. Wright, J. Kundycki and a radio operator. Named *Merchant Trader*, ZK-CAL started commercial operations on 12 May 1962. Registered alphabetically later on 7 June 1961, ZK-CAM was delivered much earlier to Woodbourne than ZK-CAL. Arriving in Karachi on 30 July 1961, the delivery crew (K. Beattie, R. McKenzie, J. Kundycki plus a radio operator) spent almost three weeks waiting to take the aircraft down to New Zealand. Departing from Karachi on 18 August 1961, the aircraft was finally delivered to Woodbourne on 3 September 1961. Named *Merchant Venturer*, the aircraft started commercial operations on 30 October 1961.

Five more aircraft arrived from the PAF in 1965–66: ZK-CLU, ZK-CLT, ZK-CRK, ZK-CRL and ZK-CRM. A further two Bristol 170s came from the Pakistan Government (one was also ex-PAF before service with the Pakistan Government) in 1966 via Ansett-ANA after being in service with the Australian airline.

ZK-CLU was delivered to Auckland for SAFE on 1 June 1966. After taking the registration ZK-CLU on 1 July 1966, it entered service with the airline on 3 May 1967, named *Merchant Buccaneer*. ZK-CLT was registered to SAFE on 1 June 1965 and delivered to Auckland on 24 August 1965 by its crew, J. Fleming and N. Pirie. The aircraft was named *Merchant Hauler* and entered service on 17 December 1965. This aircraft and ZK-CRK would be used on the Chatham Islands service, under contract from the Department of Internal Affairs, from Wellington and later from Christchurch. DME (distance-measuring equipment) and HF (high-frequency) radio were installed in the aircraft, which retained its windows. The 'capsule' the passengers travelled in to the Chathams was a specially designed 'box' which accommodated the passengers with airline-type seats, lighting and air conditioning. It too ran on the aircraft rails and took up the rear half of the hold. The windows in the capsule lined up with the aircraft windows to provide a view. The forward part of the hold carried freight.

ZK-CRM had been registered to SAFE on 9 August 1966 and arrived at Woodbourne from Pakistan on 13 August 1966. This aircraft was partially rebuilt after arrival with the centre section from ZK-AYG and the wings from ZK-BMA, finally entering service with SAFE over a full year later, on 16 August 1967, named *Merchant Herald*.

Two of the Bristol 170s bought from the PAF had been the personal aircraft of the PAF Chief of Staff. These were ZK-CRK and ZK-CRL. ZK-CRK was delivered to SAFE by a Pakistani crew, with the aircraft still in its camouflage colours, on 6 July 1966. It was registered ZK-CRK on the same day and entered service on 13 December 1966, named *Merchant Wayfarer*. In 1968, DME equipment and HF radio was installed in the aircraft (as with ZK-CLT) for flights to the Chatham Islands. The windows were also kept. However, ZK-CRK had its name changed from *Merchant Wayfarer* to *Merchant Islander* for the Chatham service.

ZK-CRL was delivered to Woodbourne from Pakistan on 3 October 1966 and registered on 24 October 1966, named *Merchant Porter*. The aircraft did not enter service and was used for spares.

Two further Bristol 170s purchased by SAFE had Pakistani origins but both arrived via a more circuitous route. Both aircraft also had very similar service histories. ZK-CVK and ZK-CVL had both been PAF aircraft fitted with a paratroop door rather than a freight door, and had gone on to the Pakistan Government and Ansett-ANA before being purchased by SAFE. The first aircraft was registered ZK-CVL on 27 October 1967 and delivered to Woodbourne in Ansett colours on 5 November 1967 with its new registration.

The second aircraft was registered ZK-CVK on 3 November 1967 and delivered by G. Powell and G. Stuart to Woodbourne also in Ansett colours on 11 November 1967 with its new registration. Both ZK-CVK and ZK-CVL, however, were only ever used for spares and both registrations were cancelled on 5 April 1972, although the wings of ZK-CVL were used in the rebuilding of ZK-CVY in October 1967, which was registered to SAFE on 23 November 1967 before entering service on 18 December 1967.

FLEET CHANGES 1966/67

One Bristol 170 Mk 31E which had a short-lived service in SAFE colours was ZK-CPU. After being purchased from Aviation Traders, the aircraft was registered to SAFE on 8 July 1966 and flown out to New Zealand by a West London Air Charter crew and entered commercial service on 23 July 1966. The Wahine storm (named after the ferry that sank), which hit Wellington on 10 April 1968, lifted ZK-CPU from its restraints and it was damaged badly enough for the aircraft to be written off by an insurance assessor. The registration (ZK-CPU) was cancelled on 31 May 1968 and the aircraft was used for fire training before being scrapped. Its fin was kept behind SAFE's depot at Wellington Airport for some time.

Bristol 170 Mk 31 ZK-CQD had been rebuilt in 1966 by Aviation Traders before being sold to SAFE. The aircraft arrived at Wellington on 14 November 1966 in SAFE colours and had been flown out from Britain again (as with ZK-CPU) by a West London Air Charter crew.

Another purchase from Aviation Traders was Bristol 170 Mk 31E ZK-CPT. The aircraft was registered to SAFE on 2 May 1966 and flown from Britain to Woodbourne on 26 May 1966 by its crew, J. Howard and R. Alexander. Named *Merchant Courier*, the aircraft started operations with SAFE on 18 July 1966.

PURCHASE OF SAFE BY NAC

Airwork's link with SAFE was finally terminated in September 1972 when their shareholding was bought out by New Zealand National Airways Corporation (NAC). SAFE Air Ltd thereafter became a wholly owned subsidiary of NAC.

Owned by Air New Zealand, SAFE Air Ltd is now a maintenance and repair organisation with subsidiary companies in New Zealand and Australia.

20

NIGERIA

NIGERIAN AIR FORCE

After independence in 1962, an Anglo-Nigerian defence agreement was abrogated and, although a number of countries had helped Nigeria with the inception of its own air arm, it was West Germany that had been the principal provider of expertise. The commander of the Nigerian air force was a West German, Colonel Katz. After the start of the civil war in 1967, the West Germans suspended their help and Airwork stepped in to fill part of the breach.

In 1968 a formal agreement was reached between the Nigerian Federal Government and Airwork to provide technical assistance to the Nigerian air force for five years. There were four main areas of support:

1   The expansion of the existing aircraft engineering facilities to provide additional workshops at the Kaduna Air Force Base in order to enable the overhaul of aircraft and ancillary equipment.
2   The rationalisation of the procurement of spares and overhaul of components.
3   The expansion of the Technical Service School at Kaduna.
4   Flying training on the Piaggio P.149D aircraft at Kaduna.

The Nigerian air force operated a fleet of twelve Piaggio P.149D basic-training aircraft. They were dispersed in bush areas and operated in a harsh environment. The result of this was that they required extensive refurbishment. On completion they were test flown by an Airwork test pilot and brought back into service.

During the period of the five-year contract, the flying school at Kaduna was commanded by a Nigerian air force OC (officer commanding) and was staffed by twelve ex-RAF-qualified flying instructors provided by Airwork. The engineering programme also covered maintenance of Dornier 27s and Douglas DC-3s, and upgrading of their avionics equipment.

BIAFRAN WAR

During the 1967–70 Biafran War, Airwork assisted the Nigerian Government in procuring two Jet Provost T.51s (serials 143 and 157) from the Sudan air force. They were flown from Khartoum to Kano in August 1967. They flew on to Kaduna and then Makurdi, which was their operating base against Biafra, and given the Nigerian air force serials NAF701 and NAF702. Airwork provided technicians to service and prepare them for combat.

OTHER NIGERIAN CONTRACTS

Airwork were involved in three other areas separate to the Nigerian air force. AST at Perth trained pilots and engineers to CAA standards for Nigeria Airways.

A separate training contract was also provided by AST Perth for helicopter pilots and engineers for the Nigerian navy prior to type training on the Westland Lynx provided by the manufacturer.

Finally, AST at Perth undertook the training to private pilot's licence standard of ATC assistants for the Nigerian Federal Aviation Authority.

21

OMAN

BACKGROUND TO THE INSURGENCY & DHOFAR REBELLION

There has been a long history of British influence in Oman and the sultanate has long been kindly disposed towards the United Kingdom. British forces assisted Oman in its quarrel with Saudi Arabia which started in 1945 over their border centred initially on the Buraimi crossroads. In 1957 the newly formed and Saudi backed OLA (Oman Liberation Army) attacked Muscat and captured a large area. The ruler, Sultan Saeed bin Taimour, requested British help.

Oman began to form its own air force and the sultanate of Muscat and Oman air force (SMOAF) was duly established on 1 March 1959. The air crew was seconded from the RAF; at the same time Airwork gained their first contract in Oman and were with the Omani air force from the start. Airwork were responsible for the maintenance and technical support for the fledgling air force.

A great impetus to the expansion of the SMOAF (and subsequently Airwork's operations there) resulted from the trouble in Dhofar. The insurgency problem had never really gone away. The rebellion against the rule of Sultan bin Taimour started in the province of Dhofar. There had been discontent since 1962 but the momentum gained, culminating with attacks against police and army outposts on 9 June 1965. The trouble lasted from 1965 until 1975. The DLF (Dhofar Liberation Front) or *Adu*, as the rebels were known, received backing variously from Saudi Arabia, Egypt, Iraq and later South Yemen. In 1967 the DLF reorganised themselves, with the aid of South Yemen, into the Popular Front for the Liberation of the Occupied Arabian Gulf (PFLOAG).

The security situation deteriorated with the withdrawal of British forces from Aden in 1967. Ironically, Airwork had gained a three-year contract from the new government of the South Arabian Federation, as it was first called, to provide technical support for their military air wing and naval patrol boats. Airwork staff in Aden and Oman found themselves not exactly supporting military forces of two opposing sides, but certainly providing technical support to two states that were ideologically opposed to each other. On 7 August 1967, the British base at Salalah was attacked by the insurgents and a Provost was damaged in the attack. The insurgency gained ground and by 1969 they had captured the town of Rakhyut and the SMOAF moved to counter the increasing threat by shifting their centre of operations to Salalah.

In August 1970 the SMOAF name was changed by dropping 'Muscat' to become the SOAF (Sultan of Oman's Air Force), although it had been referred to as the SOAF as early as 1965.

With the increasing encroachment of the PFLOAG and their control over much of the Dhofar region, a strong response was required. The first was the staged coup d'état on 23 July 1970 with Prince Qaboos bin Saeed Al Saeed assuming power from his father, Sultan Saeed bin Taimour. Prince Qaboos had attended Sandhurst and was a young, forward-looking man who knew that decisive measures were needed to defeat the insurgency. Regarding the day of the coup, Airwork employee Ted Weinel recalled:

> The same day as Qaboos's father was deposed, he was shipped out to Bahrain by RAF Argosy, after treatment to a self inflicted gun-shot wound (in his foot) that occurred during the father/son confrontation in the palace at Salalah. The whole of the Sultan's army Brigade (under the command of Brigadier J.S.Fletcher OBE) in the Salalah zone was on alert and the SOAF Strike aircraft flew low 'top cover' over the town just about all afternoon on that day.
>
> Clearly, Airwork was involved in turning the aircraft around for rotating-sorties over the town and up and down the coast. The Beavers were on standby for additional troop movements or CASEVAC operations, in the event, along with the helicopters. It was a very exciting afternoon, especially as none of us really knew what was going on. We (the Airwork staff) only learned of what had happened, hours after the event. It was after midnight before we put the aircraft to bed.

With his autocratic father exiled to London (spending his remaining years in the Dorchester Hotel, London), Sultan Qaboos set about introducing a number of social and administrative reforms to deprive the rebellion of support.

On the ground, British forces, including members of the SAS, launched an offensive in the Salalah area on 21 February 1971, freeing the town of Sudh from the insurgents. Operation Jaguar was launched in October 1971 in order to establish strong fortified positions in Jibjat and Medinah. Air support from the SOAF was vital to these operations, with Beavers, Skyvans and Caribous proving logistical support and the Strikemasters providing air support to ground operations. The border area of Yemen presented problems of a different kind in that not only did the insurgents infiltrate through the mountainous border and use supply routes, they also used what they thought would be a safe haven to bombard the sultanate with artillery and mortar fire. This was especially dangerous to the SOAF Skyvans and helicopters providing support in the small, rough border landing strips. The response to this threat was for the Strikemasters to launch attacks on the positions over the border in Yemen which led predictably to protests from the Yemeni Government. Border towns in Yemen attacked by the Strikemasters included Hauf, Jaadib and Habarut.

Probably the most significant engagement occurred at what came to be known as the Battle of Mirabat. As long as the PFLOAG kept to low-intensity guerrilla tactics, they were moderately successful. However, on the night of 18/19 July 1972, they launched a major attack with 250 fighters on the city of Mirabat. Omani and British troops (including eight members of the SAS), along with Omani policemen, fought the insurgents. Once again close air support helped to repel the invaders, who were forced to retreat. The SOAF had flown in reinforcements of another twenty-three SAS troops. Despite beating off the attack, two members of the SAS had been killed.

Salalah Detachment
c. early 1960s. The
flight office-cum-living
room in the picture is
a fly-screened, covered
terrace looking out on
to the 'pan' and airfield
beyond. Sleeping
accommodation was
in curtained spaces
on the left. (Edward
Weinel)

The strong response from the sultan with the assistance of the UK and (at various times) Jordan, Pakistan and Iran ensured the defeat of the threat. On 11 December 1975 Sultan Qaboos declared the war over, although there was occasional sporadic trouble in later years.

It should be noted that although the Airwork staff were mostly ex-military personnel (including ex-Fleet Air Arm), they were technically employed as civilians in Oman. In May 1974 a number of the Airwork staff in Oman were awarded the Sultan's Commendation in recognition of their service. In 1977 Airwork staff were informed that they were also eligible to receive the Dhofar Medal in recognition of Airwork employees who had been closely involved with SOAF operations in Salalah between 1965 and 1975. Civilians up until that point had not been eligible for the award. The Dhofar Medal, though, was never physically received in many cases.

AIRCRAFT & OPERATIONS

There was considerable overlap between the RAF and Airwork personnel. Many Airwork personnel had served in the RAF or Army Air Corps and all the pilots were serving RAF officers who had volunteered and been seconded for special or unusual duties. Although Airwork were contracted to carry out the maintenance work on the aircraft and helicopters, there was overlap here as well. For instance, in 1966 seconded RAF air-frame specialists carried out major wing modifications on the four Beavers in Muscat.

The main air force base was set up at Bait Al Falaj near the Omani capital Muscat. The first arrivals to join the SMOAF were two RAF Scottish Aviation Pioneer CC1s XL518 and XL554 in March 1959, which were transferred on secondment from 78 Squadron Khormaksar in Aden and served until 1962, with two more joining shortly after the arrival of the first pair. Shortly after the arrival of the Pioneers, three Percival Piston Provost T.52s (XF682, XF683 and XF688) arrived in 1959 and were followed by XF868 in 1960 (WW452 crashed on delivery), WV501 and WV678 in 1961, WV476 in 1963 and XF907 in 1965. These aircraft were converted for ground-support operations. By 1966, at least two of the Piston Provosts were based at Muscat and one at Salalah, and these would alternate when major servicing came up for each aircraft.

Four ex-British army de Havilland Canada Beavers were delivered in 1962 to replace the Pioneers. The Pioneers and the Beavers were ideal aircraft for operations in Oman with their rugged airframes and STOL capabilities. Much of Oman's terrain was covered in jagged hill formations and had a poor road network. It was terrain which suited insurgents and required air operational capabilities to counter them. One of the main functions of the SMOAF was to provide troop transportation and logistical support to army and police outposts throughout Oman. Many of the outposts lay in remote areas with the most basic facilities, including landing strips rarely longer than 984ft (300m) and composed of sand and crushed rock.

At the time of the arrival of the Beavers at Salalah, there were normally around four Airwork technical staff based there (it was still an RAF base at this point) and eighteen at Muscat. The Airwork men were on a three-month tour at Salalah. They dined in the sergeants' mess and lived on the job in what was then an old customs building dating back to the 1920s. By 1974, the number of Airwork technical staff had grown to around seventy in total.

Piston Provost T.52 WV476, displaying a new sand camouflage which had just been applied in 1965 as an experiment for the Salalah region, was the only Piston Provost to wear this scheme. (Edward Weinel)

With the completion of Seeb Airport and the military facilities in 1970, the SOAF headquarters was moved there (initially from 1969) from Bait Al Falaj, along with the Airwork Maintenance Service. A helicopter element was established which eventually comprised twenty Agusta-Bell AB.205, three Agusta-Bell AB.206s, two Agusta-Bell AB.212s and five Bell 214B helicopters by 1977. Some of these were initially used by the Omani police. The military helicopters and crews alternated their duty between Muscat and Salalah.

BAC 167 Strikemaster Mk 82s were delivered in 1969 and were to replace the Piston Provosts. The Strikemasters were a major step up in capability from the Piston Provosts as they could carry a greater weapons load. Airwork had suggested the use of the Hispano Suiza SURA ground attack rockets to Wing Commander John Severne when he was in the process of establishing the new South Yemen air force in Aden during 1966–67. Wing Commander Severne, in turn, recommended to his counterparts in the SMOAF that the SURA rockets be used in place of the unreliable Second World War vintage 4in (10cm) rockets. Subsequently, the Strikemasters were the first aircraft to carry them.

In 1969 the Beavers were given a camouflage scheme as they were by then becoming more involved in CASEVAC and MEDEVAC operations in the war zone, along with troop deployment and retrieval operations.

Two Douglas C-47s (serials 501 and 502) were delivered via Hurn in 1969 and 1970. However, they were not ideal aircraft for Oman and they were quickly replaced by Caribous.

Three de Havilland Canada Caribous (801, 802 and 803) were delivered in 1970, with the first being delivered on 9 April that year. These rugged aircraft brought a greater carrying capacity to operations in rough and remote areas. Unfortunately two of the Caribous (802 and 803) crashed and were written off, to be replaced by two more (804 and 805).

Continuing the upgrade in logistics capability, from 1970 the SOAF started taking deliveries of Short Skyvans. Deliveries were through Airwork at Hurn and started in June 1970. Skyvan G-14-67 passed through Heathrow in September 1971. The Skyvans were returned to Hurn in 1982–83 for a complete overhaul which included conversion of seven of them to a maritime surveillance role, with Racal ASR.360 Surveillance Radar installed, and renamed Seavans.

There were five Vickers Viscounts delivered to provide internal transport services, with the first (501) departing Hurn for Oman on 30 September 1971. Although there were five Viscounts delivered, the serial 504 was used by two different Viscounts after one replaced another. The Viscounts were also used for transportation of Omani businessmen, Airwork staff (departing and returning from leave), as well as the transportation of military personnel between Muscat and Salalah.

The year 1974 saw the arrival of three types of British aircraft. A £900,000-plus order was placed for eight BN-2A-21 Defenders to replace the Beavers. In fact, the 500th model of the BN-2A variants to come off the production line was G-BCEK, delivered to the SOAF as 301 on 14 August 1974. A BAC VC10 was delivered for use by the Royal Flight and three BAC 1-11 series 485GD were ordered as replacements for the Vickers Viscounts. At the time of ordering, it was envisaged that the new BAC 1-11s would also provide forward air support for army operations. However, other than two demonstration landings for senior SOAF officers at a strip south of Salalah, they were never used in this role. The three were delivered on 18 December 1974 (1001), 29 January 1975 (1002) and 1 November 1975 (1003). The reason for the later delivery of 1003 is that, after its first flight at Hurn, it was returned to have a modification made to allow a large cargo door to be fitted. All three BAC 1-11s were given this modification as they were original built as standard BAC 1-11 frames. On 22 November 1975, shortly after its delivery, 1003 had a severe cockpit fire at Seeb when the oxygen supply was being replenished. The damage was so bad that the aircraft was dismantled and returned to Hurn via sea for repair. The airframe arrived at Poole Harbour and was then taken through the streets of Bournemouth to Hurn on 23 May 1976. The damage was repaired and 553 (the serial had changed from 1003) flew back to Oman on 26 February 1977. The three aircraft were operated in various 'Combi' configurations once the doors had been modified. The serials

BAC 167 Strikemaster 416 after being hit by ground fire. The canopy has been removed and ejector seat made safe, plus detonator caps have been removed from the rockets. (Edward Weinel)

of all three were changed in 1976 to 551 to 553 respectively, 551 being fitted with long-range fuel tanks in the rear of the forward hold in summer 1983, the work carried out by Dan Air Engineering at Lasham. Seating seventy-nine passengers (551 could seat fifty-nine with a palette by the cargo door for luggage), the BAC 1-11s were used to transport personnel and cargo from Seeb to Masirah, Salalah and Thumrait. They also flew regularly all over the Middle East and to India and Pakistan, as well as Europe. Major maintenance was undertaken at both Lasham and Hurn.

Air support was not without risk as many aircraft sustained bullet damage. One Strikemaster (413) was shot down and another (406) was hit by a SAM-7 missile on 19 August 1975 while on support operations in the hills. The pilot tried to recover to Salalah but the damage caused was quite severe. The Strikemaster crashed before the main runway, with the pilot ejecting at close to zero feet; he ended up on his hands and knees, with a badly damaged back, amongst the boulders and rocks of the coastal plain. After the RAF ambulance had picked up the injured pilot, Ted Weinel of Airwork took a Tilly wagon (a Mini Moke with large wheels) and drove out to the crash site with a number of Airwork engineers immediately after the event. At the same time an RAF recovery team with a crane and low-loader also drove out to the crash site to start recovery of the wreckage. Just after they arrived, half a dozen mortar rounds, fired by the *Adu* from the surrounding hills, landed close by, which entailed an immediate response from the RAF regiment. The Airwork team neutralised the remaining munitions and beat a hasty retreat.

The ex-Army Air Corps de Havilland Beavers were sold to Canada in 1976 after being overhauled by Airwork at Hurn.

Despite the help from Britain, Sultan Qaboos also enlisted the aid of Pakistani and Jordanian forces and also considerable help arrived from Iran by November 1972. These involved substantial numbers of Iranian troops along with F-4 Phantoms and helicopters, including Agusta-Bell 205s and 206s plus CH-47C Chinooks. Between 1972 and 1977, when they withdrew, well over 14,000 Iranian troops, marines and members of the Iranian air force had served tours of duty in Oman. At the same time as the IIAF (Imperial Iranian Air Force) were deploying troops and aircraft, a decision was made to enhance the offensive capability of the SOAF. In 1975 a total of thirty-one Hawker Hunters were received as a gift from King Hussein of Jordan. These aircraft were all flown to Thumrait between March and May 1975 by Royal Jordanian Air Force pilots. The intention of the SOAF was to use sixteen of them in 6 Squadron, with the balance of the aircraft being used for spares, airfield decoys and to cover attrition. Jordan also provided air crews and support staff in the early stages prior to the SOAF being able to take over the full running with the assistance of Airwork. Airwork engineers were involved

Hawker Hunter F.9 817 – some of the Hunters were 'hybrids'. In this picture, taken at Thumrait in September 1976, 817 has the rear fuselage of 851 after its original section became badly corroded and was replaced, but it kept the serial 817. (Ian Hawkridge)

from July 1975, with the Jordanian personnel, in bringing the aircraft up to operational standard. A further two Hunters were added to the force when the SOAF took delivery of two T.66Cs from the Kuwait air force in late 1978. These were 803 and 804. Airwork engineer Ian McGrory and a pilot were tragically killed in a high-speed taxiing accident which wrote off one of the Hunters (800) on 30 September 1976 at Thumrait.

In October 1975, the SOAF Hunters flown by British and Jordanian pilots, in association with the IIAF Phantoms, made the final offensive against the insurgents. Supported by IIAA CH-47C Chinooks to bring up supplies, troops and artillery, plus the IIN (Imperial Iranian Navy) destroyers providing bombardment of the targets, attacks were launched against the insurgents in the Sarfait area, at the same time also attacking rebel artillery positions over the South Yemen border. The threat from SAM-7s was always present and the Hunters made dive-bombing runs with turns designed to reduce the potential of being hit by the ground-to-air missiles. One Hunter was hit during the operation but managed to return to base.

By late 1979, the Hunter force consisted of twelve operational aircraft with six in reserve. By 1993, this figure was down to nine operational aircraft, with the last operational flight being flown in the border dispute in 1987.

During 1977, five of the Strikemasters were sold to Singapore as the war had been declared over on 11 December 1975.

From 1977 onwards, with the end of the war, the SOAF involved itself in a major upgrade of facilities and aircraft. Twelve SEPECAT Jaguar Internationals were ordered in 1977 which replaced the Strikemasters of 1 Squadron. A new air base had been built at Thumrait and officially opened on 1 July 1975, although it had previously been a diversion airfield and refuelling post known as Midway in the 1960s. Other airfields were expanded and improved, including landing strips in the desert as well as Salalah, Masirah and Bait Al Falaj.

The Jaguars were primarily concerned with ground-to-air operations but would also carry AIM-9 Sidewinders for air defence and could carry R.550 Matra Magic air-to-air missiles. They were placed at Thumrait with 8 Squadron and 20 Squadron at Masirah.

In the late 1980s eight BAe Hawk Mk 103s and eight BAe Hawk 203s were ordered. The SOAF was renamed RAFO (Royal Air Force of Oman) in 1990.

In 2000 the Jaguars were given an upgrade to 'Jaguar 97' standard. This involved improved avionics and navigation systems, enhanced thermal imaging, along with the capability to carry TIALD (Thermal Imaging Airborne Laser Designator) pods on the centreline station and ability to carry LGBs (Laser Guided Bombs).

The first of three Lockheed C-130H Hercules was delivered in March 1981. By mid-1983, a further two C-130s had been delivered, along with a Douglas DC-8-73CF for long-range transport plus two AS.332C Super Pumas. By this stage helicopters and transport aircraft were allocated to squadrons as required depending on task loads in the north and south of the country.

Further upgrading took place in 2002 when Oman ordered twelve Lockheed Martin F-16 C/Ds. This was followed by an order for C-27J Spartans to replace the Skyvans and Caribous, which like the Strikemasters had seen long service in Oman. Having given a good account of themselves, the Strikemasters were finally retired in 2001.

The Royal Oman Police also upgraded their capabilities by placing an order for six AB.139 helicopters. The RAFO also placed an order for twenty NH.90 helicopters.

From 1959 the contract was run by Airwork Services Ltd, which changed to Airwork (Oman) Ltd in 1980. After the takeover by VT Aerospace in 2000 it became Airwork Technical & Partners LLC (which included local Omani involvement) and continues under that name after the July 2010 takeover by the Babcock International Group.

OTHER AIRWORK ACTIVITIES IN OMAN

In 1976 Airwork won a completely new contract to provide engineering design and manufacture to equip Thumrait ATC tower and airfield. The contract included navigation aids.

In 1978 Airwork secured a contract to design, build and commission a new ATC desk, communications and equipment for SOAF Masirah Island off the coast of Oman following severe cyclone damage. Emergency repairs were undertaken by Airwork technicians from Muscat. The Masirah ATC project was commissioned in 1979.

In 1987 Airwork gained another military Omani contract to take over the engineering support of the Rapier missile defence system.

Early Years of Oman Contract: Social & Working Conditions

By Edward Weinel

Airwork technical staff lived on the SAF army camp close to Bait al Falaj airfield. The airfield was also the official civil airport of entry for Oman.

Each man had his own air-conditioned cabin in a prefabricated billet block with ablution facilities next to the company Mess. In 1966 there were 18 staff members.

The Mess comprised a dining room, with kitchen attached, and a lounge cum bar room where the men could relax.

There were other accommodations next to the lounge where the then manager/chief engineer lived along with a spare room for visiting, head office people.

Later, as a more senior manager was recruited, these accommodations were used by a new chief engineer and one of the technical chaps as staff increased. The new manager had a married-quarter 'up the hill' where the senior SOAF and SAF officers (commanders) lived.

The kitchen, waiter and house-boy service was provided by the company under the supervision of a Pakistani steward who was also responsible for purchasing the victualling supplies from the town. His spending was under the control of the 'Messing Rep' (one of the volunteer mess committee members) who held the monthly funding into which staff members paid approx £25 per month.

The kitchen was manned by two Pakistani cooks and table was served by the Steward and one of the two houseboy/waiters.

Meals were:

Breakfast at 8 AM (after two hours work, starting at six AM)
Lunch at 2.30 PM, after normal working hours finished at 2 PM.
Tea and stickies at 4 PM.
Dinner at 6PM.

Food was normally standard British fare except for Fridays when the best curry this side of the Equator was served.

Also under the supervision of the Steward, two houseboys would clean rooms and make beds (with frequent changes of bed linen).

Personal clothing and sheets etc were washed and ironed on a daily basis by a couple of local, company employed 'dhobi boys'.

The bar was run by the committee bar member who was responsible for stocking with beer and spirits which were obtained from the Gray Mackenzie supply company, by special permission.

Ample supplies of Double Diamond draught beer were always available along with the usual brands of tinned beer and spirits.

The bar was obviously a popular social meeting point for the men after an afternoon at the beach or, for some, after the afternoon siesta.

Various games were played around the bar, dominoes and dice for example, with cards and darts in the lounge.

Entertainment comprised beach-trips for swimming, water-skiing and fishing. A special beach was set aside by the Sultan for British SAF and SOAF officers (and families) and Airwork technical staff use.

Once or twice a week there was Cinema on the army camp for officers, Airwork and all ranks and followers living on the camp.

Four week leave periods were normally taken at six or eight month intervals, usually by roster so as not to deplete the technical staff numbers too much. One day for every week worked.

Trades comprised: Airframe & Engine technicians (normally 8 or 9, not counting the C.Eng), Electrical & Instrument technicians (normally 2 or 3), Air Radio techs who sometimes double for E&I techs (normally 2 or 3) and Armourers (normally 3).

There was always a detachment of one A&E, one Air Radio and one Armourer under a permanent Leading Hand A&E to Salalah. They normally rotated on a two or three monthly basis. The LH A&E was permanent by choice at that time.

Detachment technicians dined in RAF Salalah's Sergeants mess and slept in a building next to the aircraft dispersal pan. Later the planes were kept overnight in concrete blast-pens nearby.

On those occasions, if and when insurgent mortar shells fell within the RAF camp fences, Airwork staff were paid a special bonus of £1 a day for two months. (Classified as Danger Money.)

In Muscat off-camp entertainment amounted to inter-company darts matches with companies like Wimpies, a pipe laying company, and the Dutch operators of PDO (Petroleum Development, Oman), bathing as mentioned and shopping in town. Sight seeing was also popular, visiting various localities along the coast from the twin towns of Mattrah and Muscat.

In-house entertainment, aside from the bar, revolved about music, with tape recorders, record players or LW, MW radio or reading and writing letters. Mail moved to and from UK by courtesy of the BFPO system via the RAF aircraft movements from Bahrain and between the Gulf States, Muscat, Masirah and Salalah.

The only telephonic communication with the outside world was by telephone in the British Consulate in Muscat. Calls to UK could be made (for instance at Xmas) by prior booking. Such calls were limited to 3 minutes.

There were no televisions and no computers.

At work, the engineers (starting at 6 AM) followed a military regimen of servicing on the Provost and Beaver aircraft. First off, Before Flight inspections on planned aircraft for continuation training or army out-post support in the Northern region. Technical documentation was normally controlled through the F.700 (technical log).

Thereafter, work continued on the various tasks involving heavier scheduled-servicing on other aircraft.

Upon the return of planned sorties, After Flight inspections and refuelling were carried out before picketing the aircraft for the day. BP provided the refuelling service.

Salalah Detachment: Social & Working Conditions

By Edward Weinel

The SOAF's Salalah Detachment during 1966–68, consisted of two Provosts (and eventually one Beaver) and was supported by four Airwork technical people (One Leading Hand Airframe & Engine, I/C, one A&E, one Armourer and one E&I who doubled as Air Radio although sometimes it was an Air Radio man who doubled as E&I).

The detachment personnel were rotated on a two month basis so that the Airwork people at Muscat shared in the harder living/working conditions that were then typical at Salalah. However, detachment duty was not obligatory; but purely on a volunteer basis. During my time, not many people refused, when asked.

As it happened, the Leading Hand I/C had elected to stay on a permanent basis. He was an ex-RAF Flt Sergeant who preferred life on the RAF Station, even though conditions were harder than at Muscat.

The SOAF Detachment Pilots were accommodated in the station officer's mess because they were all (at that time) still serving RAF officers who had volunteered for the special duties with SOAF.

The Airwork detachment supporting SOAF aircraft at Salalah lived 'on site' in a building next to the dispersal hard standing just outside the station perimeter-wire, on the Southern end of the camp.

The accommodation served as a flight (despatch) office, a lounge area with easy chairs and a fridge, along with the flight-office furnishings. There were four partitioned and curtained sleeping areas where the engineers could keep their personal things and clothing, etc.

The main room was open at the airfield side with fly-screened arches, and no air-conditioning was provided.

Behind the accommodation there was an open yard surrounded on the three other sides by weaponry store rooms and a small armoury. Only 1st line and some minor 2nd line servicing was conducted on the aircraft.

At one end of the building a room was set aside as a communications centre, housing two Baluch signallers detached from the Dhofar Brigade headquarters at Salalah. These signallers were rotated on an eight hourly roster so that the communications room was manned 24 hrs a day.

Both SOAF and Airwork used this facility to send and receive messages to and from HQ at Muscat or to Army Brigade HQ etc. The signals were sent by morse over the radio on SAF (army) frequencies.

(Later, Airwork had a small contract, briefly, to service Brigade ground radio services. This was eventually taken over by directly contracted, uniformed personnel.)

The Airwork technical fellows dined in the station Sergeants mess. Food was therefore free of charge, which was a small compensation for the hard-living conditions.

The RAF supplied a canvas-covered, field hangar which provided space for one aircraft on scheduled servicing. This was erected on an open area of ground, only a short distance from the dispersal pan and in the lee of the Southern perimeter wire.

As the insurgency escalated and mortar attacks on the camp increased, concrete blast pens were built near the canvas hangar in which to accommodate the two Provost aircraft overnight. This facility was also extended to the Beaver and became a permanent feature of the SOAF detachment (most attacks at that time occurred at night). An armed guard was provided by the Dhofar Brigade which comprised a small platoon of Baluch soldiers and a 'Ferret' scout-car under the command of a British officer.

Air support for the Brigade in the hills of Dhofar became more frequent and recce patrols were a constant daily routine. The Beaver was used with increasing frequency for Med-evac, Cas-evac and general transportation duties for supplies and troops.

Towards the end of 1968, after I had decided to become 'permanent' at Salalah, a new accommodation facility was built to house the Airwork detachment technicians. More staff were detached to the location and each had an air-conditioned room. A small bar/lounge room was also provided.

Some time later, a kitchen and dining room were added; but the food remained free of charge.

A new hangar was built and the aircraft fleet was increased by the introduction of the Strikemasters and helicopters.

By that time the detachment staff had also been receiving a form of danger-money as an incentive to stay on at Salalah in spite of the mortar bombing. The rule was, if one round (out of a usual 5 or 6 rounds fired in the direction of camp) actually landed inside the camp-perimeter, then the sum of two pounds a day was paid to each engineer, for the subsequent two months thereafter.

Thumrait: Social & Working Conditions

By Ian Hawkridge

Arriving on the SOAF Viscount, the oppressive heat rolled into the cabin. The SOAF arrivals unit was a large corrugated iron, open-ended hangar, which made the heat even worse. Welcome to Thumrait in May 1976! After driving in the Airwork bus with the windows open (air conditioning not working) to the Admin and Domestic site, I was dropped off at my 'bungalow'. The bungalow was a four-man prefabricated type (no individual *bayts* in those days) and came complete with small colonies of both cockroaches and 'camel spiders'.

We had a mess near to the Hunter flightline (no Jaguars or hangars then). Food was plentiful and was cooked by Asian staff and a good selection was available at each mealtime. The Airwork Catering Manager worked wonders with the funds available. There was always a roast joint or a fish main course in the evening, backed up with a curry and a salad. Vegetables and fruit were always available, as much as you wanted of fresh fruit. Other times there would be 'lobster thermidor' with lobsters fresh from Salalah market, also swordfish and tuna steaks on many occasions.

T3 bar at Thumrait. An attempt was made in 1982–83 by Airwork to take photographs of facilities and improve induction procedures to better help new employees to be aware of life in Oman. (Bob Lawson)

The cinema was next door and films were shown every night. We were able to use the SOAF swimming pool, but most of the socialising was in either our bar or the SOAF one. Our bar was small but served its purpose well as there weren't too many 'Airworkies' in those days. There were also 'private' bars in some of the bungalows. We also had a detachment of Iranians at Thumrait, and some of their officers liked a drink. Some very interesting evenings took place with those gentlemen, and often something would appear a few weeks later on one of their regular C-130 re-supply flights that you'd just happened to mention when drunk, that you liked. Very generous people.

On a Friday we travelled over to RAF Salalah with someone as a 'designated sober driver'. The NAAFI shop was popular at certain times and had 'gentlemens' magazines hidden under the counter, then it was off to the bar. Many an interesting trip back to Thumrait later in the afternoon, when looking out of either the bus or Land Rover at vehicles that had slipped over the edge of the cliff road, and were just mangled wrecks way below you.

I stayed at Thumrait until May 1977 when I had to return to UK on compassionate grounds. However I returned in the October of that year and stayed until being transferred up to Seeb in 1979. In December 1983 it was back to Thumrait again for another two years, so this time I was able to sample the new *bayts* and of course the world famous T3 bar.

Working conditions varied as to whether you were in the Armoury, on the Hunter line, hangar or in one of the offices. Normal shifts were 07.00–13.00 Saturday through

I February 2009: RAFO Jaguar S 210 flown by Squadron Leader 'Skids' Harrison makes a low pass along Thumrait's southern taxiway. Harrison was one of a number of RAF 'Loan Service' officers. (Peter R. Foster IDMA)

Thursday, Friday being the Muslim weekend. Flying commitments meant that most days the Armoury and Hunter line were manned throughout the day. Working outside wasn't too bad at all even in the high temperatures of 40C plus, during the humidity free months. However the humid months were very bad. In the armoury the conditions were bad 'all the time'. The armourers were in a building that attracted the heat, this coupled with the heavy manual work and again the humidity, made every day very hard work indeed.

My shifts varied on a daily basis as I was employed to set up the Transit Aircraft Flight. This meant that any aircraft that basically wasn't a fighter aircraft was handled by ourselves, at whatever hour of the day. We dealt with all SOAF, Iranian, Jordanian, USAF and RAF aircraft that visited. We also had quite a few civilian aircraft passing through for various reasons, Jordanian Airlines, Gulf Air, Swissair, Trans Mediterranean to name but a few.

Looking back I'm glad to have experienced all that I did in Oman whilst also having been just a very small part of the 'Airwork' story.

Tarqa Beach Shootings, 1978

Tarqa Beach is located near a small village called Tarqa and was a popular spot on Thursday afternoons and Fridays for barbecues, fishing and swimming for Airwork staff from Thumrait and Salalah. The beach was approximately 15 miles (24km) along the coast, north-east from Salalah. On 1 June 1978 a group of seven Airwork staff left Thumrait to go to the beach as normal. However, during the night the *Adu* insurgents set up an ambush and opened fire on them while they were around a camp fire. Five of them were killed (Thomas Hothersall,

Thomas Leavey, Terence Waite, Alan Pullen and John Street). Two of the group (Chris Filmer and Martin Fowler) escaped using the darkness and confusion as cover and ran into the sea to swim away from the ambush and eventually managed to raise the alarm.

The killings underlined the dangers faced by Airwork staff in Oman during the insurgency.

22

RHODESIA

THE NIGEL NORMAN REPORT & FOUNDATION OF A NATIONAL AIRLINE

Early Aviation Activity

The development of commercial aviation in Rhodesia proceeded in fits and starts. There had been limited attempts up to 1929 to put aviation on to a firm footing. These included Air Road Motors, established on 8 April 1920, which only had a brief existence. This was followed by Rhodesian Air Tours, a one-aircraft company, in the winter of 1922. Little then happened until the establishment of the Rhodesian Aviation Syndicate in 1927, which was a group of miners and ranchers who held a meeting in Bulawayo in October 1927 to discuss the establishment of a company called the Rhodesian Aviation Co. Ltd. Plans were made to engage the Southern Rhodesian Government to establish internal air services along with possible services to South Africa. However, despite the best intentions of those concerned, nothing happened for two years, although the Rhodesian Aviation Syndicate continued in its then current form.

The next step was a letter in the *Bulawayo Chronicle* on 24 January 1929 from Aston Redrup, the secretary of the Rhodesian Aviation Syndicate, announcing the absorption of the Rhodesian Aviation Syndicate by the Rhodesian Aviation Co. Ltd. It stated that Cobham/ Blackburn Co. (Sir Alan Cobham's airline association with the Blackburn Aeroplane & Motor Co.) had acquired a large interest in the Rhodesian Aviation Co. and that an aircraft and pilot would shortly arrive from England. The pilot was Captain Benjamin Roxburgh-Smith DFC, who farmed near Bulawayo but was an ex-First World War pilot and who also had a close involvement with Sir Alan Cobham and Robert Blackburn of the Blackburn Co. (also known as Blackburn Airlines). The Rhodesian Aviation Co. Ltd was formally registered on 17 April 1929. The first aircraft purchased was DH.60X Moth VP-YAA (registered on 1 April 1930) and a regular weekly service was started between Bulawayo and Salisbury. There were financial problems and the £395 loss in the year 1929–30 was covered by a grant from the Southern Rhodesian Government and the Beit Railway Trust.[1] There were further problems in 1931 when Imperial Airways took over the African interests of Sir Alan Cobham/Blackburn Airlines. Whilst Sir Alan Cobham/Blackburn Airlines were prepared to put finance into the Rhodesia Aviation Co., Imperial Airlines were not prepared to do so until their main air route through Africa was up and running. All financial support was therefore withdrawn.

At the second AGM of the Rhodesia Aviation Co. Ltd on 17 July 1931, the financial problems were discussed but it was stated that the Southern Rhodesia Government and the Beit Railway Trust would continue to provide financial support.

---

1 The Beit Trust is still in existence today and continues its philanthropic work through offices in Zimbabwe and the UK.

In July 1931 Nyasaland's first aviation company started operations at Blantyre with two DH.80 Puss Moths VP-YAP and VP-YAR. This was Christowitz Air Services, owned by a cartage contractor Mr C.J. Christowitz, who had been the first passenger to arrive by air in Nyasaland in a Cirrus Moth of the Rhodesian Aviation Co. in October 1930. The Christowitz Air Services DH.80s were to feature in later developments.

Two major developments then followed. The first was the opening of the Imperial Airways Nairobi to Cape Town segment of the Cairo–Cape route at the end of January 1932. The second involved the Beit trustees. As in the UK at this time, the railways had a great involvement in the development of commercial aviation. The Beit trustees had a more benevolent view than their British counterparts. Sir Alfred Beit, one of the Beit trustees and a director of Rhodesia Railways, made an important announcement in Bulawayo on 10 February 1932. He stated: 'The principal duty of the Beit Trust is to improve all communications in Rhodesia and Africa generally.'

Two weeks later the Trust made a grant of £50,000 for 'facilitating air transport (in Southern Rhodesia and Northern Rhodesia) on the Imperial Airways route'. The route through the two Rhodesias at the time was (Mbeya–Mpika–Broken Hill–Salisbury–Bulawayo–Pietersburg). The expenditure was to be phased over a two-year period. Spelling out exactly what the money was intended for, Sir Alfred Beit wrote to the Trust Secretary H.H. Hitchcock in February 1932 stating that it was not intended to use the grant as a subsidy for Imperial Airways and that the sum was intended to benefit all aviators.

The Appointment of Nigel Norman

The Trust decided that, in order to ensure that their grant was put to the most advantageous use, a competent authority should be consulted. This competent authority to be appointed was Nigel Norman. He was described in the announcement of his appointment as 'Technical Adviser to the Trustees' as a director of Airwork Ltd and Aerofilms Ltd. He was asked to visit Africa and to prepare a report upon aeronautical conditions in the Rhodesias. His appointment was not a foregone conclusion as the Aircraft Operating Co. of South Africa had made overtures that they were best placed to advise on aviation in that part of Africa. There was also opposition to his appointment from the Chief Secretary's Office of Northern Rhodesia, who made overtures to the Beit Railway Trust on behalf of Major Charles Cochran-Patrick of the previously mentioned Aircraft Operating Co. of South Africa. However, a personal letter from Roderick Denman (who became an Airwork director in 1931) to his Uncle Freddie (i.e. Baron Frederic d'Erlanger, who had many useful contacts) asked for his assistance in helping to push the potential business their (Airwork's) way.

Once Norman's appointment was settled, preparations were made for his visit and a conscious attempt was made by the Beit Railway Trust to impress upon all parties that the finance was not just to be provided and spent. The Trust expected, quite correctly, value for money and they also made it clear that they would be active participants throughout the period of improvement and development work. On the subject of value for money, a letter dated 28 February 1933 from the Trust to Nigel Norman after his arrival hoped that his work was proceeding satisfactorily and put it to him that on his return to the UK in April 1933 they would prefer him to travel by steamer from Cape Town. However, they knew his wife was expecting a child and suggested that he fly to Cairo and select the cheapest route from there 'even though it be the slowest'.

The year before Nigel Norman was appointed as an adviser and consultant to the Trust, the Directorate of Civil Aviation in Southern Rhodesia had appointed Lieutenant J.A.B. Grylls as an adviser and consultant to carry out a survey of landing grounds and make a report and recommendations on their condition and improvement. The Grylls Report and his recommendations were issued on 18 October 1932. This was very similar to the work which Norman was expected to carry out for the Beit Railway Trust. Grylls was an experienced pilot and Air Ministry expert. Whilst it could have been expected that there would be some rivalry or

Sir Alfred Beit and his wife Clementine who accompanied him on most of his trips abroad. The Beit Railway Trust was the prime mover in the establishment of Rhodesia's national airline using Nigel Norman's report as the foundation of its plans. (Beit Trust)

conflict between them, both Grylls and Norman worked in conjunction with each other and it had been planned for Grylls, who was in London in January 1933, to accompany Norman on his flight south but he had to leave slightly earlier than planned.

Eventually, Nigel Norman flew solo down to Southern Rhodesia in DH.60G Gipsy Moth G-ABND, leaving Heston on 11 January 1933, after having been delayed from his planned departure on 9 January by bad weather. He flew via Marseilles, Rome, Sicily, Tunis and Tripoli to Cairo and arrived in Bulawayo on 27 February 1933 after passing through Broken Hill and Livingstone. By coincidence, just over three years earlier, on Thursday 20 March 1930, Nigel Norman had watched the preparation for departure to Bulawayo from Heston of Mr and Mrs A.S. Butler and engineer D.S. Milward. They were flying out on a delivery flight taking G-AADO, the prototype Gloster AS.31 Survey, to Bulawayo for the Aircraft Operating Co.

Norman came highly recommended to the Beit Railway Trust (quite apart from the influence of Baron Frederic d'Erlanger). Prior to his departure for Southern Rhodesia, he was asked for his opinion by the civil aviation authorities in Salisbury on the fatal crash of a Lockheed Orion 9A Special NC12229 *Spirit of Fun*, which had crashed at Victoria Falls Aerodrome on 17 December 1932. He was also asked to comment on the plans for the new Lusaka Airport, to which he made some suggestions but gave his overall approval. In fact, the drawings of the Lusaka Airport terminal building which were produced later by Norman, Muntz and Dawbarn were displayed in the Royal Academy in London in 1935. The new terminal building for Lusaka Airport was constructed partly with funds from the Beit Trust grant.

The Report

Nigel Norman set to work as soon as he arrived and undertook an intensive programme of visiting all landing sites in Northern and Southern Rhodesia, along with Nyasaland and

Mozambique. He visited numerous individuals, as well as companies and government officials connected with aviation, to listen to their views and take account of the widest possible range of opinions before preparing his report and making recommendations. His report (known as 'The Nigel Norman Report') was presented in mid-1933. His calculations of proposed expenditure to improve aviation facilities in Northern Rhodesia and Southern Rhodesia amounted to £8,855 (£3,805 for Southern Rhodesia and £5,050 for Northern Rhodesia). He also made recommendations for revising the local aeronautical map and providing pilots' handbooks (£300 and £200 respectively). His suggestion of a gift of a light aircraft to the governments of both Rhodesias (to carry out airfield inspection work at a total cost of £2,950 for two aircraft) was not met with any enthusiasm by the Beit Railway Trust. The areas of meteorology, night lighting and wireless equipment were left for further investigation after taking note of Nigel Norman's views and recommendations, although a long-wave transmitter was installed at Salisbury as recommended in the report.

Norman stated:

My recommendations are the result of a visit by air to the Rhodesias made during the period of the rains in 1933. On the journey out and in the course of my visit, I flew 18,000 miles in a Gipsy Moth specially converted for this purpose. I inspected 69 Landing Grounds and sites in the Rhodesias and examined the whole of the Imperial Airways route from Cairo to Cape Town, and also subsidiary routes extending from the colonies to Nyasaland, Portuguese East Africa and the Belgian Congo.

Among his recommendations were the following:

a) Construction of additional aerodromes and landing grounds and provision of a government-operated light aircraft to supervise their maintenance.
b) Provision of aviation maps and pilots' handbooks.
c) Establishment of additional meteorological and wireless stations.
d) Provision of night-flying equipment at the main aerodromes and en-route flashing beacons between Salisbury and the Limpopo River.

The report included detailed maps, sketches of landing grounds plus aerial photographs, taken by himself, of several aerodromes.

Probably the most important recommendation in his report was:

The establishment of a properly constituted aviation company to operate feeder services etc in S. Rhodesia., N. Rhodesia and Nyasaland. This is considered desirable for the following reasons:

1) To protect the interests of Rhodesia Railways by assuring them a controlling interest in future air activity.
2) To supply aviation facilities required by:
    a) The respective governments.
    b) The public wishing to travel by air.
    c) Private owners of aircraft, including expert maintenance and repair service.
3) To ensure co-ordinated development of aviation in the area and to put an end to unsatisfactory competition between a number of local companies working without proper technical control and with inadequate financial backing.

In order to place the operation of the new company as soon as possible upon a profit-earning basis it is essential:

a) To secure the whole of the turn-over resulting from aviation in this area to the company.
b) To obtain for the company the permanent backing of all the governments concerned and the whole of the financial aid available in the form of subsidies.

It must be said that despite the sum of £50,000 being substantial, the cost of improving facilities all over Rhodesia was considerable and it was normally the function of the government to undertake this. The money was therefore aimed primarily at the facilities on the Imperial route with everything else being secondary to this. For example, in June 1934 the acting town clerk of Bulawayo informed Sir Henry Birchenough, a Beit trustee, that the cost of improving facilities at Bulawayo Aerodrome would be £27,250 (new buildings, a large hangar, night-landing lights, tarmac). This figure alone was over half of the grant available. In the event, in 1935 the Beit trustees gave £2,400 and £1,600 respectively towards night-landing facilities at Bulawayo and Salisbury aerodromes, with further assistance coming from the government.

After his return to the United Kingdom in April 1934, Nigel Norman continued in his capacity as consultant to the Trust until the grant was completely spent the following year. Shortly after his return, he recommended to H.H. Hitchcock that they consider the Meteor Garage (designed and built by the Horseley Bridge & Engineering Co. of Tipton, Staffordshire) as the most suitable type of hangar for use in the Rhodesias.

By 1935, after the majority of the recommendations in the report had been put in place; an aircraft flying over the Imperial Airways route over the Rhodesias was never more than 25 miles (40km) from a suitable landing ground, which had been the primary purpose of the Beit trustees' grant. In 1935 alone, thirteen new landing grounds had been opened and Umtali enlarged, primarily with the aid of the grant.

Rhodesian & Nyasaland Airways Ltd[2]

Nigel Norman's report was treated with great respect and his recommendations given all due consideration. Shortly after the submission of his report in mid-1933, on 4 August 1933 a meeting of the Rhodesian Aviation Company shareholders was held in Bulawayo. It was decided that the company affairs were to be handed over to a new company whose main shareholder would be the Beit Trust, and who would also have the controlling interest in the new company. Imperial Airways were also to become smaller shareholders in the new company as well as providing technical support. Rhodesia Railways were given the option of taking up shares should they wish to do so. The chairman of the new company was (later Sir) Henry Chapman CBE, who was the general manager of Rhodesia Railways. It was also pointed out at the meeting that the company in its current form was still losing money. Some of the loss was due to the provision of a new Salisbury–Johannesburg service.

In all, £25,000 in £1 shares was issued. The £1 shares in the Rhodesia Aviation Co. Ltd issued before 1 December 1932 were allowed to be purchased at 5s each, whilst shares purchased after that date had to be at the rate of £1. The sale took effect from 1 August 1933. The new company was to be known as Rhodesian and Nyasaland Airways Ltd, with its new headquarters initially at the Railway Offices in Bulawayo. The new airline (shortened to RANA) was formally incorporated on 12 October 1933. A subsidiary office was opened at 57 Stanley Avenue, Salisbury. Imperial Airways seconded Captain G.I. Thomson DFC as operations manager for the new airline and he was based in Salisbury.

Despite the fact that Nyasaland was included and would be served within the new airline, the grant of £50,000 made by the Beit Trust was explicitly for the improvement of facilities within

---

2 Rhodesian and Nyasaland Airways Ltd is the correct title, not Rhodesia and Nyasaland Airways Ltd.

Northern and Southern Rhodesia. Up to the formation of RANA, the Rhodesian Aviation Co. had received a yearly government grant of £500 plus a further £500 (also yearly) from the Beit Railway Trust. Financing had also been sought from the Mozambique Co. as it was proposed to operate a mail service (which it was hoped they would subsidise) from Blantyre and Salisbury to Beira under a concession which required permission from the Portuguese Government.

At this point Nigel Norman was still active in Rhodesian aviation matters and was regularly consulted for advice. The terms of his original appointment were that his period of tenure was to run until the grant of £50,000 from the Beit Railway Trust had been spent. It is perhaps surprising that Airwork were not invited to participate in the operation of the new airline. A letter from Nigel Norman to H.H. Hitchcock dated just prior to his return to London stated that he had been approached by individuals with a view to co-operation in the same way Airwork were then involved in Egypt, but that he had remained impartial as his position as adviser to the Beit Trust demanded. He did, however, float the idea to Henry Chapman of an outside concern like Airwork becoming involved, but neither Airwork nor any other organisation was invited to participate (other than the on/off negotiations with Imperial Airways).

Additionally, the philanthropic work of the Beit Railway Trust did not stop at the £50,000 initial grant. From the establishment of RANA, the trust had given £19,000 to the new airline in the first four years of operation.

The airline looked at possible new routes including tourist flights to Victoria Falls and to Kariba for fishing, although these did not materialise. A Midlands service was introduced linking Salisbury–Gatooma–Que Que–Gwelo–Bulawayo. However, a Bulawayo–Ndola service was discontinued in November 1935 due to poor passenger and freight figures. During 1935, the airline entered into a contract with the Northern Rhodesian Government to station a RANA aircraft at Lusaka permanently for the government's use.

The airline decided to move its headquarters from Bulawayo to Salisbury early in 1934. At this stage, the aircraft of the Rhodesian Aviation Co. formed the core of the new airline and two more aircraft (DH.80 Puss Moths VP-YAP and VP-YAR) were added in mid-February 1934 when Christowitz Air Services of Blantyre was absorbed by RANA.

By 1935, RANA employed a permanent staff of fifteen people which included seven 'B'-licensed pilots and four licensed ground engineers. During that year, the airline flew 2,315 flights with a route mileage of 315,249 miles (507,344km) carrying 3,351lb (1,520kg) of mail, 3,005lb (1,363kg) of freight and 2,319 passengers. Other activities undertaken by the airline included carrying out surveys for the Roads Department and searching for any missing aircraft. RANA was also called upon to assist in moving government officials and military stores during the 1935 riots in the Ndola Copper Belt.

The new airline was keen to acquire a large multi-engined aircraft and, pending delivery of their first DH.89A Dragon Rapide, a Westland Wessex G-ABEG was loaned by Imperial Airways. The Wessex was used by RANA until the first DH.89A Dragon Rapide, VP-YAU, was delivered in August 1935 (the first multi-engine aircraft to be registered in the colony). The Wessex G-ABEG was then loaned to DBR of Northern Rhodesia and written off in an accident at Chirundu in 1937.

RANA gradually expanded with further deliveries of aircraft in the following years: DH.90 Dragonflys YP-YAX in 1936 and VP-YBR in 1938; DH.89A Dragon Rapides VP-YBJ, YP-YBK in 1938 and VP-YBT, VP-YBU, VP-YBY and VP-YBZ in 1938; and DH.85 Leopard Moth VP-YCH in 1939.

In 1937 there were two developments, both involving Imperial Airways: the first was a new operations manager in January, when Captain Charles A. Barnard succeeded Captain Thomson; the second and more important was the introduction of the Empire Air Mail scheme in June. Imperial Airways had discontinued their Atalanta Class aircraft Central African route and replaced it with their C Class flying boat service on the East African coast route. Air mail has always been a good source of income for airlines and this was particularly so for new airlines during this period which were looking for income from any source as commercial passenger flying was in its infancy. Under the Empire Air Mail scheme, all first-class mail on empire routes was to be carried by air (where possible) and it was to be un-surcharged. Imperial Airways was appointed as contractor to the British Government and RANA became a sub-contractor to Imperial Airways. RANA operated a service to Beira to connect with the flying boat service to collect and deliver mail.

Up to this point in 1937, the role of the Beit Trust in assisting RANA to become a financially independent and viable airline cannot be understated. Then, as now, sufficient finance was the one ingredient that was vital to any new airline. Once the Empire Air Mail scheme was in operation, RANA became financially independent.

The introduction of larger-capacity aircraft in the form of the DH.90 Dragonfly and DH.89A Dragon Rapides enabled RANA, by 1938, to build up a scheduled route network. A Monday–Saturday service, operated in conjunction with South African Airways (SAA), linked Salisbury–Bulawayo–Pietersburg–Johannesburg with passenger-request stops at Gatoma, Que Que and Gwelo. The aforementioned Midlands service (Salisbury–Gatooma–Que Que–Gwelo–Bulawayo), introduced shortly after the formation of the airline, continued with a Leopard Moth flying the route in both directions twice weekly. However, this was primarily an empire mail-carrying service by 1938, although there was a limited passenger-carrying service operated.

The grandly named Empire Route Connection (London), although the UK terminus was actually Southampton, left Salisbury for Beira on Sundays and Thursdays, with the return flights on Mondays and Thursdays. The journey took two and a half hours in each direction and connected with the twice-weekly Imperial Airways C Class flying boat Southampton–Durban service. RANA also operated the following scheduled services at this time: a once-weekly Blantyre–Beira service; a twice-weekly Salisbury–Lusaka service; a twice-weekly Salisbury–Blantyre–Lilongwe–Fort Jameson (with a passenger-request stop at Zomba); and a twice-weekly Salisbury–Umtali–Beira service (with a passenger-request stop at Rusape).

With the exception of the Blantyre–Beira service, the other three were all advertised as connecting with the Imperial Airways service either directly or through immediate connections. A timetable note reminded all passengers using their own transport to arrive at least fifteen minutes before departure.

With the arrival of the Second World War, RANA and its assets, along with its staff, was taken over by the Southern Rhodesia Government on 1 February 1940 to become Southern Rhodesia Air Services (SRAS), in effect becoming a combined communications and airline squadron for the air force. The name of RANA lay on the register of companies with the intention of reviving it later. However, at the end of the war, the Federation of Rhodesia and Nyasaland formed Central African Airways Corporation (known as CAA) on 1 June 1946 and RANA went into voluntary liquidation on 8 July 1946.

RANA occupies a special place in commercial aviation history. Although there were mishaps and accidents with the aircraft during its six years of operation, there was not one fatality or serious injury to any passenger or staff member. A remarkable achievement considering the hazards of flying in the bush in Central Africa, plus the fact the aircraft were basic and not equipped with the modern aids of today.

After the break-up of the Federation in 1963 and the independence of Northern Rhodesia (Zambia) and Nyasaland (Malawi), three separate subsidiary companies of CAA were formed: Air Malawai, Zambia Airways and Air Rhodesia, with CAA continuing to operate on behalf of each airline. After the Unilateral Declaration of Independence by Rhodesia in 1965, the tripartite airline system became unworkable and CAA was broken up into its separate national entities in 1967. Air Rhodesia continued until 1979, when it became Air Zimbabwe Rhodesia and then changed to Air Zimbabwe in 1980 after independence.

The Role of Imperial Airways

Despite the fact that the original purpose of the Beit Railway Trust grant had been to improve facilities for the Cape to Cairo route within Rhodesia, with the 'spin off' of improving aviation and aviation facilities within the colony itself, a number of parties in Northern and Southern Rhodesia viewed Imperial Airways with ambivalence at best.

The route to both the Cape and London was obviously of great benefit, but many felt that the airline had little interest in the colonies and only looked to what would benefit themselves, particularly in the case of any joint ventures. Early correspondence between the Beit Railway Trust and the chairman of Imperial Airways shows that the airline wanted finance to improve the landing grounds in Tanganyika first, followed by Sudan rather than Rhodesia – something the Trust was not prepared to consider. A letter dated 1 March 1933 from Nigel Norman to H.H. Hitchcock discusses the breakdown of negotiations between Imperial Airways and local aviation interests (the Rhodesian Aviation Co.) in Bulawayo. In the letter Norman states:

> I find that negotiations with Imperial Airways for their acquisition of this company have fallen through and that responsible people here think it is not unfortunate. Personally I also am inclined to the view that were this local company to be entirely in the hands of the Imperial Airways the local flying requirements of the colony might be subjugated to the interests of the Trunk Line Service, whose object would, of course, be to bring traffic to their own line, and would not be prepared to take any risks in providing local facilities which would stimulate the development of the country.

In fairness to Imperial Airways, they wished to provide the best service they could and a letter from them to the Trust dated 7 March 1932 expressed concern at the condition of landing grounds between Kenya and Rhodesia during the rainy season, which reduced loads to such an extent that it meant passengers could not be carried on occasions. The airline hoped that a portion of the £50,000 grant would go towards improving the landing grounds and bring them up to an acceptable condition. This view was a departure from their first standpoint of wanting the finance to go to improving landing grounds in Sudan as well as Tanganyika.

In the separate matter of a partnership with a new Rhodesian airline, a memorandum of a meeting in Salisbury on 3 April 1933 between Sir James McDonald, Major Hudson (Minister of Defence and Air for Southern Rhodesia) and Nigel Norman again discussed approaches by Major Walker of Imperial Airways and the view prevailed that, as far as aviation was concerned, the colony would be better served by a company which was not under the financial or technical control of Imperial Airways.

The 1937 move to the Mozambique coast of the trunk route from Rhodesia showed that Imperial Airways had a fairly short-term view and acted only in their own interests, albeit whilst still providing a service. However, operational criteria came before the interest of the colonies.

Conclusions

It is sometimes said that Airwork 'started' the Rhodesian national airline, which is not correct in the same sense that say Airwork had a substantial involvement in the establishment of the current Egyptian national airline EgyptAir. It would, however, be fair to say that Airwork in the form of Nigel Norman played a significant role in the establishment of the Rhodesian national airline and that his visit and survey, and his report, along with his later advice and suggestions during the implementation phase, brought a focus and acted as a catalyst to establishing the airline.

If any credit is to be given for starting the Rhodesian national airline, then that credit should really go to Sir Alfred Beit and the Beit Railway Trust, who provided the finance and a guiding hand in the shape of their tireless secretary, H.H. Hitchcock, who seemed to be anywhere and everywhere in both London and Southern Rhodesia arranging meetings, providing reports, making suggestions and pulling all the disparate parts together with the sole principle of what was best for Rhodesia.

AIRWORK & THE ROYAL RHODESIAN AIR FORCE

Airwork had formed a holding company (Airwork Holdings Ltd, registered on 4 April 1935) to deal with Rhodesian interests. The company was used for the start of their contract in 1959 servicing RRAF (Royal Rhodesian Air Force, later Rhodesian Air Force or Air Force of Zimbabwe) aircraft in a hangar belonging to the air force at the New Sarum Base, which was part of Salisbury Airport. The first general manager was Wing Commander Tidy RAF (Ret.). The aircraft serviced were initially RRAF Douglas C-47s and Percival Pembrokes, upon which minor and major servicing was carried out. The servicing of the C-47s and Pembrokes had previously been carried out by the RRAF at New Sarum Air Base at Salisbury Airport and Fields Aviation Company at Bulawayo before being taken over by Airwork. Airwork then moved to their own hangar on the civilian side of Salisbury Airport in around 1964. The work carried out for the RRAF expanded to include servicing the RRAF's Vampire FB.9 and T.11, and Hawker Hunter FGA.9. Most of the Airwork technical staff were ex-RAF with a few civilian trained personnel.

UDI & the Insurgency

The Unilateral Declaration of Independence (UDI) on 11 November 1965 brought many changes. The maintenance and servicing work carried out by Airwork was always supplementary to that carried out by the Rhodesian air force (RhAF) which had its own staff and facilities for carrying out its maintenance. However, once UDI was declared and the insurgency started in earnest, the operations and flying hours carried out by the air force shot up accordingly, leaving the air force having to pass on more and more of the work to Airwork. In later years (up to 1980) a useful source of recruitment was ex-RhAF technicians who had retired but had the knowledge required, having worked on air force aircraft during their service. The size of the

English Electric Canberra B.2 R2510 returning to the Airwork hangar at Salisbury Airport after a flight test in April 1971. This aircraft crashed off the end of runway 06 at Salisbury on 16 November 1971. (Robin Norton)

Airwork facility at Salisbury grew to occupy three hangars with a work force which varied from time to time, but as a rule at the busiest periods consisted of up to sixty-five staff comprising thirty staff working on airframes, one radio fitter, four instrument technicians, six electrical engineers, one spray painter, six engine technicians/engineers, three administration staff, ten general labourers, two armourers and one storeman.

UDI also brought other problems in the political arena. The Southern Rhodesian Government under Ian Smith was declared an 'illegal regime' by the British Government. As a British company, Airwork were forced to distance themselves from the operation in Rhodesia, but still carried on operations as normal with no dilution of its shareholding in the Rhodesian company. The political arguments are, however, well covered elsewhere.

Although Airwork were originally handling work on the C-47s and Pembroke C.1s, with the huge increase in work caused by the insurgency, the full range of aircraft in the RhAF came to be handled by Airwork. These included Vampire FB.9 and T.11, Hunter FGA.9, Canberra B.2, Canberra T.4, Reims Cessna FTB337G 'Lynx', Aermacchi AL-60-L2l 'Trojan', Hunting Percival Provost T.52, Douglas DC-7CF, Cessna 421A, BN Islander and Cessna 185 Skywagon (two were impressed into service).

All rotary maintenance and servicing work for the air force was carried out by Rhotair, a completely separate private company with no connection to Airwork.

The three hangars (most recently commissioned in April 1982) which were owned by Airwork, mostly for their air force work, were sold to Huntings in December 1995 and subsequently demolished in 1997 to make way for the new terminal building at Harare Airport.

Post-Independence

After independence in April 1980, the new Air Force of Zimbabwe either lost or got rid of its experienced technical personnel. Airwork then took over the daily running of squadrons at New Sarum and Thornhill (Airwork owned a block of flats for personnel at Thornhill). Airwork also at that point provided technical lecturers for No. 1 Ground Training School at New Sarum (which was renamed Manyame Air Base). Eight BAe Hawk Mk 60s were delivered in 1982 to join the nine remaining Hunter FGA.9s. These were followed by 12 F-7s (export version of the Chengdu Jian-7).

The Airwork link with the Air Force of Zimbabwe was finally terminated in December 1993 after local interests had formed an organisation to take over the functions performed by the company.

RUAC/UAC

RUAC (Rhodesia United Air Carriers) was formed in 1957 from a number of small charter companies: Air Carriers Ltd, Flights (1956) Ltd of Salisbury and Fishair of Victoria Falls. Victoria Falls Airways joined later. Air Carriers was owned by Hunting Clan Africa Airways, a subsidiary of the maritime Clan Line. In August 1960 Commercial Air Services (Rhodesia) of Bulawayo was integrated into RUAC following the formation of British United Airways. Airwork Ltd in the UK had a 50 per cent shareholding (acquired in 1948) in Commercial Air Services, Bulawayo, Rhodesia through their ownership of Commercial Air Services, South Africa. This gave Airwork Ltd in the UK a 51 per cent shareholding in RUAC through their holding company, which was Air Carriers. The remaining 49 per cent was held by UTOS (United Transport Overseas Services), who had their Head Office in London before being transferred to their subsidiary, the United Tour Group. This 49 per cent had originally been split with another company which was bought out by UTOS in the 1960s. RUAC was to become the biggest and most successful business air charter operator and tourist pleasure flight company in Central Africa.

From 1957 to its sale to Hunting Airmotive in 1995, RUAC was run by three people: Colman Meyers, who had started the company in 1957 to 1978; Charles Paxton (an ex-RRAF group captain) to 1986; and Carole Brooks until 1995. Carole Brooks stayed with the company for two further years to oversee its merger with Zambesi Air Services (the charter company already owned by Hunting). RUAC was the dream of Colman Meyers, an aviator of Jewish descent who started flying during the Second World War and had great experience of flying in Africa. Immediately after the war, he had been involved in the flying training in Johannesburg of new pilots for the fledgling Israeli air force.

After the merger with Comair in 1960, the fleet was increased to ten aircraft and was poised to expand further. RUAC also became the Beechcraft agents for Central Africa. There were three bases at the start of RUAC's operations: Salisbury Airport was the main base and maintenance centre, with further bases at Bulawayo Main Airport and Victoria Falls. The main airport at Victoria Falls was some miles away in Livingstone (now Zambia), but through its prior acquisition of Victoria Falls Airways, RUAC became the leaseholder of Sprayview Aerodrome, which was less than a mile from the Falls. Sprayview had originally been the main airfield for the region and had become too short for scheduled passenger flights, but was eminently suitable for light aircraft operations.

Despite the problems created by UDI, RUAC continued to prosper. There were concessions to the growing insurgency as the aircraft were all painted in matt grey and, where practical, engine exhaust outlets were moved above the engines of the aircraft to avoid SAM-7 Strela shoulder-launched missiles supplied to the insurgents.

RUAC's three main areas of business were:

1   The Head Office and main base at Salisbury, which was devoted to business light aircraft charters and general aviation maintenance.
2   The second branch at Victoria Falls, which was for tourist flights and was also a maintenance base.
3   The third branch at Bulawayo, which concentrated on scheduled flights to the Lowveld. Business charter and general aviation maintenance was also carried out at Bulawayo.

Operations & Aircraft

From the above areas of business, the most lucrative for the company were the tourist flights at Victoria Falls known as 'The Flight of Angels'. These flights of ten to fifteen minutes' duration over the Victoria Falls from Sprayview were so popular that RUAC took out a trademark on the term 'Flight of Angels', which had come from explorer David Livingstone's description of the Victoria Falls when he first discovered them in 1855: 'Scenes so lovely must have been gazed upon by Angels in their flight.'

During the mid-1990s, the Victoria Falls operation ran into difficulties when the government informed United Air that they wanted the Sprayview airfield for housing and terminated the lease. The carrier was forced to use the Victoria Falls Airport which was some considerable distance away and added ten minutes' flying time in each direction, which obviously impacted on running costs. The loss of Sprayview airfield almost killed off the operation at Victoria Falls. The immediate problem was solved by the lease of a helicopter (Bell Jet Ranger Z-WLY) which could still operate out of Sprayview for sightseeing flights. By the time of the sale of the business in 1995, Sprayview was closed to all flying operations and is now covered with houses.

In the early days, the scheduled flights from Bulawayo to the Lowveld were operated on behalf of the national airline, Central African Airways. These were later suspended and replaced by their larger aircraft. Business charters were also operated from Bulawayo. After a break of many years and after the Bulawayo operation had been closed down, the Lowveld flights were reinstated and operated by BN2 Islanders and, latterly, BN3 Trislanders. Scheduled flights from Bulawayo to Kariba were also carried out but were not successful. A twice-daily service was

Two BN3 Trislanders Z-AIR and Z-UTD. Both were ex-Botswana Defence Force aircraft and arrived in Harare still in their original military camouflage. (Carole Brooks)

also operated from the late 1970s until 1995 between Kariba and Bumi Hills Safari Lodge, which was a fifteen-minute flight. The aircraft used for this service would vary depending on the passenger load and were originally sent up from Harare until a permanent base with offices and passenger lounge was established in 1990.

Cloud seeding was also carried out from Harare Airport. The contract was with the Meteorological Department and was to seed clouds over the catchment area of the newly built Kyle Dam, which was to supply irrigation for the Lowveld. Cessna 210 VP-YLT was bought specifically for this purpose. It was so successful that the contract was extended to the whole country during the rainy season, when two or three aircraft were used. Beech Baron BE-55s with specially modified doors were used in addition to the Cessna 210 VP-KLY.

The BN3 Trislanders (ex-OE 1 and OE 2, carrying civil registrations A2-AGX and A2-AGY) were bought from the Botswana Defence Force and, despite their age, they had very low flying hours. As the sale was from the Botswana military to a civil Zimbabwe operator, it was not without problems. Carole Brooks, the managing director of RUAC, travelled to Gabarone with two BN2 Islander pilots and an engineer to collect the aircraft and bring them to Harare, but it took over a week to complete the formalities in Gabarone and fly the aircraft to their new home on 21 February 1991. The Trislanders finally arrived in Harare still in their Botswana military camouflage to be repainted in the United Air colours and given registrations Z-AIR and Z-UTD. After a Check III, both aircraft were given their first air test in their new livery on 11 March 1991.

Having the main base at Harare International Airport gave UAC (United Air Charters) an advantage as they were the only general aviation operators there, with any competitors having to use Charles Prince Airport (formerly Mount Hampden, an ex-Second World War base) on the other side of the city, although UAC also had a smaller base at Charles Prince Airport. Latterly, the largest of the GAA hangars at Harare International Airport (leased by the company from Airwork) was known as the Light Aircraft Terminal and provided facilities for resident and visiting corporate aircraft. Altogether there were six GAA hangars grouped together at Harare Airport. Two were owned by UAC, three by Airwork and the sixth by Anglo American Corporation, but leased by UAC for many years as a maintenance facility. By 1994, the company was using all six for its operations. By 1997, they were removed to make way for the new international terminal.

Independence

After independence in 1979 and the adoption of Zimbabwe to replace Rhodesia, the name Rhodesia United Air Carriers was unacceptable to the new government. The proposal only to use the abbreviated name of the company RUAC (Pvt) Ltd was also turned down as it still contained the initial for Rhodesia. The name United Air Charters (Pvt) Ltd was settled upon. The camouflage scheme on all aircraft was replaced and they were all painted in the same standard fleet colours, which was a blue lines colour scheme on a white background with the name 'United Air' painted in blue on the fuselage.

Reorganisation by Airwork

Despite being a majority shareholder in RUAC, Airwork had no representation on the Board of Directors. Generally Airwork Ltd was satisfied with an overview of the company's proceedings and regular visits from the Head Office in Britain. Airwork Zimbabwe had nothing whatsoever to do with the running of RUAC or indeed any involvement with Airwork's shareholding in the company. This situation changed in the 1980s with the reorganisation of the company over the 1988 to 1991 period. Carole Brooks, who had been made deputy general manager then general manager, was made managing director. Of the five directors, two of the positions were given to Airwork Zimbabwe representatives, with the remaining three director positions given to representatives of the United Touring Company, who were the company's biggest customers in the Victoria Falls operation.

End of Airwork's Involvement

As the tourism industry in Zimbabwe was changing, UTC had decided to dispose of their 49 per cent shareholding in the company. In November 1995 the entire 100 per cent shareholding in United Air Charters was sold to Hunting Airmotive in Zimbabwe, which was part of the Hunting Group in the UK. At the same time the three hangars belonging to Airwork were also sold to Hunting.

In 1988 Airwork became part of Bricom Group Ltd. Prior to 1993, Bricom became indebted to the Swedish bank Nordbanken and was one of its $8.67 billion worth of un-performing assets. As part of the Nordbanken rescue, Securum AB (Sweden) was formed in 1993 with Swedish Government backing. Its mandate was to act as a specialised company that either reorganised or disposed of these toxic assets to extract maximum value from them for the ultimate benefit of the Swedish taxpayer.

In 1993 Short Brothers of Belfast (which had been bought by the Canadian company Bombardier Inc. in 1989) acquired Airwork as a wholly owned subsidiary from Securum Industrial Holdings. Bombardier decided that they did not want the Zimbabwean part of the operation and thus the Airwork-owned companies and 51 per cent shareholding in United Air Charters became the property of Securum. Because of the loss of the Air Force of Zimbabwe contract, the political uncertainty and the declining value of the Zimbabwe currency, Securum decided to disinvest in Zimbabwe.

Carole Brooks, the managing director of United Air Charters, was given the responsibility of managing the disinvestment project, which took two years to complete (1995–97). This extremely complex exercise involved nine companies (Air Carriers, United Air Charters, Airwork Services, Air Holdings, Embankment Investments, Dalmatia House, Union Castle Mail Steamship Company, Hunting Clan (Africa) Airways and Manbeira). Embankment Investments was a wholly owned Airwork Zimbabwe subsidiary which had been formed after UDI when strict exchange control measures were put in place. This meant that profits from Airwork operations, apart from an annual management fee, were not allowed to be repatriated. The profits and any buildings owned by Airwork were put into Embankment Investments, who continued to invest in property until the early 1990s and were the most asset-rich company in the group.

The properties involved were the three Airwork hangars at Harare Airport, a large warehouse in the industrial area of Harare, a large three-storey double shop and offices in the Harare central business district, two very large residences in the Harare suburbs, one block of four prestigious townhouses in Harare city, one block of fourteen flats in the Harare suburbs and one block of flats in Gweru. The latter two blocks were occupied by Airwork staff at New Sarum and Thornhill air bases.

23

SAUDI ARABIA

TRAINING MISSION AT TAIF, SAUDI ARABIA

In February 1947 approval was given for BOAC to conduct a two-year mission at Taif in Saudi Arabia in order to promote flying training and hopefully also to promote an interest in British-made aircraft for purchasing. The intention was for BOAC to provide an Avro XIX and two DH.82A Tiger Moths with two pilot instructors and a ground engineer. The Avro XIX was to be used for administrative purposes as well as demonstrations. Training on the Tiger Moths was to be *ab initio* up to 'A' licence standard for between eight and ten pupils in each of the two years. It was envisaged that eight of the most promising students would go on to the UK for further training up to 'B' licence and Second Navigation Certificate standard. The total estimated cost of the proposed programme was £84,500 with a capital outlay of £27,000 plus £7,500 for the training in the UK at £750 each per pupil.

The Saudi Arabian Government accepted the offer and proposals in mid-March 1947. However, BOAC ran into various difficulties with the project and delays started to build up. Basically, BOAC were unable to meet their commitments. The MCA, who had been handling arrangements for the government, agreed that Airwork should take over the contract from BOAC. The situation was almost tailor-made for Airwork with their long experience of training along with considerable overseas experience and, in particular, Middle Eastern experience.

Captain Charles Pritchard of Airwork flew out to Taif on 13 May 1947 to meet the Saudi Government representative, Amir Mansour. He returned at the end of May with an agreement he had reached with the Amir to establish the British Civil Air Training Mission to Saudi Arabia.

An Avro Anson, G-AIXY (ex-MG966) was purchased and registered to Airwork on 7 August 1947, plus two Tiger Moths from the Middlesex Flying Club at Denham, which were all earmarked for the new endeavour. Two engineers left for Saudi Arabia via sea on board the SS *Lycaon* on 13 September 1947 with the Tiger Moths on board.

At the same time as the departure of the engineers and Tiger Moths, Wing Commander R. Black, the chief instructor of Airwork, also left for Taif to become the head of mission and chief

DH.89A G-AKTZ was used by the British Civil Air Training Mission at Taif, Saudi Arabia, prior to use by Birkett Air Services. (John Havers collection)

pilot. Finally, on 11 November 1947, the Anson G-AIXY arrived at Jeddah en route to Taif. On board were: Lieutenant Commander Herbert Frank Bromwich RN (Ret.), who piloted the Anson and was the second-in-command of the new mission; Squadron Leader P.W. Herbert; W.W. Cook (navigator); R.W. Wisson (radio officer); and C.W. Stapleforth (engineer). The Anson left for Taif and returned to Jeddah the following day, with Wing Commander Black and two instructors (Bromwich and Herbert) to collect the two Tiger Moths.

Further staff arrived during this period: J.N. Wilson (the Link Trainer instructor); chief engineer Geoff Lawson; and his assistant W. McLoughlin. The two engineers who had arrived on the SS *Lycaon* with the Tiger Moths were R.W. Ross and Mr Stapleforth. Further staff followed: Pilot Mike Collins; navigator and radio operator Arthur Parnell; engineer Bill Spavin; and another engineer Gerry Tonkin, who replaced Geoff Lawson. Some wives of the staff joined their husbands in what must have been fairly basic conditions.

Official training with the first intake of Saudi trainee pilots began on 16 November 1947 at Hawiya airfield, which was 18 miles (29km) from Taif. The airfield was 4,500ft (1,372m) above sea level on the edge of the Hejaz Mountains, which were 5,000ft (1,525m) above sea level. There were no hangars at Hawiya airfield and accommodation was mainly in tents.

By the end of November 1947, Amir Mansour, the Saudi Government representative, had requested that the scope of the mission be extended by Airwork. The flying continued in the arduous conditions and by August 1948 a further Tiger Moth was added to the mission's inventory. As all the aircraft were still British registered, they had to be inspected by Oliver Smart, the Air Registration Board surveyor based in Cairo. He arrived at Hawiya in August 1948 and described the conditions as deplorable, stating that the landing strip was a flat piece of desert miles away from the town with no buildings.

In February and March 1949 high winds had curtailed flying, but up to this point seventeen of the nineteen cadets had flown solo, although there had been accidents and incidents. Tiger Moth G-AITH was damaged beyond repair at Hawiya on 2 February 1949 by a solo pupil flying too low. A further problem occurred on 4 April 1949 when Tiger Moth G-AITI damaged its propeller and the only replacement had been damaged in a fire, so the propeller from G-AKCM (which was on its CoA renewal) was used to replace it. Only four days later, G-AITI was again damaged when a pupil lifted the tail and it slipped from his hand, which caused the aircraft to stand on its nose and damaged the replacement propeller. With no spare propellers, flying training on the Tiger Moths ceased until two replacements were flown out at the end of April 1949. Once the propellers arrived and G-AKCM had its CoA renewed, two Tiger Moths were back in use for training. A third Tiger Moth, G-AKCG, arrived to replace G-AITH. However, when G-AKCG was being unloaded from the ship at Jeddah docks, the box was dropped from the crane unloading the Tiger Moth, and some damage was caused.

Avro Anson G-AIXY, which was being used as a navigation trainer, also had its share of problems. In April 1949, it suffered an engine failure on take-off. It then went to Jeddah and was detained there awaiting spares. G-AIXY was also experiencing other mechanical difficulties and a decision was taken to replace it.

In May 1949 the contract for the operation of the mission was extended for a further year and in July 1949 ten Saudi pupils were sent to the UK for further advanced training to enable the trainee pilots to operate the Bristol 170s that had just been bought by Saudi Arabian Airlines. Five of the trainee pilots went to air service training at Hamble and the other five went to Airwork's school at Perth's Scone Aerodrome. Training continued at Taif with a proposal that the establishment should change from an EFTS (Elementary Flying Training School) to a Grading School.

The CoA on Anson G-AIXY expired in September 1949 and it was replaced by one of Airwork's DH.89A Rapides G-AKTZ. The fate of Anson G-AIXY remains a mystery. On the one hand, it was recorded as having been scrapped at Hawiya airfield; however, one of the mission members, Gerry Tonkin, stated that the Anson was being flown back to the UK for overhaul. After leaving Cairo, it developed engine trouble. To save weight as much as possible was thrown out of the aircraft, including personal items, to keep it in the air so they could reach Tobruk or El Adem. It was to prove fruitless and the Anson had to make a forced landing in the desert. The landing area turned out to be a minefield, but the crew were able to evacuate safely and the aircraft was left to its fate.

In September 1950 a valuation was made of the aircraft and spares prior to the termination of the contract at the end of that month. In October 1950, the Saudi pilots had completed their training and, despite having had civilian training, the intention of the Saudi Government was to use them as the nucleus of the new Saudi air force. Wing Commander Black hoped that the pupils at Perth would be used for civilian purposes. Sadly, Black died suddenly on a visit to London on 6 November 1950.

Shortly after this, Squadron Leader Herbert became adviser to Amir Mansour. As a result, many of the Saudi pilots training in the UK were attached to the RAF for further training. Thus ended Airwork's training mission to Saudi Arabia at the end of 1950, but it would not be the end of their involvement with the desert kingdom.

THE SAUDI ARABIAN AIR DEFENCE SCHEME, 1966–73

Background

There were two main elements driving the establishment of the Saudi Arabian Air Defence Scheme. The first was the problem with the Egyptian support of the regime in Yemen. The Saudis have always been acutely aware of the unique position they occupy in the Arab world as the heartland of Islam, and have always maintained an obsessive concern in protecting their borders. The second was the desire of Harold Wilson's Labour government to try to maintain British influence east of Suez, to put it bluntly, as cheaply as possible and at the same time to sell British arms, equipment and associated services to help pay for the purchase of the US General Dynamics F1-11s for the RAF. In northern Yemen, a civil war had broken out in which the Saudis gave their backing to the royalist Muhammad al-Badr against the Egyptian-backed republican Abdullah al-Sallal. The Egyptians sent military help in the form of 20,000 troops and Egyptian air force Ilyushin Il-28s and MiG-17s. The Egyptian air force aircraft made a number of incursions into Saudi territory, attacking the Saudi-backed northern Yemen royalists. This was a situation which was intolerable to the Saudis, who had no real means to defend the border. There were greater concerns underlying the problem of the incursions. Egypt was backed by the USSR and the Yemen Arab Republic, with its Egyptian patrons representing a threat not only to the Saudis but also to the south, to British interests in Aden.

John Stonehouse, the Parliamentary Secretary to the Ministry of Aviation (later to fall into disgrace in 1974) in the first Wilson government, was a strong supporter of arms sales to the Saudi Government. He was supported by Geoffrey Edwards, a former RAF officer who was then living in Saudi Arabia with links to Prince Sultan bin Abdul Aziz, the Saudi Minister of Defence and Aviation. Edwards acted as a middleman to set up the deal involving BAC, Associated Electrical Industries and Airwork Services Ltd, with Airwork providing ground support and pilot training. The pivotal issue was the purchase of the F1-11s for the RAF and scrapping of the TSR2 programme, which left Britain badly needing the contract to provide finance for the purchase of the US aircraft. This in turn led to US Government support for a joint Anglo-American bid which would provide British aircraft and radar along with a US missile defence system.

The package was worth £100 million and included the purchase of forty BAC Lightnings, twenty-five BAC 167 Strikemasters, radar stations and the Hawk SAM system provided by Raytheon. Airwork were to provide training and technical support services with the Airwork 'slice' estimated at £30 million (shared with Raytheon).

The Magic Carpet Scheme, 1966–67

Whilst the incursions died down during the period of negotiations regarding the Air Defence Scheme, relations between Saudi Arabia and its southern neighbour and Egypt were very low. Prior to the finalisation of any deal, the Saudi Government were anxious to meet any renewed attacks on their territory. However, although there were Saudi F-86s stationed at Dhahran, there was neither the will nor the support to enable them to challenge the Egyptian Il-28s and MiG-17s. Khamis Mushayt was the only base near the border area (54 miles [87km] away) and had only the most basic of facilities with no road links.

Prince Sultan paid an urgent visit to London in February 1966 and requested the loan of an RAF squadron to fly under Saudi colours. It was a request which the British Government could not agree to in light of Britain's attempts to disengage itself from the imperialist role. However, it left the government in a quandary as they were keen to help and did not wish to jeopardise negotiations for the Air Defence Scheme. Additionally, the announcement in that February, that Britain was withdrawing from Aden, made the Saudis understandably nervous of the situation on their southern border. Equally nervous were members of the British Government who were worried that the potential £75 million purchase of BAC Lightnings might not go ahead. Burke Trend, the Cabinet secretary, outlined the dilemma in a memo to the prime minister in which he stated at the end that 'We are therefore under a moral obligation to give them a minimum of military support'.

Whilst Prince Sultan's request for an operational RAF squadron was turned down, he was offered the inducement of Airwork flight instructors to operate Saudi aircraft. With the pressing need for air defence being the top priority of the Saudi Government, a preliminary contract was signed ahead of the main Air Defence Scheme contract to provide the Saudis with some reassurance that their requirements would be met with the by-product of keeping them interested in following through with the main contract.

This preliminary contract was known as 'Magic Carpet' and was signed on 28 March 1966. It provided for six BAC Lightnings (four single-seat and two two-seat trainers) and six Hawker Hunters to be refurbished and made available as quickly as possible. Additionally, under the contract, a Thunderbird anti-aircraft missile would be provided by the British army and AEI would supply four radar systems. Airwork were to provide all necessary personnel to operate and maintain the equipment and aircraft, including '12 operational pilots'. All the aircraft and equipment were earmarked for the airfield at Khamis Mushayt.

Equipment and personnel began to arrive in Saudi Arabia in early 1966, with the first twenty Airwork service technicians arriving in January of that year. However, they had to be stationed at Riyadh as facilities at Khamis Mushayt were still not ready and, in fact, did not become available until early 1967. Riyadh was too far from the border with Yemen for any effective response to Egyptian attacks, of which there were more in October 1966. The force started moving into Khamis Mushayt in early 1967. By this time there were over 250 Airwork staff (mainly technicians and controllers) based at Khamis Mushayt.

Four Hawker Hunter F.6s, which had the designations F.60 assigned to them, arrived along with two two-seater T.66 trainers designated T.70. The Hawker Hunters were to act as a transition platform between the BAC Strikemaster and the BAC Lightning. The Hunters arrived in 1966 ahead of the Lightnings, and although they were intended as a kind of midway trainer to the Lightning, they were also intended to act initially as a show of force to the Egyptian incursions and they saw some action on the border.

However, there was Saudi dissatisfaction with the preparedness of the force as only one Lightning and one Hunter was operational. In effect, the Saudis felt that Airwork were not fulfilling their contractual responsibilities. In January 1967, after attacks by the Egyptians on Saudi towns near the Yemen border, Prince Sultan complained to the British ambassador (Morgan Man) on 30 January that apart from only one aircraft of each type being operational, Airwork pilots were not prepared to fly combat missions. The threat was made to cancel both the Magic Carpet contract and the much larger Air Defence Scheme contract if Airwork did not start to meet their contractual responsibilities.

The MCA looked to Airwork for their side of the story, which was that basically the Saudi Government wanted results at speeds which could not be delivered. There was great pressure to put the aircraft into service without any delay. This, combined with the lack of facilities at Khamis Mushayt and poor road links to the air base, left Airwork struggling to satisfy the Saudis' wish for an immediate air defence system that worked. To be fair to the Saudis, they had paid their money and wanted to see something for it. Airwork pledged to have eight pilots operational by mid-February 1967.

BAC 167 Strikemaster Mk 80A 1120. A total of forty-five Strikemasters were sold to the RSAF; 1120 was built in 1974 and eventually came on to the British register as G-RSAF. (Via Bob Pugh)

However, finding operational pilots for advanced fighter aircraft was not so easy. There was also the murky question of the term 'mercenary'. In the event, the solution found by Airwork was to encourage a number of pilots to leave their Airwork contract and sign up directly with the Saudi Government through the agent ex-RAF officer Geoffrey Edwards. The pilots were paid through Edwards by Airwork using proceeds from the Magic Carpet contract. In the event it was possibly the only solution, with Airwork and the British Government seemingly distancing themselves partially from the unsavoury allegations of aiding and abetting mercenary or imperialistic activities. Some of the pilots complained that they had signed up as instructors and not to take part in combat operations. However, substantial tax-free salaries of £10,000 p.a. helped to smooth ruffled feathers. The British Government view was officially that the pilots were not to engage in any combat, but their tacit approval was evident as the overwhelming desire was not to jeopardise either contract at any cost. In any event, by the third week of February 1967, patrols were mounted along the border with the Yemen Arab Republic and the Egyptian incursions ceased.

The ground crews were not so handsomely rewarded, however, and when orders were issued in late February 1967 for aircraft to be prepared for possible combat operations, they realised they were going to have to support offensive operations from the Khamis Mushayt base. There were a number of complaints from the Airwork staff to Members of Parliament, the Ministry of Defence and the British Embassy in Saudi Arabia. Their concerns were that by arming aircraft and generally preparing and servicing aircraft for offensive operations, they were leaving their status open to misinterpretation that they were simply mercenaries. Their fear was that, in turn, this would lead to loss of their pension rights (many were ex-British servicemen) and potentially loss of citizenship. Sixty of the Airwork staff had signed a letter which was sent to the Airwork Services general manager J.H. Hopkins in mid-February 1967 which stated that they had not been hired to service 'operationally armed aircraft' and demanded a re-negotiation of their contracts.

The ground crews were given assurances that their positions were legally separate from that of the pilots. In truth, little distinction could be made but the government was keen to play the situation down. The assurance was given by the Foreign and Commonwealth Office that:

> While we naturally hope that their personnel will not become engaged in any hostilities, we assume that the risk is in practice confined to their involvement in defensive operations in the event of an attack on Saudi Arabian territory. In such circumstances their pensions should not be at risk. Still less is there any risk of loss of UK citizenship.

In spite of the problems, the airfield was brought up to operational status by Airwork. The Hunters were first to arrive at Khamis Mushayt. The first two Lightnings arrived there on 7 August 1967, with two more arriving on 9 August 1967. The final two arrived just over a week later. Full operational status was achieved with all aircraft, air crew and support on 13 November 1967. By February 1968, Khamis Mushayt had six BAC Lightnings, five Hawker Hunters, fourteen pilots, a working radar system, over 170 supervisory and ground-support personnel, along with a full range of storage and domestic buildings. Notwithstanding all the aforementioned problems and the logistical issues associated with the remoteness of Khamis Mushayt, it was a considerable achievement by Airwork. Despite the achievement, the RAF had to give up two Thunderbird squadrons and thirteen of its BAC Lightnings. There was also considerable British Government involvement with the Saudi Government and Airwork, which had been the opposite of what had been the intention at the outset.

The Magic Carpet contract ended on 31 March 1968 with the arrival of Pakistani administrative and technical personnel at Khamis Mushayt.

The Main Contract: The Saudi Arabian Air Defence Scheme, 1967–73

Despite the ongoing problems with the Magic Carpet contract, negotiations for the main Air Defence Scheme continued. Although BAC had signed a contract in early 1966 to supply the aircraft to the RSAF, the negotiations continued for a year and a half over the required servicing and training portion of the contract. The Saudis put pressure on to get as much as possible out of the deal whilst driving a very hard financial bargain. Prince Sultan threatened to cancel the entire contract in September 1966 when it was found that Airwork's costs, and therefore prices to the Saudis, had risen considerably. Airwork representatives pointed out that the increased costs were due to additional items and services requested by the Saudis. However, the Saudis stuck to their position and asked the government to intervene to reduce the costs. The government was reluctant to get too deeply involved but with negotiations dragging on into 1967 and no progress being made, John Stonehouse (by now Minister for Technology) encouraged Airwork to make a commitment to the Saudis that they would not make 'excessive profits' from the deal. In order to break the deadlock in June 1967, Airwork made a pledge, as a gesture of goodwill, to try to limit its profits within a margin of 10 per cent and to repay the Saudis 75 per cent of any profits in excess of that figure.

Once the issue of finance was agreed, the Saudis then requested that within twenty-two months of the contract being signed, they wanted to have a fully trained and operational squadron of Lightnings. Quite simply, this was beyond Airwork's capabilities, due to the condition of the rudimentary facilities and airfields in Saudi Arabia. The only option was for Airwork to approach the RAF, who agreed to undertake to train sixteen Saudi pilots within the twenty-two-month period, with two additional pilots after that period was complete.

Prince Sultan pressed for another bargain by requesting that the training be carried out free of charge in view of the friendly relations between the two countries. John Stonehouse politely rejected the request but offered that the training would be carried out at cost which was agreed.

The final part of the contract was thus signed on 18 September 1967. The contract provided for Airwork to undertake technical support for the RSAF aircraft for a five-year period and to operate a flying training school as well as two more advanced OCUs (Operational Conversion Units) to train pilots on military aircraft. Additionally, Airwork would undertake to train 1,000 Saudi nationals to become RSAF ground crew.

Under the contract to the Saudi Arabian Ministry of Defence, Airwork were to provide comprehensive technical training which could be broken into five main areas: (1) the establishment of the King Faisal Air Academy at Riyadh which provided *ab initio* and basic jet-flying training, along with English language and ground school training; (2) the establishment of the Technical Training Institute in Dhahran which provided English language training, academic technical training, along with basic, advanced and on-the-job training in thirty trades; (3) the provision of the Lightning flying operational conversion unit at Dhahran including pilots, ground instruction and in-flight simulators; (4) the provision of type flying operational conversion units at Dhahran; and (5) on-the-job training at Khamis Mushayt. The scale and scope of the training was very large. For instance, the Technical Training Institute at Dhahran comprised classrooms, common rooms, printing rooms and eighteen teaching laboratories which covered training in airborne and ground radar units, plus facilities for technical training on engines, airframes, electrical and electronic, instruments and basic metal-working trades. There were 240 expatriate Airwork instructors and eighty English language teachers employed at the institute. Airwork's technical library produced training notes, text books, lecture notes, instructors' hand-outs, examination papers and student records. Over one three-year period, the average output of printed material was 120,000 A4 sheets of text per month. Over and above the training, there was accommodation, catering and messing for 1,200 students.

Despite the final formalisation of the contract, problems started to occur from the start. The delay in the signing of the contract meant that the different phases of the contract were not synchronised. The BAC Lightnings and Strikemasters which should have been delivered in the spring of 1968 had to be stored in the UK until the facilities and buildings in Saudi Arabia were completed in September 1968. The RSAF pilots who were completing their RAF training were left without the opportunity to practise their skills until everything was in place in Saudi Arabia. Airwork once again came under intense pressure to put everything in place and to do it quickly.

A further problem faced by Airwork was the lack of suitable Saudi nationals as candidates for ground-crew training. With a small population of only 3.5 million, many of the most suitable candidates had already been snapped up by other firms such as Raytheon, who had already signed their part of the contract with the Saudis much earlier. Additionally, there was a great demand for educated young Saudi men in all areas of government and commerce in Saudi Arabia.

With the lack of suitable candidates, Airwork had selected eighty-one students from an initial ninety-four for entry to British universities to study scientific and technical subjects; thirty-one were rejected as unsuitable. The Saudi Government pledged to screen another 120 candidates. Out of the promised 120, only seventy were provided and of this number only seven qualified. Despite this, the Saudis ignored the test results and insisted that thirty-one of the candidates be sent to the UK.

There were further problems caused by interference from the Saudi royal princes. In October 1967 Prince Mashari called on Airwork without any notice and asked to be given an introduction to civil and military aviation. The Airwork staff passed the request to the British Government who suggested he be given a tour of RAF facilities in the UK.

On top of this, a number of Saudi princes were also actually going through Airwork's training programme and there was a concern that safety might be prejudiced. There were frequent groundings on the slightest pretext by the RSAF, certainly in cases where there would have been no such action by the RAF in similar circumstances. This had the effect of reducing the amount of time for training within the limited time frame already available.

More problems were to be found in the relationship between Airwork instructors and members of the Pakistan air force (PAF) who ran the OCU prior to Saudi pilots progressing to the LCU (Lightning Conversion Unit) to qualify for flying the Lightning. The OCU was an intermediate stage of training where pilots learned combat tactics before moving on. Airwork were supposed to have taken over the running of the OCU from the PAF officers, but a decision was made by the RSAF after the signing of the Air Defence Scheme contract to allow the PAF officers to continue to run the OCU. Tension emerged between the two groups because Airwork instructors were concerned that a number of the pupils being passed from the OCU to the LCU were not of a sufficient enough standard to cope with Lightning training, and that a number of them could not hope to qualify. The view of the RSAF and PAF was that these pupils should be passed and there were suggestions that pressure was being applied by Saudi princes.

This conflict led to a high turnover of Airwork personnel which consequently slowed down training. At the visit of a British MP (Gerald Fowler, the Parliamentary Secretary to the Ministry of Technology) to Saudi Arabia in June 1969, the commander-in-chief of the Saudi air force complained about the insufficient numbers and below-standard quality of Airwork employees. Gerald Fowler felt concerned enough to recommend a greater oversight of the Air Defence Scheme contract. A second RAF officer was assigned to Saudi Arabia to join the RAF officer already in place to assist in overseeing the contract and to help resolve problems.

In late 1969, the Lightning squadron was deployed to the Yemen border to meet renewed incursions. Once again there was Saudi pressure on Airwork staff to engage in operations which led to the resignation of three Airwork flight instructors. The episode corroded Airwork's reputation among ex-RAF personnel, which was the pool from which they recruited their staff, and led to further recruitment problems.

Problems continued for Airwork in March 1971 when the equivalent of £50,000 in Saudi riyals was stolen from Airwork premises in Dhahran. Although salaries of Airwork staff were paid overseas, the missing money formed the cash salary which was paid in-country for the staff's day-to-day living expenses. Part of the investigation involved a Saudi tracker brought in by police to look at the footprints in the sand near the window where the money had been stolen from. Airwork staff were required to walk in the sand nearby so the tracker could compare footprints. Despite this farcical element, the investigation launched by the Saudi authorities uncovered a number of misdemeanours by Airwork employees, including brewing and sale of illicit liquor. Airwork employees were aggravated by the heavy-handedness of the Saudi police and also felt aggrieved at the police attitude that the robbery had been perpetrated by an Airwork employee as opposed to a Saudi national. There were arguments on both sides, however, as there had been burglaries from Airwork staff accommodation that had gone unreported as there were illegal stills on the premises. Airwork staff were detained without charge and not allowed to leave the country whilst investigations continued. However, this element of Saudi police work applied to everybody, not just Airwork staff, and continues to be the case today.

Shortly before the disappearance of the money, relations between the Saudi Government and Airwork had reached a low point. General Hashim of the RSAF complained to the British air attaché in Jeddah that the shortage of Lightning instructors was 'unnecessary and avoidable'. He also commented that Airwork staff were unable to anticipate problems and difficulties or to plan ahead effectively. Furthermore, he said that they took corrective action only when pressed and more often than not the remedy applied was too little, too late.

Harsh and possibly somewhat unjustified criticisms given that many problems arose as a result of the Saudi Government's policies. Nonetheless, the fact remained that the only way to move forward was for far greater involvement than previously by the British Government. The RAF was becoming increasingly involved in the Air Defence Scheme. In 1967 and 1968 the RAF had trained Saudi pilots to fly the Lightning and also provided fifty-three places for Saudi students on their ground training course. They also made their aircraft available for Airwork instructors to refresh their skills in addition to allowing Airwork ground crews on to their technical courses to enable them to reach the standard required as stipulated in the terms of the Air Defence Scheme contract.

The RAF also assisted in recruiting suitable staff for Airwork, as well as releasing their own personnel to work as flight instructors. The Ministry of Defence provided support administrative staff to help monitor the programme, with more staff deployed to the British Embassy in Jeddah to also assist the programme. Despite this intervention and additional support, the condition of the RSAF Lightnings began to deteriorate considerably, mainly due to 'wastage in skilled maintenance personnel' at Airwork.

Once again there were more complaints from the RSAF. This time they complained of staff shortages at Airwork's Technical Training Institute and at the flight school, the King Faisal Air Academy. At this point, British officials decided that things could not carry on in their present form. The British ambassador stated:

> One of the reasons for our failures in Saudi Arabia is that we were responsible (under some very vague assurances) for the condition of the cart and its load without having any control over the horses. In future, therefore, we should ensure that the reins are firmly in our own hands.

The British Government moved to replace the contract with a government-to-government agreement. Britain henceforth would agree to provide Saudi Arabia with aircraft, training and support services. All of this would be provided by the British Government, who would contract British companies to supply everything required.

This would give the government much greater control, which is what the Saudi Government had pressed for from the beginning. What was also driving the change was the possibility of further sales to the Saudis of Jaguars and helicopters worth £100 million.

In April 1973 the governments of the UK and Saudi Arabia signed a government-to-government contract under which the Ministry of Defence took over the Saudi Arabian Air Defence Scheme. Airwork were not included in the new contract and all the work previously undertaken by them was handed to BAC. In early February 1973 the British ambassador stated to a senior member of Airwork:

I hoped Airwork were in no end of term spirit of insouciance and conversely, would seek to go out, if not in a blaze of glory, then with some shred of goodwill left and this not only because it would make it easier for BAC to pick up the practical running of the operation, but because it might stand Airwork in good stead in some future situation which we could not at the moment foresee.

Certainly not easy words for anyone in Airwork to have to listen to. In the summer of 1973, a Ministry of Defence team of a dozen officers arrived in Saudi Arabia to 'monitor the progress and performance of the British Aircraft Corporation's task in Saudi Arabia'. In addition to this, BAC requested a loan of 100 RAF personnel to help fulfil the terms of the contract.

Despite all these efforts, the Saudis opted for the Northrop F-5E over the Jaguar for their next major arms purchases.

From the beginning it is possible to take the view that Airwork had been handed a poisoned chalice. The Saudis had wanted a government-to-government contract and whichever company had taken the contract probably would have failed to meet what the Saudi Government was looking for. There are not too many commercial organisations that have the resources equivalent to that which a government could provide. The Saudi Government had set standards which were quite simply unrealistic for Airwork to comply with, despite all their years of overseas contract work in the Middle East and elsewhere. Harold Wilson's Labour government wanted maximum returns for minimum financial outlay and ended up losing out in financial terms, although they maintained a good relationship with the Saudi Government. It could also be said that the proof of the pudding would have been for the Saudis to order the Jaguar and British helicopters had they been happy with the final intervention of the government and the implementation of the substantial help to BAC to run the Air Defence Scheme after they had taken over from Airwork. In retrospect, Airwork did the best they could under very difficult circumstances and perhaps not enough credit has been given to them for this.

52-656. One of three Lightnings on a ferry flight for delivery to the RSAF in July 1966, after it made an emergency landing at RAF Muharraq with a fault. (Peter Hamlin)

The Aircraft

When Airwork staff arrived at the start of the Magic Carpet contract, the RSAF were using Lockheed T-33s and F-86 Sabres which had been maintained with American support. Airwork staff took over the support of these aircraft, although more pressing matters were the introduction of the Hunters and Lightnings under this contract. One Airwork QFI, Bob Pugh, went to Myrtle Beach in the USA to convert on to the T-33 to continue their use in the inventory. Pugh was an ex-RAF man who spotted an Airwork advert for pilots in Saudi Arabia. He spent some time at Warton familiarising himself with the Strikemaster, being shown the flight characteristics by BAC pilots, though this was not a conversion course. He then flew one of the first Strikemasters out to Saudi Arabia via Malta, Cairo, Luxor and Jeddah before arriving in Riyadh. He became the first squadron commander for the Strikemaster, of which the RSAF purchased a total of twenty-five Mk 80/80As. On arrival they found that the Saudi students had completed their first stage of flying *ab initio* on Cessna 172Gs and were ready to move on to the next stage of their training. There were eight Cessna 172Gs (not the export T-41 Mescaleros) used for *ab initio* training.

Pugh trained the first Saudi student to fly solo in a Strikemaster at Riyadh. He moved on to Dhahran to fly the T-33s, though these were eventually phased out in favour of F-5s after the Airwork contract.

The RSAF bought a total of thirty-four BAC Lightnings F.53s (based on the F.6). The multi-role aircraft carried air-to-air missiles and also could be used for ground attack using bombs. The Lightnings were considered a mechanic's paradise as far as overtime was concerned as they were always breaking down with fuel leaks, engine problems and radio problems. There were initial issues over overtime as it was time off in lieu, but then payments were made available and overtime became very popular. Nose docks were built for the Lightnings, which were three-sided buildings to provide shade from the scorching sun. The aircraft would be too hot to touch after landing.

Whilst the Lightning was intended as the main strike force of the RSAF, the Hawker Hunters and BAC 167 Strikemasters provided a very useful back-up force. Despite the difficult start and ongoing political problems, once the force was established it provided the deterrent against the Egyptians that the Saudi Government was looking for.

24

SUDAN

SUDAN AIRWAYS

Organisation

Following a decision by the government of the Sudan in May 1946, Sudan Airways was formed with the intention of developing an internal airline network within the large country's 1 million square miles. The Sudanese Government provided the capital for the new airline and Airwork Ltd was appointed to provide flying, maintenance and technical services on a management basis. Airwork had recommended that basic services, such as air taxis and survey work, should be offered initially with light aircraft within the country itself. Initially all traffic and promotional activities for the fledgling airline were undertaken by Sudan Railways. Accounting and other commercial activities were undertaken by the Sudan Finance Ministry. In 1949 the airline was granted some autonomy by being given control over its own budgets and accounts. Despite the greater freedom this allowed, the control exercised by Sudan Railways was felt to be over-restrictive, particularly in cases where the railway served the same routes as the airline. In 1951 Sudan Airlines came under the control of the Finance Ministry and the link with the railways was severed. Shortly after this, control of the airline passed to the Ministry of Communications.

The airline grew from 104 staff in 1949 to 625 in 1960.

Aircraft & Expansion of Routes

Sudan Airways started operations with four DH.104 Doves: SN-AAA, SN-AAB (later ST-AAB), SN-AAC (later ST-AAC) and SN-AAD (later ST-AAD). Proving flights began in April 1947, with formal operations starting five months later.

From the beginning, it was planned to have four main routes opened and developed. The new routes were:

a) Atbara, Kareima,* Dongola* to Wadi Halfa
b) Kosti,* Malakal, Wau, Yirrol* to Juba
c)   El Obeid, Nahudi, El Fasher to El Geneina
d) Tabara, Port Sudan, Kassala to Gedaref*

All the above routes radiated from Khartoum and those destinations marked with an asterisk were request stops.

Alterations were made to the above planned routes and stops, and finally it was decided to start with three routes radiating from Khartoum to Port Sudan and Asmara in the east and Juba in the far south. The new air route to Juba was a considerable improvement over journey by river. The journey down the White Nile to Juba by steamer involved a gruelling twelve-day transit, whereas the Dove could reach Juba direct in five hours' flying time. The journey was obviously somewhat longer with the planned stops at Kosti, Malakal, Wau and Yirrol, but nonetheless it was a substantial saving in travelling time.

De Havilland Dove SN-AAC flew the first Sudan Airways service from Port Sudan and Atbara to Khartoum on 22 September 1947. This was weekly and increased to twice weekly the following month.

The arrival of DH.104 Doves G-AHRJ and G-AIIX at Khartoum Airport for Sudan Airways on 22 February 1947. (John Havers collection)

A new weekly service was started in October 1947 linking Khartoum, Malakal and Juba.

By the end of 1947, Sudan Airways was operating 1,572 unduplicated route miles (2,530km) and the scheduled aircraft miles per week totalled 5,444 (8,761km).

A strike by Sudan Railways in May 1948 was a timely reminder of the importance of the fledgling airline to communications. In a thirty-day period, one de Havilland Dove had carried a total of 450 passengers along with mail, freight and medical supplies, completing 40,000 air miles (64,374km) within the period and travelling to all parts of the Sudan.

During the same year, new routes were opened from Khartoum to El Geneina and Wadi Halfa.

A fifth Dove, SN-AAE, was delivered in 1952. By this time the number of passengers carried in the Doves (carrying up to eight passengers each) had grown from 4,000 in 1949 to 7,000 in 1952. The small capacity of the aircraft and the far-flung and diverse nature and number of airports and landing strips meant a very low density factor in passenger numbers. For instance, the daily passenger figure per station was 3.1 and 1.9 in 1953 and 1954 respectively. The majority of the passengers were civil servants and passengers needing medical treatment.

The Sudan was then Africa's largest country in area and not all of the routes opened were considered in any way viable, but air communications were a vital necessity considering the poor ground transport network. However, the route which had been opened to Asmara on the Red Sea via Kassala in 1947 was suspended in 1953.

Despite these low figures and perhaps less than promising beginnings, in 1953 two Douglas DC-3s (SN-AAG and SN-AAH) were bought which provided considerably more capacity. A number of routes showed promise for development and a further two Douglas DC-3s (SN-AAI and SN-AAJ) were added to the fleet in 1954, followed by a fifth and sixth (SN-AAK and SN-AAL) in 1956. A seventh Douglas DC-3 (SN-AAM) was added in 1958.

The addition of the larger-capacity DC-3s over this five-year period from 1953 to 1958 enabled Sudan Airways to open several new routes. The first was an extension of the airline's main western route from El Geneina to Abéché in the Chad Territory of French Equatorial Africa in 1953. Abéché was an important transit and trading centre on the Muslim pilgrim route through Sudan to Mecca in Saudi Arabia. The following year, another international service was opened when the service to Port Sudan from Khartoum was extended to Jeddah in Saudi Arabia. However, the most important route opened in 1954 was the extension of the service from Wadi Halfa to Cairo in November. The effect of these additional routes was to increase the unduplicated route network of the airline to nearly 4,200 miles (6,760km) by 1955.

During 1959, the service from Khartoum/Wadi Halfa to Cairo was extended to Beirut and another link to Cairo was added when a direct service was started from Port Sudan. Some of the flights from Khartoum to Cairo and Beirut were made direct in 1959, with the stop at Wadi Halfa being dropped.

The next major step for the airline came in 1959 when Vickers Viscount 831 ST-AAN was delivered on 5 June 1959. The arrival of the new Viscount enabled a new weekly service to be opened to London via Cairo, Athens and Rome, which added a further 2,250 route miles (3,621km) to the airline's network. The Viscount would receive maintenance checks and servicing on its trips to the UK. Viscount ST-AAN was highly utilised during its time with Sudan Airways, being used on a number of routes, and at one point was carrying more passengers annually than the airline's Doves and DC-3s combined.

SUDAN AIR FORCE

Airwork gained a five-year contract starting in 1962 to provide maintenance and support for the Sudanese air force Fokker F.27s, Percival Pembrokes and Jet Provosts.

All Airwork staff who stayed for the full term of the contract were offered a very generous end-of-term bonus. Life was basic but enjoyable for the staff, although there were anti-

Sudan air force Fokker F.27M; 899 was part of the first export order military model F.27s (troopship) ordered by the Sudanese air force from Fokker in 1964. The aircraft was written off in an accident in Sudan on 10 November 1969. (Ray Shoebridge)

government riots in Khartoum in 1964. However, Airwork staff were untouched by the events (that left twenty-seven dead), which could be observed from the balconies of their flats in the city. The relationship with the Sudanese military was very cordial and occasionally Airwork staff would fly on operations countrywide across Sudan, such as casualty evacuation or dropping leaflets over rebel areas. One flight in a Pembroke required the Airwork engineer Ray Shoebridge to shut down an instrument panel after a fire started which left the aircraft without any navigation aids. However, the flight was from Kosti to Khartoum and was completed by the simple expedient of following the River Nile.

Airwork staff would also accompany the air force F.27s and Douglas DC-3s on their supply flights to RAF Khormaksar in Aden to collect, amongst other items, RAF standard oxygen for the Sudanese Jet Provosts. The flights were routed via Asmara and the DC-3s, which were unpressurised, were supposed to make a detour around the 15,000ft (4,600m) mountains before Asmara, but regularly the DC-3s would ignore this standing instruction and fly over the mountains to save time.

The contract ended in 1967 and the Russians moved in to take over.

RAF, RN, ARMY TRAINING & MAINTENANCE

25

BOOKER & DENHAM

BOOKER

Whilst Booker is not necessarily the best known of Airwork's various operations, it was certainly one of the most important for a period, with eighty employees spread between the two main areas of Airwork's UK operations (after Gatwick) in 1948 at Blackbushe and Booker.

No. 21 EFTS

No. 21 EFTS (Elementary Flying Training School) was formed on 1 June 1941, taking over from No. 13 ERFTS at White Waltham, which was run by de Havilland and disbanded on 3 September 1939. The workshops, catering and ancillary services were all under the control of Airwork. No. 21 EFTS inherited a large fleet of thirty-six Miles Magisters and seventy-two DH.82 Tiger Moths from No. 13 ERFTS. The first course consisted of 120 pupils and lasted seven weeks, which was later extended to eleven weeks. With the amount of activity, relief landing grounds were established at Bray (from 5 July 1941 to 15 December 1941) and Denham (20 October 1941 to 9 July 1945). In May 1942 the school became responsible for training Glider Regiment pilots to solo standard. No. 21 EFTS continued as the only wartime school still operating and was disbanded on 28 February 1950.

No. 1 BFTS

On 20 December 1950 Airwork established No. 1 BFTS (Basic Flying Training School) at Booker with eighteen de Havilland Chipmunks, replacing No. 21 EFTS. This was to assist the regular flying training schools with the instruction of National Service men who had been selected for air-crew duties. No. 1 BFTS at Booker was the first of the basic flying training schools.

Pupils entered the school after training at one of the recruitment centres and initial-training schools where, after passing the air-crew selection board tests, they were given the acting rank of pilot officer.

The period of training at Booker was for twelve weeks with successful candidates at the end of this period moving on to flying training schools to attain their 'wings', which entailed a further six months of training.

At any one time, approximately forty-five pupils would be undertaking training at the school; an average of eleven pupils would have completed the course and be preparing to leave immediately. The age range of the pupils was predominantly 18½ to 19 years old. The training was split into three main areas: ground training (flying) which consisted of lectures and demonstrations; flying training; and ground training (general service) which covered more general areas such as games, drill, range firing, physical training and leadership skills.

No. 1 BFTS was organised into flights and echelons, and placed under the command of an RAF squadron leader assisted by a course commander (held by the rank of flight lieutenant) and an adjutant (held by the rank of flying officer). The school was run along service lines, with the commanding officer responsible for general overall supervision including instruction in service administration, law and discipline. Airwork were responsible for all flying training in the air and on the ground. The Airwork manager and chief instructor, R.M. Hackney, was a former squadron leader with over 6,000 flying hours. Reporting to Mr Hackney were sixteen instructors. The school was equipped with an average strength of thirty Chipmunks, although forty-nine were actually used overall.

The No. 1 BFTS was disbanded on 21 July 1953.

Maintenance Contract: Bomber Command Communications Squadron

In March 1947 Airwork were given a contract for the operation and maintenance of the HQ Bomber Command Communications Squadron at Booker. Included in the contract was the airfield management of Booker, which involved motor transport operations, maintenance and catering. The Bomber Command Communications Squadron comprised various aircraft at various times, some of which were the Percival Pembroke C.1, Avro Anson, Miles M.14 Magister, Miles M.38 Messenger, Airspeed Oxford, Douglas C-47A, Percival Q.6 and de Havilland Devon C.1.

From 1956 to 1963, as well as continuing the aerodrome management, maintenance of three university air squadrons, catering, motor transport and RAF motor transport, Airwork also undertook maintenance of civil aircraft at Booker and movement of AOG spares for the 'V' Bomber fleet.

All the contracts held by Airwork at Booker ceased in 1963.

AIRWORK DENHAM & AIRWORK FLYING CLUB

The Airwork Flying Club was formed at Heston on 29 October 1938 as a subsidiary of Airwork Ltd and was run by Myles Wyatt from March 1939. Flight Lieutenant B.A. Davy, the club's chief flying instructor, was secretary, and its registered address was Westbrook House, 134 Bath Road, Hounslow. In addition to Davy, the other instructors in March 1939 were Mark Lacayo, M.W. Kimpton, W.B. Fordham and P.B. Elwell. Brian Davy left Airwork in the same month they moved to Denham (March 1939).

Many of the Airwork employees joined the club under the Civil Air Guard scheme which allowed people to learn how to fly at the cheap rate of 5s an hour, thereby providing a ready

DH.82A Tiger Moth G-AHRU was with the Airwork Flying Club, alternating between Langley and Denham from May 1946 to 11 February 1949. (Alan Holloway)

pool of potential pilots for the RAF. A branch of the club was established at Denham airfield, Buckinghamshire, in March 1939, due to pressure on space at Heston. The club had purchased Moths to be used for their participation in the Civil Air Guard scheme. The owner of Denham airfield was a rather eccentric gentleman called Mr Bickerton who would not allow the use of aircraft with tailskids on the airfield. The Moths did not have wheel brakes so they were used by the Airwork Flying Club at Heston and the Airwork Avro Club Cadets were therefore used by the club at Denham, with the club's activities split between Heston and Denham due to the two types of aircraft. The club's Avro Cadets were considered to be fine training aircraft and Airwork had replaced their Armstrong Siddeley Genet engines (which were expensive to maintain) with Gipsy Majors. The Gipsy Major was a less powerful engine but performance was not reduced due to the cleaner lines.

A number of the trainee pilots preferred learning to fly on the Cadet at Denham as it was a smaller airfield compared to 'the endless acres at Heston', as one trainee put it. Due to the small size of Denham (which is now much larger than it was in the late 1930s), no trainee was allowed to undertake his first solo without a dual check circuit first.

After the war, the club restarted operations on 16 September 1946, with its base over at Langley rather than Heston, but Denham was still used. Denham was popular with aviation enthusiasts in the area and it was reported that from April to September 1947, nineteen new pilots gained their 'A' licences after training at the club and nineteen old 'A' licences were renewed. During this same period twenty ex-service members qualified for their 'A' licences and eleven 'B' licences were renewed. The total number of flying hours for this six-month period was 663.

26

DUNSFOLD

When the RAF started replacing the Sabre with the Hawker Hunter, Airwork were one of the organisations responsible for refurbishing many of them for other NATO air arms.

Airwork used facilities at Speke, Ringway and Dunsfold for the work. Two Bessonneau hangars were leased at Dunsfold for part of the work to be carried out.

The Sabres were being returned to their original specifications before being flown out to Europe. After the work was completed, an Airwork pilot would make a test flight before a USAF pilot would make a final check of the aircraft on behalf of their air force and then making its delivery flight. One of the Airwork pilots was Joe Tyszko, later to become Airwork's chief test pilot after the death of Claude Trusk in 1953.

Under the auspices of the MDAP (Mutual Defence Assistance Programme), the London Air Procurement Office was the US organisation which handled the refurbishment and transfer of the Sabres, and was based close to the US Embassy in London. Major Gary Sparks was a USAF acceptance pilot under the programme and was assigned to Airwork. During the three years he spent at Dunsfold he got to know many of the staff, not just at Airwork but also Hawker Aircraft, who were working and tuning up the Hunter for RAF service. Among the Hawker test pilots he was on good terms with was Neville Duke.

Major Sparks' first delivery flight from Dunsfold took place on 4 January 1956, when he delivered the first Sabre to Italy. The receiving air base in Italy was at Pratica de Mari near Rome. Most flights were made with one refuelling stop en route, but many flights could be actually flown non-stop due to tail winds. For a short period Major Sparks held the unofficial speed record from London to Rome. One of the Hawker pilots actually set the official speed record between the two cities using data from Major Sparks' flights. Once the delivery was completed to Italy, the return flight was usually first class on a Pan Am DC-7C from Rome to Paris and then BOAC or Air France from Paris to London (there was no direct Pan Am service from Rome to London). As Major Sparks put it, on Pan Am 'There were free drinks, Steak or Lobster and the stewardesses were always young, pretty and friendly – all courtesy of the MDAP!'

Of the forty-three delivery trips Major Sparks made from Dunsfold to Pratica de Mari, one stands out in particular. He had been given a weather forecast for Pratica de Mari of scattered clouds at 5,000ft (1,500m) and 5 miles' (8km) visibility. Instead he arrived in the vicinity out over the sea in the middle of a snowstorm with the cloud base at 600ft (183m) and 2 miles' (3.2km) visibility. There was no GCA at Pratica de Mari and while trying to home in on the beacon, the Sabre was losing height rapidly before finally breaking out over a 10,000ft (3,048m) runway which was covered in trucks and heavy machinery. It was obvious the airport was not open (it was Rome's new airport – Fiumicino). However, he was so low on fuel he had to attempt a landing or bale out. He made contact with the airport and advised them of his predicament so the runway was immediately cleared and he landed safely. He then contacted a TWA Constellation and asked them to contact Rome ATC to let them know he was safely on the ground and to close his flight plan. His next problem was to explain, without any knowledge of the language, that he was delivering a plane to the Italian air force and that he needed a phone to call the American Embassy in Rome. He organised everything from a nearby bar and with a generous measure of Canadian Club. By the time the car from the embassy arrived, he was ready to promise everyone who had bought him a drink that he would land his next Sabre on the same spot again. The events were photographed and recorded in a local newspaper – something not appreciated by his superiors!

By 1957, a number of the Sabre 4s which had been refurbished by Airwork at Ringway and Speke were left at Dunsfold without going on to the USAF. This was possibly due to a shortage of engines. Most of them were struck off charge in December 1958 and moved over to Lasham in 1959.

Dunsfold Aerodrome was not far from Gatwick and had hard runways whereas Gatwick was still a grass aerodrome. In addition to the work carried out by Airwork at Dunsfold, jets like the Attacker and Sabre were flown into Dunsfold, dismantled in the Bessonneau hangars there and brought over to Gatwick by road, with the process being reversed once they had been refurbished.

27

FLYING TRAINING: RAF, RN, ERFTS, EFTS, AONS

THE FORMATION OF THE ERFTS (ELEMENTARY & RESERVE FLYING TRAINING SCHOOLS)

A review of the RAF in 1935 found a need to expand rapidly against a backdrop of an increasingly powerful Nazi Germany which was continuing to build up its forces in complete disregard of the Versailles Treaty. A target of 1,500 front-line RAF aircraft was set for March 1937, and to supplement this figure, increases were required in pilots from a figure of roughly 420 to 2,500. An increase in aircraft hands and aircraftmen from 3,700 to 20,000 was also envisaged, along with an increase of fifty new stations.

This expansion led to changes in the operation of flying training for the RAF. Although the number of RAF flying training schools was also increased from five to eleven, their duties were cut down. The elementary flying training element was no longer to be undertaken at the RAF schools but at civil training schools instead, which would leave the RAF schools to concentrate on advanced training. As a result the number of civil schools was increased from four to thirteen. Among the first batch of new civil schools was Perth, to be run by Airwork Ltd.

To tie in with these new civil schools, in August 1936 Lord Swinton, the Air Minister, announced that a new class of reserve would be formed from January 1937, to be called the RAF Volunteer Reserve (RAFVR). Instruction was to be split at these new schools between 'Town Centres' and 'Aerodrome Centres' with ground instruction given at the town centres and flying instruction given at the aerodrome centres. By March 1937, arrangements were in place for the entry of trainees, with a requirement for 800 pilots in the first year. Training began in April at the aerodromes, the number of which had risen to twelve.

Candidates were expected to be between their eighteenth and twenty-fifth birthdays, physically fit and have an education up to the standard of the School Certificate (or the Leaving Certificate in Scotland). Flying experience was not a requirement. Selected candidates were enlisted as airmen pilots and given the rank of sergeant with further opportunities for promotion. The initial period of service was for five years, with pilots having the opportunity to extend the period of service. Candidates were expected to be available for training at weekends and evenings and also had to attend annually a continuous training period of fifteen days.

Pilots were given a retaining fee of £25 p.a. and pay and allowances were given for periods of continuous training. An allowance was given for out-of-pocket expenses at other times. Travelling expenses were also refunded.

In January 1937 Airwork had announced plans for an ERFTS at Kenyon, Manchester, and also at Langley, but neither of these were proceeded with.

NO. 11 ERFTS PERTH (SCONE)

The idea of civilian-run reserve flying training schools had been discussed for some time prior to the formal announcement of their establishment. As early as August 1935, Perth Town Council had already given permission for such a school to be operated from the new aerodrome being prepared at Scone.

Twelve training aircraft were envisaged with 3,200 hours of flying instruction per annum. Airwork planned for a staff of six flying instructors with additional instructors in armaments, air navigation, photography and parachuting. Under contract to the Air Ministry, Airwork opened the new RAF reserve training school on 27 January 1936 at Perth Municipal Aerodrome at Scone, which was still yet to be formally opened. New hangars, classrooms, pupil and staff accommodation, workshops and canteens were built. The new school was equipped with twenty DH.82 Tiger Moths (eight more than originally planned). The RAF provided Hawker Hart trainers (including K3844/98/4766/68/5816) and Hawker Hinds (including K6642/6724/6829) for existing reserve pilots.

Shortly after the establishment of the ERFTS, in January 1936 prolonged frost retarded the growth of the grass and thawing affected the ground to such an extent that it was unsuitable for operations. In order to allow time for the ground to be made suitable, the ERFTS relocated to RAF Abbotsinch at the end of February to early March 1936, with the assistance and co-operation of the Air Ministry to gain temporary accommodation at Abbotsinch. The ERFTS moved back to Perth in mid-April 1936.

There were two notable visitors to the reserve training school in Scone in September 1936: Roushdy Bey (the Egyptian deputy director of Civil Aviation) and Kamal Elawi Bey (the managing director of Airwork associate company Misr-Airwork). The two had just returned from an IATA Conference in Sweden and on their visit to the UK wished to inspect the Scone operation to see if something similar could be undertaken in Egypt.

No. 11 ERFTS became No. 11 EFTS on 3 September 1939.

NO. 14 ERFTS CASTLE BROMWICH

No. 14 ERFTS started operations on 1 July 1937 using six Miles Magisters, DH.82 Tiger Moths, Hawker Hart trainers (including K3843/48/3902) and Hawker Hinds (including K5506 and L7176). On 3 September 1939 the unit was disbanded and merged with No. 44 ERFTS and No. 20 ERFTS Gravesend into No. 14 EFTS on the same date.

NO. 17 ERFTS BARTON

In August 1936 there was a proposal to base an ERFTS at either Barton or Ringway with up to thirty-five aircraft. Four firms put themselves forward to the airport committee to operate the school. These were Reid & Sigrist, Airwork Ltd, the Herts & Essex Aero Club and Surrey Flying Services. However, it was decided by the Air Ministry that Barton was too small for intensive flying training with thirty-five aircraft. The Manchester City engineer put forward a plan costing £67,000 to expand Barton to a size large enough to allow three separate runs of 3,000ft (914m). This was considered to be too expensive and the proposal for the ERFTS lapsed temporarily. In June 1937 the plans were scaled down to allow for up to ten based aircraft to use the main Barton hangar. Temporary wooden buildings were constructed for instruction and administration. Part of the main hangar workshop was partitioned to create parachute, medical and rest rooms.

No. 17 ERFTS Barton, October 1937: DH.60M Moth K1112 with DH.60M K1890 on the left of the picture. (R.A. Scholefield)

A contract was granted to Airwork to run the new establishment; No. 17 ERFTS and the school opened on 1 October 1937. The chief flying instructor was Flying Officer S.J.H. Carr, although the rest of the staff were civilians.

The unit's first HQ was located at Sunlight House in Quay Street, Manchester.

Three DH.60M Gipsy Moths (K1208, K1835 and K1897) arrived on 1 October 1937 from Cardington. Flying training operations began on 9 October 1937 with three RAF Tiger Moths visiting from the Airwork-run No. 14 ERFTS at Castle Bromwich. By September 1937, sixty-three pilots were being trained. Of the full establishment of twelve Tiger Moths, there were two (non-fatal) crashes: K1112 on 18 July 1938 and K1890 on 22 July 1938. The last Gipsy Moth departed on 7 March 1939. The unit was re-equipped with ten DH.82 Tiger Moths from 1 February 1939, with N5458 and N5459 arriving that day from 27 MU (Maintenance Unit) at Shawbury. Tiger Moth N6470 was damaged beyond repair in a forced landing on 27 June 1939.

Advanced twin-engine training was added to the unit's responsibilities from February 1939 and more temporary wooden buildings were constructed to cater for this. The new buildings were completed in the late summer of 1939. The first two Avro Ansons (N5257 and N5258) arrived from Cosford on 19 July 1939. The training involving the Ansons rotated between Ringway and Barton due to Ringway being more suited to operations by these heavier aircraft.

With the outbreak of war No. 17 ERFTS was disbanded on 2 September 1939.

NO. 44 ERFTS ELMDON

No. 44 ERFTS started operations on 1 May 1939 at the brand-new aerodrome at Elmdon (the architects of which were also linked to Airwork through Nigel Norman). The unit was intended to be supplementary to No. 14 ERFTS at Castle Bromwich, which had already been in operation for nearly two years. Applications for training were invited from not just pilots but also air observers, wireless operators and air gunners. After a fairly short period of existence, the unit was disbanded on 3 September 1939 and merged with No. 14 ERFTS (see Castle Bromwich above) and No. 20 ERFTS Gravesend, to form No. 14 EFTS on the same date. No. 44 ERFTS operated Miles Magisters and Hawker Hinds (including K5426/5506/L7213).

NO. 50 ERFTS RINGWAY

No. 50 ERFTS was operated by Airwork at Ringway, with the first aircraft (Hawker Hinds K5515 and L7195) arriving on 24 May 1939. The intention was to use the main 1938 RAF hangar until the RAF station and two associate hangars for No. 50 ERFTS and 613 (City of Manchester) Squadron were completed in spring 1940. From 24 May 1939, No. 50 ERFTS movements at Ringway were relatively few and far between and the unit alternated between Ringway and Barton. The agreement between the Manchester Airport Committee and Airwork was to have twenty-nine aircraft based at Ringway, but in the end only eight aircraft were based there between May to August 1939; as stated, these aircraft (four Hawker Hinds, two Hawker Audaxs and two Tiger Moths) alternated between Ringway and No. 17 ERFTS at Barton.

The unit was closed down on 3 September 1939.

REORGANISATION OF ERFTS INTO EFTS

With the outbreak of war, the infrastructure of flying training underwent a dramatic change. No. 17 ERFTS at Barton and Ringway were closed. No. 44 ERFTS at Elmdon was combined with No. 14 ERFTS at Castle Bromwich and, with another (No. 20 ERFTS from Gravesend), formed a new school, No. 14 EFTS, which was formed at Elmdon on 9 September 1939 under Airwork management dedicated to producing Fleet Air Arm pilots for the rest of the war. A relief landing ground at Leamington was used to cope with the considerable activity. No. 14 EFTS was disbanded on 1 February 1946.

No. 11 ERFTS at Perth remained but was renamed No. 11 EFTS. The civilian DH.82 Tiger Moths of No. 11 EFTS were allocated serials BB672–92 in September 1940. In the autumn of 1940 No. 11's Hart Trainers were withdrawn and Miles Magisters arrived with further DH.82 Tiger Moths.

All these schools were expanded and the numbers of DH.82 Tiger Moths were increased in some cases to over 100 per school. Flying instructors were mobilised into uniform for the duration of the war, although most ground staff remained civilians. All these schools were absorbed into RAF groups under a flying command structure. These changes all took place from 3 September 1939.

With the focus on flying training at the EFTS, the considerable amount of work carried out on maintenance and repairs by Airwork tends to be overlooked. As much work was undertaken on this side of the operations as there was on flying training.

NO. 6 CANS (CIVIL AIR NAVIGATION SCHOOL) STAVERTON

On 15 May 1939 the Martin's School of Air Navigation (formed by the C.W. Martin Co. on 26 May 1938) at Shoreham, Sussex, which was run under an Air Ministry contract, was taken over by Airwork and was moved to Staverton in Gloucestershire, becoming the Airwork Civil School of Air Navigation. A fleet of eighteen DH.89A Rapides from overseas work, including Airwork's Iraq petroleum contract, was assembled to undertake the training of RAF navigators and observers, with nine of the DH.89A Dragon Rapides being used initially at Staverton. On 6 August 1939 the school came under the control of the RAF, becoming No. 6 Civil Air Navigation School, then later No. 6 AONS (Air Observer & Navigation School). Airwork also set up a civilian repair and modification workshop for RAF aircraft at Staverton.

The school's civilian DH.89A Dragon Rapides were impressed by the RAF in August 1940 as Z7253-66. By the end of 1940, most of the Rapides had been replaced by Avro Ansons. By the summer of 1941, sixty-three Ansons were on strength, training 240 pupils. Impressed aircraft used as hacks included DH.87 Hornet Moth X9326, Miles M.11A, Whitney Straight DR612 and Percival Q.6 X9328. In June 1942 the RAF took over the running of Staverton and later, in September 1942, the Wigtown Observer Training Schools absorbing them into the new larger Observer Advanced Flying Unit organisation and the schools were subsequently staffed with RAF officers and NCOs.

NO. 7 CANS PERTH

No. 7 CANS was formed at Perth in January 1939 to train navigators on Avro Ansons. In November 1939 the school was redesignated No. 7 AONS and the fleet of Ansons was added to by the arrival of eight DH.89A Dragon Rapides from No. 6 AONS at Staverton, which returned to Staverton in June 1940. With changes in training requirements, the school was disbanded on 1 June 1940.

NO. 11 RFS (RESERVE FLYING SCHOOL) PERTH

In 1947, with Airwork's RAF training having ceased, a new contract was given to the company to provide RAFVR training at Perth (Scone). No. 11 RFS started operations on 18 March 1947.

The intention was to provide training for 550 reserve air crew using Tiger Moths, Avro Ansons, de Havilland Chipmunks, Harvards, Hawk Trainers and Airspeed Oxfords. The numbers of aircraft reduced as time went on. Reserve training ceased in 1954 and No. 11 RFS Perth was disbanded on 20 June 1954.

NO. 13 RFS GRANGEMOUTH

Under an Air Ministry contract to provide refresher training to reservists, Airwork opened the No. 13 RFS at Grangemouth Aerodrome in Scotland on 1 April 1948 using six DH.82 Tiger Moths (N6539, N6925, T6553, T7445, DE775 and NL779). The squadron commander was Wing Commander F.D. Nugent and the chief flying instructor was Squadron Leader A.F. Underhill. Recruitment of RAFVR and WAAF (VR) pilots was carried out through No. 101 Reserve Centre, RAF Bishopbriggs, Glasgow, and candidates from the east of Scotland applied through No. 66 (Scottish Reserve) Group Headquarters at RAF Turnhouse. It had been intended to open a town centre location for the squadron in Edinburgh but this did not happen.

Grangemouth itself was, however, an airfield without a future. Despite the money that had been spent on the facilities by its previous owners, Scottish Aviation, neither Edinburgh nor Glasgow city councils were interested in using the facilities as a future airport for either city. Scottish Aviation had also moved their operation from there to Prestwick. In November 1948 the Ministry of Aviation advised Grangemouth town council through the Department of Health (Scotland) that they were prepared to relinquish the airfield for an £11 million industrial development scheme. After being in occupation for only one year, and with forty air crew in training and another 150 more in various stages of entry, No. 13 RFS was disbanded on 19 April 1949 and merged into No. 11 RFS at Scone. RNAS Abbotsinch and the civil airport at Renfrew both rejected requests to move the RFS to either location.

The 521-acre Grangemouth airfield was also finally closed in April 1949.

NO. 23 RFS SUNDERLAND (USWORTH)

No. 23 RFS Usworth was formed on 1 February 1949 with DH.82 Tiger Moths, although these were replaced by de Havilland Chipmunks. The unit was operated by Airwork. No. 23 RFS also operated the Percival Prentice, Airspeed Oxfords and Avro Ansons. Due to reorganisation of flying training units, No. 23 RFS was closed on 31 July 1953.

NO. 1 AOS (AIR OBSERVERS' SCHOOL), WIGTOWN

On 19 September 1941 No. 1 AOS was reformed and Airwork were tasked with the setting up of the unit. A group of Airwork engineers was assembled from various locations including Staverton, as well as two from Airwork Perth (Messrs MacPherson and Bell) plus Joe Connolly who transferred from Airwork at Renfrew. They were all sent to Wigtown in Scotland, where a new airfield was being constructed, to assist in the foundation of the new school and facilities. No. 1 AOS started operations under the command of an RAF officer, Captain Openshaw, with Paul Terry acting as general manager for the Airwork operation there.

There were four flights of Ansons at Wigtown, along with Westland Lysanders and Bristol Blenheims, all maintained by Airwork. Airwork were also responsible for provision of catering at the airfield. Amongst the regular exercises conducted at Wigtown was a flight every morning of eight Ansons which would take off and fly to Castle Bromwich for navigation training and return the same day.

The school was redesignated No. 1 (O)AFU on 1 February 1942, still under Airwork control. On 13 September 1942 No. 1 (O)AFU was absorbed into the new large observer advanced flying unit organisation and was staffed with RAF officers and NCOs.

NO. 2 BANS (BASIC AIR NAVIGATION SCHOOL)

No. 2 BANS was formed at Usworth, Sunderland, on 18 April 1951, to be managed by Airwork who carried out maintenance and overhauls of the approximately twenty-five Avro Anson T.21s on strength at any point. The student navigators were regular RAF personnel and the pilots and instructors were from the RAFVR. Most of the student navigators were on National Service. The unit was disbanded on 30 April 1953.

NO. 1 GRADING UNIT (AIRWORK) RAF DIGBY

On 3 January 1951 the No. 1 Grading School was formed at Digby to train pilots of No. 2 ITS Digby, Lincolnshire. Just over a year later, on 15 January 1952, it was renamed the Airwork Grading Unit before being redesignated the No. 1 Grading Unit on 9 June 1952, with an eventual establishment of fifty-six DH.82 Tiger Moths. The No. 1 Grading Unit was disbanded on 31 March 1953. Both Nos 1 and 2 (below) Grading Units provided grading for air crew at Cranwell College.

NO. 2 GRADING UNIT (AIRWORK) RAF KIRTON-IN-LINDSEY

Airwork also set up No. 2 Grading Unit at Kirton-in-Lindsey, Lincolnshire, in No. 54 Group, from part of the Airwork Grading Unit (which had been formed at Digby on 15 January 1952) with DH.82 Tiger Moths on 9 June 1952. No. 2 Grading Unit was disbanded on 31 March 1953.

AAC MIDDLE WALLOP

A major contract was gained in April 1963 for the training of AAC (Army Air Corps) pilots at the AAC Centre, Middle Wallop in Hampshire. The large contract also included ground support and maintenance for fifty-four helicopters, twenty-four de Havilland Chipmunks and seven Auster 9s, as well as provision of ATC and communications services. The contract was run by Bristows on behalf of Airwork Services. In October 1970 Bristow took over the direct running of the contract with twenty helicopters and fifteen QFIs. Airwork remained directly responsible for the running of Middle Wallop's airfield services and for providing ground instruction.

RAF LINTON-ON-OUSE

In December 1984 Airwork were awarded a contract for the operation of No. 1 Flying Training School at RAF Linton-on-Ouse which included all services on the station except flying instructors, air traffic controllers and defence. The contract started on 31 March 1985 with fifty-four Jet Provosts and seventeen Scottish Aviation Bulldogs to be operated and maintained. The contract included the support for the Royal Navy Initial Training Squadron, the maintenance and servicing of Bulldogs and ground and electronic services at Topcliffe airfield and at the relief landing ground at Dishforth airfield. There were still approximately sixty Jet Provosts being maintained at Linton-on-Ouse in early 1989.

RAF CHURCH FENTON

Another major training contract was the awarding of a contract in August 1987 to operate No. 7 Flying Training School at RAF Church Fenton with Jet Provosts. The contract started in April 1988 and was run in parallel with the Linton-on-Ouse school contract, along with the reserve landing ground at Elvington. All services were provided with the exception of flying instructors and air traffic controllers. The Jet Provosts started to be replaced with the introduction of the first Embraer Tucanos to the RAF training programme in 1989. Due to defence cuts in 1992, the Church Fenton contract was reduced to reserve landing ground status only and the ground at Elvington was closed.

28

HURN

Although the FRU had been at Hurn for several years by 1959, Airwork decided to move their headquarters from Langley down to Hurn Airport in 1959, occupying the wartime huts and hangars. The engineering facility at Lasham was also closed down and transferred to Hurn, along with operations at Blackbushe, including the Cessna agency which had only been fairly recently established at Blackbushe.

Piper PA-23-250 Aztec 5B-CBG was used for communication duties in Saudi Arabia from 1971 to 1974, along with Aztec 5B-CAH. Both were Riyadh-based. (John Havers collection)

With the changes brought about by the formation of British United Airways and the Air Holdings Group, Airwork at Hurn were known as Airwork Services Ltd. In addition to being the company's new headquarters, Airwork Services' activities at Hurn were split into three main areas: the Aircraft Engineering Division; the Design Organisation; and the Radio Division. Hurn's 102 hangar housed the Engineering Division, which carried out major overhauls, the manufacture and provision of spares, modifications and crash reclamation. The Engineering Division was also responsible for providing on-site working parties in the UK and overseas. The Design Organisation carried out design, drawing and experimental flight-testing for a number of UK aircraft manufacturers with the emphasis on structural work plus radio, electronics and instrumentation. The Radio Division was an important part of the Airwork organisation and dealt with airfield communications systems as well as radio and navigation equipment for aircraft.

The new head office building at Hurn was ready for occupation in October 1961.

As part of the large reorganisation with the formation of the Air Holdings Group, many of the staff who had transferred to Hurn from other locations such as Lasham were offered positions within the Air Holdings Group of companies as it was decided to close down Airwork Services Ltd. A number of staff decided to leave, however, as not all could find employment at Hurn.

The Radio Division at Hurn achieved major sales and servicing, in July 1967, of American airborne electronics equipment for King Radio Corporation and Narco Avionics Inc.

The Engineering Division at Hurn designed and manufactured an access ladder for the new Jaguar fighter.

After the departure of the FRU to RNAS Yeovilton in 1972, the operations at Hurn were reorganised. The three separate operations, consisting of the College of Air Training (Hamble) Baron Flight contract, the Civil Aviation (CAA) Flying Unit Dove contract and the Hangar 45

The Airwork Services Head Office at Hurn in 1965. Pikes which had been manufactured by Airwork General Trading for the Home Guard in 1940 were on display in the reception area. (Babcock International Group)

Civil Aircraft Maintenance work, all came under one manager. The Airwork Radio Department provided support services to all three.

In 1983 the Airwork motor transport and maintenance section moved out of the old wartime huts to new purpose-built accommodation.

An airborne radar surveillance set was developed in 1982 in Airwork's Radio Division. On the supply side, the Supplies Division, which had been based at Stony Lane in Christchurch before moving over to Ferndown, close to Hurn, had for many years been supplying numerous overseas governments and companies in Dubai, Lesotho, Sudan, Brunei, Malta, Chile, Singapore, India and Peru. Also, in 1982, a Prototype Digital Simulator (PDS) contract for the RAF and RNAS started. A new department was set up for this at Hurn.

AIRCRAFT & OPERATIONS

Hurn was never used as an airline base in the same way that Blackbushe was; the new BUA made their base at Gatwick. Nevertheless, there was a steady throughput of aircraft through the years of both civil and military aircraft that were connected with Airwork and their associates, particularly overseas. These aircraft would be at Hurn for major overhaul, maintenance and servicing, repairs, refurbishment or passing through on delivery flights, in many cases with Airwork providing the air crews for delivery. Some very brief examples through the years will give an idea of the diversity of aircraft involved.

1960s

The early 1960s saw a wide range of both civilian and military aircraft arriving for maintenance. These ranged from Air Condor Bristol 170 G-AGPV, which was serviced by Airwork at Hurn and test flown on 29 July 1960 before being delayed by one further day due to technical problems and returned to Air Condor at their Southend base on the morning of 31 July 1960, to Vickers Valetta C.1 VW860, which went to 5 MU at Kemble on 17 November 1961 after work at Hurn.

Airwork were closely involved with a number of Middle Eastern air forces with various aircraft either passing through Hurn on delivery or having major overhauls. These included Caribous and Islanders for the Abu Dhabi defence force, Douglas C-47s for the SOAF and South Arabian Federation air force, Jet Provosts for the Sudanese air force and Bell 47Gs for the South Arabian Federation air force.

1970s

The College of Air Training moved their Beech Barons to Hurn in February 1971 with the maintenance of these aircraft being undertaken by Airwork.

A number of Britten-Norman Islanders, which had been damaged in a gale after being blown over at Bembridge in December 1978, were repaired and rebuilt in hangar 102. G-BESE and G-BFNL were beyond repair and used for spares.

1980s

Fifteen of the ROAF Skyvans were returned to Hurn in 1982–83 for a complete overhaul. The work was carried out in hangar 102 and involved seven of the aircraft being converted to a maritime surveillance role with radar installed by the Radio Division.

Ghana air force Skyvan SC7-3M-400. Four Skyvans were brought back by sea through Poole Harbour to Hurn for refurbishment by Airwork. (Jim Halley via Air Britain)

1990s

A Skyvan contract gained in 1990 was to recover four Ghana air force Skyvans for a complete overhaul. They were returned by sea to Poole in September 1990 and transferred to Hurn in a road convoy. The Skyvans were G.450, G.452, G.454 and G.455.

29

LANGLEY

After the announcement on 13 March 1946 of the closure of Heston by Lord Winster, the Minister of Civil Aviation, Airwork prepared for their move over to Hawker's airfield at nearby Langley. Langley airfield had been laid out by Hawker Aircraft Ltd in 1936 and a satellite manufacturing plant was added to boost production from their Kingston factory in 1938, when production of the Hawker Hurricane had started. The grass airfield suffered from severe water-logging in winter and spring which limited the size of aircraft that could use the airfield. Initially Airwork started operations in the former Hawker hangar in the woods, splitting the hangar between the Airwork standard maintenance section and Airwork's experimental section. They moved over to the main area of the airfield into another Hawker hangar with four bays. One bay was used by British South American Airways, two were used by Hawker and one was used by Airwork. Airwork's research and development engineering section moved into four hangars on the Richings Park side of the airfield. There was also the problem of traffic at nearby Heathrow.

An overview of the Airwork hangars at Langley Aerodrome. (Alan Holloway)

As the Heathrow traffic increased, Hawker moved their flight-testing to Dunsfold. Airwork, however, continued at Langley where they undertook repair, overhaul and conversion of smaller aircraft types (with Gatwick handling the majority of larger aircraft) on behalf of aircraft manufacturers, airlines and private owners. Langley was also used for their experimental and development work with a total of around 200 employees working at any one point.

AGT (AIRWORK GENERAL TRADING) CONTRACTS

Whilst Airwork General Trading was carrying out a considerable amount of work at other locations (principally Gatwick and later the large Sabre refurbishment contracts at Ringway and Speke), the division also sought work for their Langley site. This included a number of RAF DH.89A Dominies which were converted to civil use (Rapides), the maintenance of the Denham Flying Club aircraft and major overhauls of the Sudan Airways Doves. Airwork General Trading at Langley were also responsible for the inspection and repair of all ATC gliders in the south of England (i.e. south of Hull). Airwork were responsible for transporting the gliders from their airfields to Langley where they would be inspected, patched and rebuilt. After checking and rebuilding they would be returned to the gliding centres. Each glider was brought to Langley after 1,000 launches and at any one time there would be up to thirty-five gliders present in the workshops.

Among the work carried out at Langley was a contract for fifty London buses which were painted for London Transport, each requiring no fewer than sixteen coats of paint and all by hand. An inspector from London Transport came out from Chiswick to inspect and pass the work. There was a considerable amount of paint left over and so all unopened tins were returned to London Transport, while the remaining opened tins were used to paint more than one Airwork employee's house.

The quest for work included contracts such as one for de Havilland Hornet power units which were then being overhauled at Leavesden. Another contract gained was for the repair of fuel tanks for the Bristol 166 Buckmaster. The constant quest for work led to very competitive pricing, resulting in low profit margins on occasions.

Royal Pakistan Air Force Ferry Flights

One area that Airwork always looked for business was in ferrying aircraft on delivery flights. They were put out at losing a contract to Mayfair Air Services to ferry Hawker Tempest IIs from Langley to the Pakistan air force. When the contract came up for renewal Airwork were determined not to be beaten and quoted a very low price to ensure they gained the contract from Mayfair. The contract now involved the ferrying of Hawker Fury 60 and 61s to the Royal Pakistan Air Force. Among the pilots taken on from Mayfair was John Judge, known as 'Pee Wee' in aviation circles. Once Airwork had gained the contract for the ferrying of the Furys they took on all the former Mayfair pilots with the exception of Veronica Volkersz, as Airwork's policy at the time was not to employ female pilots. This policy, however, was to the detriment of Airwork, who took on a number of questionable second-rate pilots despite there being a shortage of pilots at the time.

Bristol Brabazon Elevator Control Testing

A number of interesting projects were carried out by Airwork at Langley with aircraft one would not normally expect to see arriving and departing.

Avro Lancaster RE131 is dwarfed by the size of the Brabazon. RE131 was flown over to Filton from Langley by Claude Trusk. (*Flight International* via Alan Holloway)

One of the first major projects was the design and installation of the power controls for the Bristol Brabazon. Four Avro Lancasters were allocated to use in testing connected with the Brabazon, although two of them (ME540 and PP755) were not connected with Airwork. The Lancasters used by Airwork were RE131 and RF286 and were used to test the Lockheed and English Electric power controls in the Bristol Brabazon I elevator control assembly. In addition, RE131 went on to test the pitot tube for the Brabazon. Lancaster RF286 was with Airwork Langley from 20 May 1948 to 28 January 1949. It arrived at Langley direct from Hullavington after a Middle East tour. Engineer and designer Syd Holloway (who had been put in charge of experimental work at Langley) had arrived at Langley after starting with Airwork at Heston and then going to Renfrew, Loughborough and back to Heston during the war years. He had overall responsibility for fitting the power controls in the Lancaster's tail at Langley. RE131 was the main aircraft used as the powered controls test bed for the Brabazon. After RE131 was modified at Langley, much of the initial testing was carried out at Blackbushe and Farnborough because of the waterlogged airfield at Langley. The problems with waterlogging there continued through the summer of 1949 and well into the following year.

On a number of the Blackbushe and Farnborough test flights, Syd Holloway flew as flight test engineer and sat in the aircraft's cockpit on the starboard side, next to the manual override controls. When the initial testing phase was complete, RE131 departed to Filton for further test flying on 16 July 1948. To await RE131's arrival at Filton that day, Syd Holloway departed Langley in the works' Miles M.38 Messenger G-AHXR, which he landed within one of the large turning circles at the end of Filton's main runway without entering the runway proper.

Magnetic Survey, Vickers Wellington

At approximately the same time as the Brabazon elevator work was being carried out, another unusual aircraft arrived early in 1948 to undergo modification by Airwork at Langley (and was also the only example of its type to go on to the British civil register for a short period). This was Vickers Wellington B.X RP468. This Wellington had been built at Blackpool by Vickers-Armstrong as a B Mk X. On 18 July 1945 it was delivered to 12 MU Kirkbride and then transferred to 27 MU Shawbury on 27 October 1946. On 22 January 1948 the aircraft was allocated to Airwork General Trading at Gatwick but was delivered to Langley on this date. The conversion work involved the fitting of instruments for airborne magnetic surveys on behalf of the Department of Scientific and Industrial Research (DSIR), to whom the aircraft was loaned. Syd Holloway was involved in installing a Smith's SEP 1 electric autopilot and magnetometer along with a Decca 'Navigator' system to plot the exact location of the aircraft whilst carrying out magnetic surveys. On 22 July 1949 the Wellington was given the civil registration G-ALUH, with the owner given as the Ministry of Supply. The application of the civilian registration was believed to be for the purposes of making survey flights with the newly fitted equipment along the coast of Norway, operating out of Stavanger.

Avro Lincoln B.II RF342 TRE Test Bed

With the advent of the Cold War, an interesting military project in the early 1950s included the prototype radar installation for use in Britain's V-bomber force. Airwork's contract was to install the prototype TRE (Telecommunication Research Establishment) system in an Avro Lincoln B.II bomber. The aircraft used was RF342. Once the 12ft diameter TRE radome had been built, it was installed on the underside of RF342. Syd Holloway oversaw the installation of the equipment and flew on the Lincoln as flight engineer for the forty hours of flight-testing required for the equipment. As well as acting as flight engineer, he was also unofficially allowed to fly the aircraft. The TRE's system used centimetre wavelengths produced by a magnetron to give pinpoint ground pictures of targets from high altitudes. The test flights were carried out in the spring and early summer of 1950. Once again, as with the problems encountered with the Lancaster test beds, a large portion of the test flying took place from Blackbushe due to the ever-present problems of waterlogging at Langley. The test flights of RF342 at Blackbushe were under the command of Airwork's chief test pilot, Claude Trusk.

On 17 October 1950 Claude Trusk and Syd Holloway flew RF342, departing and returning to Langley after a four-hour fifty-minute test flight. The Lincoln was flown from Langley to Blackbushe on 7 February 1951, again commanded by Claude Trusk with Syd Holloway as co-pilot.

The Lincoln returned to Langley from Blackbushe and was given a forty-minute local test flight from Langley by Claude Trusk and Syd Holloway on 6 July 1951. There was another two-hour local Langley flight on 1 May 1952.

Many aircraft used as flying test beds were at the end of their useful service life and usually scrapped once the test-bed programme was complete. However, RF342 can today be viewed in the RAF museum at Cosford after a varied history following its test-bed flying programme.

Ferranti Flying Unit, De Havilland Vampire WG801

A smaller but nonetheless interesting modification was carried out on de Havilland Vampire WG801. The Vampire had a new type of light fitted to the wingtips, which was not a landing light as such but to help monitor the aircraft's position for the research work being carried out by Ferranti. The Vampire was to be delivered to the Ferranti Flying Unit at Turnhouse in October 1952 and was on strength with the unit from 28 October 1952 to 16 October 1953. As a matter of interest, engineer Syd Holloway was asked to collect Proctor Mk I G-AHMV from Croydon and deliver it to the Airwork AST at Perth on the same day as the Vampire was to be flown up to Turnhouse from Langley by an Airwork test pilot. On the day, the whole of eastern England up to York was blanketed with thick fog. Nonetheless, Syd was able to take off from Croydon in G-AHMV despite the murky conditions and arrived at Perth safely after a refuelling stop at Newcastle's Woolsington Airport. The Vampire was still fogbound at Langley and didn't reach Turnhouse until the following day.

OTHER EXPERIMENTAL & MODIFICATION WORK

Vickers Valetta VL249 was used for auto-landing testing on behalf of Smiths; some of the testing was carried out at nearby London Aiport (Heathrow). Claude Trusk and Syd Holloway took VL249 for local test flights on 25 April, 5 May, 14 and 18 June (all 1951) and 7 May 1952. Seymour Lee and Syd Holloway made a test flight in it on 25 May 1951.

However, in addition to the heavier military aircraft that were worked on, Airwork General Trading also carried out modifications and maintenance work on a variety of smaller aircraft. Some examples were Beechcraft 17 Traveller (Staggerwing) LN-HAK, Beech Expeditor N79848, DH.89A Rapide G-AKTZ, Airspeed Consul G-AIIN, Gloster Meteor WS111 (which was converted to a two-seater trainer) and Percival Proctor P.34 III G-AHGA, which was prepared for use in air racing. G-AHGA had been loaned to Airwork staff for air racing for the cost of a new CoA by owner Charles Hughesdon, husband of actress Florence Desmond. G-AHGA was entered for the 1952 *Daily Express* South Coast Air Race, flown by Airwork chief pilot of the Air Transport Division, Robert McIntosh. Both Syd Holloway and Airwork engineer Jock Graham prepared the aircraft at Langley for the race. The previous year McIntosh had achieved fourth place in the King's Cup Air Race flying Percival Proctor P.30 III G-AIEH. Syd Holloway acted as mechanic and had plenty of experience with Proctors, flying them regularly between Langley and the Airwork Central Drawing Office at Gatwick. For the 1951 King's Cup Air Race, McIntosh won £100 for coming fourth in the event in G-AIEH. In the 1952 *Daily Express* race, McIntosh had more luck in G-AHGA and won the race, giving £200 each to Syd Holloway and Jock Graham for preparing the aircraft and acting as ground crew. After the *Daily Express* race, they took

Beech DI7S LN-HAK at Langley on 8 April 1949, when it was taken for a one-hour test flight by Claude Trusk and Syd Holloway after maintenance work was carried out. (Alan Holloway)

G-AHGA back to Langley and made modifications to the engine cowling. The modifications produced a neat row of louvres below the inverted engine which provided the only exit for cooling airflow from around the exhaust stubs, lowering the Gipsy Queen engine temperature during pre-race taxiing and added 20mph (32km/h) to its average speed. The extra speed gave the edge when G-AHGA was entered for the 1953 Welsh Air Derby on Swansea Common, which Syd Holloway won as he piloted the aircraft for this race.

OVERSEAS LIAISON

The overseas headquarters for Airwork operations was also established at Langley. In April 1952 they began recruiting engineers for Sudan Airways which was then operating DH.104 Doves.

AIRWORK FLYING CLUB AT LANGLEY

The Airwork Flying Club was a limited company formed as a wholly owned subsidiary of Airwork Ltd. Post-war, the operational side of the club was based at Langley Aerodrome and restarted operations after the war on 16 September 1946. The club owned three DH.82A Tiger Moths.

Beneš-Mráz Be.550 Bibi G-AGSR. This aircraft arrived at Heston pre-war as OK-BET. It crashed at White Waltham on 25 October 1951, tragically killing its owner, Michael C. Chorlton, a film editor and director. (Alan Holloway)

TEST FLYING AT LANGLEY

The servicing and maintenance which had been such an important function pre-war was carried on at Langley with the emphasis on commercial aircraft, although private fliers were still catered for. Claude Trusk was Airwork's chief pilot in the earlier days at Langley and, along with Syd Holloway, who was in charge of experimental work, they would take many of the aircraft for a local test flight after work had been carried out on them. Some examples include Percival P.34 Proctor V SU-ACH owned by Prince Omar Halim of Egypt on 28 and 29 June 1948; Percival P.34 Proctor G-AHFK on 4 July 1947; de Havilland Tiger Moth DF192 flown to Langley from Kemble for a CoA overhaul on 14 August 1947; Avro 652A Anson LT939 (at Langley for autopilot testing) on 17 February 1948 which was taken on a local flight; Iraq Petroleum Co. DH.89 Rapide G-AJVA on 28 February 1948, normally based in Tripoli, was taken on a local flight after being prepared for its CoA which was issued the following day on 1 March 1948; Miles Gemini G-AJOA was taken on a local test flight on 14 March 1948; Beechcraft Traveller G-AJJE was flown on a number of local test flights on 27 March 1948 and 3/4 May, 23 and June, and 5 July 1949; Beechcraft Traveller LN-HAK was flown after work on 8 April 1949; Beech Expeditor N79848 was test flown on 28 August 1949; de Havilland Rapide G-AKTZ was flown on 3 October 1949 locally; Airspeed Consul G-AIIN was flown twice on 12 October 1949; Airspeed Consul G-AUIT was flown three times locally on 14 October 1949; and de Havilland

Rapide G-ALGO was test flown locally on 2 December 1949. An example at the heavier end of the scale was Vickers Viking EI-ADH (one of the Aer Lingus batch sold to Misr Airlines), test flown on 21 October 1948 after being refurbished by Airwork General Trading.

Avro 652 Anson G-AIRX emerged from the Airwork hangars in mid-April 1952, after having spraying equipment fitted for Airwork's tsetse fly-spraying contract in East Africa. G-AIRX was taken for two local test flights from Langley on 19 and 22 April 1952 by Claude Trusk, with Syd Holloway acting as observer on both flights. The aircraft then departed for A&AEE Boscombe Down for testing with the new spraying equipment from 24 April 1952 before departing for East Africa in May 1952, where it was registered VP-KJK.

D. HELMORE TEST FLIGHTS

Syd Holloway also undertook some test flights with D. Helmore, again in most cases acting as an observer. These included a thirty-minute trip on 20 May 1953 in Gloster Meteor WS111 on a local Langley flight. This Meteor had been converted by Airwork to a two-seater. On 8 July 1953, D. Helmore and Syd Holloway made three flights in Meteor WS111: from Langley to Moreton Valence; a local flight at Moreton Valence; and returning to Langley that same day. On 11 August 1953 WS111 was flown back to Moreton Valence, with D. Helmore and Syd Holloway returning later that same day.

Airspeed Oxford DF413, on 29 July 1953, flew from Langley to Aston Down with D. Helmore commanding followed by a number of flights between the two airfields on 6 and 7 August 1953, and later in August 1953 between Langley and Moreton Valence, plus a local flight on 14 October 1953 commanded by D. Helmore.

COMPANY BUSINESS FLYING

In addition to the flying of aircraft for tests, and after overhauls and CoAs, there was a considerable amount of flying by the Airwork Flying Club and company hacks.

In particular, on inter-company liaison work, there were regular trips between Langley and Airwork's main Drawing Office at Gatwick and numerous other locations. The aircraft used were Percival P.34 Proctor G-AHMV and Miles M.38 Messengers G-AHXR and G-AHFP. For example, G-AHXR and G-AHFP put in three round trips in one day (20 December 1948) between Langley and Elmdon. They were also used during the early period of Airwork's Langley residence for trips from Langley to Anthorn, Bembridge, Blackbushe, Christchurch, Defford, Dunsfold, Leavesden, Elstree, White Waltham, Elmdon, Leeds (Yeadon), Croydon, Filton, Shoreham, Stretton, Plymouth (Roborough), St Mary's (Scilly Isles), Perth (Scone), Swansea (Fairwood Common) and Newcastle (Woolsington). The Airwork pilots included Claude Trusk, Syd Holloway and A.S.P. Paine.

AIRFIELD CLOSURE

In May 1955 Airwork were given six months' notice to leave the airfield by the owners, the Ministry of Supply. Whilst this was disappointing news which meant that Airwork would have to find a new engineering base, it was not entirely unexpected as Heathrow was only 2 miles (3.2km) away. In addition to the increasing traffic at Heathrow, the circuits of both airport and airfield overlapped each other. Further pressure on the Langley airfield was added by housing development that had taken place on the edge of the airfield. At this point Slough Council had approached the Ministry of Supply with a view to obtaining the airfield land for municipal housing purposes.

30

LASHAM

In April 1956 Airwork General Trading Co. set up a repair and maintenance facility at Lasham airfield as they were moving their work away from Gatwick. Approximately a dozen staff moved from Gatwick to Lasham, including Lasham's general manager Graham Corner, foreman Mr Collins (replaced by Roy Thomas) and future Airwork MD, Denis Wareham, who worked on radios. The chief inspector was Bill Starkey. The total number of Airwork staff was around forty personnel.

At this point Lasham had T2 hangars occupied by the RAE, Dan Air (two hangars) and the Lasham Gliding Society. Airwork's facility was in a T2 hangar built just after the war, which was actually built off the airfield to the north of the road running along the perimeter, called the Avenue, and to the west of Back Lane. A taxiway was built from the T2 hangar across the Avenue to access the airfield. The hangar had previously been used by Handley Page to store Marathons.

The first aircraft that arrived for repair work was Britavia's Handley Page Hermes G-ALDI.

Amongst the aircraft regularly serviced there were a Trans Arabia Airways Douglas DC-6B, Sudan Airways Douglas DC-3s (ST-AAH to ST-AAM inclusive, which came for major checks and CoA renewals) and Iraq Petroleum DH.104 Doves (G-AJJF, G-AMUZ and G-AKJP). One long-term visitor was Ministry of Supply HP.74 Hermes 2 VX234 (ex-G-AGUB), which was

HP.74 Hermes 2 VX234/G-AGUB parked outside the Airwork hangar at Lasham. It suffered damage to its wing caused by taxiing Miles M.38 Messenger G-ALAI whilst at Lasham. (Peter Carter)

being modified for the Royal Radar Establishment at Defford to carry SLAR (Side-Looking Airborne Radar) for the TSR2. This tail-wheel Hermes was with Airwork at Lasham for eighteen months.

The Marconi Doppler Vickers Viking G-AHOP was also a visitor.

On 9 February 1958 two more Sudan Airways Douglas DC-3s, ST-AAG and ST-AAM, were present undergoing maintenance, along with Miles Marathon XV229/G-AILW. Sudan Airways Douglas DC-3 ST-AAH was present on 11 April 1958. A further two Miles Marathons, G-AMHS and G-AMHV, arrived from Farnborough on 18 September and 2 October 1958 respectively for overhaul on behalf of Air Navigation & Trading Co. Ltd of Squires Gate.

Bristol 170 Freighters were aircraft that Airwork had considerable experience with and a number of these were overhauled at Lasham, including RCAF Bristol 170s 9697, which was present on 13 October 1957, and 9699, which had been overhauled just prior to this. Both had flown in from Filton and among the modifications was the installation of stretcher rails. Two other Bristol 170s worked on were G-AGPV and G-AGUT, which were present in June 1957.

The first ex-RCAF Canadair Sabres arrived on 26 October 1958. These were eventually transferred to Staravia at Church Crookham and scrapped.

On 2 January 1959, a further five Canadair Sabres arrived. Ex-USAF Sabres also passed through (two examples are 19472 and 19772) on their way to being scrapped by Staravia at Church Crookham. On one occasion, Airwork's chief test pilot Joe Tyszko overran the Lasham runway on landing one of the Sabres.

The last aircraft to leave the Airwork facility at Lasham was Handley Page Marathon G-AMHS. This aircraft was transferred to Hurn on a Queen Mary trailer after it was decided to close Lasham at the beginning of September 1959. Peter Carter was the last Airwork employee to leave, putting the lock on the hangar door before going in the Queen Mary trailer with the Marathon down to Hurn. With Airwork's departure, Staravia took over the facility to use it as a scrapyard.

In the 1960s the site became an agricultural store and the T2 hangar was gone by the 1980s. The area is now agricultural land with no traces of its previous aviation use.

31

LOUGHBOROUGH

The Airwork General Trading facility at Loughborough was an aerodrome, known as Derby Road and built on the site of a former racecourse. The well-known local firm of Brush also occupied the former racecourse grandstand building on the new airfield for assembly of DH.89A Rapides, which were manufactured at their works in the town and transported in parts out to the airfield for assembly.

Students from Loughborough College (now the University of Loughborough) helped to prepare the site for the aerodrome. Reg Cantello and Larry Lafone of Airwork both travelled up from London by car to visit the site and assess its suitability in 1941.

Airwork moved on to the site shortly after Reg Cantello and Larry Lafone's visit and initially occupied a hangar which was shared between themselves and the Aero Engines Section of the college, with a partition separating the two functions. The work carried out by Airwork started with repairs to Westland Lysanders (damaged tail-planes, fins and control surfaces) under Contract B83835/40. The Lysander repair work was all brought in by road in sections and parts. Four Cunliffe-Owen engineers were flown in from Eastleigh and billeted in Loughborough to assist with the Lysander repair work. Eventually, once the Boston programme was fully under way, a total of 400 Airwork staff were employed at its peak, with many employed locally.

Following the work carried out by Airwork's design office at Hounslow and in the remaining workshops at Heston and the Heston Aircraft Co., the first modifications were successfully made to enable Douglas Bostons to carry nose-mounted searchlights. This was preliminary work and not in conjunction with later work carried out at Burtonwood. A contract had also been given to Airwork for Douglas Boston modification and repair work. The work, which was under the auspices of the Ministry of Aircraft Production, was to modify a large number of Douglas Bostons for RAF use from 1941. Additionally, Bostons came in for repair work which was for damage primarily from belly landings, but battle and other damage was repaired under the same contract. In order to accommodate this large contract for the Douglas Bostons, a much larger 60,000sq. ft (5,574sq. m) hangar was constructed for Airwork alone and was completed at the end of 1942. Airwork then vacated the smaller hangar they had shared with Loughborough College. A new flight shed hangar for final painting and preparation of the Douglas Bostons was also built and completed in early 1943. A 2,040ft x 120ft (622m x 37m) tarmac runway was built shortly after this with an additional 1,260ft (384m) of grass at the western end.

Airwork employee Steve Needham worked on the Bostons from leaving school in 1942 and he recalls much of the repair work involving the belly landings which severely damaged the aircraft, as well as battle damage and more mundane repairs.

At the peak of the work, between eight and ten aircraft would be worked on at one time. The Bostons would be arranged in a herringbone fashion, with four or five aircraft on each side of the hangar and one in the middle (the most advanced in repair) with the nose pointing towards the hangar entrance waiting to be wheeled out. The aircraft would arrive on Queen Mary trailers, the fuselages on one trailer and the wings and other parts on another. The aircraft that had belly landing damage required a considerable amount of metal sheeting to replace the damaged areas. A room full of Airwork staff (all female) worked solely on metal sheeting sections from drawings. On arrival the fuselage would be placed on a stand in the hangar with the wings on stands on each side, and the repairs would commence with the aircraft gradually being rebuilt and the wings and engines being bolted back on last before the aircraft was ready to go to the finishing shed for repainting.

Material stripped from the aircraft was sent to an outside depot used for salvage. The depot was located at the village of Sileby outside Loughborough and was owned by Airwork. Any material or sections from Bostons that were deemed 'Not Repairable' were sent to the Sileby depot for dismantling and cannibalisation or to be eventually disposed of.

TURBINLITES

From 16 March 1943, all the Turbinlite Bostons and Havocs started to arrive at Loughborough to have the Turbinlite equipment and batteries stripped out and the aircraft converted to other uses.

QUEEN OF DISHLEY BROOK

Boston III BZ217, which had been repaired and repainted, was collected by an ATA pilot on 19 February 1944. The aircraft was taxied to the end of the runway in preparation for take-off. As the runway was relatively short, there was little room for error for an aircraft the size of a Douglas Boston. As it sped down the runway, the pilot felt he was not going to clear the trees at the end and he aborted the take-off. The aircraft swung hard left and ended up in Dishley Brook after the port wing demolished part of the wall of a bridge which carried the A6 over the brook. Airwork employee Kathleen Ridgeway, who saw the aircraft being recovered, recalled that a number of Airwork employees remarked that the aircraft had been named

Queen of the Skies and that it had gone from being *Queen of the Skies* to *Queen of Dishley Brook* in one afternoon.

PETER CLIFFORD

Once the Bostons were ready for delivery, they were test flown from the Derby Road airfield by local test pilot Peter Clifford, who lived at the time in Beacon Road in Loughborough. He gained a reputation for some feisty flying both over the airfield and over the town of Loughborough itself. Steve Needham recalls going up as a passenger on some of the test flights and being treated to a display of aerobatics including looping the loop, and, as Peter Clifford said to him at the time, 'if it can do that, it can do anything'. On another occasion, he was a passenger when Clifford stalled the Boston at 15,000ft (4,571m) and the aircraft fell to 9,000ft (2,743m) before he then started putting it through its paces.

LANCASTER WING REPAIRS

The Douglas Boston modification and repair programme was completed in 1945 (BZ199 and BZ376 were the last two Bostons to depart for 38 MU on 1 July 1945). However, the site had already started the repair of trailing edges and wings for the Avro Lancaster under Contract C/Acft/5510. The contract for Lancaster wing repair was short-lived, from 29 June 1945 to 29 March 1946. Airwork engineer Syd Holloway, who had been transferred from Airwork at Renfrew to be closer to his ill father, was in charge of wing-jig installation for the centre section from main spar to trailing edge, which required six heavy-duty castings supplied by Avro to act as a base for each work platform. When a shortage of the base castings threatened the Lancaster repair schedule, Syd designed a fabricated alternative that was accepted and approved by the works management. His alternative used steel channel and angle, and so, armed with a priority purchasing authority for the material and sub-contracting machining, he began a search across the Midlands. The search took him to some strange rural workshops where he was amazed to find heavy machining facilities capable of milling 18ft x 6in x 3in (5.5m x 15.2cm x 7.6cm) sections of steel angle. The alternative jigging soon put Airwork back on schedule on the wing repair. At the end of the Lancaster repair contract, Syd returned to Airwork at Heston.

Today, one can see the main building on Derby Road which was built around the structure of one of the old hangars. Riker Laboratories, as it was then named, was not allowed to construct a new building so the hangar was used and re-clad and rebuilt inside. The other hangar, which had been used as a warehouse by Riker Laboratories, was demolished in the late 1960s to early 1970s.

32

PERTH AST 1936–91

Scone Aerodrome at Perth is another name that has become linked with Airwork, as much possibly as Heston. The aerodrome was originally to have been called Newlands Aerodrome, but Scone was settled upon instead. The original instigator of an aerodrome for Perth in the early 1930s was the Lord Provost of Perth, Thomas Hunter, who later became the local MP. Nothing came of the idea until the expansion of the RAF was announced in 1935 and Sir John

Ure Primrose once again pushed for an aerodrome at Perth. He received support from many Perth Council members and a scheme valued at £20,000 was put forward. An Aerodrome Committee chaired by Sir John Ure Primrose was set up and assistance was sought from experts in the field.

As happened with a number of budding aviation ventures in the 1930s, the advice of Airwork at Heston was sought (among others), along with the associated architectural company Norman, Muntz and Dawbarn. A number of proposals were made which revised and enlarged the original scheme of £20,000. The new proposals doubled the cost to £40,000.

The site chosen at Scone was 400ft (122m) above sea level and generally fog free. One hundred and seventy acres of pastureland was purchased from Scone Estates, with a further 80 acres being purchased from J. Patrick Cuthbert of Barclayhills, this 80 acres mainly consisting of heather and cleared woods. Work began on the aerodrome in June 1935. Fifty acres had to be cleared of 780 tree stumps, which took six weeks and so the building work began in September 1935. The ground contractors were Maxwell M. Hart & Co., and the building contractors were William Taylor & Son. Both companies were Glasgow based. Along with various sub-contractors, there were approximately 300 labourers and 130 tradesmen involved

16 August 1947: Airwork and the Strathtay Aero Club organised the Perth Air Display with 10,000 spectators. The show was opened by the Lord Provost of Perth, Sir J. Ure Primrose. (Royal Aero Club)

in the project. The original buildings comprised six cottages along the main drive and a large hangar. Terminal buildings were also constructed and included offices, rest rooms, dining rooms and a kitchen. Further purchases of land were made in April 1936 when 40 acres were bought from Westfield Farm along with 40 acres of woodland and pasture from Gretna Green Farm. A further 41 acres were leased from Gretna Green Farm. There were two runways of 3,000ft (915m) and 4,200ft (1,280m), and a direction-finding tower was installed after the aerodrome opened.

Despite the fact that by its opening date the construction costs had climbed to £60,000, there were great hopes for the new aerodrome, including a training school for the RAF, the attraction of airlines (in particular Railway Air Services & Highland Airways) and the attraction of air mail services. The aerodrome officially opened on 5 June 1936, although flying had been taking place from January of that year with thirty-three pupils. Present at the opening ceremony were the Duke of Hamilton, Viscount Swinton, Provost and Mrs Nimmo, Lord Mansfield, Mr T. Hunter MP, Lord Provost and Mrs Gumley of Edinburgh, Sir Francis Norrie-Millar, Treasurer Lindsay and Sir John Ure Primrose. Councillor Primrose presented Viscount Swinton with a salmon rod made in Perth and after the ceremony was over a luncheon was held at the Station Hotel in Perth.

Although Scone was the municipal aerodrome for Perth, it was considered to be very much Airwork's aerodrome. Eighty-three people were employed from the start of operations and the firm Scottish Grass Products Ltd set up a scheme to produce cattle feed from the compressed grass cuttings from the airfield.

The assistant general manager of Airwork, P.J.B. Perkins, became aerodrome manager. Airwork's occupation and position as managers of the aerodrome came under scrutiny when the Lands Valuation Appeal Court in Edinburgh set a valuation for rates and rental purposes of £3,002 10s p.a. compared with the nominal figure of £230. This was a substantial difference and a considerable sum of money for the time. The issue was the Court's view as to whether the money paid by Airwork Ltd represented a lease on Scone Aerodrome or not. Perth Council's view was that the money paid to them by Airwork included landing fees. The Court, however, felt that Airwork were in exclusive occupation of Scone Aerodrome (actually correct for the most part) and therefore leasing from the council. In the end a compromise was reached and the figure was reduced to £1,200 p.a.

North Eastern Airways flew through Scone to Newcastle, Leeds, Doncaster and London, as well as Aberdeen, Inverness and Renfrew. Railway Air Services also flew an experimental flight from Renfrew to Perth on 10 September 1936.

POST-WAR

In March 1946 Airwork negotiated with Perth Town Council to purchase Scone Aerodrome, offering £54,000 for the aerodrome and all the land associated with it, including buildings, fittings and all other equipment owned by the council. The offer was accepted on 11 March 1946 and the completion of the sale followed with the title deeds being handed over by Sir John Ure Primrose (now Lord Provost) to R.L. Cumming, an Airwork director, on 31 July 1946. This formalised Airwork's position and the company was able to plan for the future on a secure basis. Part of the reason prompting the sale was the announcement that RAF Errol was to become a joint airport for Perth and Dundee – something which eventually failed to materialise but it was enough to cause Perth Council to feel that the long-term future of Scone would be more secure under Airwork ownership rather than fighting for an airport status that may or may not have materialised in the distant future.

A summer service to Renfrew started on 1 July 1950. This was run by BEA with the intention of linking up at Renfrew with flights to Belfast, London, Dublin and the Western Isles. However, the experiment was not a great success and it was not repeated.

Military training at Scone continued for some years after the war. Up to the 1950s, Scone Aerodrome provided flying training mainly for the RAF, the RAFVR and the university air squadrons. In addition, by November 1954, Airwork were also organising flying, engineering and navigational training on behalf of the Admiralty and Air Ministry. This included the conversion training of all naval pilots to heavy twin-engine aircraft. Radio overhaul work was also carried out at Scone which gave a broad scope to the activities covered.

CIVIL TRAINING

With the rundown in military requirements, Airwork had to look to other areas to fill the shortfall. As early as 1954, the view was that the logical place to look for business was in the expanding civil airliner market. In 1955 the Perth Airwork Flying School received approval for commercial pilot licence training and instrument refresher courses (IRC), becoming the first civil school of flying to have an approved instrument rating (IR) course.

The Airwork School of Aviation, as it was known, negotiated its first contract with an overseas airline in 1955 when it concluded an agreement to train pilots for Sudan Airways. There had been earlier overseas pilots trained at Perth (from Saudi Arabia and Denmark), but this was the first formal contract with an overseas airline. Messrs Saieed, Gizouli and Ati of Sudan Airways began training at Scone in November 1955. By the end of the 1950s, courses of twenty to thirty students at a time were being formed at two-monthly intervals.

Once British United Airways was formed, the airline looked to AST for *ab initio* training for the majority of their students. Other British airlines also sent their trainees to Scone. In recognition of the school's high training standards, in 1961 the Ministry of Aviation issued the

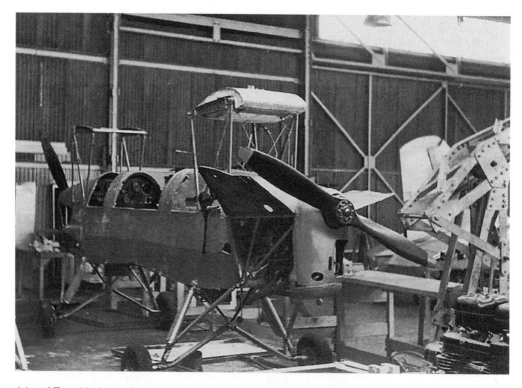

A 'twin' Tiger Moth used for instruction at Perth in the late 1950s. (Neil Aird)

training school with a special 'illuminated' certificate confirming its exceptional status in the UK, something which had not been granted to any other school.

In April 1960 the Airwork School of Aviation became Airwork Services Training and took over the School of Aeronautical Engineering from Air Service Training, Hamble (which had ceased operating because the government had set up the College of Air Training at Hamble), and moved it to Perth, along with the staff (including the manager Stan Bull) and eighty students. There were ninety-six students to start on the first course held at Scone. Once established at Scone, the Engineering School introduced a number of new electrical, turbine and rotorcraft courses, with an impressive array of associated equipment for use by instructors and students.

The move of the engineering facility placed extra demand on space at Scone, with additional student accommodation required along with ancillary facilities for the school.

In order to protect the airfield and its boundaries from outside encroaching development, Airwork purchased Gairdrum Farm with its 340 acres in 1967.

Air Service Training

In August 1969 the title was officially changed to Air Service Training Ltd. The 1970s and early 1980s was a period of expansion at Scone. By this time, average student numbers were between 120 to 150 for trainee pilots and 300 to 400 for trainee engineers. The number of countries sending students for training had also expanded and included Algeria, Ghana, Iraq, Kenya, Kuwait, Lebanon, Nigeria, Singapore, Sudan, Syria, Tanzania, Uganda and Zaire (now Democratic Republic of the Congo). There were also private students from Greece, Malaysia, Hong Kong and Pakistan. Over 100 nationalities have received training and at any point in time up to fifty nationalities would be receiving instruction.

The increase in student numbers required considerable expansion of the facilities. In 1970, construction of the Stormont Hall complex started. This was a two-storey building which included student dining rooms, reading rooms, television rooms, sick-bay facilities and a staff club. One wing contained a large assembly hall and another wing student bars.

One major development which took place in 1968 was the construction of two hard runways. Runway 04/22 (length 2,798ft [853m]) was completed in October 1968 and runway 10/28 (length 1,998ft [609m]) was completed in November 1968, making AST the only flying school for commercial pilots to have this facility.

Helicopter training, under the control of manager Cyril Sweetman, started at the school in 1963 with two Hiller UH-12Cs. The first course, commencing on 30 September 1963, consisted of three pilot officers from the Ghana air force. Cyril Sweetman was to have a moment of fame flying Hiller UH-12 N780ND in the James Bond film *From Russia with Love*.

From 1972 there were three schools at the aerodrome: the School of Aeronautical Engineering (the largest); the School of Flying; and the School of English. Mike Stanford had been chief engineering instructor for over twenty years and, under his guidance, the number of instructional staff grew to over forty members, with the student population reaching a peak of 435 at one point.

There was a constant eye on the future at AST and attempts were made to diversify by running a number of courses for RNAW Almondbank, as well as training ex-servicemen for civilian licences. One particularly useful area of expansion was in offering English language courses as an adjunct to the aeronautical courses. A School of English was established in 1972 which operated as a wing of the ground school but became a separate school in its own right in 1974 under the management of John Beech. With the English Language school running as an independent unit, not all of the students stayed at Scone after their course. With general and technical English taught, roughly one-third of the students would move on to other training establishments such as Bristow Helicopters at Redhill, the Britannia Royal Naval College at Dartmouth, HMS *Raleigh* at Plymouth and the Offshore Petroleum Training Centre at Montrose. The remaining two-thirds of students would split fairly equally between moving on to flying or engineering courses at Scone. In 1976 the School of English took over the whole building which had previously held the club bar and dining rooms, whilst a new building was constructed that year for the warden's office.

Another important development took place in 1981 when a new ATC tower was opened with improved equipment.

In 1988 AST, as part of British & Commonwealth Holdings, was sold as part of a management buy-out to Bricom Group, which was then acquired by the Swedish Rochfield Group. The Rochfield Group had intended to sell Bristow (along with AST) but the Group itself then failed in 1991. In November 1991 the long connection with Airwork was finally broken when Bristow Helicopters was finally sold in a management buy-out. Up to this point the link with Airwork had always been maintained (separately to Bristow). The deal, which included AST being bought by Bristow, had a total value of £200 million. Bristow was acquired by Caledonia Investments and Morgan Grenfell Development Capital, with a 45 per cent stake each and the balance held by management. Whilst still retaining the name, AST became part of a new holding company: Bristow Aviation.

Aircraft & Maintenance

Up to 1960, single-engine training had been carried out on DH.82 Tiger Moths, Miles Messengers and de Havilland Chipmunks, and twin-engine training had been carried out on Airspeed Consuls and de Havilland Rapides. The single-engine aircraft were replaced in 1960 by Cessna 150s.

A selection of AST Cessna tails in February 1968. Reims Cessna 150G G-AVEM had a number of owners after AST and was still flying on the UK register forty-four years later. (Colin Lourie)

Two aircraft which arrived for use by the School of Aeronautical Engineering were ex-British Airways Trident G-ARPX and ex-Air Inter Vickers Viscount F-BGNR, which both flew into the aerodrome, arriving on 23 October 1982 and 8 October 1973 respectively. G-ARPX was broken up in September 1996 and F-BGNR was sold in December 1996.

In April 1966 AST bought a further eight more Cessna 150s to bring the training fleet at Perth up to twenty-one Cessna 150s. The Cessna fleet was destined to become the largest in Europe. Between 1961 and 1967, over thirty Cessna 150s and Cessna 310s were delivered to AST at Scone.

One of the Airwork core activities at many locations was the servicing of private aircraft and this was also undertaken at Scone, in addition to the training activities. The flying school aircraft were already maintained at Scone originally under the guidance of the chief engineer Charlie Delbridge for twenty-three years from 1954 until his retirement in 1977. The new chief engineer was Bill Bremner, who by the mid-1980s was responsible for overseeing the maintenance of over sixty privately owned aircraft covering forty different types.

MAIL DROPS TO HIRTA ISLAND

Airwork were contracted to provide mail drops to the personnel of the Royal Artillery Guided Weapons Range (Hebrides) detachment on Hirta Island in the Outer Hebrides. Air currents, clouds and very uneven ground made the island unsafe for landings by aircraft or helicopters. The mail service by RASC landing craft and trawlers was infrequent and a constant source of complaint by the personnel on the island. Although helicopters had indeed carried mail and moved sick personnel, it was decided in the summer of 1959 to try to carry out free-fall drops of mail and some supplies by air. Airspeed Consul G-AJNE (registered to Airwork Ltd at this point, re-registered to Airwork Services Ltd on 29 June 1960) had already been chartered by the army from Airwork at Perth to fly army co-operation services between St Kilda and South Uist. For the month of September 1959, a number of flights were made by G-AJNE, flown by pilot Donald Pow, with the first experimental free-fall drop containing 280 letters being made on 3 September 1959. The experimental service continued for a year and was replaced by an official contract placed by the army with AST in August 1960. The service was sub-contracted to Loganair from 1963 to 1965 and then went to Strathair, but the contract was again placed with Airwork from 1969 to 1973 (with a sub-contract to Strathair in 1970–71). Over the years, various operators besides AST were contracted to provide the air drop, including Loganair and Edinburgh Flying Services.

STRATHTAY AERO CLUB

The Strathtay Aero Club was formed at Scone on 29 May 1936 as a result of the efforts of three ex-RFC/RAF fliers from Dundee. One of them, E.A. Powrie, had already bought an Avro Avian G-AAHK and this aircraft became the property of the club. The club was unable to secure the services of an engineer, so a maintenance contract was agreed with Airwork. Flying operations commenced on 9 June 1936. Due to the war, the club's activities were suspended and its activities were resumed in July 1946.

On Saturday 16 August 1947 Airwork and the Strathtay Aero Club organised the Perth Air Display at Scone with a good sized crowd of 10,000 spectators attending.

The club thrived and had a membership of 270 by 1948. By the end of June 1949, there were seventeen pupils under instruction. In the previous year fourteen pupils had gained their 'A' licences after 635 hours of instruction. Close co-operation with Airwork continued throughout the years.

SCOTTISH FLYING CLUB (SFC)

Airwork came to the rescue of the Scottish Flying Club after they had been forced out of their premises at Renfrew. The club had built up the facilities at Renfrew and ran the aerodrome there on behalf of the council. They were moved out (apart from a small presence during the war) and had expected to pick up where they had left off at the end of the war, but this was not to be. There were a number of fruitless attempts by the SFC to find a new base but none could proceed due to the high costs involved. On hearing of their plight, Airwork offered the use of their facilities at Scone on a contract basis, with a set figure for dual and solo flying. All the members of the SFC became honorary members of the Airwork Club, which was also used by the Strathtay Flying Club, and from August 1947 the SFC's two Australian-built DH.82A Tiger Moths resumed flying from Scone. Members were charged the same rates that were paid to Airwork which meant that no profit was made on these.

The SFC returned to Renfrew in 1952 before going back to Perth and merging with the Strathtay Flying Club to become the Scottish Aero Club and leasing their aircraft from Airwork rather than owning them.

33

RAF ST ATHAN TORNADO CONTRACT

BACKGROUND

The Panavia Tornado F.2 had initial flight clearances which allowed the aircraft to reach Mach 1.8 at altitude and 800 knots at 2,000ft (610m). The design criteria were ultimately for BVR (Beyond Visual Range) engagements against multiple targets such as the Mya Bison, Tu-95 Bear and Tu-22M Backfire, but had not allowed for close air combat. Initially the Tornado F.2s were used by 229 OCU to train instructor crews. At the time, due to performance and production difficulties, no AI 24 Foxhunter Radars were available. As a result, the infamous 'Blue Circle Radar' (actually steel and lead ballast, not concrete) were installed. As Foxhunter Radars and the up-engined Tornado F.3 became available, the F.2s were flown to St Athan and placed in storage at the Pickerston site.

THE FATIGUE PROBLEM

As the OCU turned out the first qualified crews, the first operational squadrons were formed. These were 29 and 5 Squadrons at RAF Coningsby in 1987. Frequent DAC (Dissimilar Air Combat) sorties were flown against the USAF McDonnell Douglas F-15 Eagles from Lakenheath. It soon became apparent that the FIs (Fatigue Indices) were being consumed at too high a rate and stress corrosion cracking was starting to occur in the centre wing-boxes. A modification was then developed to strengthen the wing-boxes by DASA (Deutsche Aerospace), the centre section design authority. The German company had overall responsibility for the mid-fuselage area including the wing-box. Further limitations were placed on the magnitude of the G manoeuvres the aircraft could pull.

THE TORNADO MODIFICATION CONTRACTS

In 1992 Airwork gained a contract from the Ministry of Defence to carry out fatigue-indexing maintenance and modification work on a batch of twenty-five Tornados. Known as FI 25, the contract was to update the Tornados at a quarter of the way through their service life. Airwork Services had submitted a very competitive tender and once this was accepted they started recruiting staff for the work, with a number of employees being recruited locally.

Under the terms of the contract, 134 Tornado F.3s (at this point the RAF operated 165 Tornado F.3s, F.2Ts and F.2s) were to be modified and Airwork's bid was for the second tranche of twenty-five aircraft. BAE had already undertaken the work on the first tranche of Tornados.

The FI modification work involved installing the DASA-supplied modification kits in the aircraft's centre fuselage.

The problem regarding incorrect work carried out was first reported by an RAF SAC at St Athan who was a member of the RAF team involved in the preparation and recovery of the aircraft before and after the F.3 FI 25 programme. Suspicions were aroused after the completion of four aircraft, and the RAF called in DASA to examine the airframes. The airframes were inspected and DASA refused to pass the work done because of the damage. At this point the remaining twenty-one Tornados of the tranche were all at varying stages of completion at St Athan when work was halted. It was stated after inspections were carried out that the damage included drill holes which had been made in the wrong areas when the DASA-supplied modification kits were installed by Airwork Services. Sixteen of the aircraft were found to have damage caused by the removal of rivets from the centre wing-box. Some areas were found to have had damage caused by attempts to remove the rivet heads with an air chisel, along with attempts to remove the rivets with oversized drills.

What does appear odd is that there was no quality assurance system in place which would probably have picked up the extent of the problems much sooner than it actually came to light, i.e. before sixteen aircraft had been affected. There were a number of 'Trojan Horse theories' which included stories of Airwork being supplied with incorrect drawings, although any experienced engineer would have immediately noticed incorrect drawings. Another theory was that 'plants' had carried out the work to discredit Airwork, but this was fanciful.

The Ministry of Defence stated that the degree of damage was so serious as to reduce the safe life of the aircraft and followed up by saying that major remedial work would have to be carried out to restore fatigue life and allow the aircraft to be flown safely. The contract with Airwork Services was cancelled by the Ministry of Defence on grounds of breach of contract and they prepared a claim for damages. The Ministry of Defence stated at the time of cancellation that they felt the company was no longer considered capable of meeting the contract requirements and would face a claim for the costs incurred for rectification of the damage. The DRA (Defence Research Agency) was brought in to provide independent advice on the structural assessment for the relevant sections of the affected airframes. This independent assessment had been requested by the structural design authority, DASA.

Airwork Services made a statement in which they expressed their unhappiness with the cancellation of the contract. After a number of articles in the press, Airwork felt compelled to issue the following statement:

> You will understand that, in the case of a potential legal situation, the company is not at liberty to discuss specific issues or details. However, allegations made in the national press have been so erroneous that the company feels obliged to make some limited comment. Airwork has a very long and successful history of supplying services to the RAF and other customers around the world. The company has been an approved supplier to the MoD under the original Def Stan 05-21 quality standard, then the revised MoD AQAP-1 Quality Standard and, most recently under BS5750 and ISO9001 international quality standards.

Panavia Tornado F.3 ZE288 at Edinburgh Airport on 11 June 2007. ZE288 was one of the affected St Athan Tornados which had its mid-section replaced with the mid-section of Tornado F.2 ZD940. (Martin Third)

In conforming to such standards, the company always prepares a comprehensive quality plan, together with the customer, to meet the specified requirements precisely.

AFTERMATH

The aftermath had potentially far-reaching consequences, not least being that the damage to the aircraft affected front-line availability of Tornado fighters. The contract was taken from Airwork and given to BAe. Whilst it is difficult to quantify the actual overall effect on Airwork, it cannot be doubted that the whole episode was a public relations disaster for the company.

On 28 February 1995 the MP for Bridgend, the Rt Hon. Win Griffiths asked the Secretary of State for Defence, Roger Freeman, the following questions:

Mr Win Griffiths: To ask the Secretary of State of Defence if he will make a statement about the role of RAF St Athan and the maintenance of Tornado and other aircraft since 1983.

Mr Freeman: RAF St Athan provides overhaul, repair and manufacturing facilities for fixed-wing aircraft of all three services, and many of their mechanical, structural and engine components. Currently Tornado accounts for around 48 per cent of St Athan's work.

Mr Win Griffiths: Will the Minister confirm that work done at RAF St Athan by the company Airwork has cost a minimum of £300 million so far in botched and damaged

Tornados? Will the Ministry receive compensation from the Bricom Group? Was anyone in the RAF or Ministry directly responsible for seeing that the work was properly done, and will anyone lose his job or be admonished?

Mr Freeman: The hon Gentleman's estimate of the amount involved is wildly inaccurate. We have not yet costed the amount, and I would not be able to give the hon Gentleman the figure if we had, because we intend to take legal proceedings against Bricom in connection with the work done by Airwork.

I am glad to say that the damage to the Tornado aircraft that has been identified is being rectified by British Aerospace, the cost being a mere fraction of the sum mentioned by the hon Gentleman. I am glad to say also that RAF St Athan won the competition for the fatigue index at No 25 – a quarter of the way through the fatigue life – to repair about 100 of the remaining Tornados. I congratulate the service men and women involved, some of whom are the hon Gentleman's constituents.

In 1995 a trial installation was carried out using one of the donor Tornado F.2 centre wing-boxes on one of the damaged Tornado F.3s. This was a success and the recovery programme went ahead on the remaining fifteen aircraft.

Like an ill-omened albatross, the matter continued to involve the Airwork name with the crash of a Tornado F.3 in the following years. On 28 September 1996, Tornado F.3T ZE759 was being flown on a shakedown flight from BAe Warton by an MoD crew when it crashed off Blackpool beach. Both crew members ejected safely but concerns were raised as ZE759 was one of the batch that had been worked on by Airwork at St Athan in 1993 and had its mid-section replaced by Tornado F.2 ZD904. This was the first flight after modification work had been taken over by BAe from Airwork. Whilst the cause of the crash was eventually identified as control problems due to a foreign object jamming control surfaces, the Airwork aspect of previous modifications carried out was looked at by investigators.

Unfortunately the problems incurred at St Athan continued to hang over the company for a considerable time and the reputation of the Airwork name never really recovered.

34

RENFREW

Airwork's move to Renfrew, near Glasgow, in 1939 was caused by the pressure on facilities at Whitchurch after the newly formed BOAC moved in. With the approach of war, the intention of Airwork had been to set up an MU at Whitchurch in addition to their other work carried out there. Initially, a number of the Whitchurch Airwork staff moved back to Heston (ironic in view of the fact that they were being forced out of Whitchurch by BOAC moving in from Heston as well as Croydon). However, the facilities at Heston were far too overcrowded and the unit was moved to a newly created facility at Renfrew Aerodrome.

On 2 September 1939 approximately thirty Airwork employees were told to report to Heston at 2 a.m. with their gear as they were being immediately transferred to a new repair depot. On their arrival at Heston they were instructed to help pack machinery and equipment for the move. Once this was completed, they were taken to Euston station and put in three reserved carriages on a train bound for Glasgow Central station.

Airwork employees Syd Holloway and Joe Connolly recalled being part of the first batch of Airwork employees to travel up to Scotland from Heston. The majority of the group chosen to help set up the MU at Renfrew were young unmarried men, chosen because they had fewer family ties. Syd Holloway found life hard in Renfrew at first. The new Renfrew employees arrived in Glasgow tired and hungry and were allocated 'digs' in private houses where they were treated with coolness, particularly if a member of the resident family had been called up for active service. Many locals regarded the men from the south as 'draft dodgers', not realising their work was classed as a 'reserve occupation'. The day after their arrival, the men were taken through the heavily industrialised Clydeside area to Renfrew Aerodrome, where Airwork occupied the four-bay Belfast Truss hangars along with the two-bay hangar behind them in the south of the airfield. A separate building next to the four-bay hangar was used as a canteen and another small building nearby was used for stores. These hangars and buildings displaced the Scottish Flying Club, who had been using them for a number of years. There were no workshop facilities as such and the men had to make benches and trestles from whatever materials were available. A freight train then arrived with workshop equipment from London. Also within the consignment were five civilian aircraft which had been in the process of being worked on at Heston and had been dismantled and packed then sent up to Glasgow by train. The aircraft were an Avro Cadet, Vega Gull, a French DH.82A Tiger Moth F-AQOX, a Miles Merlin G-ADFE and a DH.89A G-AFFF. All the equipment and the parts of the five aircraft were manhandled off the train and taken by road to the new workshops at Renfrew.

Workshops were set up with what basic equipment was available. Once this work was completed, the men had little to do other than fill sandbags. As the first Scottish winter built up the lack of heat for the newly arrived employees was a constant source of discomfort.

At this stage Renfrew airfield itself only had grass runways. The operations of the Westland Lysanders of the Polish 309 Squadron had caused the mud to rut. The intense cold had then frozen the mud, creating a hazard as the hard, rutted surface created vibrations that caused the small bombs to fall off the wing struts of the taxiing Lysanders.

The first tasks undertaken at Airwork Renfrew were the completion of the overhaul of the civilian aircraft and Avro Cadet mentioned previously. The Cadet was sent off to an RAF station for allocation to a training unit and the civil aircraft were returned to their owners. However, there was a serious mishap with the DH.89A Dragon Rapide G-AFFF. During the repairs, heat from an electric lead-lamp ignited the aircraft's fabric, setting fire to the fuselage. Armed with only hand-held fire extinguishers, the staff fought the fire as it spread and the flames shot upwards, fanned by the up-draught of the lofty hangar's dimensions towards the wooden roof trusses. Eventually the blaze was brought under control but not before it had consumed most of the port fuselage. G-AFFF later crashed near Milngavie, with the loss of five passengers and crew on 27 September 1946.

Many of the men who had arrived at Renfrew from Heston had worked mainly on wooden and fabric aircraft. As such, the arrival of the first all-metal aircraft for repair required rapid developments of new talents. Bristol Blenheim Mk Is were the first to arrive, followed by Bristol Blenheim Mk IVs. Although Airwork had been preparing a new building at Whitchurch (before they had to leave) to construct wings for Bristol Blenheims, at Renfrew they were given a contract, B83835/40 (which ran to 11 July 1941), to repair Bristol Blenheims (plus Lysanders at Loughborough and Whitleys at Gatwick). This was replaced by contract C/Acft/1176/C37b to repair Blenheims and Tarpons/Avengers from 12 July 1941 to 30 June 1945.

The first Blenheim (actually a fuselage) arrived on a horse-drawn trailer. The arrival was a surprise to the Airwork staff and they were informed by the owner of the horse and trailer that there was a whole trainload of aircraft to be brought up and he didn't think his horse was up to the task. A lorry was quickly hired to bring the rest of the aircraft to the aerodrome from Fulbar Street station, Renfrew. There were twenty Bristol Blenheims in all, mostly partly dismantled and all were damaged in one way or another. The remaining Blenheims and their parts were offloaded with the help of a small crane at Fulbar station and taken back to Renfrew Aerodrome.

The process of repair was to strip the aircraft down completely, with useable parts being placed around the hangar floors in their respective groups and then being used, where possible, to rebuild the damaged Blenheims. The result of this was that one aircraft could be rebuilt from parts from a number of aircraft. The first damaged Blenheim to be repaired at the new depot was L6644.

Thereafter, a number of the damaged Blenheims arrived at Renfrew on the beds of 60ft (18.3m) articulated Queen Mary trailers. The majority of the damage to the aircraft was caused mainly by pilot error involving the incorrect selection of hydraulic controls, for there were three identical levers mounted side by side in the cockpit. The levers activated the power-controlled gun turret, wing flaps and undercarriage. The gun turret lever had to be turned off before selection of wing flaps or undercarriage. Failure to do so caused the Blenheim to sink slowly on to idling propellers as the undercarriage retracted during pre-flight checks. In addition to this, the Blenheim Mk I's instrumentation was underdeveloped, so there were problems with the air compressors, vacuum and hydraulic pumps and the twin vertical rev-counters. The rev-counters vibrated so badly that maintenance crews had great difficulty in adjusting accurate throttle settings. Most of the instruments were made by different manufacturers so there was no interchangeability.

Syd Holloway had been promoted to workshop foreman and was given the task of overcoming these problems on the Blenheims at Renfrew. In this position he also had the task of training new labour drawn from local industries in the Clydeside area. However, there were many shipyards in the vicinity and the Ministry of Labour redirected workers that were not suitable as they failed to appreciate the difference between ship and aircraft riveters. The biggest problem faced by the unit, though, was the shortage of spare parts and materials supplied by regional RAF MUs. The MUs had only recently been established and were still struggling to gain some kind of order in their procedures and systems. In a word, it was chaotic. Many stocks held were either unchecked or not coded which led to supply delays and the supply of incorrect items. One order from Airwork Renfrew for 7lb (3.2kg) of rivets arrived as seven single rivets. Airwork staff at Renfrew had permission to go to any MU in the country to seek parts and equipment

Bristol Blenheim (Bisley) Mk V DJ702 was repaired at Renfrew between 14 April 1944 and 27 September 1944 after a flying accident with No. 12 (Pilots) Advanced Flying Unit at Spittlegate, Lincolnshire. (Alan Holloway)

for repair work, although the nearest MU was at Carluke and much extra material came from there. The work at Renfrew was considerable and arduous. The staff worked seven-day weeks, with Joe Connolly recording one ninety-two-hour week. The throughput of repaired aircraft was at the rate of one a week for both Blenheims and Avengers, with occasionally two being turned out in one week, which would then be five per month.

Another contract gained by Airwork during the period of the Blenheim repair contract was to equip de Havilland Dominies and Avro Ansons with a new bombsight for use by the RAF's OTC flying training schools. On the Dominie, the device was positioned on the floor of the aircraft between the aircraft's legs, where the bomb-aimer's window quickly became obscured by mud and debris thrown up by the aircraft's wheels when operating from grass airfields. Syd Holloway, who by this time had been promoted to works superintendent at Renfrew, overcame the problem with the Dominie's window by designing and making prototype double-acting, sliding doors to the window for the bomb-aimer's position. The modification worked well and was adopted on all the Dominies modified by Airwork.

The Blenheim contract proceeded smoothly with only two mishaps. The first was the arrival of a Blenheim being delivered to Renfrew by a ferry pilot. Coming in over the familiar landmark of Arkleston Cemetery, the aircraft approached too steeply and ploughed into the soft perimeter boundary where the propellers dug into the earth, tearing the engines out of their housings and rolling away across the airfield. The second accident occurred when another Blenheim overshot on landing after a test flight and crashed into an empty air-raid shelter where it burst into flames. Airwork staff were first on the scene and once again, as in the Dominie blaze mentioned earlier, used hand-held fire extinguishers until the arrival of the fire brigade. However, every time the flames were doused and the pumps turned off, the fire reignited because the Blenheim's bomb doors were clad in Electron, a metal that self-ignited when it reached flammable temperature.

Airwork continued their work unabated at Renfrew whilst tarmac runways were laid and building work commenced on additional hangars and buildings, notably for Lockheed Overseas during 1942/43. Scottish Airways also continued flying out of the airfield under the auspices of the AAJC.

By 1940, Airwork had pioneered the use of fixed-price contracts to repair aircraft which led to considerable savings in costs and manpower. When the Blenheim repair contract came to an end in 1944, Airwork were awarded a further contract to prepare Grumman Avengers for service and carry out repairs. These aircraft were delivered under the Lend-Lease aid programme. This contract lasted from 1942 to 31 December 1945. The first Avengers arrived on USS *Wasp* at nearby King George V Dock. Each aircraft arrived with its own workshop and service manual, along with a tool kit that made its preparation for service a relatively easy task. Syd Holloway devised a test rig to speed up the servicing of the aircraft's hydraulic systems and built a maintenance trestle to house it. The test rig was powered by a mains electric motor driving the aircraft's hydraulic pump that was swung out on to the test rig, leaving the system intact and thereby eliminating airlocks and the need to bleed the system.

The majority of the repairs to the Grumman Avengers related to broken firewalls due to wheels-up landings. Once declared airworthy, they were test flown by 'Dutch' Holland, an old airline pilot. After the war many of these Avengers were put on an aircraft carrier, taken out to sea from the River Clyde and lowered over the side into the sea to meet Lend-Lease requirements.

Apart from the main contract work of repairing Blenheims and Avengers, Airwork also carried out other ad hoc work. One interesting example was a Vickers Wellington which carried a degaussing ring for sweeping mines. The Wellington had landed at Abbotsinch to be dismantled and crated before being taken out to a vessel on the River Clyde for shipment to the Middle East. The RAF at Abbotsinch asked the Airwork Renfrew general manager if they could provide someone at very short notice to go over to repair the magnetic ring which had been damaged as they were waiting to transport the aircraft out to the waiting vessel.

Grumman Avenger Mk II JZ489 inside one of the Belfast Truss hangars at Renfrew. The last flight of a Grumman Avenger repaired by Airwork took place at Renfrew on 29 December 1945. (Lou Curl)

Once the war had ended and the contract for the Avengers had finished, the Airwork depot at Renfrew had to look to other areas for business, especially in the civil field as military work was winding down. The general manager, James Brent, gave an interview to a local paper at the end of the war in which he stated that he was positive there would be work forthcoming in civilian aircraft maintenance and repair. In the early part of 1947, Automobile and Aircraft Services Ltd entered into an agreement with Airwork that anyone who purchased an aircraft from them would have an after-sales service provided by Airwork at their airfields including Renfrew. The company offered also to arrange maintenance and servicing facilities to any private owners who had bought aircraft from them prior to their agreement with Airwork in March 1947. Unfortunately, in the austere post-war years in Britain, there was not enough civil work to keep the depot open at Renfrew and it was closed down by spring 1949.

35

RINGWAY

A contract was awarded to Airwork General Trading to refurbish and modify the Canadair Sabre Mk 2s before they were passed to the Greek (Royal Hellenic Air Force – RHAF) and Turkish air forces (TAF) under the Mutual Defense Aid Program (MDAP). Airwork initially looked at the possibility of using the two Bellman hangars by Ringway's 1938 control tower.

However, a much larger hangar became available located in the centre of Ringway's southside hangars. This was hangar No. 522 and the company moved into it in early 1953. At this stage Airwork had already commenced work on refurbishing Sabres at Speke.

A number of interesting aircraft visited Ringway in connection with the overhaul work carried out by Airwork. These included RCAF C-45 Expeditors, C-119 Flying Boxcars, DC-4M North Stars, along with Greek and Turkish C-47s. The C-47s would bring in pilots from the respective national air forces to perform the delivery flights to their new bases once each batch of Sabre 2s became ready.

CANADAIR SABRE 2

The first Canadair Sabre 2s to arrive for overhaul on 7 April 1954 were 19371, 19375 and 19383 of 421 (Indian) Squadron and coded 'AX', previously based at Grostenquin Air Base in France. Within two months of these first arrivals, work built up quickly, to the extent that the Sabres were parked outside hangar No. 522 awaiting attention. In the following twenty-four months, 202 Sabre 2s (including sixty-two also taken over to Speke) were to pass through Ringway. Various modifications were carried out including an extended leading edge before the aircraft were flown on to be used by the Greek and Turkish air forces with the designation of the aircraft changed to F-86E(M) after completion of refurbishment and modifications.

Once testing of the aircraft was complete, the RCAF markings would be replaced by Greek and Turkish air force insignia with 19408 being the first Turkish aircraft and 19220 being the first Greek aircraft to have their insignia applied on 13 June 1954. Some of the Sabres were switched between the two air forces (thirteen Turkish were changed to Greek and five Greek were changed to Turkish). From February to June 1955, batches of Sabre 2s arrived from Canadair's factory at Cartierville after overhaul and repainting in Greek and Turkish air force insignia before arrival at Ringway for checking and onward delivery.

A source of interest for onlookers was some of the test flying carried out on the Sabres. On 3 July 1954, 19222 in Greek air force markings took off and climbed to 30,000ft (9,100m) then made a supersonic dive, aiming the 'boom' at the Airwork hangar, but the 'boom' hit the nearby village of Styal instead. The Sabre then performed a loop and 'beat up' the Airwork hangar at low level, then went into a vertical climb with ten upward rolls, turned over on its back and rolled out into a subsonic dive before landing.

Other examples of air-show-type aerobatics included the arrival on 2 July 1954 of four Sabre 2s from Zweibrücken, which proceeded to perform an impromptu display before clearing to allow the arrival of a KLM Convair 340 and then landing themselves.

Despite these impressive aerobatic displays, there were problems. A Sabre 2, 19344 in RCAF markings, made a fast touchdown on 3 July 1954 (the same day as 19222 created its sonic boom) on the relatively short 5,900ft (1,800m) 06/24 runway and its port brake was smoking before coming to a halt.

What made these particular flights all the more memorable was that they were performed at a fairly busy commercial airport which would include normal commercial aircraft arriving and departing in between the Sabre antics!

More tragic, however, was the loss of 19234 on a test flight on 15 December 1954 when it crashed on Holme Moss killing the pilot, Flying Officer P.V. Robinson, of the RCAF 137 (Test) Flight. Another tragedy was the loss of 19289 when it crashed on 11 July 1955 near Chaumont in France on its delivery flight to the TAF, killing the US delivery pilot.

One incident during a test flight, which fortunately did not result in loss of life, took place on 2 September 1954 when Sabre 2 19267 collided in mid-air with an RAF de Havilland Vampire FB.5 (VV616 of 613 Squadron). Both aircraft managed to land safely.

CANADAIR SABRE 4

Between July 1954 and September 1956, forty ex-RAF Sabre 4s were modified by Airwork at Ringway before being painted in USAF markings and flown to the Italian and Yugoslavian air forces. At the time of their arrival there were still Sabre 2s being worked on for Greece and Turkey. The duly refurbished Sabre 4s started to come out of the Airwork facility from March 1956 onwards in their old-style NATO camouflage scheme, which had been touched up. Each one had a USAF and Canadian serial number applied in white. After test flying by Airwork pilots, these Sabres were designated F-86E(M) and delivered to USAF charge at Dunsfold and Burtonwood. USAF pilots took the aircraft for onward delivery to the Italian and Yugoslavian air forces.

The last Sabre 4 to depart Ringway, on 30 September 1956, was 19782.

CANADAIR SABRE 5 & 6

The majority of the refurbishment work on the Sabre 5s and Sabre 6s was carried out by Aero & Engineering Merseyside at Hooton Park. However, a small number of Sabre 5s (nineteen) were refurbished by Airwork at Ringway for the RCAF, plus ten Sabre 6s. The ten Sabre 6s which Airwork refurbished in March and April 1956 were the only ones refurbished in the north-west.

LOCKHEED & CANADAIR T-33AS

A small number of Lockheed-built T-33A Shooting Stars were overhauled by Canadair in Montreal and given Turkish and Greek air force (Hellenic) markings. These were ex-RCAF

A group of RCAF Lockheed T-33A Shooting Stars for the Turkish air force. The first four to be refurbished for the Turkish air force had arrived at Ringway by 30 March 1955. (R.A. Scholefield)

aircraft which had been transferred to the RCAF from the USAF. They were officially transferred to the Turkish and Greek air forces on 3 February 1955. They were then delivered to Airwork at Ringway in two batches between late March and late May 1955. Nearly all these aircraft retained their original RCAF serials as well as USAF serials in a couple of cases.

In addition to the T-33A Shooting Stars, a small batch of Canadair-built T-33A Silver Stars were also brought in for repairs and servicing. Some of these were later transferred to the French air force.

Whilst work was being carried out on the Sabres and Silver Stars, a number of RCAF, TAF and RHAF aircraft visited, bringing in pilots and personnel. In Ringway's case these included RCAF C-54GM North Stars, Beech C-45 Expeditors and a C-119F Flying Boxcar, plus Greek and Turkish air force C-47s.

Airwork General Trading Ltd moved out of Ringway in 1956 across to Speke where extra hangarage was taken on to accommodate the work on the F-86 Sabres.

36

ROYAL NAVY TRAINING

AIR DIRECTION SCHOOL/ADTU/ADS

There is a differentiation between the terms Air Direction School, ADS (Air Direction Squadron) and ADTU (Air Direction Training Unit) which is taken by some to be the same thing at different times. The Air Direction School was formed in 1941 to train Royal Naval personnel in the control of fighter aircraft and based initially in the control tower at RNAS Yeovilton before it moved to Kete. The aircraft that were used to support this school was initially the ADS from 1950, which was run by Airwork (after taking over from 790 Squadron), and the ADTU upon its establishment at Yeovilton in 1961.

RNAS Brawdy & St Davids

In 1949 Airwork had received a contract to operate aircraft on behalf of the RN Aircraft Direction Centre at Kete in Pembrokeshire. The school, which had started in the Yeovilton control tower, was close to the old wartime airfield at Dale on St Ann's Head and gave radar training to Royal Naval fighter directors for aircraft carriers.

Airwork Ltd formed the ADS at RNAS Brawdy on 5 January 1950. This squadron took over from 790 Squadron, which had operated from RNAS Dale and then RNAS Culdrose using de Havilland Sea Mosquito TR.33s.

Airwork also operated a heavy twin conversion course using de Havilland Mosquito T.3s and Sea Hornets from December 1949 to September 1956. These aircraft were also used for interception exercises.

On 8 September 1951, due to the Royal Navy's expansion plans for Brawdy, Airwork and the ADS had to move over to St Davids. St Davids was never actually commissioned as a Royal Naval air station. It was an RAF airfield but was loaned to the Admiralty for Airwork's Royal Navy training. It was staffed and run by civilians of Airwork Ltd, though most of the civilians were ex-navy personnel. Airwork's local manager at this time was Mr F.B. Tomkins, a former RAF group captain and one-time commanding officer of RAF Stoke Orchard (glider pilot training). The Airwork chief flying instructor was Mr T.P. Aldous, who later went on to become managing director of Airwork Overseas Ltd at Hurn. Aldous was transferred to the FRU at

Air Direction Squadron de Havilland Sea Venoms line up at St Davids. (Babcock International Group)

Hurn as manager, just as it was beginning operations and his place as chief flying instructor was taken by Reg Leach. Airwork carried out full operational and instructional tasks as well as the servicing of aircraft, airfield control, transport and catering. Despite the very full flying programme the move from Brawdy to St Davids was accomplished without any interruption to the programme.

Jet Conversion Course Aircraft

The first two Meteor T.7s to be used were WA600 and WS104 which were allocated to the unit on 18 September 1953. These were followed by WL332, VW446, WS115 and WS117, which all arrived in late 1953. Further Meteor T.7s were used from 1954 onwards. A total of twenty-two Meteor T.7s were used at varying times by November 1957.

Air Direction Squadron Aircraft

The aircraft used by the ADS consisted of a mixture of Supermarine Attacker F.1, FB.1 and FB.2s which were all used between September 1955 and November 1957, with the first arrival being Attacker F.1 WA526. From October 1955 to 12 August 1958, the unit used de Havilland Sea Venom FAW.20s, with WM567 being the first and last Sea Venom FAW.20 used.

The ADS remained at St Davids from September 1951 until October 1958, when they moved back to RNAS Brawdy. Brawdy became the home for the ADS for three years, until January 1961, when the unit moved to RNAS Yeovilton, becoming the ADTU.

By 1956, the Airwork Royal Navy operations at St Davids and the FRU at Hurn were putting in 400 flying hours per month on average. The ADS and the Air Direction School moved back to Yeovilton in January 1961 with the Sea Venoms, which were replaced by Hunter GA.11s and T.8s.

In December 1965 the ADTU at RNAS Yeovilton had a complement of eight pilots and twenty engineers.

When the ADTU Sea Venoms were retired in December 1970, de Havilland Sea Vixens were used to form an FRU outstation at Yeovilton (see below).

FRU

Background

The decision to form a civilian-operated FRU at Hurn was made in late 1951. In June 1952 Mr T.P. Aldous, Airwork's chief instructor at St Davids, was appointed manager of the new unit, which was named 'Airwork Services FRU (Hurn)'. It is sometimes incorrectly referred to as '776 FRU'. The main purpose of the newly formed FRU was to supplement the duties of the 771 Squadron FRU (based at RNAS Ford) by providing target aircraft for HMS *Boxer*, which was the Royal Navy radar operators' training ship.

A close-up view of the ML Aviation winch and sleeve target-towing equipment on Gloster Meteor TT.20 WM292. (Babcock International Group)

Much experience in this type of work had been gained by Airwork over the previous two years as a result of their unit at Brawdy (St Davids from September 1951). Airwork (St Davids) was equipped with Sea Mosquito TR.33s for FAA air crew twin piston conversion training and Mosquito T.3s used as 'fighters' and 'targets' in conjunction with the Aircraft Direction School at Kete (HMS *Harrier*), Pembrokeshire.

During July 1952, Sea Hornets began to arrive at St Davids, releasing the Sea Mosquito TR.33s for the FRU at Hurn. The Sea Mosquitos continued in service at Hurn for just over a year until they were replaced by Sea Hornets.

In February 1957, 700 Squadron at RNAS Ford transferred its target-tug aircraft to the Airwork FRU. In May 1967, 728 Squadron at Hal Far, Malta, was disbanded and Airwork then also covered Mediterranean fleet requirement tasks and several detachments were made to locations such as Cyprus and Gibraltar.

By March 1967, FRU operations were being restricted by the airport opening hours at Hurn. There was talk in 1968 about a possible move to Yeovilton but lack of space precluded this move until a later date. By 1967–68, the FRU was utilising every available hangar at Hurn.

The FRU remained at Hurn until November 1972 (with the Sea Vixen FRU outstation at Yeovilton).

Mosquito/Sea Mosquito

Two PR.16s arrived at Hurn on 10 August 1952 just prior to the delivery of the TR.33s from St Davids. Both variants were used almost exclusively in conjunction with HMS *Boxer* off the south coast.

Sea Hornet

Sea Hornets started replacing Mosquitos from February 1953. They continued doing the same work with HMS *Boxer* but increasingly FRU duties were carried out with other ships. The newly formed (on 17 August 1955) 700 Squadron used Firefly TT.4s for FRU duties but worked closely with the Airwork FRU.

It was decided that the Sea Hornets would be replaced at the end of 1955 by Attackers. However, in July 1955, serious corrosion had been discovered in the mainplane spars of some Sea Hornets. All aircraft were inspected whilst investigations commenced on a possible rectification programme. Aircraft cleared after inspection continued flying until 13 October 1955, when it was decided to ground the type once and for all. Sea Furies were used to take over from the Sea Hornets.

Sea Fury

The first Sea Furies arrived at Hurn on 14 October 1955, with five aircraft on strength by 18 October 1955. The FRU Sea Furies served until 1962, when they were finally superseded by Sea Hawks. Between 1955 and 1960, three separate batches were delivered to the FRU. The first batch was withdrawn from use from October 1957, due to old age. Their replacements lasted until March 1960, by which time they too were worn out. The final batch comprised refurbished examples and represented the last piston-engined, fighter-type aircraft to see service in Royal Navy colours. In this last batch was TF956, the first production FB.11 and a veteran of the Korean War.

The Sea Furies were considered obsolete long before the FRU finally relinquished them.

Attacker

The late autumn of 1955 was a very busy time for the FRU with two new types being assimilated, one of which was the unit's first jet aircraft. The initial plan to replace Fireflies with Sea Hornets had been dropped and instead Attackers were scheduled as replacements with effect from November 1955.

They were to be operated on a trials basis with a view to taking over the gunnery and tracking role from 700 Squadron, with the eight Sea Furies covering general FRU duties. The premature departure of the Sea Hornets meant that the Sea Furies would be covering for the Attackers until they were ready for FRU service.

The Attackers were intended as a stopgap measure, the obvious successor being the Sea Hawk.

A total of six Attacker FB.2s were delivered to Hurn between November 1955 and January 1956. At the same time Attackers (F.1, FB.1 and FB.2s) were delivered to Airwork at Brawdy/St Davids.

Sea Hawk

From November 1956, Sea Hawk F.1s began to supersede the Attackers. By late February 1957, the Airwork FRU had taken over the responsibility for all FRU duties, including those carried out by 700 Squadron at Ford.

There were eight Sea Hawk F.1s on strength by March 1957. The F.1s were progressively replaced by the FB.5 version from April 1958. In June 1961 the first of the FGA.6s arrived and they initially replaced the Sea Furies and then the FB.5s.

The Sea Hawks were very successful and the last two examples did not leave the Airwork FRU until February 1969.

The Sea Hawks were used for radar calibration work as well as for gunnery tracking and training. The Sea Hawk had such a small profile that it was difficult for gunnery training and calibration crews to pick up visually a target Sea Hawk. It was decided to install a powerful Harley Light at the tip of the port under-wing tank as a standard fit. The conversion seems to have been applied initially to the FB.5s by RNAY Fleetlands and/or NARIU Lee-on-Solent (Naval Aircraft Radio Installation Unit) prior to delivery to Airwork FRU. The FRU Sea Hawk F.1 WF161 appeared to have served as the prototype conversion aircraft for both the Harley conversion and the overall black paint scheme. In operation the Sea Hawk pilot would switch on his light and fly towards the ship and the gunnery operator would line up his sights on the light quickly and easily.

The FRU Sea Hawks exercised frequently with the Fraser Gunnery Range at Portsmouth, also the home of the Fleet Photographic Unit which provided a processing and analysing service for the 35mm cine films aligned with the tracking system with the guns. The negative film from a successful gun crew's film would be analysed by Wrens. The Sea Hawks were painted black overall so that they would show up very clearly on the negative film under all conditions of light.

Firefly

With the merger of 703 (STU) and 771 (FRU) Squadrons into 700 (Trials and FRU) Squadron at RNAS Ford on 17 August 1955, the Firefly TT.4 target-towing element of the old 771 Squadron was retained by 700 Squadron whilst all other FRU duties were passed on to the Airwork FRU at Hurn.

By the end of 1956, the target-towing requirements were transferred to the FRU, leaving 700 Squadron as a purely trials and evaluation squadron. Firefly TT.4s began to arrive at Hurn from 4 February 1957 and the full complement of six aircraft was achieved by 15 March 1957.

The Firefly TT.4 was equipped with a ML Aviation ML4G winch and could tow sleeve or banner targets out to a length of 6,000ft (1,800m) and operate up to 10,000ft (3,048m). TW723 seen here served with the unit from 11 December 1957 to 9 December 1958. (Babcock International Group)

Although the TT.4s had mostly been refurbished prior to joining Airwork FRU, they were obsolete long before arriving at Hurn. About the same time as the first aircraft arrived with the FRU its replacement the Meteor TT.20 prototype WD767 first flew at Bitteswell. The first Airwork FRU Meteor TT.20 (WM292) arrived in May 1958 and the last Firefly TT.4s departed in December 1958.

Dragonfly

701 Squadron (Ships' Flights and Helicopter Trials) disbanded at Lee-on-Solent on 20 September 1958. One of the squadron's tasks was to provide a helicopter for torpedo tracking. This involved the helicopter following the path of the torpedo through the water to facilitate easy recovery of the round for analysis. It was decided that the Airwork FRU would fulfil this role. Secondary tasks were SAR and general hack duties. One Dragonfly was to be provided. Crew training was provided by Ford Station Flight both at Ford and Hurn using Dragonfly HR.3 WG709 prior to the arrival of Airwork FRU's WG724 from Ford on 22 September 1958. WG724 was replaced by WG719 which itself was replaced by VZ965.

The FRU's Dragonfly was not utilised to any great extent although it remained on strength until July 1961, when 771 Squadron was reformed at Portland and took over the main role.

Meteor

The Meteor TT.20s were employed in the ground/ship-to-air firing role and were equipped with a ML4G wind-driven winch operated from the rear cockpit. Four sleeve targets were available for use. The aircraft operated between 5,000ft (1,523m) and 10,000ft (3,048m) with the sleeve streaming out to about 18,000ft (5,486m). Flight duration was about one hour and thirty minutes, and generally only up to two sleeves could be streamed per sortie before the aircraft began to run out of fuel. It was common to see a TT.20 doing a low pass over Hurn and release its sleeve on to the airfield, where it could easily be recovered after a flight.

In 1963 Flight Refuelling Ltd acquired manufacturing rights for the Hayes TA7 target system using a Del Mar Winch. The company developed it into the now familiar Rushton high-speed target system which operated in the Canberra TT.18. This sophisticated dart-shaped metal target was installed in some of Airwork FRU's TT.20s (e.g. WM242) in 1968 and continued in service until Canberra TT.18s began to replace them in September 1969. Meteor TT.20s were retained at Hurn until March 1971.

Prior to 1962, rating and type familiarisation checks had been carried out by Airwork (St Davids) Meteor T.7s. However, on 18 January 1962 a Meteor T.7 was delivered to the Airwork FRU specifically for these purposes. In addition to these primary tasks it was used as a target aircraft and as a hack. Three T.7s passed through the FRU between 1962 and 1971. A Harley Light nose fitment was available when the T.7 was used in the target role. It is believed that WF791 Meteor T.7 from 5 CAACU, Woodvale, was used on loan for a short period from 10 July 1967.

The winches used on the TT.20s were allocated individual letter codes which were purely for identifying serviceable ones.

Supermarine Scimitar

In 1964 Scimitar F.1s were offered as the future replacement aircraft for the Sea Hawks, there being no surplus Hunters available for FRU duties. The Scimitars delegated for Airwork FRU were put through a long modernisation programme at RNAY Fleetlands, starting with XD246 in October 1965. Operational support was provided at NASU Brawdy (Naval Aircraft Support Unit) and also the Airwork FRU. Harley Lights were also fitted in the noses of most aircraft. However, the Scimitar caused numerous maintenance problems.

764 Squadron at RNAS Lossiemouth trained up the Airwork pilots during most of 1965. When this task was completed in November 1965, one of their aircraft (XD267) was flown to Hurn to provide continuation and familiarisation training until the first of the refurbished machines arrived in June 1966 (XD246).

By October 1967, only a handful of Sea Hawks remained, although the latter remained in service until February 1969. One month later, the first Hunter GA.11 arrived to replace the Scimitar. The last Scimitar to depart from Hurn was XD244.

Hawker Hunter

The first Hunter GA.11 WV382 complete with Harley Light in the nose arrived on 27 March 1969. Prior to the arrival of Airwork FRU's own Hunter T.8C in December 1969, T.8s were detached from time to time to the FRU from Brawdy and Yeovilton.

The Hunters fulfilled the same role as their predecessors, the Scimitars. All the Hunters were equipped with a Harley Light in the nose, including the T.8C.

With the final departure of the Scimitars in January 1971, the complement of GA.11s was built up to eight plus a single T.8C.

BAC Canberra

The first TT.18 (WK123) was delivered to the Airwork FRU on 15 September 1969. Four TT.18s were on strength by November 1970 and the aircraft was a considerable improvement over the

Meteor TT.20 (which left FRU service in March 1971) as it could tow two high-speed targets at a cable length of about 22,000ft (6,705m) to 30,000ft (9,143m) and operate at a height of 15,000ft (4,571m) and stay on station for much longer.

In addition to TT.18s, the FRU operated a T.4 as a radar target and calibration aircraft when not employed in crew training and checking. A single B.2 was also employed on target and calibration duties but it left the FRU for conversion to TT.18 and eventually joined the FRADTU at Yeovilton.

Canberra TT.18 WK123, which was Airwork FRU's first Canberra, was the last aircraft to leave Hurn on 29 November 1972 when the FRU disbanded to become FRADTU at Yeovilton.

De Havilland Sea Vixens

In 1970 five Sea Vixens replaced the ADTU Sea Venoms and formed an outstation known as Airwork FRU (Yeovilton). These were flown initially by 890 Squadron pilots, giving the Airwork ground crews valuable experience on the type. The main purpose of these aircraft was to provide a service to FOST (Flag Officer Sea Training) for the calibration of Royal Navy vessels' radar and missile systems. They also provided an in-flight refuelling role for the F-4 Phantoms of 767 and 892 Squadrons during 1971–72. A total of twelve Sea Vixens served with the FRU outstation at various times.

FRADTU/FRADU

On 16 October 1972 the Hunters and Canberras from Hurn joined the Sea Vixens at Yeovilton, becoming Airwork FRU Yeovilton. On 1 December 1972, the FRU and the ADTU were merged at Yeovilton, becoming known as the Fleet Requirements and Air Direction Training Unit (FRADTU). The word 'training' was dropped from the title in 1973 and the unit became the Fleet Requirements and Air Direction Unit (FRADU). The role of the unit was the same as before, which was to provide the Royal Navy fleet with realistic targets for exercises. The Canberra also played the role of Soviet Tu-95 Bears.

Aircraft Operations

After the formation of FRADTU/FRADU, the initial complement of the unit was thirty-one aircraft: twenty-one Hunters, five Canberras and five Sea Vixens.

The Sea Vixens retained their '75z' identities throughout their service until they retired from the FRADU in February 1974 after some 5,000 flying hours with the unit.

The Hunters of the ADTU that had been assigned call signs 731–748 were gradually reassigned new FRADU identities with numbers in the 8xx range.

One of the training tasks undertaken by the Hunters was to simulate sea-skimming missiles. The grim reality of such attacks was to become apparent during the Falklands War. The training would involve two Hunters flying in close formation with a Canberra towards a vessel and the Hunters accelerating away towards the ship to simulate missile launches.

The Canberras continued their high-speed target-towing role, as they had at Hurn. FRADU also used Canberra T.4 WJ874 for currency training and the annual visit of a team from 231 OCU, which checked the operational standards of the FRADU. The first (WH780) of seven T.22s arrived in 1973. Five more arrived at Yeovilton in 1974, with the final aircraft (WH803) arriving in July 1976. These T.22s were modified PR.7 photo reconnaissance aircraft which were used initially to train operators for the Blue Parrot radar in Buccaneers. These radar units were installed in the nose of the T.22.

A line-up of FRADU Canberras at RNAS Yeovilton. (Kevin Slade)

Blue Herons

In 1975 Airwork pilots formed the 'Blue Herons' aerobatic team with Hawker Hunters at RNAS Yeovilton. By this time FRADU was flying up to sixty sorties a day, with the 'Blue Herons' practising their display flying after hours. Under the leadership of Derek Morter, the team first flew on 6 September 1975, becoming the first ever civilian aerobatics team using military aircraft. The skill of the Airwork crew is shown in the fact that the team won the premier (Shell UK Trophy) aerobatic trophy at the 1977 International Air Tattoo at RAF Greenham Common after being placed second the previous year. Due to defence cuts the team disbanded in 1981.

Flight Refuelling bid for the contract when it came up for renewal in 1983 and took over from Airwork. However, Airwork involvement was not completely over with FRADU, as a contract was obtained in April 1988 to overhaul the FRADU Hunters at Hurn.

37

SPEKE

The primary work carried out at Speke by Airwork was the refurbishment of Canadair-built Sabres. An Airwork advert at the time described their work at Speke as follows: 'The erection, modification and servicing of Sabrejet aircraft operated by the RCAF from UK bases.'

During the five years Airwork spent at Speke they occupied the No. 1 (Art Deco) hangar throughout the whole period and at various times hangar Nos 2 and 6, depending on how much pressure there was on space. Prior to the start of the refurbishment work, Airwork staff were sent to Canada for training in the year prior to work starting and in addition Airwork teams travelled to RCAF bases in Europe.

CANADAIR SABRE MK 2

After intensive Sabre Mk 2 operations in Europe, a contract was given to Airwork General Trading in late 1952 to overhaul the RCAF Sabres, with the first three arriving on 17 November 1952 from RAF North Luffenham. A small stream of Sabre Mk 2s arrived over the following months, with these being used in training up the workforce. On 9 October 1953 two Canadair-built Sabre Mk 4s arrived. These were the first of a number of Mk 4 aircraft which had been used by the RCAF and were to be overhauled and repainted by Airwork before being passed on to the RAF. By early 1954, the hangar used by Airwork was full of Sabres (sixty had arrived at Speke by April 1954).

With the introduction in service of the first Canadair Sabre Mk 5s to replace the Sabre Mk 2s, the last of the earlier Sabre Mk 2s had left and on 23 April 1954, a new batch of RCAF Sabre Mk 2s arrived as Airwork began a new contract (under the Mutual Defense Aid Progam) to overhaul these aircraft for the Greek (Royal Hellenic) and Turkish air forces. The work was carried out jointly with the Airwork facility at Ringway and involved work such as the fitting of extended wing leading edges. With the completion of the work, the designation of the aircraft was changed to F-86E(M). A few Sabre 2s were transferred from Ringway to Speke as work on the Sabre 2s started to draw to a close. The work lasted just over a year from April 1954 to May 1955. A total of sixty-two Sabre 2s for the three air forces (RCAF, RHAF, TAF) passed through Airwork's hands at Speke between November 1952 and October 1955.

CANADAIR SABRE MK 4

From October 1953 to October 1954, a batch of sixty Canadair Sabre Mk 4s, which had been allocated to the RAF and given RAF serials, were loaned to the RCAF to use as a stopgap measure pending arrival of their (RCAF) Sabre 5s. Most of these Sabre 4s supplied to the RAF had been supplied by the USA under the MDAP (Mutual Defense Aid Program). These Sabre Mk 4s began to arrive for servicing and modification with Airwork at Speke. Many of these aircraft arrived at Speke with mixed RCAF/RAF markings. In early 1954 the Sabre Mk 4s were flown on to 5 MU Kemble after work was carried out on them. At this point (from mid to late 1954) Hawker Hunters were starting to equip the RAF and thereby release the Sabre Mk 4s. Overall there were a total of 121 Sabre 4s overhauled at Speke from October 1953 to 4 January 1958, with the last one being 19472.

A further contract involved overhaul of eighty Canadair Sabre 4s for delivery to Italy and Yugoslavia. These particular aircraft left Speke in USAF markings with Canadian serials as the deal was being financed by the USA.

In an effort to consolidate the work and reduce costs, Airwork General Trading Ltd moved out of Ringway in 1956 over to Speke, where extra hangarage was taken on to accommodate the work on the F-86 Sabres.

The first large group of RCAF Sabre Mk 4s after arrival in March 1954, parked in front of No. 1 hangar at Speke, the centre of Airwork's operations from 1952 to 1958. (Phil Butler)

CANADAIR T-33A SILVER STAR

A much smaller number (five in total) of T-33As were dealt with at Speke compared to Ringway and the number at Ringway was small. These were Canadair-built T-33A Silver Stars, with two of them (21016 and 21022) in such a damaged condition that they arrived by road on 19 March and 6 April 1955 respectively. Three of the five aircraft were later delivered to the French air force.

As for Ringway, there were also visits by Greek and Turkish Dakotas, bringing in pilots and support personnel, plus visits by RCAF aircraft including Bristol 170 Freighters for the Sabres and T-33As.

DE HAVILLAND VAMPIRE NF.10

Additionally, Airwork General Trading were given a contract to modify RAF night fighter Vampire NF.10s to navigation trainer standard. The first batch arrived on 5 March 1954. In a fifteen-month period, thirty-six passed through the facility. The Vampire NF.10s acquired served with the RAF from 1951 to 1954, equipping 23, 25 and 151 Squadrons.

OTHER WORK

After the Sabre contract was finished Airwork carried out work on a small number of RCAF T-33s in 1955. Other than the storage of a few Bristol 170s for the manufacturer in 1957–58, there were only two other small pieces of work. This was the overhaul of DH.104 Doves for the Iraq Petroleum Co. in 1956–57 and the overhaul of two Sudan Airways Douglas DC-3s in 1957–58.

Airwork closed down their Speke operation in February 1958 after their bid to overhaul ex-RAF Lockheed Neptunes for Argentina was rejected and no other work could be found. As with much of Airwork's business, there was only work as long as new contracts kept coming in. Once they stopped, there was little option but to close the facility.

38

UNIVERSITY AIR SQUADRONS & BRITANNIA FLIGHT

The university air squadron (UAS) contracts were held at different times and for varying times in most cases.

BRITANNIA FLIGHT PLYMOUTH AIRPORT

In January 1965 the Ministry of Defence awarded a contract to Airwork Services to provide experienced ex-service flying instructors and aircraft technicians to undertake the initial grading (screening) of potential pilots for the Fleet Air Arm.

Based at Plymouth's Roborough Airport, the flight initially consisted of six Royal Navy DH.82 Tiger Moths (T6296, T8191, BB694, BB814, BB852 and XL714). XL714 (ex-T6099 and G-AOGR) was one of four DH.82As reconditioned for the Royal Navy.

Student pilots were given twelve hours' flying over the period of a fortnight to cover basic flying exercises and to bring them up to solo standard. Airwork staff introduced standardised mass pre-flight and post-flight briefings to ensure that objective assessments were made of the student's potential for further fixed-wing and rotary flying training up to wings (Brevet) standard. The students included Royal Navy engineering cadets as well as *ab initio* for Dartmouth College cadet pilots and observers.

In June 1966 the DH.82 Tiger Moths were replaced by de Havilland Chipmunks. DH.82 Tiger Moth BB814 made the last landing on 23 June 1966.

The standards and assessments of the unit were tested over a twenty-year period from the unit's inception and were found to be correct. Great emphasis was placed on the flying instructional standards and these were maintained by the RAF's Central Flying School (CFS).

GLASGOW UAS

In December 1950 Glasgow UAS moved to Scone due to runway work at Abbotsinch and Airwork became responsible for maintenance of the squadron's aircraft. Airwork Ltd were running the aerodrome at Scone and in 1951, they presented a trophy (called the Scone Cup) for an annual competition to be held amongst the Scottish university air squadrons. The first competition was held in October 1951 and was won by Glasgow.

The title of the squadron changed on 1 January 1965 from Glasgow University Air Squadron to Universities of Glasgow and Strathclyde Air Squadron. On the same date, the servicing of the squadron's motor transport vehicles was transferred from Airwork Services at RAF Turnhouse to Glasgow.

DURHAM UAS

From February 1949, Airwork provided maintenance for the Durham UAS. In March 1949 the squadron moved to Ouston and again Airwork were contracted to provide the maintenance for Durham UAS and for No. 11 AEF (Air Experience Flight) also based at Ouston. From 1955, Airwork were offered a contract to continue to operate the Durham UAS, which had now moved to Sunderland's Usworth airfield. The contract included catering and motor transport.

LONDON UAS

Airwork were contracted to maintain the London UAS Chipmunks at Booker from September 1951. They were still being maintained in 1953 and continued from 1956–63.

OXFORD UAS

Oxford UAS had their second-line maintenance carried out at Booker by Airwork. This continued from 1956–63.

BRISTOL UAS

Bristol UAS had their second-line maintenance carried out at Booker by Airwork. This continued from 1956–63.

MANCHESTER UAS & LIVERPOOL UAS

No. 10 AEF

As part of a major contract won in 1962 for operating No. 5 CAACU and providing a number of services, at RAF Woodvale, Lancashire, Airwork were additionally responsible for servicing the de Havilland Chipmunks of the Manchester and Liverpool UAS, along with No. 10 AEF.

No. 4 AEF

Airwork had taken over the running of Exeter Airport on behalf of Devon County Council in 1964. At the same time the company also began the support and servicing for No. 4 AEF. The closure of No. 3/4 CAACU at Exeter in December 1971 did not affect the Airwork contract to continue servicing the two Chipmunks of No. 4 AEF.

EAST LOWLANDS UAS & NO. 12 AEF

Airwork gained a contract in 1969 to provide engineering support to three Scottish university air squadrons (Edinburgh, Glasgow and Aberdeen), plus No. 12 AEF which was based at RAF Turnhouse.

A contract was obtained in 1992 to maintain the East Lowlands Universities Air Squadron aircraft at RAF Turnhouse.

UGSAS & ABERDEEN UAS

The long relationship that Glasgow (UGSAS from 1965) enjoyed with Airwork at both Scone and Glasgow was finished in 1969 with the centralisation and transfer of the work to RAF Turnhouse, where the Bulldogs and Chipmunks belonging to the universities of Edinburgh, Glasgow & Strathclyde and Aberdeen were maintained with No. 12 AEF.

SOUTHAMPTON UAS

In 1978 Airwork secured a contract which started in December of that year to operate the Southampton University Air Squadron, which consisted of six Bulldogs plus the four Chipmunks of No. 2 AEF at Hurn. The student pilots from Southampton University often used RNAS Lee-on-Solent for their training flights in the Bulldogs.

NO. 1 AEF MANSTON

Airwork secured a contract which started in August 1985 to provide engineering support for the de Havilland Chipmunks of No. 1 AEF at Manston.

DHC.1 Chipmunk WG482 of Southampton UAS was maintained by Airwork Services at Hurn. (John Blake via Air Britain)

MISCELLANEOUS

39

MISCELLANEOUS CONTRACTS

The nature of Airwork's business was essentially contractual with limited time spans. This meant that it was a constant task to look for new work. Some of the contracts lasted for a long period and others for fairly short periods. Some contracts were large and some were small but the following listing gives an idea of the nature of the very varied work undertaken by the company through the years. It should be remembered that for every new contract gained, there would be several which had been bid for, but lost.

1933

Avro Cadets, Persia (Iran)

Once Misr-Airwork was established, Alan Muntz made a visit to Tehran, Persia, on behalf of A.V. Roe Ltd. A.V. Roe had authorised Airwork to act on their behalf to sell Avro Cadet training aircraft to Persia. With the backing of the British ambassador, Sir Rex Hoare, Alan Muntz had meetings with the Shah's Minister of Court, Abdolhossein Teymourtash. Teymourtash was greatly interested to hear about the use of Avro Cadets in the Airwork School of Flying and foresaw that they could be useful training aircraft in Persia. Before any deal could be concluded, however, Teymourtash was imprisoned, never to re-emerge. It was generally felt that he had become too powerful and posed a threat to the then Shah.

1934

Newtownards 'Ards Airport'

A new civil aerodrome (the first in Ulster) was officially opened on 31 August 1934 at Newtownards. Known as the 'Ards Airport', Airwork leased the airport and managed it. It had been built on part of the estate of Lord Londonderry who was a keen aviator and owned an Avro 638 Cadet G-ACTX and GA Monospar ST-4 G-AEPG; his daughter Lady Mairi also owned DH.87B Hornet Moth G-ADMR. Lord Londonderry had also been closely involved with the planning of the airport. In effect the airport was a joint venture between Airwork and Lord and Lady Londonderry.

There was a large crowd of an estimated 15,000 spectators for the opening ceremony which was attended by Viscount Castlereagh MP, W.H. Simms (chairman of Newtownards Urban Council), Dr D'Arcy (Primate of All Ireland) and Lord Abercorn who formally opened the airport. Taking part in the opening ceremony was 502 (Special Reserve) Squadron from Aldergrove with three Vickers Virginias contributing to a small flying display. There were a number of civil and military flying displays including two Hawker Furys of 43 Squadron and No. 5 Flying Training School. Alan Muntz was present and gave a display in an Avro Commodore.

The aerodrome manager was F. McNally and Airwork opened a branch of their School of Flying with a resident instructor, Flight Lieutenant Reginald W.E. Bryant. The flying school's resident aircraft was Avro 638 Cadet G-ACTX which was named *Finian the White* by Lady Londonderry at the opening ceremony.

The North of Ireland Flying Club was also offered a home at the new aerodrome. The airfield was twice a checkpoint in the famous King's Cup Air Race in 1935 and 1937.

On 27 September 1934 the managing director of Airwork wrote a letter to the Lord Mayor of Belfast asking for financial assistance in the running of the aerodrome.

However, Airwork's time at Ards was fairly brief (sixteen months) as Lord Londonderry terminated the agreement with effect from 1 January 1936 and took over the management. The Airwork School of Flying was also closed down on the same date and replaced. G-ACTX *Finian the White* was sold to Lord Londonderry in July 1936. Commercial activities at Ards grew from 1936 onwards and the termination by Lord Londonderry was possibly as a result of the growing estrangement between himself and Alan Muntz over the problems in the marriage between Muntz and his daughter.

Airwork assisted in the establishment of the Weston-super-Mare Aero Club.

1937

Airwork became involved with Dunkley Prams, which were Birmingham based, but some production was moved to Airwork's 'National Works' at Bath Road, Hounslow, under the auspices of Airwork General Trading Ltd. Later, however, the entire output of Dunkley Prams was given over to war work with emphasis on the fabric which had previously made the prams. This was under government direction and a source of great bitterness to the Dunkley family in later years as the company never recovered its pre-war fortunes.

1939

Airwork were contracted in August 1939 to start a new RAFVR School at Marlow but war intervened and the contract was put on hold.

1940

Pikes were manufactured for the Home Guard along with landing craft. Some of the Pikes were put on display many years later in the Airwork headquarters at Hurn.

1942

In June 1942 the War Office gave Airwork a contract to produce a large number of collapsible boats and snow sledges for commando and special operations purposes. A number of factory locations were found and set up in West London to produce 120 boats a week by mid-1942. At the same time Airwork also received a contract to produce the prototype rotachute for airborne army experiments.

1944

The company was now involved in the design and manufacture of aircraft fuel, oil and hydraulic tanks for the aircraft industry in addition to its aircraft repair work.

1945

The Ministry of Aircraft Production awarded new contracts to Airwork to dismantle and break up hundreds of unwanted aircraft in the Solway Firth area and Scotland with many being reduced to spares.

By 1945, Airwork were now starting to place orders for post-war designs of British aircraft still on the drawing board.

1946

The post-war sales and service organisation expanded to promote new designs such as the Bristol 170 Wayfarer, Vickers Viking and Airspeed Consul. As an example, Airwork managed the 1946 North and South America sales tour of Bristol 170 G-AGPV in conjunction with Bristol.

1947

The Catering Division of Airwork Ltd opened the first licensed bar at the new London Airport (Heathrow) on 25 April 1947. At the announcement of the opening, comment was made that it was hoped that the opening of the bar would provide better service than that of the tea and coffee bar at the time.

In 1947 Airwork operated Vickers Viking G-AJFT on behalf of the Pakistan Government with the aircraft being based in Karachi.

1948

Airwork established an office in April 1948 in the terminal at Croydon Airport. The office was open on Tuesdays, Wednesdays and Thursdays and manned by Airwork representative Mr H. Smith.

In November 1948 Airwork provided five of the six pilots required by Hawkers to ferry six Hawker Tempest IIs to the Indian air force at Cawnpore.

Airwork acquired a 50 per cent interest in Comair in South Africa which operated a flying training school. Commercial services were started with a Cessna 195.

1949

In December 1948 Airwork Ltd signed a three-year contract with Pakistan Aviation Ltd of Karachi to provide assistance and to act as technical consultants in the establishment of an aircraft and engine overhaul shop and training school. Airwork were also to advise on technical standards as these had not yet been established in the country. The workshops were established at Drigh Road, Karachi, in the giant airship hangar built originally for the R.101 which was modified for use as workshops. Airwork sent 200 technicians out to Karachi and locally employment was provided for between 400 and 500 unskilled and semi-skilled Pakistani nationals. Pupils for advanced training were provided from this pool of local labour.

1950

The company received contracts to manufacture large trailer bodies for the motor industry and for large commercial refrigerators of which 6,000 were built at Loughborough. This contract ceased in 1963.

Airwork leased three aircraft and gave technical assistance to Channel Islands Air Services in 1950. The airline was based in Guernsey and its brief period of operation was from early 1950 to October 1950 when operations ceased. The leased Airwork aircraft were DH.89A G-AESR and DH.104 Doves G-AHRJ and G-AKSS.

1951

In November 1951 Airwork took a 25 per cent shareholding in the Princess Air Transport Co. Ltd, with Saunders-Roe holding the majority share of 75 per cent. The aim of the company was to study the factors affecting the operation of the Saunders-Roe Princess flying boats and to be in a position to tender for their operation should the opportunity arise. Myles Wyatt of Airwork became the new company's chairman and Sir Archibald Hope of Airwork was a director. Only one (G-ALUN) of the three Princess flying boats ever flew. The remaining two G-ALUO and G-ALUP were built and broken up eventually.

1953

Airwork Ltd became an executive member of the Aerodrome Owners Association, replacing Handley Page Ltd in April 1953. The Executive Committee consisted of eight municipal and eight commercial members.

De Havilland Vampire Mk Vs at Hatfield prior to delivery to the Egyptian air force in August 1950. The ferry pilots were (from de Havilland) G.E. Thornton and (from Airwork) Squadron Leader D.R. Turley George. (Royal Aero Club)

The RNAS Northern Communications Squadron (782 Squadron) which was based at RNAS Donibristle was operated by Airwork from 1953. The unit provided de Havilland Dominies for communications work and naval air transport in the north. In 1955 the squadron took delivery of Sea Princes. In 1956 there was a further change of equipment when de Havilland Sea Devons replaced the Sea Princes and Dominies. The Sea Devons ran a service (known as the Clipper Service) to connect at RNAS Anthorn with a twice-weekly southern service linking the southern naval air stations. The northern side of the schedule was run by 782 Squadron. The contract was finished on 15 November 1958 and RNAS Donibristle was closed in 1959.

1954

Deliveries, Hatfield

Airwork delivery crews flew the first four of eight de Havilland Vampires for the Burmese air force out to Burma from Hatfield on 6 December 1954, covering the first 620-mile leg to Marseilles in one hour and thirty-five minutes.

Deliveries, Blackbushe

Airwork were constantly involved in delivering both civil and military aircraft. Some examples include the delivery of Handley Page Marathons JA6009 and JA6010. The first left Blackbushe for delivery with Far Eastern Airlines in Japan on 7 August 1954. Flown by Airwork personnel, Senior First Officer Riley and Radio Officer Rylands, the 10,000-mile flight took nine days routed via Nice, Bari, Athens, Tripoli (Lebanon), Basra, Bahrain, Sharjah, Karachi, Delhi, Allahabad, Calcutta, Rangoon, Tourane, Hong Kong, Tai Pei, Okinawa and Iwakuni.

Other Activities

The company took over the running of the Fighter Control School at Hurn.

In 1954 Airwork were contracted to provide servicing and maintenance for the Gloster Meteor T.7 and F.4s, plus the Vampire T.11s of No. 4 Flying School at Worksop, Nottinghamshire. As with many of these contracts undertaken by Airwork, the contract was also to supply catering and motor transport operations.

1955

The Durham UAS contract also included the running of the ATC at Usworth.

An army co-operation unit was set up with DH.89A Rapides and Percival Proctors.

1956

A new drawing office facility was opened in Brighton.

The Airwork facilities at Disley and Loughborough received a major government contract for radio-controlled cars and conversions of searchlight vehicles from the Ministry of Supply. This contract ceased in 1963.

1958

Airwork Services Ltd took over the Stansted facility at Hangar 1 of Aviation Traders (Eng) Ltd in March 1958 along with the remains of the Ministry of Supply Sabre contract. The intention was to make Stansted their main overhaul base but, after six weeks, the base reverted to AT(E) L. All Airwork employees had been told they were going to get a pay rise but when the base reverted to AT(E)L, the rise was rescinded, believed to be due to the repurchasing of AT(E) L by Freddie Laker and the transfer of the operation to Southend. The only work carried out during the relevant period at Stansted was a repaint of Hermes 2 VX234 (G-AGUB) and a small amount of care and maintenance on the twenty remaining Sabres.

1961

In January 1961 Airwork Services at Panshangar Aerodrome, Hertfordshire, were appointed the sole UK distributors for the Cessna range of aircraft. Airwork then appointed regional dealers for sales service and spares. The Cessnas which passed through Panshangar had the radio installations carried out on site by Airwork engineers.

The Cessna concession was transferred to Perth's Scone Aerodrome in May 1962, becoming a regional dealer, and the main Cessna dealership under Airwork Services, based at Panshangar, was transferred to Hurn.

In October 1961 Airwork gained the contract to operate RNAS Lee-on-Solent ATC, navigation aids, fire and rescue service, plus motor transport and engineering support to the RNAS fixed-wing fleet of de Havilland Sea Herons and Sea Devons of 781 Squadron. The Lee-on-Solent contract ceased in March 1981.

A contract starting in December 1961 was gained to provide engineering support at RAF Andover, Hampshire, for the eight Avro Ansons and one VIP de Havilland Devon of 21 Squadron. In 1964 the Ansons were replaced with Percival Pembrokes and Devons. The strength of the squadron was increased to fourteen aircraft at the same time. The contract to provide engineering support to 21 Squadron ceased in October 1975.

1962

In February 1962 the company obtained a new type of contract which was to provide engineering support on a twenty-four-hour, seven-days-a-week basis, throughout the year for the first two Air Traffic Control Radar Units (ATCRU) at RAF Sopley, Hampshire, and RAF Hack Green, Cheshire. These radar sites were a joint civil and military operation and included the Joint Area Radar School. The Hack Green station was closed in October 1966 and the staff were relocated. RAF Sopley (known as Southern Radar ATCRU) closed in November 1974 and the contract ceased.

A contract was gained at Aldergrove Airport, Belfast, to service and maintain the navigation aids from May 1962.

Another major contract won in 1962 was at RAF Woodvale, Lancashire. This was to operate the No. 5 Squadron Civilian Anti-aircraft Co-operation Unit (CAACU) which operated Gloster Meteor T.7s and T.8s. The aircraft were used for target towing at the Tycroes Range on Anglesey. The contract included servicing the Western Sector Flight as well as airfield management, ATC, catering and motor transport. The RAF Woodvale contract finished in 1975.

1963

Airwork obtained a contract in June 1963 to provide services at RAF Northolt which included catering, motor transport and RAF SIB motor transport maintenance. The contract included runway de-icing for which two Rolls-Royce Derwent engines mounted on a frame (pushed by a fuel bowser) were used. The main part of the contract, however, was the servicing and maintenance of the Metropolitan Communications Squadron. These were de Havilland Devons, Percival Pembrokes, four Vickers Valettas and Sycamore helicopters. Approximately twelve Airwork personnel were employed at Northolt including management. The contract ceased in December 1972.

Although not one of its largest contracts, the company were given a contract in 1963 to provide the Watch-keeping Bus Service for RAF Fylingdales in Yorkshire.

A larger new contract gained in October 1963, however, was to operate No. 231 OCU (Operational Conversion Unit) at RAF Bassingbourn. This contract involved the servicing of over sixty Canberra air rafts along with maintaining ground equipment, navigational aids, communications and photographic equipment at the base. RAF Bassingbourn closed in 1968 and the Canberra contract ceased.

A step in a new direction in 1963 was the gaining of a contract to provide technical support for R/T communications and control of naval aircraft on manufacturer's gun-laying trials for Vickers Ltd at Stonehouse, Gloucestershire, and Crayford, Kent.

1964

A completely new contract obtained in 1964 was to set up and operate the maintenance and servicing of three new ATCRU (joint civil and military) which were operated on a twenty-four-hour, seven-days-a-week basis at Lindholme, Lincolnshire, Watton in Norfolk and North Luffenham in Rutland. The Watton and North Luffenham radars became operational in December 1965 and Lindholme became operational in May 1966.

Another useful area of work for the company was the transfer of simulators. In December 1965 the Airwork engineering support team arranged for the transfer of simulators from St Davids and RNAS Brawdy to RNAS Yeovilton and RNAS Lossiemouth. A contract was given to Airwork to service the Yeovilton simulators (cockpit trainers for the Hunter and Whirlwind) and this contract continued well into the 1980s. The Whirlwind cockpit trainer was transferred from RNAS Yeovilton to RAF Shawbury in January 1988. Design work was undertaken for the simulator at the time of its move and this was undertaken by the PDS Section at Airwork Hurn.

Exeter Airport Ltd was bought out by Air Holdings to become a wholly owned subsidiary of Airwork Services, but it remained autonomous. Basically the airport was managed and run on behalf of Devon County Council. This included operating the resident No. 3/4 CAACU unit as well as supporting civil operations.

In December 1971, No. 3/4 CAACU, with its resident Meteors, Vampires and Hunters, was disbanded, although there was plenty of civil work available for Airwork as well as continuing the support for the No. 4 AEF Chipmunks.

Airwork Services also became involved with another Devon airport in 1964. The company set up Plymouth Airport Ltd as a wholly owned subsidiary which, as well as running the Britannia Flight, operated and serviced the aircraft of the flying club and the resident Royal Marine Helicopters. Airwork operated the airport until 1975 when Brymon Aviation Ltd (trading as Brymon Airways) took over.

1965

In 1965 Airwork assisted in the setting up and operation of the Flying Doctor Service in Zambia. From 29 September 1966, Beagle 206S G-ATZP was put on the Zambian register as 9J-AAM and was used in the role until 15 July 1969.

A contract was awarded to the company to provide engineering support to the RAF Manby College of Air Warfare and its associated airfield at RAF Strubby in Lincolnshire. This included support for the RAF School of Refresher Flying (senior officers' air course). This support was for the four squadrons of Vickers Varsities, Jet Provosts, plus Canberras and Meteors. RAF Strubby closed in 1971 and that portion of the contract ceased. RAF Manby closed a couple of years later in 1974 and again the contract ceased on the closure of the base.

1966

After the success in obtaining the AAC Middle Wallop training and maintenance contract in 1963, further Army Air Corps work followed when Airwork won a contract in 1966 to provide ATC services and engineering support for communications and navigation aids at the AAC base at Netheravon in Wiltshire.

Marconi Vickers Viking G-AHOP was used as a test bed from 1951. The first installation was Ekco VHF TR/CE/1140/24 equipment. (Babcock International Group)

1968

Another different line of work arrived in March 1968 when Airwork Services gained a contract to provide full engineering and operational services at Winkfield for the US satellite tracking station there. This was the first operational NASA station on foreign soil.

Further work involving simulators was undertaken in 1968 with the removal of the Gannet simulator from Brawdy to Lossiemouth and its continued maintenance after installation.

A technical training school was set up for the Singapore Defence Force in 1968.

In March 1968 the company gained a contract to take over the maintenance of the helicopter training squadrons at RNAS Culdrose in Cornwall.

Contracts were signed in August 1968 to provide technical and operations services for the European Space Agency (ESA). This was at a number of different locations: the European Space Research Organisation (ESRO) at Darmstadt in West Germany; Estrack at Redu in Belgium; European Space Research & Technology Centre at Noordwijk, Holland; and Frascati, Italy.

A contract was obtained to provide technical support for the new ADDF (Abu Dhabi Defence Force) which started with two BN2 Islanders in September 1968.

1969

As part of a new contract to provide engineering support to three Scottish university air squadrons plus 12 AEF, which was based at RAF Turnhouse, Airwork were also tasked with providing engineering support for a de Havilland Devon of 207 Squadron at RAF Turnhouse.

1970

At very short notice, Airwork undertook a contract to service the Canberra TT.18s of 7 Squadron at RAF St Mawgan in Cornwall. These Canberras performed target-towing duties for the RN and RAFR ranges off Cornwall and Devon using the Rushton target winch system. In November 1971 there was a permanent Airwork staff detachment from RAF St Mawgan to RAF Kinloss with 7 Squadron Canberras which were using the ranges in the Hebrides. The contract to provide engineering support to 7 Squadron ceased in March 1981 when the squadron and the task were transferred to RAF Wyton. However, Wyton had no experienced staff to deal with the Rushton winch system as fitted to the Canberra TT.18, so the contract was extended to provide the engineering support at St Mawgan on the winch system.

1971

A contract commenced in 1971 to provide ATC and engineering support services at RAF Leconfield in Yorkshire. The RAF moved out of Leconfield in 1977 but the SAR helicopter flight remained; the ground communications for this and Strike Command continued to be maintained by Airwork Services. The Leconfield contract ceased completely in 1982. It was, however, resurrected in December 1988 in order to man communications for the SAR flight (at Normandy Barracks) and to service range electronics at Cowden bomb and firing range.

In South Africa, the company undertook the running of the SAAF Central Flying School at Dunnottar AFB, which had over forty Harvards on strength. The contract was a sensitive one due to the political and international situation with South Africa at the time. Airwork also provided support for the airfield services at Dunnottar.

1973

A Dassault Mystère 20 (Fan Jet Falcon) was delivered to Oman for the Sultan on 17 July 1973. This was the first aircraft on the Omani civil register and was registered as A40-AA. This was later re-registered A40-GA in December 1976 after the arrival of a Grumman Gulfstream 2 which took the registration A40-AA. The Dassault Mystère 20 was maintained by Airwork and was a regular visitor to Hurn.

In 1973 Airwork Services took over the engineering support operation at Lydd Airport which was owned by BUA subsidiary Silver City Airways.

1974

In January 1974 the contracts which Airwork held with the European Space Agency were expanded to include space documentation.

New Middle Eastern support contracts were obtained for the Qatar police (support for two Aerospatiale Gazelles) and air wing (support for Hawker Hunters), Sharjah Airport and the Dubai Police Air Wing (this was mainly for helicopter maintenance). The Qatar and Sharjah contracts all ceased in 1977. The contract for the helicopter maintenance of the Dubai Police Wing ceased a year later than the others.

In March 1974 a contract was obtained to provide second-line electronic services at the Combined Signals Organisation Station at Bude in Cornwall (satellite monitoring station).

In December 1974 Airwork were involved in setting up the UN ICAO Flying School at Soroti, Uganda.

1975

A contract was gained to provide engineering support at the International Press Centre in London.

From October 1975, the 750 Squadron Sea Princes at RNAS Culdrose were maintained by Airwork Services.

The maintenance contract with the ADDF (Abu Dhabi Defence Force) ended and pilot training and maintenance was taken over by Pakistani personnel.

1976

Airwork at Hurn were contracted by British Airways to strip completely and refurbish three Sikorsky S-61 helicopters from the USA for North Sea Oil Operations.

The Airwork Services Medical Division (Mediservice) won a contract to provide technical services at Wellington Hospital, in St John's Wood, London.

1977

In January 1977 Airwork acquired a substantial part of freight forwarder Gulfsped which had been operating a transport service to the Middle East for some time. From the time of the acquisition, Gulfsped worked closely with the Airwork Supplies Division.

Also, in December 1977, Airwork obtained a contract to operate the new airfield at Scatsta in the Shetland Islands on behalf of the Sullom Voe Consortium.

1979

Airwork gained a number of varied new contracts in 1979. They included a contract to maintain and operate new navigation aids and communications equipment, such as a weather satellite system at Brunei International Airport; and a contract to operate all services (except ATC) at RAE Llanbedr airfield, such as radar and Jindivik pilotless aircraft plus the mother control aircraft, Canberras and Meteors. Both the Llanbedr and Brunei contracts started in May 1979. The Llanbedr contract was expanded in 1982 to include provision of ATC services. The Brunei contract ceased in March 1984.

In March 1979 the company had started a contract to operate Unst Airport in the Shetlands for the Shetland Islands Council and Chevron Oil. Three other unusual contracts during the year were a contract to provide electronic engineering support for the Royal Navy Language Training School (HMS *Mercury*) at Petersfield in Hampshire; a contract to manufacture galley units and equipment for large hovercraft; and a contract to design and build an underwater TV system for the Royal Navy.

In recognition of the amount of overseas work undertaken, Airwork were awarded the Queen's Award for Export in July 1979.

1980

A contract was obtained to maintain the Auto Triangulation System and TACAN Beacon at Ouston, Northumberland.

At Exeter Airport, Airwork took over the share capital of West Country Aircraft Servicing and West Country Air Radio.

In Germany, a contract was secured to supply staff to Electluft to refurbish NATO radar equipment whilst another radar contract obtained in the same year was to provide operational and engineering support for the long-range radar installation at Blake Hill Farm in Wiltshire for Appleton Laboratory (Science Research Council). This contract was later extended to a similar installation at Cobb Hill, Surrey. The Blake Hill Farm contract ceased in 1982.

1981

A contract was obtained to provide engineering support to T424 airfield radars for BAC (British Aircraft Corporation) at Bitteswell in Leicestershire and Dan Air at Lasham. A similar contract in the same year was to remove T424 radar at Leavesden, and then install and commission the equipment at Sunderland's Usworth airfield.

On the catering and medical side, Airwork were contracted to provide catering and medical staff to a new hospital during its initial setting-up phase in Dhahran, Saudi Arabia.

1982

Airwork provided a number of ad hoc contract personnel for Plessey installation contracts in Kenya, Gabon, Eire, the Falkland Islands, Libya and Zanzibar.

During 1982 and 1983, a contract was obtained to take delivery of and to maintain and operate the presidential aircraft for the President of Malawi. The aircraft was HS.125/800B MAAW-J1 and a hangar and stores for the operation were set up at Zomba, the previous capital in Southern Malawi. The HS.125 became part of a controversy in 2009 when it was sold for US$4 million to purchase a new presidential jet at a cost of US$13.26 million, causing a foreign-exchange crisis in the country. This caused the UK to reduce its foreign aid to Malawi by £3 million.

1983

A contract was awarded to provide resident airfield engineering support for navigation aids and radar on behalf of Rolls-Royce at Leavesden.

1984

A contract was awarded to take over the maintenance and servicing of navigation aids, radar and communications equipment at A&AEE Boscombe Down from MoD staff. A further contract was obtained in 1992 to provide full ATC services for Boscombe Down in 1992.

Another Scottish airport contract was gained in 1984 for servicing and operation of navigation aids and communications at Dundee Airport.

Airwork and the US company Vinnell were awarded a contract to provide engineering and logistic support to the US forces in the Arabian peninsula. This contract was operated and run from Oman.

1985

A contract was given to Airwork in August 1985 to take over the army Military Air Target System 'A' (known as MATS A) at Larkhill, Wiltshire, with worldwide operational detachments.

The following month, in September 1985, Airwork formed Technical Services Shetland to operate the Unst and Scatsta contracts.

Also in September 1985, a small contract was gained to provide support for the Short Skyvans of Lesotho's police mobile unit.

1986

Airwork gained a number of varied contracts in 1986. These were a contract to refurbish Jetstream aircraft for the RAF starting in April 1986; a contract in January 1986 to provide ATC services including engineering support at Bournemouth International Airport; one for Airwork to take over the running of the ATC at Dounreay Atomic Power Station airfield for the UK Atomic Energy Authority; the acquisition, in July 1986, of Alvair, an aircraft maintenance company at Coventry Airport; a contract, also in July 1986, to provide storage maintenance for RAF VC10 (ex-British Airways) at Abingdon airfield; a contract in the same month to carry out a Tornado modification programme at RAF Cottesmore; and in September 1986 a contract for Shackleton AEW2 aircraft of 8 Squadron to reduce to sub-unit overhaul and to refurbish to operational standard.

1988

A contract was gained in January 1988 to provide range engineering and photographic services at the Proof and Experimental Establishment at Pendine.

In August 1988 another offshore oil contract was gained to operate the then new heliport at Dimlington in Humberside for British Petroleum. This included ATC services and the processing of gas rig personnel transiting offshore.

1990

In 1990 Airwork gained two West Country contracts. The first was to provide management and ATC services at St Mary's Airport on behalf of the Scilly Isles Council. The other was to provide ATC services at Plymouth Airport.

1991

There were some small contracts won in 1991. The first was to provide refuelling services for the USAF at RAF Fairford in Gloucestershire; the next was to provide engineering support for the Ministry of Defence facility at Northwood from December 1991. Overseas there was a contract from Nepal to repair one Skyvan in Kathmandu which involved sending a crew out to effect the repairs in August 1991. The final contract was to modify AAC helicopters at Detmold in Germany in August 1991.

1992

A contract was gained to provide engineering support and domestic services to HMS *Gannet* at Prestwick.

Airwork were given a contract to maintain airfield systems at Staverton as well as provide services (the non-directional beacon was serviced from Hurn).

APPENDICES

AIRCRAFT REGISTERED OR USED BY AIRWORK AND ASSOCIATES, 1928 – 3 SEPTEMBER 1939

Here, and in the following appendices, is only a selection of the aircraft that Airwork and associated companies were involved with.

Avro 638 Club Cadet

Reg.	From/To	Reg.	From/To	Reg.	From/To	Reg.	From/To
G-ACHN	01/06/33–05/11/45	G-ACHO	01/06/33–10/06/41	G-ACHP	01/06/33–24/08/42	G-ACTX	11/06/34–07/36
G-ACTY	11/06/34–03/06/36	G-ACTZ	19/01/39–20/02/41	G-ACNY	25/04/35–10/06/41	G-ACZS	31/01/39–10/41

Avro 641 Commodore

Reg.	From/To	Reg.	From/To
G-ACUA	11/06/34–02/35	G-ACRX	08/05/35–09/35

Avro 643 Cadet

Reg.	From/To	Reg.	From/To
G-ACZA	03/08/35–07/36	G-ACXJ	16/10/35–06/36 and 06/07/36–11/36

Avro Avian IVM

Reg.	From/To	Reg.	From/To	Reg.	From/To	Reg.	From/To
G-ABDP	07/30–09/30	G-AAVP	02/31–04/32	G-AACV	03/31–02/33	G-AAWI	08/??/35–12/35
G-ACKE	18/05/37–09/38						

Avro Five (operated jointly with Air Taxi)

Reg.	From/To
G-AASO	05/30

Avro Ten

Reg.	From/To	Reg.	From/To
G-ABSP	12/31–12/31	G-ABSR	12/31–12/31

BA Eagle II

Reg.	From/To						
G-AENE	30/03/37–05/37						

Bellanca P/maker

Reg.	From/To						
G-ABNW	22/03/34–03/36						

BK Eagle

Reg.	From/To						
G-ACPU	08/07/38–02/39						

BK Swallow

Reg.	From/To	Reg.	From/To				
G-ACUF	06/12/35–06/36	G-ACUF	30/04/37–10/38				

Blackburn Bluebird IV

Reg.	From/To						
G-AASU	??/30–07/06/30						

Cierva C.30

Reg.	From/To	Reg.	From/To				
G-ACKA	??/33–09/33	G-ACUT	19/06/34–18/09/34				

Comper Swift

Reg.	From/To	Reg.	From/To				
G-ACGL	15/07/35–12/35	G-AAZC	26/05/38–28/05/38				

DH.60 (Various)

Reg.	From/To	Reg.	From/To	Reg.	From/To	Reg.	From/To
G-AACY	21/11/28–??/34	G-AAEB	02/29–02/29	G-EBMP	06/06/29–11/29	G-AALX	09/29–27/09/29
G-AAIV	01/30–01/30	G-AAKC	10/30–04/31	G-ABGP	13/05/31–03/32	G-EBQH	??/??–06/31
G-ABEO	11/31–08/33	G-ABCS	10/32–07/34	G-ABND	05/01/33–05/33	G-ABBO	04/09/33–10/33
G-AASY	10/33–10/34	G-AABK	29/10/34–11/36	G-ABLZ	28/10/35–03/36	G-ABNE	16/11/35–01/36

Reg.	From/To	Reg.	From/To	Reg.	From/To	Reg.	From/To
G-ACIA	19/12/35–07/36	G-ABDK	31/01/36–06/36	G-AAKW	14/02/36–31/07/36	G-EBLV	17/02/36–06/36
G-AEDZ	02/36–12/36	G-ABOA	08/12/36–04/37	G-AAAS	23/09/36	G-ACPI	12/36–05/37
G-AAJL	13/03/37–05/37	G-ABMA	21/08/37–4/10/37	G-ABCG	27/05/38–07/03/39	G-EBOI	29/06/39–12/39
G-ABOE	25/02/39–16/01/40	G-AAMS	03/04/39–16/01/40				

DH.80

Reg.	From/To	Reg.	From/To	Reg.	From/To	Reg.	From/To
G-AAVB	12/30–05/31	G-AAXS	04/31–11/32	G-ABLD	04/31–06/31	G-ABDI	08/32–10/32
G-ABGS	04/33–08/35	G-ABMP	03/07/35–10/36	G-ADLP	10/07/35–08/36	G-ABOC	03/08/35–01/36
G-AAKN	09/08/35–06/36	G-ABNC	03/09/35–07/36	G-ABEM	30/03/36–08/36	G-AEOA	01/10/36–05/37
G-ABNC	14/10/36–08/37	G-ABKG	13/06/39–02/01/40				

DH.82

Reg.	From/To	Reg.	From/To	Reg.	From/To	Reg.	From/To
G-ADOF	19/09/35–18/12/35	G-ADOG	19/09/35–11/01/36	G-ADOH	19/09/35–11/01/36	G-ADOI	19/09/35–11/01/36
G-ADOJ	19/09/35–11/01/36	G-ADOK	19/09/35–11/01/36	G-ADOL	19/09/35–11/01/36	G-ADOM	19/09/35–11/01/36
G-ADON	19/09/35–11/01/36	G-ADOO	19/09/35–11/01/36	G-ADOP	19/09/35–13/01/36	G-ADOR	19/09/35–13/01/36
G-ADVN	25/10/35–06/01/36	G-ADVO	25/10/35–07/01/36	G-ADVP	25/10/35–08/01/36	G-ADXK	03/12/35–31/01/36
G-ADXN	03/12/35–06/02/36	G-ADXO	03/12/35–08/02/36	G-ADXP	03/12/35–13/02/36	G-ADXR	03/12/35–04/02/36
G-AEEA	17/03/36–07/04/36	G-AEUV	18/03/37–02/07/37	G-AFDC	19/11/37–03/12/37	G-AFDD	19/11/37–03/12/37
G-AFGW	25/01/40–09/02/40	G-AFNM	09/02/40–02/40	G-AGAP	19/02/40–03/40		

DH.83

Reg.	From/To	Reg.	From/To	Reg.	From/To
G-ABWF	13/04/33–09/34	G-ABYO	16/02/34–28/04/34	G-ABZN	29/07/35–14/08/35

DH.84

Reg.	From/To	Reg.	From/To	Reg.	From/To	Reg.	From/To
G-ACLE	31/10/33–09/35	G-ACHV	05/05/35–08/35	G-ACEU	13/01/36–03/37	G-ACEV	23/01/36–08/36

G-ACMC	23/01/36–08/36	G-ACMJ	25/01/36–07/36	G-AEKZ	07/36–12/08/36	G-ACNI	31/12/36–18/03/37
G-ACIE	28/05/38–28/05/38	G-ADOS	06/40–?				

DH.85

Reg.	From/To	Reg.	From/To	Reg.	From/To	Reg.	From/To
G-ADCO	20/02/35–27/02/35	G-ADUL	10/35–11/35	G-ACLZ	24/03/37–16/06/40	G-AFZG	29/08/39–01/07/40

DH.86

Reg.	From/To	Reg.	From/To	Reg.	From/To		
G-ADEC	02/09/37–17/09/37	G-ADEA	11/10/37–06/38	G-ADMY	14/10/37–06/38		

DH.86B

Reg.	From/To	Reg.	From/To	Reg.	From/To	Reg.	From/To
G-ADYC	08/37–07/38	G-ADYD	08/37–08/38	G-ADYE	08/37–12/37	G-ADYH	08/37–12/37
G-ADYI	08/37–01/38	G-ADYJ	08/37–10/37	G-ADYG	12/37–08/38		

DH.87

Reg.	From/To	Reg.	From/To	Reg.	From/To	Reg.	From/To
G-ADJX	30/08/35–27/09/35	G-ADUL	10/35–11/35	G-AFHX	09/06/38–21/06/38	G-ADKM	15/06/38–10/38
G-ADKV	16/01/39–03/39						

DH.89

Reg.	From/To	Reg.	From/To	Reg.	From/To	Reg.	From/To
G-ADCL	19/12/35–08/36	G-ACPN	01/36–09/36	G-ACPO	01/36–05/36	G-ADAL	01/36
G-ADAK	08/36–08/36	G-ADAI	28/08/37–15/07/40	G-ADAE	28/08/37–05/38	G-ADIM	28/08/37–15/07/40
G-ADDF	31/08/37–09/37	G-ADAH	31/08/37–05/38	G-ADAG	02/09/37–15/07/40	G-ADBW	30/01/39–15/07/40
G-AFLY	22/11/38–15/07/40	G-AFLZ	22/11/38–15/07/40	G-AFMA	22/11/38–15/07/40	G-AFME	09/12/38–15/07/40
G-AFMF	09/12/38–15/07/40	G-AFMG	09/12/38–15/07/40	G-AFMH	09/12/38–15/07/40	G-AFMI	09/12/38–15/07/40
G-AFMJ	09/12/38–15/07/40	G-ACZE	17/03/39–15/07/40	G-ACZF	17/03/39–03/39	G-AEMM	21/10/39–?

DH.90

Reg.	From/To						
G-AFVJ	12/06/39–13/07/39						

DH.94

Reg.	From/To	Reg.	From/To	Reg.	From/To	Reg.	From/To
G-AFOD	09/05/39–16/01/40	G-AFOE	09/03/39–16/01/40	G-AFOF	31/07/39–28/08/39	G-AFOG	23/08/39–09/10/39

GAL ST.4 & ST.25

Reg.	From/To	Reg.	From/To
G-ADLT	27/08/36–05/37	G-ACJF	01/03/44–12/12/45

Hawk Major

Reg.	From/To
G-ADLO	15/07/35–05/37

Klemm L.27A

Reg.	From/To	Reg.	From/To
G-ABOR	15/07/35–12/35	G-ABJX	11/10/40–01/44

Miles Falcon

Reg.	From/To	Reg.	From/To
G-AFAY	29/07/37–24/08/37	G-AFBF	14/10/37–03/02/38

Miles Monarch

Reg.	From/To	Reg.	From/To
G-AFGL	12/04/38–30/06/38	G-AFTX	12/09/39–30/11/39

Percival Gull

Reg.	From/To	Reg.	From/To	Reg.	From/To
G-ACHA	25/07/33–12/35	G-ACLG	07/09/33–10/33	G-ADFA	21/04/38–11/40

Short Scion

Reg.	From/To
G-ACUZ	21/03/35–05/38

Spartan Cruiser II & 3-Str II

Reg.	From/To	Reg.	From/To
G-ACBM	12/32–02/33	G-ACAD	15/07/35–05/36

Tipsy Trainer 1 & Tipsy B

Reg.	From/To	Reg.	From/To				
G-AFSC	15/07/39–05/41	G-AFGF	06/12/38–03/39				

Vega Gull

Reg.	From/To	Reg.	From/To				
G-AEPS	26/08/38–10/38	G-AETE	07/11/38–06/02/39				

Whitney Straight

Reg.	From/To	Reg.	From/To	Reg.	From/To	Reg.	From/To
G-AERS	01/37–20/01/37	G-AEVA	20/05/37–08/37	G-AFJJ	19/08/38–29/09/38	G-AEYJ	19/09/38–12/38
G-AFGK	29/08/40–19/02/43						

Zlin XII

Reg.	From/To						
OK-TBK	04/37						

APPENDIX II

GATWICK

Armstrong Whitworth Whitley Mk I–IV inc. modified and/or repaired by AGT Gatwick 1939–42

Serial	Arr./Dep.	Serial	Arr./Dep.	Serial	Arr./Dep.	Serial	Arr./Dep.
K7188	17/12/40–17/12/40[1]	K7189	11/09/42–08/12/42	K7196	18/05/42–26/07/42	K7203	03/05/38–22/02/39
K7218	02/07/39–01/06/40	K7220	31/12/39–01/06/40	K7221	24/02/39–06/07/39	K7230	27/06/39–08/06/40
K7231	24/07/39–24/05/40	K7233	18/08/41–25/01/42	K7239	14/06/40–03/08/40	K7240	?–06/03/39
K7242	20/06/39–01/06/40	K7246	28/11/38–05/03/41	K7252	12/08/38–10/11/40	K7255	25/04/39–21/10/39
K7258	25/04/39–01/10/42	K7259	?–08/04/41	K7262	03/07/39–23/05/39 & 22/09/41–18/02/42	K8937	22/09/39–08/12/40 & 18/05/42–02/08/42
K8938	02/04/42–24/07/42	K8944	09/04/42–16/06/42	K8972	27/04/42–11/06/42	K8974	05/04/42–11/06/42
K8978	07/08/42–11/10/42	K8979	03/02/42–21/02/42	K8992	18/08/41–26/11/41	K8995	05/09/39–04/09/40
K8999	05/05/42–13/08/42	K9003	16/01/42–14/02/42	K9004	18/09/40–13/04/41	K9006	22/05/42–01/07/42
K9012	04/04/42–16/05/42	K9014	30/01/42–30/04/42	K9017	17/06/40–02/06/41	K9019	05/09/39–10/05/40
K9023	09/11/40–05/41[2]	K9024	17/06/40–18/10/40	K9026	5/04/40–08/02/41		

1 K7188 SOC 17/12/40.

2 K9023 to instructional airframe 3302M 5/41.

APPENDIX III

HESTON

Airwork School of Flying Aircraft

Aircraft	Reg.	From/To
Avro Avian IVM	G-AAVP	02/31–04/32
Avro Avian IVM	G-AACV	01/31–?
Avro 638 Cadet	G-ACTX[1]	11/06/34–07/36
Avro 638 Cadet	G-ACTY	11/06/34–03/06/36
Avro 638 Cadet	G-ACTZ	11/06/34–03/12/38
Avro 638 Cadet	G-ACNY	25/04/35–11/38
Avro 638 Cadet	G-ACZS	12/08/38–12/38
Avro 641 Commodore	G-ACUA	11/06/34–02/35
DH.60G Gipsy Moth	G-AACY	28/11/28–15/05/36
DH.85	G-ADCO	20/02/35–27/02/35
DH.85	G-ACLZ	24/03/37–16/06/40
DH.87A	G-ADJX[2]	30/08/35–04/37

Pre-War Airwork Flying Club Aircraft

The following were registered to the Airwork Flying Club from Airwork Ltd (i.e. the School of Flying) on the following dates and continued to be used for instruction. Some of the Avro 638 Cadets were moved from Heston to Denham in December 1939. G-ACHP was impressed as HM570 in 1942:

Avro 638 Cadet	G-ACNY	29/11/38–10/06/41
Avro 638 Cadet	G-ACZS	12/08/38–14/12/38
Avro 638 Cadet	G-ACTZ	19/01/39–20/02/41
Avro 638 Cadet	G-ACHO	29/11/38–10/06/41
Avro 638 Cadet	G-ACHP	29/11/38–24/08/42

Post-War Airwork Flying Club Aircraft

DH.82A Tiger Moth	G-AHRT	28/05/46–15/02/49
DH.82A Tiger Moth	G-AHRU	28/05/46–11/02/49
DH.82A Tiger Moth	G-AHRV	28/05/46–24/09/48
DH.82A Tiger Moth	G-AITH	13/08/47–18/02/49

1 Based at Newtownards.
2 Probably operated for Airwork School of Flying, April 1936.

APPENDIX IV

AIRLINE FLEET TO 1 JULY 1960 (BUA FORMATION DATE)

Bristol Freighter Mk 11A & 21A

G-AHJD	dd	7/8/46–sold 20/05/50
G-AICS	lsd	01/49–returned 10/49 (leased from Bristol A/c Co. Ltd)
G-AICT	lsd	10/47–returned 04/52 (leased from Bristol A/c Co. Ltd)

Douglas DC-3

G-AGKC	dd	10/49–sold 02/52
G-AGIS	dd	11/53–sold 12/53
G-AGYZ	dd	05/54–sold 03/57
G-AMBW	dd	06/50–sold 11/53 (carried trooping serial XB246)
G-AMRA	dd	11/04/53–to BUA (operated by Transair from 11/56)
G-AMZD	dd	10/04/53–crashed Barcelona 11/04/60
G-AMZW[1]	dd	29/05/53–sold 01/07/53 (to Sudan Airways as ST-AAH)
G-AMZX[2]	dd	29/05/53–sold 04/09/53 (to Sudan Airways as ST-AAG)

Handley Page Hermes 81

G-AKFP	dd	08/52–w/o Calcutta 01/09/57 (carried trooping serial XD632)
G-ALDA	dd	31/12/56–sold 10/59 (carried trooping serial WZ838)
G-ALDB[3]	dd	??/52–w/o Orleans 23/07/52 (carried trooping serial WZ839)
G-ALDC	dd	31/12/56–sold 06/59 (carried trooping serial WZ840)
G-ALDF	dd	02/52–w/o Sicily 25/08/52 (carried trooping serial WZ841)
G-ALDG	dd	08/57–sold 10/59
G-ALDO	dd	08/52–wfu 03/59

Vickers Viking

G-AHOP[4]	dd	10/52–31/07/67 (carried trooping serial WZ972)
G-AHOR	dd	27/03/53–03/11/55
G-AHOT	dd	09/03/53–10/08/54
G-AHOW	dd	03/53–sold 25/10/54
G-AHOY	dd	Leased 1948
G-AIXR	dd	04/47–sold 05/59 (carried trooping serial WZ355)
G-AIXS	dd	05/47–w/o Blackbushe 15/08/54 (carried trooping serial WZ354)
G-AJFP	dd	06/47–sold 12/48
G-AJFR	dd	07/47–sold 04/58 (carried trooping serial WZ311)
G-AJFS	dd	09/47–sold 02/58
G-AJFT	dd	09/47–sold 03/60 (carried trooping serial WZ306)
G-AKTU[5]	dd	02/48–sold 03/60 (carried trooping serial WZ356)
G-AKTV	dd	02/48–sold 05/59 (carried trooping serial WZ357)

1 G-AMZW and G-AMZX did not enter Airwork airline service.
2 G-AMZW and G-AMZX did not enter Airwork airline service.
3 Leased from BOAC.
4 Also used as test beds.
5 Also used as test beds

G-AHOW was leased from Eagle from 11/01/53 before its purchase by Airwork.
Airwork also leased G-AHON for brief periods from 1949 to 1952, and it was stated as the primary aircraft to start operating the new Central African service in 1952. It was written off on 25/07/52 with Crewsair in Malta.

Vickers Viscount series 736 & 831		
G-AODG	dd	03/01/58–transferred to Transair 02/59, to BUA 01/07/60
G-AODH	dd	03/01/58–transferred to Transair 02/59, to BUA 01/07/60
G-APND	dd	23/02/59 to BUA 01/07/60
G-APNE	dd	17/03/59 to BUA 01/07/60
G-ASED	dd	Leased to Sudan Airways 05/06/59

Three Vickers Viscounts series 755 on order (G-AOCA, G-AOCB and G-AOCC) were resold in December 1955 ahead of delivery to Compañia Cubana de Aviacion.

Airwork non-airline aircraft to 1 July 1960 (BUA formation date)

Airspeed AS.65 Consul					
Reg.	From/To	Reg.	From/To	Reg.	From/To
G-AHEG	05/03/46–09/04/48	G-AIKR	02/01/47–01/01/60	G-AJNE	24/10/56–01/01/60

G-AIKR and G-AJNE with AST Perth (to 14/02/62 and 31/10/61 respectively).

Avro 652A Anson					
Reg.	From/To	Reg.	From/To	Reg.	From/To
G-AIRW	09/08/48–05/07/50	G-AIRX	14/02/52–09/06/52	G-AKMV	01/07/48–27/07/50

All to Airwork East Africa.

DH.89A Dragon Rapide					
Reg.	From/To	Reg.	From/To	Reg.	From/To
G-AKTZ	09/06/48–26/09/50	G-AJDN	20/04/53–16/04/58	G-AKJS	21/09/59–03/07/62
G-AESR	18/10/47–01/02/53	G-AKRS	13/04/53–04/05/60		

G-AJDN, G-AKJS and G-AKRS with AST Perth, G-AESR with Iraq Pet. Co. 18/03/37–19/09/47 and G-AKTZ with Iraq Pet. Co. 25/08/54–04/09/56.

DH.104 Dove					
Reg.	From/To	Reg.	From/To	Reg.	From/To
G-AKSS	07/02/49–10/02/51	G-AHRJ	08/06/50–05/10/50	G-AMEI	17/10/50–14/06/51

G-AKSS and G-AHRJ leased to Channel Islands Air Services, Guernsey, in 1950.

Percival Proctor

Reg.	From/To	Reg.	From/To	Reg.	From/To
G-AHMV	01/11/1950–06/01/54	G-AIHD	13/04/53–22/04/58	G-ALCK	07/05/54–12/03/59
G-ALER	22/08/52–04/06/56	G-AMBS	28/04/52–23/06/58	G-AKWL	14/03/52–23/09/57

APPENDIX V

SHELL ECUADOR FLEET, 1947–50 (DURING PERIOD OF AIRWORK CONTRACT)

Bristol 170 Mk 1A & 21A Freighter

Reg.	From/To	Reg.	From/To	Reg.	From/To
HC-SBM	13/03/47–03/09/49	HC-SBN	?/04/47–27/09/48	HC-SBU	14/09/48–06/08/49

All Bristol 170s were given low-pressure tyres and fitted for supply drops.
HC-SBN/HC-SBZ returned to Ecuador on 14 October 1949 to replace HC-SBU, lost in accident 6 August 1949, and was given new registration of HC-SBZ. Sold to Aviation Traders Ltd as G-AICS on 28 August 1950, departed Ecuador 11 September 1950. Later crashed as G-AICS on Winter Hill, Bolton, on 30 April 1957.

Douglas DC-3

Reg.	From/To	Reg.	From/To
HC-SBR	07/02/47–?/49	HC-SBS	04/03/47–19/10/49

HC-SBR was named *Star of Altar* and HC-SBS was named *Star of Sangay*.

Grumman G-21 Goose Amphibian

Reg.	From/To	Reg.	From/To	Reg.	From/To	Reg.	From/To
HC-SBA	04/45–02/08/49	HC-SBB	01/02/45–17/02/49	HC-SBT	08/05/47–?	HC-SBV	22/04/49–28/04/49
HC-SBK	23/09/49–03/50	HC-SBY	19/08/49–26/08/49				

HC-SBA was named *Rio Napo* and HC-SBB was named *Curaray*.
HC-SBV crashed on River Pastaza on 28 April 1949 during test flight in single-engine practice, killing Airwork chief pilot V.R.H. Ferguson and chief engineer H. Riggs.

Of Note …

1   Both Douglas DC-3s in Shell/Airwork service were named after local Ecuadorian volcanoes.
2   Some of the Grumman Goose Amphibians were named after rivers in Ecuador. It is not known if all were named.
3   Ford Tri-Motors: there is some confusion over exactly what happened with the Tri-Motors after Airwork's start on the contract in early 1947. An article by Roy Pearl in *Flight* in

January 1948 on the overall Airwork operation describes an Ecuador fleet of three Grumman Goose Amphibians, two DC-3s, two Bristol Freighters and two Ford Tri-Motors. There were three Ford Tri-Motors present on the arrival of Airwork in Ecuador in early 1947: HC-SBJ, HC-SBK and HC-SBQ. It seems to be generally agreed that they played little or no further part in the operation after the arrival of the Douglas DC-3s and the Bristol 170 Freighters. All three were withdrawn from use as follows: HC-SBJ on 11 May 1948; HC-SBK was grounded on 16 July 1947; and HC-SBQ is shown as grounded on 16 July 1947 but also 'taken out of service' on 19 April 1948, i.e. nearly one year later. Two are generally listed as being grounded at Shell Mera for most of the Airwork contract: HC-SBJ and HC-SBQ. However, HC-SBQ is reported as being in Caracas at some point in 1948. The whereabouts and final fate of HC-SBK after being grounded on 16 July 1947 are unknown.

Shell-Ecuador Fleet Numbers

Fleet No.	Reg.	Fleet No.	Reg.
1	Grumman G-21 Goose HC-SBA	9	Ford Tri-Motor HC-SBI
2	Grumman G-21 Goose HC-SBB	10	Ford Tri-Motor HC-SBJ
	Grumman G-21 Goose HC-SBX	11	Ford Tri-Motor HC-SBK
3	Ford Tri-Motor HC-SBD	12	Grumman G-21 Goose HC-SBL
	Grumman G-21 Goose HC-SBY	13	
4	Ford Tri-Motor HC-SBC	14	Ford Tri-Motor HC-SBQ
5	Budd RB-1 Conestoga HC-SBF	15	
	Bristol 170 Freighter HC-SBM	16	
6	Budd RB-1 Conestoga HC-SBE	17	
	Bristol 170 Freighter HC-SBN	18	Douglas DC-3 HC-SBR
7	Budd RB-1 Conestoga HC-SBH	19	
	Bristol 170 Freighter HC-SBU	20	Douglas DC-3 HC-SBS
8	Budd RB-1 Conestoga HC-SBG		

Of Note …

1   Fleet numbers were assigned upon the aircraft's arrival in Ecuador.
2   From the above listings it can be deduced that when an aircraft crashed or was withdrawn, its replacement was assigned that aircraft's fleet number. However, using this system, it is not certain how the repurchased Grumman G-21 Goose and Bristol 170 arrived at their numbers. Nevertheless, there were five numbers which were used twice and five numbers in the sequence up to No. 20 which were unused.

APPENDIX VI

SOUTH RHODESIA: EMERGENCY LANDING GROUNDS

Nigel Norman surveyed no fewer than sixty-nine sites which included main airports and airfields such as Salisbury and Bulawayo down to strips in the bush to be used for emergency landings. He worked closely with Lieutenant Grylls of the South Rhodesia Directorate of Civil Aviation and both felt that the establishment of these emergency strips was vital. The following table gives estimated costs prepared separately by both men in 1933 on the three main routes to be operated by RANA compared to the request for financing by Colonel Parsons, the Director of Civil Aviation, to the Beit Trust for grant monies. Colonel Parsons felt the amount needed on the Bulawayo to Victoria Falls route would be higher than the estimates provided due to the larger timber on the route and the cost of removing it.

Landing Grounds	Lt Grylls' Estimated Costs	Nigel Norman's Estimated Costs	Amount requested by DCA
Route: Bulawayo–Victoria Falls			
Sawmills	£200	£100	
Intundhla	£100	£100	
Gwayi	£150	£250	
Dett	£150	£250	
Wankie	£400	£400	
Matetsi	£150	—	
Victoria Falls (telephone)	—	£100	
TOTALS	**£1,150**	**£1,200**	**£1,500**
Route: Salisbury–Blantyre			
M'rewa	£125	£200	
M'toko	£100	£100	
Makaha	£125	£300	
TOTALS	**£350**	**£600**	**£500**
Route: Salisbury–Beira			
Marandellas	£300	£300	
Russpi	£300	£300	
Umtali	£400	£400	
TOTALS	**£1,000**	**£1,000**	**£1,200**
GRAND TOTALS	**£2,500**	**£2,800**	**£3,200**

AIRCRAFT REPAIRED BY AIRWORK GENERAL TRADING CO. LTD AT RENFREW, 3 SEPTEMBER 1939 – 30 JUNE 1944

Douglas Boston III

AL684   AL735   AL737   AL739   BZ241

Bristol Blenheims (all marks)

K7113	K7115	K7116	K7148	K7157	K7161	K7162	L1110	L1135	L1139	L1146
	L1152	L1177	L1181	L1187	L1194	L1198	L1203	L1210	L1216	L1224
	L1240	L1271	L1284	L1292	L1310	L1316	L1318	L1336	L1342	L1343
	L1352	L1363	L1400	L1433	L1437	L1449	L1450	L1457	L1462	L1468
	L1470	L1506	L1513	L1518	L1519	L4867	L4870	L8660	L8663	L8684
	L8716	L8657	L8658	L8660	L8663	L8684	L8745	L8756	L8783	L8786
	L8837	L9029	L9301	L9306	L9333	L9542	L9461	L9478	N3523	N3527
	N3538	N3575	N3597	N3600	N6147	N6165	N6163	N6194	N6205	N6218
	N6235	N6237	N6239	P4839	P4840	P4845	P4847	P6931	R2781	R3601
	R3620	R3623	R3638	R3639	R3825	R3871	R3872	R3883	R3888	R3911
	T1865	T1878	T1925	T1936	T1948	T1950	T1958	T1991	T2043	T2128
	T2136	T2219	T2222	T2227	T2254	T2284	T2288	T2322	T2325	T2326
	T2334	T2335	T2336	T2351	T2434	V5396	V5434	V5454	V5459	V5501
	V5522	V5529	V5599	V5621	V5622	V5623	V5655	V5659	V5680	V5695
	V5698	V5721	V5727	V5729	V5740	V5748	V5749	V5753	V5763	V5766
	V5794	V5850	V5864	V5873	V5886	V5894	V5897	V5936	V5937	V5956
	V5957	V5958	V5998	V6000	V6005	V6007	V6011	V6021	V6072	V6123
	V6173	V6194	V6237	V6251	V6260	V6262	V6310	V6394	V6431	V6441
	V6456	V6510	V6511	V6517	V6527	Z5730	Z5735	Z5736	Z5738	Z5750
	Z5751	Z5816	Z5868	Z5873	Z5878	Z5879	Z5881	Z5951	Z5954	Z5965
	Z5971	Z5974	Z5985	Z6034	Z6077	Z6088	Z6093	Z6150	Z6162	Z6167
	Z6172	Z6173	Z6185	Z6244	Z6257	Z6265	Z6266	Z6271	Z6337	Z6341
	Z6372	Z6416	Z7297	Z7313	Z7314	Z7340	Z7348	Z7354	Z7356	Z7415
	Z7444	Z7491	Z7611	Z7615	Z7620	Z7688	Z7705	Z7758	Z7761	Z7768
	Z7770	Z7796	Z7798	Z7881	Z7892	Z7894	Z7902	Z7905	Z7911	Z7918
	Z7919	Z7921	Z7923	Z7926	Z7927	Z7965	Z7983	Z9654	Z9664	Z9666
	Z9667	Z9676	Z9710	Z9712	Z9713	Z9720	Z9723	Z9733	Z9735	Z9742
	Z9745	Z9748	Z9753	Z9792	Z9797	Z9798	Z9800	Z9801	Z9809	Z9810
	AZ869	AZ885	AZ888	AZ890	AZ896	AZ897	AZ898	AZ901	AZ927	AZ931
	AZ933	AZ947	AZ949	AZ950	AZ951	AZ959	AZ960	AZ964	AZ967	AZ970
	AZ989	AZ991	AZ992	AZ999	BA156	BA212	BA229	BA366	BA393	BA688
	BA715	BA743	BA789	BA859	BA880	BB137	DJ702			

Bristol Blenheim/Bisley

DJ702

A number of Blenheims were repaired at Abbotsinch by AGT repair teams from Renfrew.

Allotted to AGT Renfrew but cancelled

BZ321: allotted 6 June 1944
BZ352: allotted 12 March 1945

Five aircraft being worked on at Heston were transferred to Renfrew in September 1939: an Avro Cadet, a Vega Gull, DH.82A Tiger Moth F-AQOX, Miles Merlin G-ADFE and DH.89A G-AFFE.

SOURCES & FURTHER READING

The personal papers of F.A.I. Muntz, with the kind permission of his daughter Mrs Nicolette Baring, have been an invaluable guide to the early days of Airwork.

I am also indebted to the following: Alan Holloway for kindly allowing me to use his late father's unpublished autobiography, *The Prototype Man: A Profile of S.A. Holloway and his Aviation 1932–1992* by Syd Holloway plus photos and materials; Mrs Carole Brooks, the former managing director of RUAC/UAC, for details of the background of the history of the company and its Airwork tie-in and her personal reminiscences; John Hancock of Babcock International for access to what remains of the Airwork archive; and personal reminiscences of former Airwork staff listed in the acknowledgements. I am grateful to John Havers for permission to reproduce the article on the mission to Saudi Arabia in 1947–50; R.A. Scholefield for the Barton and Ringway material; Phil Butler for the Speke and Heinkel 111 details; and Mrs Jennifer Scanlan and Alison Hodge for permission to use material from *Winged Shell* by the late Hugh Scanlan.

Books

50th Golden Anniversary booklet (AST, 1985)

Amos, Peter, *Miles Aircraft: The Early Years, the story of F.G. Miles and his Aeroplanes 1925–1939* (Air Britain, 2009)

Beith, Richard, *Scottish Air Mails 1919–1979* (self-published)

Belcher, Rob, *Blackbushe* (Airfield Focus)

Burrell, David, *Furness Withy 1891–1991*

Butler, Phil, *Liverpool Airport* (The History Press, 2008)

Cameron, Dugald, *Glasgow's Airport* (Holmes McDougall, 1990)

Chorlton, Martyn, *Airfields of North East England in the Second World War* (Countryside Books, 2005)

Cotton, Sidney, *Aviator Extraordinary: The Sidney Cotton Story* (Chatto & Windus, 1969)

Davies, R.E.G., *History of the World's Airlines* (1964)

Dhekney, M.K., *Air Transport in India (Growth & Problems)* (Vora & Co., Publishers Ltd, 1953)

Doyle, Tony, *The Triple Alliance: The Predecessors of the first British Airways* (Air Britain)

Eglin, Roger & Ritchie, Barry, *Fly Me, I'm Freddie* (Futura Publications, 1981)

Fleming, Guy D., *Blue is the Sky* (W. Earl & Co., 1947)

Halford-MacLeod, Guy, *Britain's Airlines, Volume One: 1946–1951* (The History Press, 2006)

———, *Britain's Airlines, Volume Two: 1951–1964* (The History Press, 2007)

Hope, Lester, *Safe in the Skies* (Safe Air)

Hopkins, Michael J., *Feet off the Ground: Memories of Flying in Kenya and Beyond* (M.J.H. Teignmouth, 2011)

Jones, David, *The Time Shrinkers* (Beaumont Aviation Literature, 1977)

Merton Jones, A.C., *British Independent Airlines since 1946, Vols 1–4* (LAAS/International & Merseyside Aviation Society Ltd)

Noyes, Lillian Frances, *India's Domestic Civil Air Transport Policy* (University of Texas, 1971)

Phipp, Mike, *Bournemouth International Airport* (Tempus Publishing, 2002)

———, *Bournemouth's Airports: A History* (Tempus Publishing, 2006)

Robinson, Brian R., *Aviation in Manchester: A Short History* (Manchester Br., Royal Aeronautical Society, 1977)

Roy, R., *World Airline Record 1952* (Roadcap & Associates, Chicago, 1952)

Scanlan, Hugh, *Winged Shell* (Alison Hodge Publishing, 1987)

Sen, A., *Five Golden Decades of Indian Aviation: Tata's Memorable Years* (Aeronautical Publications of India Pvt Ltd)

Sen, Alka, *Glimpses Into Indian Aviation History 1910–1997* (Indian Aviation News Service Pvt Ltd Bombay & Aviation News Service, 1998)

Severne, Air Vice Marshal Sir John, *Silvered Wings* (Pen & Sword)

Sherwood, Tim, *Coming in to Land* (Hounslow Library, 1999)

Smith Jnr, Myron J., *The Airline Encyclopaedia 1909–2000, Vol 2* (Scarecrow Press)

Wakefield, Ken, *Somewhere in the West Country* (Crecy, 1997)

Watson, Jeffrey, *Sidney Cotton: The Last Plane Out of Berlin* (Hodder Headline Australia, 2004)

Wedekind, Joan, *Keith Campling and the Story of Aviation in East Africa* (Cirrus Associates, 2006)

Magazines, Newspapers & Articles

Air International, October 1978

Air Pictorial, October 2000: article by John Havers

Airwork *Heston* booklet

Al-Ahram Newspaper Archives

Flight Global Archives

Indian Aviation: Civil & Military magazine

Loughborough Echo

Newbury Weekly News Archives, Newbury Library, Newbury, Berkshire

Rapide Magazine series of articles: 'The Canadair Sabre in the North West' by R.A. Scholefield

Skyways Indian magazine

Wingspan, May 1992: article by Guy 'Flip' Fleming

Other Sources

Beit Trust Archives

Hansard

Heston Yahoo Groups

International/Merseyside Aviation Society

The National Archives

TALOA Alumni Association

Every attempt has been made to check sources of material and photographs. Please contact the publishers with any suggestions, comments, alterations or additions, or anything connected with the material in the book.

INDEX

Printed in Great Britain
by Amazon.co.uk, Ltd.,
Marston Gate.